A Few Good Books

Using Contemporary Readers' Advisory Strategies to Connect Readers with Books

Stephanie L. Maatta

Neal-Schuman Publishers, Inc.

New York

Published by Neal-Schuman Publishers, Inc.
100 William St., Suite 2004
New York, NY 10038

Printed and bound in the United States of America.

The paper used in this publication meets the minimum requirements of American National Standard for Information Sciences—Permanence of Paper for Printed Library Materials, ANSI Z39.48-1992.

Library of Congress Cataloging-in-Publication Data

Maatta, Stephanie L.
    A few good books : using contemporary readers' advisory strategies to connect readers with books / Stephanie L. Maatta.
        p. cm.
    Includes bibliographical references and indexes.
    ISBN 978-1-55570-669-2 (alk. paper)
    1. Readers' advisory services—United States. 2. Readers' advisory services—Technological innovations. 3. Fiction in libraries—United States. 4. Books and reading—United States. 5. Books and reading—History. I. Title.

Z711.55.M33 2010
028.9—dc22

                                                                                    2009040999

Contents

Part II: Reaching the Contemporary Reader

Part III: The Art and Science of Readers' Advisory

List of Illustrations

TABLES

FIGURES

Foreword

A Few Good Books takes a big-picture view of what the librarian or library school student needs to know to be an effective readers' advisor. Complementing Joyce G. Saricks's *Readers' Advisory in the Public Library* (2005) and Jessica Moyers' *Research-Based Readers' Advisory* (2008), this book brings together in one convenient place a huge range of material. "Reading" is conceptualized in a broad sense to include an encounter with a work in any format—codex book, screen, audiobook—and to include a range of forms of engagement from skimming to deep reading.

Like the reference transaction, the readers' advisory transaction is brief—often only a few minutes long. If done badly, the staff member responds to a request by saying something like, "Sorry, I don't know much about science fiction/war stories/regency romances/splatterpunk/survivor stories. But maybe if you just browse over there, you will find something." If done well, however, the outcome is a happy match between the user's interests, mood, and reading competence and the "few good books" that the staff member suggests. The library user may have experienced the encounter as an interesting discussion about books and reading interests and may not be aware of the range of expertise needed by the library professional to bring about the successful outcome. This book provides a road map to concepts and sources in key areas that the readers' advisor needs to know about: reading research and theory; types of books and genres of (mostly) fiction; communication with readers/library users; and new technological mediations.

Even experienced readers' advisors (RAs) will find something new here, especially in the emphasis given to very current technological resources and trends. Stephanie Maatta pays special attention to the ways in which emerging technologies have changed almost every aspect of the RA process. Reading itself changes when it moves from codex book to screen and includes engagement with a variety of formats, including audiobooks and downloadable books. Communicating with library users changes in a world mediated by Web 2.0 applications. And to help with the problem of finding fiction books with similar appeal factors (never easy in a traditional catalog), librarians have new electronic tools, including resources such as LibraryThing.com, that work by capturing the way real readers experience and categorize books. *A Few Good Books* provides a crash course on new technological mediations of RA work and a lot more besides.

Catherine Sheldrick Ross
Professor
The Faculty of Information and Media Studies
The University of Western Ontario
London, Canada

Preface

TO CONNECT OR DISCONNECT?

Imagine this: . . . It's a hot, summer afternoon. You're working at the reference desk when a patron eases up to you, and says . . .

Scenario 1

User: Hi! I'm really sorry to bother you, but can you recommend something good to read?

Librarian [*smiling*]: I just finished *The Guernsey Literary and Potato Peel Pie Society*. It was wonderful. Everyone I know loves it.

User: Oh, well, I don't really like books about cooking. What's potato peel pie anyway?

Scenario 2

User: Hi! I'm really sorry to bother you, but can you recommend something good to read?

Librarian [*smiling*]: You're looking for a book to read for enjoyment?

User [*nodding in agreement*]: Uh-huh. We're going on vacation and I need something to read during our flights.

Librarian: Vacation. How lovely. So, to give me an idea about the kind of story you might like, can you tell me about a book you've read that you really enjoyed?

User: I just finished *My Lady Elizabeth*, and I thought it was really good. I think it's by Alison Weir.

Librarian: What was it that you liked about it?

User: The characters. She made them seem so real. Well, I guess they were real at one time. But you really got to know Elizabeth. And the history from that time is just so fascinating. The author was good with details and describing everything so I could imagine being there. And all that political intrigue. It was set in England, and that's where we're going on vacation.

Librarian: And are there any types of books that you definitely don't like?

User: Um, I tried some of those fantasy books that are supposed to be the Arthurian legends. Thought that might set the scene for some of our travels. Didn't like them. I want my characters to really be real, you know? I don't mind a little violence and sex, but I don't like things to be, um, graphic.

Librarian: Okay. If we could find the perfect book for you today, what elements would it include?

User: You know, I think I would enjoy some more books about England. Real history so I can get into the right frame of mind. We're going to tour the Tower of London and some of the castles.

Which of the previous two scenarios would you rather be prepared to offer to people who come into the library?

Readers' advisory is a dynamic, popular service. While this traditional activity remains intact, it has also evolved with the development and implementation of robust digital and online resources. And the publishing industry has followed suit, publishing more books in more genres, available in more formats. It is impossible for readers and librarians alike to keep abreast of the bright array of books, authors, and resources.

PURPOSE

A Few Good Books: Using Contemporary Readers' Advisory Strategies to Connect Readers with Books has been written to be the most current text on readers' advisory, meeting the needs of a new generation of librarians and readers. It considers the evolution of library and information science and the emerging technologies that enhance and impact the profession. It also considers the changing variety of the readers in a multicultural society, from adult new readers to non-native speakers of English.

The overall intent is to provide a solid foundation in the theory and practice of readers' advisory (RA) along with a comprehensive examination of the tools to meet the needs of the contemporary reader. The relationship between the reader's advisor and reader is symbiotic, with each giving and taking in the transaction—understanding the reader's needs, identifying resources for good recommendations, connecting the reader with the book, and ultimately taking what has been learned from the first reader and applying it to the next.

Throughout this book the word "contemporary" is used repeatedly. The purpose is not to reiterate the other excellent texts on readers' advisory, but to explore the new technologies for meeting the needs of today's readers and the ways in which they engage with the written word. "Contemporary" readers' advisory strategies refer to current and ongoing developments in RA, especially those that are technologically mediated and that have grown out of both traditional services and innovative approaches. The focus of the book will be to provide the practitioner and the student with information on the latest developments in RA, rather than focusing attention on areas that are well addressed by other texts.

A Few Good Books: Using Contemporary Readers' Advisory Strategies to Connect Readers with Books has been written to meet the following goals:

1. To introduce the librarian and graduate student to the nature of reading and the ways readers engage with books beyond the practice of reading
2. To introduce the librarian and library and information science graduate student to the dynamic world of readers' advisory services; the readers' advisor conversation; major readers' advisor tools; general and genre fiction descriptions and suggested titles; and current and emerging trends
3. To serve as a comprehensive resource for librarians—a handy resource for finding common solutions to readers' advisory questions
4. To provide the profession with a current overview of what readers' advisory services encompasses in today's technologically enhanced world

ORGANIZATION

A Few Good Books is divided into four discrete parts. Although each part can stand alone, many links between topics exist in different chapters. Parts I and II present the necessary foundational and introductory background for the study of readers, books, and readers' advisory. For the reader who is anxious to delve into contemporary RA strategies immediately, Chapter 6, "Beyond the General Reference Interview" is an excellent starting point. Part III is the heart and soul of contemporary RA, including an emphasis on RA services that are mediated technologically and on a diverse, multicultural community of readers. Part IV concludes the text by considering many of the ancillary activities that enhance and heighten the reading experience and enable the librarian to remain current and knowledgeable about authors, books, and current trends.

Part I: On Readers and Reading

Humans were not born to read; it is a learned behavior that developed across millennia into a highly complex cognitive, social, cultural, and psychological behavior. To gain an understanding of the relationship between readers and books, and the art and practice of readers' advisory, it becomes necessary to examine the historical and theoretical foundations of reading and how humans developed as readers. Not only did the act of reading evolve, but the book as a physical artifact and the ways in which we engage with reading evolved concurrently. It is impossible to discuss readers' advisory without an understanding of what defines a reader and how the reader approaches the act of reading. It also is crucial to understand the evolution of reading to place readers' advisory in context.

Chapter 1, "From Cuneiform to Kindle," presents a discussion on the activity of reading from its earliest evidence in 4000 BC to reading in the multimedia world of the twenty-first century. More than being a recitation of history, it provides the touchstones of reading that shape and define contemporary readers.

Chapter 2, "History and Context of Readers' Advisory in the Library," turns to the activity of advising readers in the library as it has evolved over time. It considers the long-standing debate about the value of popular fiction and the evolving role of the readers' advisor in the public library. It also considers who the RA librarian is and what he or she does. The chapter also examines the values and beliefs that formed RA services and allow them to flourish in our contemporary libraries.

Chapter 3, "The Role of the Reader and the Act of Reading," is the culmination of Part I and an introduction to Part II. This chapter considers the definition of a reader and the practice of reading. It examines the social behavior we exhibit while reading, including shared reading and solitary pursuits. It also presents some of the theories that define or explore reading behavior.

Part II: Reaching the Contemporary Reader

The contemporary reader engages with reading in other ways than the act of reading a codex. With the range of options made available by Library 2.0 technologies and innovations, readers and librarians are able to engage with each other and with reading in many unique and exciting ways. Many readers seek out audiobooks and downloadable books to listen to during commutes to work and school. Younger generations of readers prefer reading online. And readers do not describe their reading preferences in traditional cataloging terms; by using resources such as LibraryThing.com, they describe books in ways that make sense to the reader, not the librarian. To this end, Part II includes the following chapters.

Chapter 4, "Tags, Clouds, and Participatory Readers' Advisory Services," begins to consider all of the Library 2.0 options for connecting with readers. Using Library 2.0 technologies invites the reader to participate in creating content and resources that are useful in meeting their needs and interests. Technology is dynamic and changes daily, but the intent of this chapter is to encourage readers' advisory staff to explore the numerous options that will enhance the reading experience.

Chapter 5, "Reading Electronically through Sight and Sound," takes a close look at the alternate formats for reading beyond the traditional print book. This chapter examines several of the digital options available for supporting the act of reading, including e-readers and audiobooks. Ultimately, Chapter 5 considers the conundrum of "What is a book?"

Part III: The Art and Science of Readers' Advisory

This portion of *A Few Good Books* comprises the heart and soul of the text. Part III is the perfect starting point for the librarian or student who is anxious to jump right into the topic of contemporary readers' advisory. The chapters focus on how to provide skilled readers' advisory for contemporary readers. Each of the listed chapters includes a brief overview of the topics and how they relate to readers and to readers' advisory service. The chapters provide practical advice, resources, and strategies as well as the theoretical underpinnings of informed practice. Resources for connecting readers with books are explored in multiple formats. Each chapter concludes with a section on further reading to enhance readers' advisory services.

Chapter 6, "Beyond the General Reference Interview," provides strategies and tools for working with readers, especially in a mediated environment. Unlike many of the excellent readers' advisory texts available, it emphasizes the new developments in RA, especially those mediated by technology. While discussed briefly, this chapter looks beyond the traditional RA reference interview, pointing the user to other works that address the practical issue of how to conduct reference interviews.

Chapter 7, "Knowing a Few Good Books," features strategies and tools for keeping current about books and authors, from visiting local booksellers to attending international book fairs (online or in person). It also explores opportunities and strategies for promoting the fiction collection and the library's readers' advisory services.

Chapter 8, "Reading in the Genres," includes in-depth discussion of popular fiction versus literary fiction and exploration of the genres in general. It provides some general descriptions of genre fiction and introduces the notion of genre blending.

Chapter 9, "Adventure, Suspense, Thrillers, and Mysteries," Chapter 10, "Science Fiction, Fantasy, and Horror," and Chapter 11, "Romance, Historical Fiction, and Westerns," provide an introduction to specific genres along with suggested authors and books. Each chapter considers elements of appeal, historical aspects and trends, and organizations and associations that support interest in individual genres.

Chapter 12, "Merging, Emerging, and Re-emerging Genres," considers other forms of fiction reading that are more topical in nature, but that form unique bodies of literature appealing to various groups of readers. Of particular usefulness, the chapter provides resources for finding information about authors and titles for emerging genres that are not yet included in traditional tools.

Chapter 13, "Readers' Advisory Services for Special Populations," explores specialized user groups within the library community, ranging from patrons with disabilities to adult new readers, and includes resources and reading suggestions to meet their unique needs. The chapter also includes strategies for using the library's whole collection to meet the unique needs of special populations.

Part IV: *Notate Bene*

Nota bene (or the plural form *notate bene*) is a Latin phrase meaning "note well," indicating that the reader should pay special attention to the matter at hand. Part IV covers many of the ancillary aspects of reading, which are of great importance to understanding the reader's interests and needs. This portion of *A Few Good Books* includes the following chapters.

Chapter 14, "List Culture," examines the array of bestsellers, reader-created and literary tastes lists, and resources for finding reading lists.

Chapter 15, "Book Awards and Award-Winning Books," discusses a variety of major literary and popular book awards, including the American Library Association Notable Books awards, the Pulitzer Prize for Fiction, and the Nobel Prize for Literature. It also describes state and regional book awards and awards for the individual genres.

Chapter 16, "Reading Groups Old and New," focuses on shared reading experiences. It examines book discussion groups from their earliest forms to contemporary online book discussion groups. It includes many print and electronic resources for supporting book discussion groups as well as strategies for forming and maintaining them.

Chapter 17, "Reading Events—A Celebration of Reading, Books, and Authors," celebrates reading within the community through events such as "The Big Read" and book festivals. At their heart, reading events create an atmosphere for open dialogue and promote understanding of diverse communities through a shared experience.

Chapter 18, "Reflections on the Future of Reading and Readers' Advisory," is the culmination of the text. The chapter brings us full circle, considering the challenges ahead in meeting the needs of an increasingly diverse community of readers.

Several extensive appendixes conclude this book. The intent is to provide access to current materials for meeting the needs of readers. Many electronic resources and Web sites are included. As of the completion of this text, all Web addresses were current and active, but keep in mind that by nature the Web is dynamic and changeable.

A Few Good Books: Using Contemporary Readers' Advisory Strategies to Connect Readers with Books is written for you, the reader, the librarian, or student, by a lover of books and advocate for reading. It is with great pleasure that the collective knowledge of many librarians and readers is passed to you, empowering you to serve the readers in your communities far and wide, from the first hesitant steps in finding a good book to the enthusiastic sharing of a "good read."

Acknowledgments

No book is ever written or completed without the support and assistance of many others. They spend time tracking down the minutiae, satisfying whims and tangents, giving advice, and proofreading (a lot of proofreading).

Several graduate assistants at the School of Library and Information Science, University of South Florida, spent an enormous amount of time scrolling through reels of microfilm, tracing citations, and photocopying. I'm especially grateful to Stacy Davis for her assistance as this project got underway, and to Kayce Horgan, who located articles and resources, built spreadsheets and tables, and above all was interested in the project as it progressed.

My research associate, Leila Martini, spent many hours preparing the chapter on reading electronically. Her greatest discovery was that she much preferred old-fashioned print books to any electronic versions. She used her research skills to my advantage and provided me with thought-provoking material that greatly enhanced my understanding of the digital environment for reading.

This book would not have been possible without the recommendation of Kathleen de la Peña McCook and the extensive generosity of her personal files. She provided a number of professional and scholarly titles to aid my research and pointed out a number of excellent resources that would be useful.

The students of the School of Library and Information Science have been my cheerleaders. They answered questions about their personal reading preferences, were interested in my writing progress, and even offered to forego assignments and exams to help me finish.

The good folk of Neal-Schuman have my heartfelt thanks and gratitude for keeping the faith and helping me throughout the process. In particular, Sandy Wood, the queen of the commas, was unfailing in advice and encouragement.

Finally, the encouragement and support of my family and friends cannot be measured. My husband, Bruce, a fellow book lover and avid reader, helped me when I bogged down. He proofread, listened, and provided insight on areas where I needed assistance. His knowledge of science fiction and fantasy made that chapter possible.

Part I

On Readers and Reading

Chapter 1

From Cuneiform to Kindle

To read: 1a (1) to receive or take in the sense of (as letters or symbols) especially by sight or touch (2): to study the movements of (as lips) with mental formulation of the communication expressed (3): to utter aloud the printed or written words of <read them a story>

—from *Merriam-Webster's Collegiate Dictionary,* 11th Edition

INTRODUCTION

Any study of readers' advisory must begin with a consideration of the history of reading and the way in which reading has evolved from the interpretation of earliest marks on a cave wall to today's black words backlit on an electronic reader. The history of reading relates intimately to the emergence and evolution of the codex, or the history of the book, into its present-day forms (one does not exist without the other) and to the development of written language. Reading did not emerge in the form that we know it in contemporary culture—words printed on a page, or other surface, which the reader decodes through cognitive and linguistic processes, frequently in silence. Rather, it developed as a method to keep accounts and records and slowly evolved.

The print-and-bound book common today did not exist in prehistoric Mesopotamia where writing is believed to have originated; stone and clay tablets were used in the process of recording knowledge rather than papyrus, vellum, or paper. Alphabetic or grammatical constructs did not exist; paragraphs and punctuation developed much later when the early Christian laity learned literacy skills. Nor did reading begin as a silent activity or shared experience as we encounter today, used for education, work, and pleasure.

An old adage says, "Necessity is the mother of invention." As the ancient Sumerians and Egyptians established trade routes and a ruling class, they needed a way to record ownership and law. It became a necessity to invent writing as a representation of the spoken word and by extension reading. And, if trade was the impetus for the development and spread of writing, then religion, predominantly Christianity, was responsible for the spread of reading and books. (Reading and writing also developed in Asia and the Middle East, though the printing press was slow to follow.)

This chapter briefly explores and touches upon the major events that impacted the development of reading across the ages and to its emergence as an organic and dynamic human activity in the twenty-first century. The history of reading begins with the notion that writing (or recording), and thus reading (the decoding of the written symbols) was used as a memory aid for information, specifically accounting and legal information, that was memorized and recited. Comparatively, in contemporary society reading allows the reader to engage with the text, respond to it, and derive meaning from the written words.

History allows us to understand the past in order to inform the future. The history of reading also leads to the history of readers' advisory. Throughout this book we will return to many of the ideas presented in the history of reading, from the aural traditions (hearing the words of the writer) to shared reading (book discussion groups and social networking). The first time an individual sought guidance or recommendations about what to read, whether for education or pleasure, the notion of readers' advisory services was born. Although the actual act of readers' advisory in a public library did not emerge until the nineteenth century when the nature of reading changed, its foundations can be seen in the evolution of readers across time.

EVIDENCE OF READING

Reading in Ancient Times

> šita (also šit, šid, šed): Sumerian, to read, also meaning to count, calculate, consider, memorize, recite, read aloud. (From Fischer, 2003: 18)

The development of reading spans millennia. Scholars argue that the first written communications may be cave paintings of prehistoric peoples, possibly relaying stories about early human existence. They served as "primitive recording systems" that conveyed "a known significance" (Fischer, 2003: 14–15). Fragments of stone tablets discovered in northeast Syria, dating to 4000 BC, provide evidence that symbols were used to convey details about daily life and indicate the emergence of writing as a form of communication. However, cave paintings and other symbols had not yet developed into phonetic, alphabetic representations of human speech (words, thoughts, and complex concepts). To comprehend the visual message or picture, the symbols had to be spoken aloud by a highly trained specialist.

Many cultures, separately and in concert, started humankind on the road to contemporary reading. Trade and commerce in particular hastened the spread of writing and reading across boundaries and between peoples. The Mesopotamians and the Egyptians created writing through pictographs; the Mesopotamians created the clay tablet and cuneiform; the Phoenicians created the first simple alphabet consisting of consonants, to which the Greeks added vowels; and the Egyptians discovered papyrus, which provided a cheap, abundant, and portable platform for writing. And with the discovery of papyrus, it became possible to easily organize and store recorded information thus the development of early libraries (scriptoriums).

Mesopotamian and Egyptian rulers saw the value in writing to communicate the sale and transference of goods, control the populace through rules and edicts, and establish religious rituals and practices. Reading and writing were established as a process for record-keeping and communication. The two activities were put to multiple uses, especially record-keeping, communication, and religious practices (see Table 1-1).

Reading had its beginning in an aural tradition; words were read aloud to serve as an "official witnessing of an oral medium" (Fischer, 2003: 28) for others to hear and to heed. Written symbols *spoke* for the one communicating the message; in other words, the symbols contained the soul of the message. Primitive readers used the written symbols to serve as memory triggers or mnemonics to provide the accounting of one's goods (sheep, goats, slaves, etc.) or to pronounce an edict from a king or ruler. Few individuals were blessed with the ability and training to memorize and interpret symbols for recitation aloud for others. Scribes were highly trained in the marking and interpretation of symbols, serving as officiates for the society's elite and ruling members and as letter writers and letter readers for the larger population.

Written symbols were marked on clay tablets using pictures and eventually cuneiform in Mesopotamia and the more highly developed hieroglyphics in Egypt (hieroglyphs giving way to hieratic writing as the Egyptian rule advanced). Interestingly, many clay tablets were small and fit within the palm of one's hand,

Table 1-1: Uses of Early Reading and Writing	
Field	Uses
Record-keeping	Codification of law Accounting of goods Formulation of tradition Inscription and lineage
Communication	Letters Royal edicts Public announcements Education, esp. of scribes
Religion	Incantations Sacred and secret texts Rituals
Source: Table 1-1 was compiled from the following texts: Graff, 1991: 15–31; Fischer, 2003: 14–43; Manguel, 1996: 27–41, 177–185.	

much like PDAs and cell phones for text-messaging today, and cuneiform used a wedge-shaped reed similar to a contemporary stylus for creating the marks.

During the fourth millennium BC, literary reading (novels, stories, poems, etc.) was unknown. As writing evolved from simple pictographs to a more complex system of characters, including consonants and syllabic symbols, the recording of laws, inscriptions, and incantations became more prevalent. Again, the written symbols were intended to be read aloud and represented the precise voice of the individual who ordered the written record. The stories and rituals of the society continued to be passed through an oral tradition while the business of the society was recorded.

For the ancient Greeks and many other classical societies, the spread of writing and reading was influenced by cultural and societal needs. Graff explains: "The spread of writing led to its employment in recording the most valued products of the culture, the orally performed poems that carried the canons of civilization and served to indoctrinate the young and to reinforce, by constant repetition, the memories of the entire population" (Graff, 1991: 22–23). It was at this point that stories and poems began to be recorded for future generations with the intent to explain and explore what was then contemporary society and culture.

With the development of an alphabet by the Phoenicians and discovery of papyrus by the Egyptians, it became easier and more efficient to maintain written records of law and lineage and to transcribe the stories, adventures, and epics of a community. But these written records continued to serve as the aide-mémoire for accurate retelling. With the advent of written records came the practice of the scribal tradition (the official reader) of adding a colophon to the written documents, certifying that he (as most scribes were indeed male) was speaking for the message's originator, and thus the identification of authorship and authority.

Early Greeks continued the tradition of reading aloud, especially through oratory. Records were written on papyrus sheets joined into scrolls. (Estimates suggest that Homer's *Iliad* comprised between 12 and 24 scrolls, representing the 24 books of the epic.) This made continuous reading difficult, with the reader viewing one sequential frame at a time (much like scrolling down a computer screen today). Most notably, the written word appeared in one continuous series without case distinction, word separation, or paragraph delineation—*scriptio continua*. Fischer explains, "The physical act of reading aloud parses the text into its constituent features, giving meaning to the tongue where no meaning is evident to the eye" (Fischer, 2003: 47). The reader must be highly skilled in interpretation of written language to provide the correct emphasis and meaning to the text.

Silent reading (or reading to one's self) appeared in the fifth and fourth centuries BC. However, it did not become commonplace until the tenth century AD. Silent reading seemed to be reserved for messages (letters on clay tablets) and "oracular responses" (Cavallo and Chartier, 1999: 7), or private communications rather than public pronouncements. Two ancient plays (*Hippolytus* by Euripides and *The Knights* by Aristophanes) provide some evidence of silent reading as well as a story relayed by Plutarch that Alexander the Great read in silence before his troops (Manguel, 1996: 43; Cavallo and Chartier, 1999: 7). The written word was intended to be spoken aloud and heard.

Most importantly, as reading transformed so did the materials of reading. As trade routes opened and papyrus became plentiful (in fact, a booming manufacturing industry in Egypt), written works became more plentiful. Written works related to professions, the thoughts of philosophers, plays and stories were transcribed and consulted for education and entertainment. While much of the written work was intended to be recited to an audience, it was now possible to read intently, and silently, for reflection and knowledge from a broad array of manuscripts.

This transformation also gave rise to deliberate book collecting and the creation of private and public libraries, with the greatest being the Library at Alexandria (established under the reign of Ptolemy I Soter in the third century BC). Although libraries were originally designed to simply house the scrolls, they became places of study where scholars could gather to read and engage in dialogue and debate. The purpose of the Library at Alexandria "was to encompass the totality of human learning: it would represent the known world's memory" (Fischer, 2003: 58). Along with the greatest collection of human knowledge ever gathered, the Library also provided attribution, editing, transcription, and, penultimately, access to information through collections and preservation.

Religion, Reformation, and Reading

If the establishment of trade routes was the impetus for the invention of the written word, then the spread of religion was the driving force for the invention of the codex, or the book, and increasing levels of literacy among the laity. Religious leaders and laypeople alike found it necessary to have convenient sources for consultation and affirmation of religious practice and dogma. Liturgical texts were reproduced in monastic workshops by cadres of scribes (most often monks). These manuscripts formed the textbooks for training novices and the texts for conducting worship. Books for the laity were produced, including Books of Hours (almanacs of the Church calendar and liturgy), Lives of Saints, Catechisms, and Psalters (Book of Psalms and other devotional texts), to encourage introspection and adherence to religiosity. Secular texts, written in Latin, were also produced at this time by the Christian Church, and the Church held monopolistic control over publishing and prescribed reading, issuing licenses for printing and publishing to only those who supported the work of the Church.

Prior to the late fifteenth century, reading was a passive activity for most people. They were told what to read by their church fathers and taught how to read the prescribed texts by their monastic scholars and tutors. Reading flowed from the top down, with readers discouraged from questioning the teachings they received. Yet transformation of the reader into an active participant began to occur as more books and pamphlets made their way into the public realm.

In the mid-to-late fifteenth century, with the development of Gutenberg's press in Germany and Aldus Manutius's development of smaller, more portable books in Italy, individual reading began to reach the masses, and print culture was born. With the creation of the moveable-type press, more books could be produced more quickly and cheaply, disseminating ideas that questioned Roman Catholic Church teachings. According to Finkelstein and McCleery, "One of the tenets of the Reformation was the unmediated relationship between the laity and God on the one hand, and the laity and the revealed Word of God—that is, the Bible—on the other. The Reformers sought to ensure that direct relationship by increasing literacy and the availability of the Bible, and other religious writings, in the vernacular" (Finkelstein and McCleery, 2005: 108–109; see also Manguel, 1996: 279, and Fischer, 2003: 169). Not only was there growth in the production of religious texts for the common population, but a rise in the printing of textbooks for schoolboys occurred almost simultaneously, thus encouraging further spread of literacy.

The general populace was now able to examine the foundations of faith and Christian teachings along with philosophy, poetry, jurisprudence, and history. Books became a source for individual enlightenment and communal knowledge (Finkelstein and McCleery, 2005: 110). Because an increasing number of printed texts appeared in the vernacular, literacy and the status of reading became more widespread, though not reaching everyone or everywhere. Significantly, with the development of introspective reading, the relationship between the reader and the text changed, with the reader "entering into an ongoing dialog with the author" (Finkelstein and McCleery, 2005: 108). The book no longer represented fact and truth, but the text allowed, even encouraged, the reader to interact and respond to the author through annotations, marginalia, and discourse (Jardine and Grafton, 1990; Fischer, 2003; Basbanes, 2006; Finkelstein and McCleery, 2005).

At this time, printing flourished, making books widely available to anyone who could afford and chose to purchase them. According to Fischer, between 1450 and 1500 approximately 27,000 known works were published, and more than ten million copies of these works were available, typically short texts and circulars (Fischer, 2003: 207, 210). With the development and proliferation of moveable-type presses, books were readily produced in the everyday language of the people, rather than the Latin of the Church. This had significant implications for the spread of literacy among the common people.

In response to the growth in numbers of readers and books, and ultimately the efforts of the Reformers, the Roman Catholic Church published *Index Librorum Prohibitorum* (*List of Forbidden Books*) in 1559, the first official list of banned books. Included among the banned books were treatises on science, philosophy, Protestant teachings, and other works that were "considered dangerous to the faith and morals of Roman Catholics" (Manguel, 1996: 287). Although the ban of books was initially effective in Southern Europe, dominated by Roman Catholicism rule, production of these same titles increased in Protestant Northern Europe. Copies then slipped surreptitiously back into Spain, France, and Italy, passing along heretical and dangerous ideas.

From the *Index Librorum Prohibitorum*: A number of novels appeared on the *Index Librorum Prohibitorum* throughout the ages, which ultimately formed the foundations of contemporary genre fiction. Among the novelists and their works that were condemned by the *Index* were:

Samuel Richardson, *Pamela* (romance), first published in 1740
Victor Hugo, *Notre Dame de Paris* (romance, historical fiction), first published in 1831
Alexandre Dumas, *The Three Musketeers* (romance, historical fiction), first published as a serial in 1844

The Rise of Novels and the Industrial Revolution

Evidence of novels as a literary genre can be found from as early as the second century AD in an extant text of an ancient Greek tale of love and adventure, which is the ancient precursor to the contemporary romance. Although fragments of novels have survived across the millennia, they did not evolve into popularized forms of reading and entertainment until the seventeenth and eighteenth centuries. Among the first "bestsellers" of modern times, readers avidly perused Cervantes' *Don Quixote* (Spain—part 1 published in 1605, part 2 published in 1615), Bunyan's *The Pilgrim's Progress* (England, published in 1678) and Madelein de Scudéry's *Clélie* and *Le Grand Cyrus* (France—published between 1648 and 1661 in multiple volumes) (Fischer, 2003: 241; Finkelstein and McCleery, 2005: 113). *Robinson Crusoe* (1719) was popular throughout Europe and North America, and Samuel Richardson's *Pamela* (1740) enthralled female readers from its first publication.

Perhaps one of the most influential publications of the early seventeenth century establishing novels as popular reading was the *Bibliothèque bleue* series, which were among the first paperbacks (as contemporary readers would recognize). According to Finkelstein and McCleery, "This series, named for its blue-paper covers, was specifically designed for a wide readership. The books were printed on cheap paper; they were short and small; they consisted often of extracts from much longer works; the texts were abridged or edited to simplify or censor" (Finkelstein and McCleery, 2005: 112). The subject of the novels was "popular": fables, tales of chivalry and romance, and fairy tales along with religious texts, etiquette guides, and practical guides, many of which make up current topics for contemporary bestsellers in fiction and nonfiction.

While the cost of the books and the popularization of literary and religious texts contributed greatly to the success of the *Bibliothèque bleue* series, levels of literacy, especially among middle-class urbanized populations, were on the rise and guaranteeing the success of popular novels. Increasingly women and girls learned to read, and they demanded materials suited to their tastes and experiences in the form of novels. With the increased reading of popular novels, echoes of more contemporary criticisms could be heard with "one index of popularity [being] the number of complaints about either the corrupting effect of so much fiction . . . or the waste of time involved in such a trivial pursuit" (Finkelstein and McCleery, 2005: 112).

Urbanization and industrialization increased the need for a literate workforce and influenced the establishment of compulsory education and public libraries. Along with industrialization came decreasing prices in print materials; paper was cheaper, and more books could be printed more quickly at less cost. Workers had an increasing amount of leisure time, allowing them to pass time reading. In fact, popular reading in the guise of novels, newspapers, magazines, etc., became an inexpensive form of pleasure and amusement for the middle and working classes. Even improved illumination through gas, oil, and electric lights influenced the increase of reading novels for pleasure.

Advances in industrialization also contributed to the proliferation of books and other reading materials. With improved printing presses and technologies came the ability to bind books faster and easier, speeding production. Improved techniques for reproducing photographs and illustrations made magazine and popular-press publication more affordable. The production of paper was facilitated by the use of wood pulp (which we're discovering today is problematic, causing brittling and decaying of paper). In addition, this era gave rise to new approaches in promoting authors and their works, making them much more visible to the reading public. Trade and industry magazines such as *Publishers Weekly* also appeared at this time (first published in 1872), further spreading the word about books and reading through announcements, publication releases, and book reviews.

Because of international growth in publishing and printing during the eighteenth and nineteenth centuries, intellectual property rights were debated by authors and publishers, culminating in the International Copyright Act of 1891 (also called the 1891 Chace Act), protecting authors and publishers from piracy abroad. Prior to the enactment of the International Copyright Act of 1891, authors were required to seek residency in foreign nations in order to protect their intellectual property and maintain control over their work. In the case of British authors, they were required to find a U.S. collaborator or publisher in order to register their publications for copyright protection. The act extended a limited protection to foreign authors to publish their works in the United States.

Along with the changing demographics of readers (middle- and working-class readers able to afford books, greater numbers of women and girls reading), there appeared a need to share reading experiences and to explore the ideas presented in both fiction and more literary works. During the eighteenth and nineteenth centuries, literary societies and book discussion groups emerged to fulfill this need. Dominated by women, literary societies presented an opportunity for intellectual growth in a time when university education was not readily available to females. The Chautauqua Literary and Scientific Circle, a derivative of the literary societies, also emerged and became the forerunner of the modern book group and contributed to the growth of the public library. While refashioned to meet the needs of the contemporary reader, book groups continue to be a popular form of communal activity for many.

The proliferation of books and literacy and the need to share the reading experience formed the foundation for readers' advisory services in the public library. Readers deliberately sought the help of library workers to find novels and popular reading that would suit their needs and tastes. Readers' advisors, on the other hand, sought to improve the reader's taste by guiding him or her to better classes (i.e., literary fiction) of literature.

READING IN THE NEW MILLENNIUM

In the nineteenth and early twentieth centuries, the physical act of reading remained much the same as it did in previous centuries. The reader scans the pages from left to right and moves from top to bottom, turning leaves as he or she goes. The book as a physical object held its familiar look and feel, becoming smaller in dimension from large folios to comfortable paperbacks, and the codex of vellum or parchment bound in wooden covers evolved to covers of cardboard or hard covers encased in cloth and pages of paper made from wood pulp and cotton rag, but essentially the same shape and function remains. Evidence suggests that during the same time frame reading became more extensive and less intensive with the increase in reading for pleasure. The popularity of dime novels surged, followed by mass-market paperbacks. Genres unexplored in earlier times emerged and caught readers' attention. Reading provided the source for both intellectual growth and personal entertainment.

With the advent of new media, including cinema, radio, television, and the Internet, the nature of reading has changed. In the late twentieth and twenty-first centuries, technology has wrought significant changes in the way in which readers interact with the written word as well as the definition of a book as a physical entity. It is not a simple matter of interpreting written symbols on a printed page and reflecting upon the text's meaning. Today we read by engaging all of our senses, including sight, sound, and touch. Public oratory and performance gave way to today's audiobooks, which can be downloaded from electronic repositories; old-fashioned print books compete with the available digital products that can be loaded onto a portable device, saving trees and space; and independent booksellers have fallen to the behemoth chains like Barnes & Noble, Borders, or Books-A-Million, and, more telling, to the world's largest online bookseller, Amazon.com.

Among the major developments in books and reading in the early part of the twenty-first century are the creation of digital medium, including e-texts and downloadable files and Web-based resources. Social networking sites, such as LibraryThing, Facebook, and MySpace, allow readers to make connections with authors, other readers, and a global community to engage in shared discourse. Initiatives such as Project Gutenberg make textual materials in the public domain accessible to anyone with a computer or compatible reading device.

Companies including Amazon.com and Sony have developed portable electronic readers, the size and shape of a modern paperback book, that allow the individual to read anytime and anywhere. These devices are being touted as the next best thing to make reading more convenient and appealing. Amazon, in fact, is unable to keep up with the demand for the Kindle, with consumers waiting 12 to 14 weeks for delivery. The e-readers are, however, not without challenges in terms of proprietary interfaces and digital media licensing, and cost to the consumer.

Other changes are occurring as well. Standards that define individual genres are blurred; it is increasingly challenging to say that a book or an author belongs in one genre or another. Despite the doom-saying, books continue to proliferate internationally, and readers have greater access to materials than any time in the past. With technological innovation readers enjoy the ability to participate in the creation of resources that meet their needs and interests. Finally, a wider array of opportunities to engage with reading through festivals, reading events, and discussion groups exists that were unheard of a decade or two ago.

CONCLUSION

Three principle evolutions occurred in the history of the book and reading: orality turning to written communication; handwritten manuscripts replaced by print and the development of print culture; and today, print medium converging with digital and extending how the reader engages with text. In the words of Bill Cope, "So, what is a book? A book is no longer a physical thing. *A book is what a book does*" (Cope, 2001: 6). Succeeding chapters of this book explore the resources and technologies that both delight and confuse the reader, examining methods to harness and employ technologies to enhance reading, redefining books and readers. It also considers myriad ways in which readers engage with the act of reading and connecting with a few good books.

WORKS CONSULTED

Basbanes, Nicholas A. 2006. *Every Book Its Reader: The Power of the Printed Word to Stir the World.* New York: Harper Perennial.

Cavallo, Guglielmo, and Roger Chartier, eds. 1999. *A History of Reading in the West.* Translated by Lydia G. Cochrane. Amherst, MA: University of Massachusetts Press.

Cope, Bill. 2001. "Chapter 1: New Ways with Words: Print and Etext Convergence. In *Print and Electronic Text Convergence* (pp. 1–15), edited by Bill Cope and Diana Kalantzis. Altona, Victoria: Common Ground Publishing.

Finkelstein, David, and Alistair McCleery. 2005. *An Introduction to Book History.* New York: Routledge.

Fischer, Steven Roger. 2003. *A History of Reading.* London: Reaktion Books.

Graff, Harvey J. 1991. *The Legacies of Literacy: Continuities and Contradictions in Western Culture and Society.* Bloomington, IN: Indiana University Press.

Jardine, Lisa, and Anthony Grafton. 1990. "Studied for Action: How Gabriel Harvey Read His Livy." *Past and Present* 129 (November 1990): 30–78.

Manguel, Alberto. 1996. *A History of Reading.* New York: Penguin Group.

FURTHER READING

Casper, Scott E., Joanne D. Chaison, and Jeffrey D. Groves, eds. 2002. *Perspectives on American Book History: Artifacts and Commentary.* Amherst, MA: University of Massachusetts Press.

Davidson, Cathy D., ed. 1989. *Reading in America: Literature & Social History.* Baltimore, MD: The Johns Hopkins University Press.

_____. 2004. *Revolution and the Word: The Rise of the Novel in America.* Expanded edition. New York: Oxford University Press.

Jackson, H. 1947, 2001. *The Reading of Books.* Urbana, IL: University of Illinois Press.

Jackson, H. J. 2001. *Marginalia: Readers Writing in Books.* New Haven, CT: Yale University Press.

Jasim, Sabah Abboud, and Joan Oates. 1986. "Early Tokens and Tablets in Mesopotamia: New Information from Tell Abada and Tell Brak. *World Archaeology* 17, no. 3 (February): 348–362.

Petroski, Henry. 1999. *The Book on the Bookshelf.* New York: Vintage.

Ryan, Barbara, and Amy M. Thomas, eds. 2002. *Reading Acts: U.S. Readers' Interaction with Literature, 1800–1950.* Knoxville, TN: The University of Tennessee Press.

Wolf, Maryanne. 2007. *Proust and the Squid: The Story and Science of the Reading Brain.* New York: Harcourt Perennial.

Chapter 2

History and Context of Readers' Advisory in the Library

Personal relations between librarian and readers are useful in all libraries.

—Samuel Swett Green, *Library Journal*, 1876

Today, advising readers in libraries about books and authors seems to be common fare and part of daily operations. Adult service librarians cull through reading lists and online resources and talk with colleagues about favorite "reads" and the specifics of genres in an effort to connect adult readers to good books. They talk with the readers using the library to find out what titles are popular and what authors are hot. For many, it is second nature to talk passionately about books and to make knowledgeable recommendations on what to read next or what books might have a particular appeal. At its very heart, readers' advisory celebrates a love of reading and the sharing of an experience.

To place the activities and tools of readers' advisory services in the context of the contemporary reader, the discussion must open with a consideration of what elements define readers' advisory services along with its historical underpinnings. Just as the book as a physical object and the nature of reading has changed, readers' advisory has evolved into a dynamic and popular service for library patrons, making use of myriad tools and resources to connect with adult readers. Today's readers' advisor takes a "whole collection" approach (Saricks, 2008: 33–34) to the process, recommending combinations of fiction and nonfiction along with audio, video, and other media, while in the past readers' advisors guided readers from fiction to the better classes of literature and nonfiction books.

DEFINING READERS' ADVISORY

How can we describe readers' advisory (RA)? Is it a conversation between a librarian and a reader? Is it an educational opportunity to guide a reader to

15

"good" books or a higher level of reading? By definition, readers' advisory is a "public library service provided by a librarian who specializes in the reading needs of the patrons" (Reitz, 2004: n.p.). More importantly, readers' advisors specialize in stories and the ways in which the story matches the needs of the reader. At its core, RA provides a public service connecting the library with its constituency through conversation. And, in the modern-day library, the conversation occurs both in person and through electronic means. Reading has many purposes, including for school and work, but the primary function of RA is leisure reading; it may revolve around a patron's desire for self-education, but the intent of the reading activity is recreational (or leisure or pleasure). RA can be described as having a dual nature or dual purposes: reader satisfaction and a literate society. These purposes go beyond the simple suggestion of a book to read to understanding the patron and his or her purposes in reading.

Readers' advisors go by many titles: fiction librarian, public services librarian, adult services librarian, and RA librarian. Regardless of job title, readers' advisors make a commitment to the interests of the reader and display an open, responsive attitude in meeting the reader's leisure reading needs. Job descriptions throughout the library literature and job announcements for RA librarians frequently include phrases such as "background in reading," "knowledge of books and authors," "public service orientation," and "people skills." The descriptions should read: A passion for intellectual puzzles that are solved through reading and sharing of books with other people. Effective RA librarians combine people skills (part psychologist, part sociologist, and part educator) with complex reading skills (part book critic, part bookseller, and part bookworm). Many of the skills of early readers' advisors are the same skills exhibited today: ability to discover and match the reader's interests to books and authors through well-developed interviewing and conversational skills; general knowledge of fiction and nonfiction collections; and understanding the importance of the relationship between librarian and reader (Saricks, 2005).

HISTORICAL OVERVIEW AND DEVELOPMENT OF READERS' ADVISORY

As early as the 1880s and 1890s, American librarians, educators, and laypeople were debating the literary value of fiction and popular novels and whether these novels had a proper place in public libraries. These early librarians believed it was their mission to lead the reader to a higher class of literature, thereby limiting the reader's dependence upon cheap and "flabby" entertainment. Ross, McKechnie, and Rothbauer summarize the late-nineteenth-century attitude toward reading and popular fiction in the following way:

> . . . reading is like eating, with classes of books that range from drugs, poisons, pabulums, and candy to strong meats and beefsteaks; that books are arranged in order

of value from dime novels and trashy fiction at the bottom to nonfictional, nonnarrative forms such as sermons and philosophy at the top; that librarians have an educational duty to help readers climb the reading ladder from the poorer to the better work; that fiction must be justified in the public library for its education value, not simply as a source of pleasure. (2006: 15–16)

In 1890 at a symposium on fiction in libraries, several librarians spoke both in favor of and argued against the inclusion of popular novels in the public libraries, including a Mr. Herbert Putnam, librarian for the Minneapolis Public Library and future president of the American Library Association. Putnam suggested in 1890 that the purpose of the public library was to be a part of the educational system and that "it is no part of our educational system to provide people with flabby mental nutriment" (1890: 263). He further suggested that the inclusion of popular fiction in the collection was only a device to attract "the reader who has not read at all," and a way to persuade readers of lower-class literature to seek out "something better" (Putnam, 1890: 264). In fact, fiction accounted for approximately 70 to 80 percent of the public library's circulation figures in the late nineteenth century, though fiction comprised less than 40 percent of the overall public library collection (Mason, 1890; Ross, McKechnie, and Rothbauer, 2006).

While fiction was a strong part of the public library collection, the debate about the value of fiction continued on for another century. Betty Rosenberg (1982: 5) legitimized the place of fiction in public libraries with her ground-breaking work *Genreflecting* and the admonishment to "Never apologize for your reading tastes." In addition, associations such as the Adult Readers' Round Table (ARRT) of Illinois solidified the importance of fiction reading in the lives of adults. Not unlike public libraries at the turn of the twentieth century, circulation continues to be the highest for fiction compared to other types of reading materials. Some estimates are as high as 90 percent of the overall circulation figures (Saricks, 2005).

Early Readers' Guidance Initiatives, 1876–1920

Along with the establishment of free libraries to serve the needs of the general public came the establishment of services to adult readers. In its early guises the public library was deemed an educational institution, designed to elevate the patrons' reading tastes and promote self-education beyond the few years of compulsory schooling many people attained. Crowley reminds us that "[r]einforcement of a library educational commitment was tied directly to the reality that fewer than 25 percent of American children older than fourteen years of age were still in school, and relatively few adults were college graduates" (Crowley, 2005: 38). It most certainly reflected the attitude of reading for education and elevation rather than reading for leisure and pleasure, as described by Putnam, Mason, and others. In his early article, Samuel S. Green (1876) suggested that readers were in need of a great deal of assistance from the library staff and it was a crucial function of the librarian to assist patrons willingly, cordially, and with sympathy.

Many arguments were made both for and against the inclusion of popular fiction and novels in the public library. (See Table 2-1 for an overview.) The common refrains for the inclusion of popular fiction suggested that fiction was an attraction for the general reader, enticing him or her into the library, and thus providing opportunities for competent and sympathetic librarians to guide the reader from popular to better literature. On the other hand, many librarians argued that public monies should be used only for the enlightenment and betterment of the working class, and only materials of a high quality should be purchased for public library collections. (Librarians assumed that better-educated readers were already selecting literature on their own.) The early readers' advisor had the responsibility of attempting to elevate the intellectual and cultural life of the reader.

During the early years of readers' guidance initiatives, public librarians separated the functions of reference services and the functions of readers' advisory services. The role of reference was to provide assistance for informational purposes and was conducted by an educated and trained individual. The role of readers' advisory fell within the purview of circulation and was provided by a library assistant or clerk who "heartily enjoys works of the imagination, but whose taste is educated" (Green, repr. 1993: S5). The role of the readers' advisor was to advise readers on stories that suited the moment and to influence the reader to make good choices of literature.

The philosophies and principles of readers' advisory service were born in these early initiatives: connecting readers to books they want to read; being sensitive to the unique needs of the individual readers; creating collections that balance fiction with nonfiction, popular novels with literature; and being responsive to both the recreational and educational needs of the patrons. These

Table 2-1: Arguments For and Against Providing Popular Fiction in the Public Library	
To Provide Popular Fiction	Not to Provide Popular Fiction
Recreational objectives	Educational objectives
Way to attract more patrons by giving public the type of books they liked and understood	Popular novels should not be purchased at taxpayers' expense
A lure to interest the "uncultivated" reader and bring him or her into the library	Elevating readers' taste
Increased recreation through reading novels and popular fiction in a time when few recreational facilities were available to the general public	Not the responsibility of municipalities to provide amusement and entertainment with public funds
Being responsive to reasonable requests for popular materials	Novels gave false ideas and expectations to the "masses"

initiatives also identified the skills necessary to provide effective readers' advisory services, including a good knowledge of books and well-developed people skills.

During the early days of readers' advisory services, many of the ancillary activities common today were initiated. Librarians began creating annotated reading lists of materials covering historical and current events, recent additions to the collection, popular-culture subjects, and best books lists on specific topics. Collection development policies were established that helped guide the acquisition priorities of popular fiction collections. Readers' advisors engaged in selected dissemination of information, sending postal cards to patrons when materials of interest were acquired. Community outreach became a common occurrence with librarians presenting programs to diverse groups, in particular debating clubs and reading circles.

In the latter part of the nineteenth century and early years of the twentieth (approximately 1898–1920), services to library patrons expanded and extended. Patron bases increased with the growth of community outreach. Librarians offered children's services to meet the unique needs of their youngest patrons, including introductions to creative and imaginative stories to encourage the development of reading, and established branch libraries in areas where they would reach the greatest numbers of readers. They also began delivering books to rural families in early precursors to modern bookmobiles (horse and wagon and trucks). From a readers' advisory outlook, it was accepted practice to include popular fiction in library collections for the purposes of recreation and amusement. Fiction collections were developed with a middle-of-the-road approach, including a range of material from popular novels requested by patrons to novels and literature selected for its quality and ability to enlighten. However, the recreation-education debate continued, but it took a divergent path to consider how much fiction should be included.

The People's University, 1920–1940

Readers' advisory services in public libraries became firmly ingrained in the mid-twentieth century. A number of major urban public libraries throughout the United States created full-time readers' advisor positions to serve their growing patron bases. The readers' advisor represented a unique position within the library separate from others and that required a specialized set of skills and tools (bibliographies especially) to match readers and books. The role of the readers' advisor was twofold: assisting adults in achieving their own learning goals and helping change casual readers into purposeful ones, both to be accomplished through the preparation of individual reading plans (Lee, 1966).

At this time, researchers for the University of Chicago, in cooperation with the American Library Association, conducted a systematic study of adult readers' interests, which helped inform the practice of readers' advisory. Two signifi-

First Urban Public Libraries with Readers' Advisory Services

1922 Detroit and Cleveland
1923 Chicago and Milwaukee
1924 Indianapolis
1925 Cincinnati and Portland (OR)

cant studies that provided the first insights into adult readers included *Reading Interest and Habits of Adults* (1929) and *What People Want to Read About* (1931). Both studies identified many factors that affected adult reading patterns, such as age, sex, marital status, and education level. (The National Endowment for the Arts current reports, *Reading at Risk*, *To Read or Not to Read*, and *Reading on the Rise*, harken back to these early studies.) These two studies, along with numerous others, laid the foundations for methods to pair book selection with the reading interests, habits, and reading levels of adults (Lee, 1966).

Reading plans prepared by readers' advisors became familiar resources within the library's reading rooms. These plans offered systematic reading on a variety of topics and were intended to serve as guides for self-education in travel, philosophy, history, humanities, and the sciences. The reading plans were a product of the American Library Association's "Reading with a Purpose Program." ALA commissioned, published, and disseminated a series of 67 bibliographic essays on an array of topics with recommendations for both fiction and nonfiction works (Crowley, 2005). Reading plans in general supported the long-time belief in the public library's role as an institution for continuing adult education.

In light of the educational role, public libraries and readers' advisors became actively involved with other agencies that offered adult education. The public library provided services in support of adult education, including preparing materials and reading lists for discussion and study groups. The local library also supplied books and materials for community organizations, university extension services, and correspondence schools and allowed access to library facilities for lectures, community meetings, and classes. Librarians also maintained specialized collections for community educational and vocational programs such as the Emergency Education Program. (This is reflected in the collections of many contemporary public libraries today; they maintain collections for continuing education and certification for emergency medical personnel, firefighters, and law enforcement as well as collections for adult basic education and English for Speakers of Other Languages.)

Throughout the 1930s, book discussion groups and community reading groups slowly evolved in the public library setting. These reading groups had a similar appeal and focus to today's "One Book, One Community" events (see Chapter 17, "Reading Events—A Celebration of Reading, Books, and Authors," for detailed discussion). Under the guidance of a librarian or other specialist discussion leader, adult readers following the same reading plans met to discuss the ideas the books presented in light of social and cultural issues of the times. While originally intended as an educational opportunity, it also allowed adults to share their reading experiences and responses to books.

Much of the popularity of readers' advisory services and the public library in the 1930s can be attributed to the effects of the Great Depression. The public library supported the general public's need to improve work skills and educational levels while also providing a place for inexpensive entertainment (free, actually) by way of reading for pleasure. The library also served as a safe haven from the elements where people could spend a few hours studying. However, the looming war changed much of this.

War and Waning Interests, 1940s–1980s

When the United States entered World War II, circulation of fiction in the public libraries declined as did the popularity of readers' advisory services. Working for the war effort became an overwhelming need; workers had little time for leisure and self-study. A longitudinal analysis of public library circulation, conducted by Herbert Goldhor (1949, 1950, and 1957) and later reported by Esther Jane Carrier (1985), indicates a decrease in median circulation of adult fiction materials nationwide from 46 to 31 percent of all circulated materials between 1939 and 1950 (Carrier, 1985). The priorities of the nation looked to maintaining the home front and supporting the troops abroad rather than simple amusements to pass time. With decreasing fiction circulation, requests for readers' advisory assistance also decreased. In fact, many libraries discontinued separate readers' advisory services, focusing their efforts on other services and resources and subsuming RA into larger adult service departments.

As in previous decades, the debate over fiction continued. Many librarians continued to argue against purchasing light or popular fiction but to maintain strong collections of literature and nonfiction. They also continued to emphasize the educational role of the library rather than the recreational one. Proponents of the library as a recreational institution compromised by providing selections of mysteries, adventure, and Westerns that were of unmistakable quality (Alexandre Dumas, Arthur Conan Doyle, Robert Louis Stevenson, for example) along with selections for popular taste, believing in the principle of "seeking to find the right book for the right reader at the right time" (Carrier, 1985: 205).

Postwar library services emphasized the informational and educational role of the library. Libraries with designated RA staffing dropped from a peak of 65 readers' advisors in 1935 to a low of ten in the 1940s and 1950s (Lee, 1966; Crowley, 2005). Librarians continued to be actively involved in outreach to community agencies and organizations in support of educational needs, but as part of the larger adult services departments. Adult programming in support of both individual and group education commonly occurred in libraries during the postwar period. Programming included lecture and discussion activities related to specific topics offered as a series, and participants were supplied with materials and related booklists. The programs were also promoted and supported by library exhibits. Some topics included in these community-wide programs were civic and current events, social issues (aging, child care, family life), and arts and humanities. The overwhelming emphasis focused on the reading of literature and educational materials and far less on popular fiction.

While readers' advisory services dwindled, library-sponsored reading discussion groups flourished. The Public Library of Washington, DC, initiated these types of programs in 1945 with their "Group Reading Program," which included reading and discussion of the works of Plato, Freud, and Emerson. Another offshoot of the library-sponsored programs included Great Books seminars at the Chicago Public Library in cooperation with the University of Chicago, which used a reading plan recommended by Mortimer Adler. The Great Books discussion group was placed under the guidance of the Great Books Foundation in 1947 and continues today with the mission to promote liberal education through the exploration of classics and great literature.

Readers' advisory services, while not disappearing altogether, became a silent partner in the public library. Many activities related to reading and providing access to popular fiction occurred during the 1960s to 1980s, but service to the individual reader was a lesser function, provided less systematically, and occasionally ignored. This was also an era of "Give Them What They Want." Libraries developed and maintained significant fiction collections that met the reading interests of contemporary library users. These collections most frequently included the national bestsellers and popular how-to books similar to what was found in local booksellers and in the grocery store's magazine aisle. Librarians certainly answered queries about books and aided readers in their selections, but they placed far less emphasis on the need for this type of service.

READERS' ADVISORY IN A MULTIMEDIA WORLD

Since the 1980s, a resurgence of interest in readers' advisory services in public libraries has occurred. The establishment of the Adult Reading Round Table in 1984, with the focus on adult reading interests, along with the publication of Betty Rosenberg's *Genreflecting* in 1982, is frequently seen as the beginning of the RA revival. Unlike the role of education of earlier activities, readers' advisory now emphasizes reading for leisure based upon the reader's interests and desired reading experience rather than guiding the reader to specific classes of literature. RA also emphasizes both works of fiction and of nonfiction and the role of genre fiction in the reading experience. The reader and his or her needs and interests reside at the heart of contemporary readers' advisory services.

Few libraries today can afford the luxury of a department solely devoted to readers' advisory, and oftentimes this activity is rolled into the broader area of reference or public services. However, more librarians and library staff are trained in helping adult readers find satisfying books to read. Library and information science schools nationwide offer classes devoted to adult services and information needs; local, state, and national conferences offer a variety of workshops, presentations, and discussion groups about serving adult readers in libraries; and many organizations offer continuing education with a focus on serving adult patrons.

Today, readers' advisory goes beyond linking readers and books. Adult services librarians now link readers to books, author resources, and multimedia resources to enhance the reading experience. Nonfiction has a definitive place in the leisure reading experience as do genre fiction and literary fiction. The focus is on providing the best-quality reading experience that meets the needs and expectations as defined by the individual reader. Readers' advisors look to the entire collection of the library—physical and virtual—to help readers make connections with books they will enjoy.

The tools of readers' advisory have expanded in scope with the rapidly advancing electronic resources. In the early days of readers' advisory, a few commercially published bibliographies and lists could be consulted, and perhaps a few colleagues could expand on books and authors. With the publishing of *Genreflecting* in 1982, a new generation of readers' resource was born, including several electronic databases that could be queried to match reading interests, authors, and genres. Today, readers' advisors consult hundreds of Web sites, listservs, blogs, databases (proprietary and public), readers' guides, and a variety of lists and books to aid the reader in finding the "right book at the right time."

Reading is a new and exciting experience for readers and readers' advisory librarians alike. Format of the book is no longer a limitation with the ready availability of digital and multimedia versions. Amazon's Kindle and other electronic reading devices as well as audiobooks that can be downloaded to mp3 players and similar devices allow readers to read anytime and anyplace. Through Web sites and social networking services, readers can engage with their favorite authors and participate in reading events. Reading has evolved into a sensuous experience allowing readers to use sound, touch, sight, and imagination to immerse themselves in books.

CONCLUSION

While much of readers' advisory has evolved over the past 100 years, much has remained the same. Many of the early strategies and readers' guidance activities echo in today's strategies, including sensitivity to the needs of the reader, conversing with the reader to determine interests, and maintaining collections that fulfill the reader's needs. At its core, readers' advisory has always intended to meet the needs of the reader by connecting him or her to books that suit the given mood and taste. The philosophy of serving the needs of the patron through nonjudgmental approaches and using well-honed strategies to start the conversation has provided the foundation for meeting those needs. The succeeding chapters of this book will explore many of the tools and strategies for readers' advisory as well as examine the ancillary resources and services to help provide a quality reading experience.

WORKS CONSULTED

Carrier, Esther Jane. 1965. *Fiction in Public Libraries 1976–1900*. New York: Scarecrow Press.

_____. 1985. *Fiction in Public Libraries 1900–1950*. Littleton, CO: Libraries Unlimited.

Crowley, Bill. 2005. "Rediscovering the History of Readers Advisory Service." *Public Libraries* 44, no. 1 (January/February): 7–41.

Great Books Foundation. 2008. Available: www.greatbooks.org (accessed September 10, 2009).

Green, Samuel Swett. 1876. "Personal Relations between Librarians and Readers." *Library Journal* 1, no. 1 (October 1); reprinted in 118, no. 11 (June 15, 1993): S4–S5.

Lee, Robert Ellis. 1966. *Continuing Education for Adults through the American Public Library 1833–1964*. Chicago: American Library Association.

Mason, T. 1890. "Fiction in Free Libraries." *Library Journal* 15, no. 9 (September): 265–267.

Putnam, Herbert. 1890. "Fiction in Libraries: Minneapolis (Minn.) Public Library." *Library Journal* 15, no. 9 (September): 263–264.

Reitz, Joan M. 2004. *ODLIS—Online Dictionary for Library and Information Science*. Westport, CT: Libraries Unlimited. Available: http://lu.com/odlis/odlis_r.cfm (accessed September 15, 2009).

Rosenberg, Betty. 1982. *Genreflecting: A Guide to Reading Interests in Genre Fiction*. Littleton, CO: Libraries Unlimited.

Ross, Catherine Sheldrick, Lynne (E. F.) McKechnie, and Paulette M. Rothbauer. 2006. *Reading Matters: What the Research Reveals about Reading, Libraries and Communities*. Westport, CT: Libraries Unlimited.

Saricks, Joyce G. 2005. *Readers' Advisory Service in the Public Library*, 3rd edition. Chicago: American Library Association.

_____. 2008. "The Conversation 101." *Library Journal* 133, no. 3 (February 15): 33–34.

FURTHER READING

Dilevko, Juris, and Candice F. C. Magowan. 2007. *Readers' Advisory Service in North American Public Libraries, 1897–2005*. Jefferson, NC: McFarland.

Flexner, Jennie M. 1938. "Readers and Books." *Library Journal* (January 15); reprinted in 118 (July 1993): S8.

Moyer, Jessica E. 2005. "Adult Fiction Reading: A Literature Review of Readers' Advisory Services, Adult Fiction Librarianship, and Fiction Readers." *Reference and User Services Quarterly* 44, no. 3 (Spring 2005): 220–231.

Saricks, Joyce. 2008. "At Leisure: Readers' Advisory—Flash in the Pan or Here to Stay?" *Booklist* 104, no. 21 (July 1): 12.

_____. 2008. "At Leisure: Hiring Readers' Advisors." *Booklist* 105, no. 1 (September 1): 42.

United States Office of Education. 1876. *Public Libraries in the United States: Part 1*. Washington, DC: Author. Reprinted by University of Illinois Graduate School of Library Science, Champaign, 1966.

Chapter 3

The Role of the Reader and the Act of Reading

What is reading, in the last analysis, but an interchange of thought between writer and reader?

—from Edith Wharton, "The Vice of Reading" (1903)

As we begin to consider the role of readers' advisory in libraries, we must also consider the role of the reader and the act of reading. The interests and needs of the reader drive collection development and fiction acquisition along with the readers' advisory activities, and the reader is, perhaps, the most important element of readers' advisory service. Understanding the reader and how each reader approaches individual choices clarifies the role of the librarian and the ability to assist the reader. This chapter surveys the definition of *the reader* and theories of reading and includes an examination of the purposes of reading. It lays the foundations for later discussions of the reader's engagement with texts.

THE READER

When you look in the mirror, who do you see? A reader? Can we easily define a reader by appearance, attitude, or actions? What makes a reader different from nonreaders? By extension we also need to ask, *Who* reads?

While the descriptions of the everyday or common (nonspecialist) reader vary, it can certainly be said that readers today are individuals who engage with words in many ways and multiple formats from print to audio and digital products. Samuel Johnson, the great British essayist and lexicographer, coined the phrase "common reader" in the eighteenth century to refer to the everyday individual (the farmer, housewife, merchant) who reads for pleasure and enlightenment. Ohmann (1983) and Kaplan and Rose (1990) believe that common readers are situated in all levels of the socioeconomic strata but are predominantly middle class, mostly educated, having spent a minimum of 12 years in formal schooling and most likely college educated. The common reader is the individual who frequents bookstores and public libraries; enjoys reading for pleasure and for information; and is "engaged with the world and socially involved" (Ross, McKechnie, and Rothbauer, 2006: 23). Readers purchase books for themselves and for others as well as borrow books from the public library and pass books between friends and family. With a simple, elegant description, Joyce G. Saricks (2005) and Diana Trixler Herald (2006) say readers are people who read, and they read everything from popular genre fiction to nonfiction to the literary classics.

Looking to the large-scale national studies of reading habits, including the National Endowment for the Arts (NEA) surveys, we can discern some demographic profiles of who reads. For example, NEA (2004) found that white American females had the highest literary reading among the racial and ethnic groups in the United States; Hispanic-American males had the lowest literary reading rates. However, the most current NEA survey (2008) reports an increase in literary reading rates by all ethnic and racial groups. Each of the last three NEA surveys (2004, 2007, and 2008) also suggest that literary reading and educational level are closely correlated with college-educated individuals more likely to engage in literary reading than individuals without a high school education. A recent Associated Press poll (Fram, 2007) found that Southerners read more books than the rest of the nation, while one in four Americans read no books in the previous year. However, in general the aggregate information from the multitude of large-scale studies invariably reports that the vast majority of the U.S. population reads something—newspapers, magazines, books, Web sites—whether defined as literary or not. (The NEA surveys define literary reading as novels, short stories, plays and poetry, discounting works of nonfiction.) British and European studies suggest similar results that the majority of adults read a variety of materials (see for example Toyne and Usherwood, 2001; Great Britain Library and Information Commission, 2000).

Other studies and surveys of readers examine the many purposes for which people read. For some it is an opportunity to exercise freedom of choice among the hundreds of available titles, selecting a book that suits a particular mood or place. For other individuals reading is purely for entertainment and pleasure. Reading provides temporary escape from the immediate world for some, while for others reading helps develop an understanding of the world at large and why events happen. Reading for information, for intellectual stimulation, and for the pleasure that rich and complex language invokes are all regularly cited reasons that readers give for their indulgences. Wayne Wiegand sums it up, saying, "[T]hey have borrowed, they have been able to fantasize and indulge, to transgress and to subvert, to appropriate and poach" (Wiegand, 1997: 36).

Types of Readers

Many attempts have been made to classify readers by type. In her book *Speaking of Reading*, Nadine Rosenthal (1995) describes eight types of readers, ranging from voracious and habitual readers to frustrated readers and adult new readers. The purpose and focus of reading for Rosenthal's groups vary widely. Voracious readers "inhale reading material . . . read[ing] magazines and newspapers . . . , literature, novels, mysteries, science fiction, history, politics, sociology, science, technology, popular psychology, repair manuals, how-to books, and cereal box tops" (Rosenthal, 1995: 77). Rosenthal suggests that voracious readers are "enraptured" by their reading. Ross, McKechnie, and Rothbauer (2006) and Toyne and Usherwood (2001) have similar descriptions of these readers, which they term "avid" readers.

On the other hand, reading for the frustrated reader is a chore to be endured. Many "reluctant readers are discouraged by their slow pace, poor attention span, comprehension failures, and inability to focus" (Rosenthal, 1995: 25). Toyne and Usherwood (2001), in their study of British readers in the public library, consider the category of nonreaders, individuals for whom reading has no significance. They identify two subgroups within nonreaders: (1) those who can but choose not to read (the common term today is aliterate) and (2) those who experience difficulties with reading (Rosenthal's frustrated readers and adult new readers). For many nonreaders, reading was never encouraged and never became part of their lifestyle. Others engaged in different leisure-time activities that they felt provided similar experiences that reading provides for readers (Toyne and Usherwood, 2001). Still others, through social and economic disadvantages, poor educational experiences, and many other instances, experience difficulties in reading or have inadequate literacy skills to cope with everyday reading or with higher-level literary reading.

Yet there is room in the library for both the avid and the frustrated reader. The avid reader wants books to fulfill a visceral need to read while the frustrated reader needs a book mentor to encourage his or her reading efforts—a role played equally well by a readers' advisor. (The notion of reading mentors will be examined in a later chapter when we look to readers' advisory services for specialized populations.)

THE PROCESS OF READING

In her book *Book Savvy*, Cynthia Lee Katona describes reading as an "unnatural" act in terms of it being a learned behavior as opposed to an instinctual, or unlearned, behavior (Katona, 2005: 11–12). Although it may seem as if we have a genetic predisposition to reading, we do not emerge from the womb as readers or nonreaders; it is a behavior that we learn over time through compulsory education, our families and caregivers, and our own intellectual curiosity. Reading can be described as an apprenticeship; as the apprentice learns a trade, he or she moves from apprentice to journeyman, from journeyman to craftsman; as apprentice readers we move from picture books to easy juvenile books, from chapter books to adult reading, and even from genre fiction to literary works, continually improving our skills along the way. We pick and choose our reading carefully to match our needs and interests and respond individually and collectively to the author's attempts to communicate with us.

Over the past several decades, educators and reading researchers have examined the practice of reading and literacy development through numerous lenses. The common element of the models is that reading is an active pursuit with the reader engaging in some form of dialogue with the author and the content of the written work. The reader brings something of himself or herself as an individual to the process while taking something from the author in fulfilling a need. Briefly examining some of the theories of reading allows the adult services librarian to understand what influences readers' choices situating reading as a transaction between the individual and the text.

Looking back to early educational practices, reading was taught as if it were a passive activity. We learned our letters, then words, sentences, and paragraphs by rote. Reading comprehension was thought to be the recognition of lists of words (remember old-fashioned spelling lists, primers, and hornbooks?) and the ability to use the lists in comprehensible, even prescribed ways. Authors gave meaning to their books through words and structure, rather than readers interpreting the content and bringing life to meaning. Reading by this description becomes an "outside-in" approach. "Meaning is thought to reside within the text, and the readers' job is to decode what's right there on the page and then take it in" (Ross, McKechnie, and Rothbauer, 2006: 48). There was little, if any, recognition of the individual reader in the early processes of literacy education and development.

During the latter half of the twentieth century, researchers began to advance new theories and thoughts on the act of reading. They posited reading as an active process with readers using their own experiences and knowledge in developing an understanding of the content and context of the text. Researchers focused on an "inside-out" approach to reading, "emphasizing the knowledge that is in the head of the reader—knowledge about the way the world works, the way language functions, and the way that stories work" (Ross, McKechnie, and Rothbauer, 2006: 49).

Several models of reading emerged from this inside-out approach, falling under an overarching series of reader-response theories. Combined, these models enable an understanding of individual choice and sociocultural influences on reading. The models describe reading as a transaction between reader and text and between reader and author.

Reader Response Theories

Reader response theories accounted for the role of the individual in the process of reading. However, the focus was not on the everyday reader as described previously, but rather looked to the "ideal" or "intended" reader. The individual had the linguistic and cognitive knowledge to interpret and understand the author's exact message and draw the same conclusions as the author. By extension, the author wrote for a specific, or intended, audience, based on socioeconomic class, educational level, or other variable of the reading community. Early studies of genre writing fell into this "intended" audience rubric, suggesting that popular fiction "carried social messages and was sometimes targeted at particular groups, such as women, working-class readers, and adolescents" (Kaestle, 1991: 71).

Schema Theory

Schema theory suggests each individual has an existing framework or pattern of understanding based upon past experiences that gives meaning to individual reading. The model emphasizes the individual's experiences and prior knowledge, and the ability to match new information to existing knowledge. According to Nassaji, "One of the major insights of schema theory lay in drawing attention to the constructive nature of the reading process and to the critical role of the reader and the interaction between the text and the reader's background knowledge" (Nassaji, 2007: 80). It also suggests "the greater our store of previously acquired knowledge on a topic and the more substance we have to connect new information to, the more we can read with fluency and a feeling of control over our reading" (Rosenthal, 1995: xviii). Schema theory allows the reader to use his or her own store of knowledge of other texts and of the world at large to construct meaning when introduced to new or forgotten information.

Metacognition Theory

Metacognition quite literally means thinking about how we think. Situating it in the reading process, Rosenthal explains, "Metacognition theory describes how active readers monitor their thinking as they read. Active readers are aware of when they are understanding the content of what they are reading and when they have lost the thread of meaning" (Rosenthal, 1995: xviii). Readers engage in specific conscious acts of controlling reading, planning and monitoring their reading, and assessing success as they reach the goals of their reading (Noushad, 2008). Most frequently used as a learning strategy, metacognition is characterized by the ability to recognize, evaluate, and reconstruct existing knowledge to explain new ideas and concepts. Rosenthal defines metacognitive readers as "process-aware" readers who are able to "provide great detail about their own unique methods of constructing meaning from print" (Rosenthal, 1995: 175).

Interpretive Communities

In its simplest explanation an interpretive community is a group of readers who share a common meaning of a text, which they arrived at individually. Interpretive communities may be best illustrated by book discussion groups, whereby group members each read the same title then come together to discuss, agree, and debate the author's intent, with members frequently drawing the same conclusion and interpretations independently of one another beforehand. The notion of an interpretive community suggests that reading is both an individual act and a social one (Fish, 2002; Iser, 2002). The reader takes a text (a novel, a poem, etc.), makes and revises assumptions, asks questions, and draws conclusions from the words as written based upon the reader's own sociocultural milieu, education, and experiences. A more significant phenomenon occurs when several individual readers draw the same or similar conclusion and interpretations from a book which they have read separately. This is a result of being members of many communities (work groups, schools, social groups, etc.) that inform thoughts and actions, and from the social and cultural forces in the individual's environments.

THE PURPOSES OF READING

Models and theories explain *how* individuals read, but in order to be effective in connecting readers to books and other forms of literary content, it becomes necessary to examine *why* individuals read. As discussed in the preceding chapters, early reading was intended for transmittal of information (accounting, edicts, and laws), for education and enlightenment, and for religious and spiritual guidance. As the novel and other forms of written entertainment enjoyed growing popularity, the purposes of reading expanded to include recreation and pleasure along with several other reasons. The categories of reading (see Table 3-1) are not mutually exclusive, but they provide a useful way to distinguish the purposes for which adults read. More importantly, readers use reading for multiple purposes simultaneously.

Reading categories can be parsed to further explore why readers choose particular types of reading. For example, information readers typically read nonfiction and take great pleasure in learning something new. They can be described as "individuals [who] find entertainment in the pursuit of knowledge" (Rosenthal, 1995: 149). Information readers are purposeful in their reading selections, choosing materials that enlighten and engage their intellectual curiosity. However, their information reading also reflects their choices for recreational reading in the form of biographies, histories, narratives, and other nonfiction works. By comparison, literature readers, or literary fiction readers, "read simply for aesthetic pleasure. They relish the sound and structure of the language, the artistry of well-crafted sentences" (Rosenthal, 1995: 1). Their understanding of the

Table 3-1: Purpose and Practice of Reading	
Type	**Uses**
Environmental Reading	Signs, billboards, external displays
Informational Reading	Instructions, research and consultation, nonfiction
Occupational/Professional Reading	Work documents (memos, letters, etc.), professional resources
Educational Reading	Textbooks and required class reading
Recreational Reading	Fiction and nonfiction for pleasure and leisure
Devotional and Ritualistic Reading	Sacred writings, religious and spiritual works
Accidental Reading	Bus and taxi side-panel advertisements, flyers and brochures, shop window and bulletin board announcements

Source: Table 3-1 was compiled from Rosenthal, 1995; Fischer, 2003; and Ross, McKechnie, and Rothbauer, 2006.

human condition is expanded and explained through the complexity of the books they choose to read. "Literary Fiction readers prefer books that demand more from them. The style, the language, and the issues considered may all require an intelligent reader willing to invest some time and effort in unraveling the puzzle these books often present" (Saricks, 2001: 134). Literature readers choose to explore and experience new literary dimensions through their reading.

Readers often describe their reading as escapist pleasures, for relaxation, and an opportunity to escape into other worlds. They also read for insight and identification—insight into their own lives through literary reading and identification with characters who find themselves in similar circumstances as well as insight into the thoughts and motivations of others. In study after study readers report that reading provides lessons about the world, from the political to the cultural, and promotes greater understanding of other backgrounds, cultures, and customs.

The notion of reading for identification and insight is particularly relevant to those Fischer (2003) calls "modern marginalized readers." Contemporary fiction, and even nonfiction, reflects the marginalized reader's unique place in society. "All marginalized readers—women, gays, blacks, exiles, and many more—read for just this reason. . . . Reading shares one's differences; it reminds that one is not alone. The demand for such reading is enormous at present" (Fischer, 2003: 315). Materials for the "marginalized" reader may be encompassed by urban street fiction, African-American fiction, GLBTQ literature, chick lit, and other genres, presented in later chapters.

CONCLUSION

Readers are a quirky and changeable group. No one definition fits except the common element that readers read, and they read for a purpose (and not a common purpose). Although the large-scale reading surveys generalize about demographics and profiles, readers come from all walks of life and interests. They choose to read for many reasons and to fulfill many individual needs. To further confound the issue, readers' tastes change across time and place, reflecting individual and societal interests. In the final analysis, the process and purposes of reading are about choice. Readers choose the time and place to read, the experience they want from the books they choose, and the purposes to which they apply the reading.

WORKS CONSULTED

Fischer, Steven Roger. 2003. *A History of Reading.* London: Reaktion Books.

Fish, Stanley. 2002. "Interpreting the *Variorum.*" In *The Book History Reader,* 2nd edition (pp. 450–458), edited by David Finkelstein and Alistair McCleery. London: Routledge.

Fram, Alan. 2007. "One in Four Read No Books Last Year." ABC News. Washington: The Associated Press. Available: http://abcnews.go.com/print?id=3507898 (accessed September 10, 2009).

Great Britain Library and Information Commission. 2000. *Reading the Situation: Book Reading, Buying & Borrowing Habits in Britain.* London: Book Marketing, Ltd.

Herald, Diana Trixler. 2006. *Genreflecting: A Guide to Popular Reading Interests,* edited by Wayne A. Wiegand. Westport, CT: Libraries Unlimited.

Iser, Wolfgang. 2002. "Interaction between Text and Reader." In *The Book History Reader,* 2nd edition (pp. 391–396), edited by David Finkelstein and Alistair McCleery. London: Routledge.

Kaestle, Carl F. 1991. "The History of Readers." In *Literacy in the United States: Readers and Reading since 1880* (pp. 33–73), by Carl F. Kaestle et al. New Haven, CT: Yale University Press.

Kaplan, Carey, and Ellen Cronan Rose. 1990. *The Canon and the Common Reader.* Knoxville: The University of Tennessee Press.

Katona, Cynthia Lee. 2005. *Book Savvy.* Lanham, MD: The Scarecrow Press.

Moyer, Jessica. 2008. *Research-Based Readers' Advisory.* Chicago, IL: American Library Association.

Nassaji, Hossein. 2007. "Schema Theory and Knowledge-Based Processes in Second Language Reading Comprehension: A Need for Alternative Perspectives." *Language Learning* 57, Supplement 1 (June): 79–113.

National Endowment for the Arts. 2004. *Reading at Risk: A Survey of Literary Reading in America.* Research Division Report #46. Washington, DC: National Endowment for the Arts.

_____. 2007. *To Read or Not to Read: A Question of National Consequence.* Research Report #47. Washington, DC: National Endowment for the Arts.

_____. 2008. *Reading on the Rise: A New Chapter in American Literacy.* Washington, DC: National Endowment for the Arts.

Noushad, P. P. 2008. "Cognitions about Cognitions: The Theory of Metacognition." ERIC Report (#ED502141).

Ohmann, Richard. 1983. "The Shaping of a Canon: U.S. Fiction, 1960–1975." *Critical Inquiry* 10, no. 1 (September): 199–223.

Rosenthal, Nadine. 1995. *Speaking of Reading*. Portsmouth, NH: Heinemann.

Ross, Catherine Sheldrick, Lynne (E. F.) McKechnie, and Paulette M. Rothbauer. 2006. *Reading Matters: What the Research Reveals about Reading, Libraries and Communities*. Westport, CT: Libraries Unlimited.

Saricks, Joyce G. 2001. *The Readers' Advisory Guide to Genre Fiction*. Chicago, IL: American Library Association.

_____. 2005. *Readers' Advisory Service in the Public Library*, 3rd edition. Chicago, IL: American Library Association.

Toyne, Jackie, and Bob Usherwood. 2001. *Checking the Books: The Value and Impact of Public Library Book Reading*. Sheffield, England: Department of Information Studies, The University of Sheffield. Available: www.shef.ac.uk/content/1/c5/ 07/01/24/CPLIS% 20-%20Checking%20the%20Books.pdf (accessed September 10, 2009).

Wharton, Edith. 1903. "The Vice of Reading." *North American Review* 177 (October): 513–521. Available: http://etext.lib.virginia.edu.modeng.html (accessed September 10, 2009).

Wiegand, Wayne A. 1997. "MisReading LIS Education." *Library Journal* 122, no. 11 (June 15): 36.

Woolf, Virginia. 1925. *The Common Reader*. Orlando, FL: Harcourt.

FURTHER READING

Along with the large-scale studies of readers and numerous texts on readers' advisory, a wonderful body of literature illustrates the reader's engagement with books. Lawrence Clark Powell's book of essays, titled *A Passion for Books* (1958), explores his personal relationship with reading, books, and librarianship. Nicholas A. Basbanes focuses on books and book collecting in several of his recent publications, most especially *Every Book Its Reader* (2005) and *A Gentle Madness* (1995), celebrating a love of reading and a love of books. Ronald B. Shwartz offers a series of individual commentaries, titled *For the Love of Books* (1999), by eminent writers of the twentieth century on the books that most influenced them. In *Books* (2008), Larry McMurtry offers a memoir of his life in books. All of these are very personal accounts of individuals' relationships with reading.

Part II

Reaching the Contemporary Reader

Chapter 4

Tags, Clouds, and Participatory Readers' Advisory Services

If you build it, he will come.

—from *Shoeless Joe* by W. P. Kinsella (1982)

Throughout this book we focus on reading and the power of community to connect readers to books. What better way to facilitate these connections than through participatory services and resources designed to enhance the reading experience? Today's buzzword and tomorrow's old hat, "Library 2.0" opens innovative ways to reach library users and nonusers alike by inviting them to participate in creating content that is useful to them. It also offers libraries the ability to do more for their constituents with less, especially less budget. Library 2.0 technologies greatly enhance the library's ability to reach out to its community and to offer the community more than a storehouse for books.

For readers' advisors the Library 2.0 concept offers alternatives for engaging readers in conversation. From Web sites offering simple reading lists to blogs with embedded audio and video of author interviews, adult service librarians solicit feedback from library users about their needs and interests and can rapidly respond to the feedback with changes and new resources. In many ways, the innovations bring the library to the reader and provide the reader with access to a range of resources beyond the library catalog and shelves. More importantly, the new technologies invite readers to contribute to the experience, making the library's Web site or catalog more robust for everyone. While too numerous to include all, several of the more robust and popular innovations will be explored in this chapter.

VERY BRIEF OVERVIEW OF WEB 2.0 AND LIBRARY 2.0

In 2003, Tim O'Reilly was credited with coining the term "Web 2.0" to describe and conceptualize the ways in which the Web has changed society and the ways individuals communicate and connect to one another. The premise of Web 2.0 is that the Web serves as a platform from which applications and software can be shared and integrated to enhance communication and offer a global reach. Its strengths are in its ability to allow users to create content and to remix existing content and applications to create something entirely new. It offers a rich, participatory experience for any Web user. Today the Web is no longer the bailiwick of Webmasters and programmers; anyone can create content and post it by using an array of easy-to-use applications and resources that are freely available online. Web users will find blogs, social networking Web sites, social bookmarking, really simple syndication (RSS) feeds, photo- and video-sharing, and podcasting among the many Web 2.0 technologies readily and freely available.

Libraries took advantage of the opportunities that Web 2.0 innovations offered by finding new ways to communicate within and outside of the library proper and by inviting library users and nonusers alike to offer evaluation and feedback. In 2005 the phrase "Library 2.0" began to be heard among forward-thinking librarians, and appeared in Michael Casey's online blog LibraryCrunch (www .librarycrunch.com) among others. Casey and Savastinuk cover the following points in their definition of Library 2.0:

- . . . a model for constant and purposeful change;
- . . . empowers library users through participatory, user-driven services;
- . . . seeks to improve services to current library users while also reaching out to potential library users. (2007: 5)

The idea of Library 2.0 is that it is user-centered and intended to meet the needs of the user and potential user. In addition, Library 2.0 has purpose and intent, and is not the use of technology for technology's sake.

In its most current "Online Trends" Survey, the Pew Internet and American Life Project (May 2008) reported that 73 percent of American adults used the Internet during their day-to-day lives. These online activities include using a search engine to find information (89 percent); visiting a government Web site (federal, state, or local) (66 percent); watching videos on video-sharing Web sites (52 percent); reading online blogs or journals (33 percent); downloading podcasts for later listening/viewing (19 percent); and creating their own blogs or online journals (12 percent). Many of these adults reported engaging in one or more of the online activities on a daily basis. In January 2009, the Pew Internet and American Life Project reported that approximately 35 percent of adults have a profile on an online social network, such as MySpace or Facebook, and 19 percent of these adults used the social networking sites on a daily basis to connect with family, friends, and other people they know. All of these Web 2.0 features play a crucial role in the lives of adults as they connect with the greater world. From a library point of view, these are all activities that can be provided through the library's Web site, encouraging patrons to find value and relevance in their library and in the services available to the community at large.

LIBRARY 2.0 TOOLBOX

As much is excluded as is included in the discussion of Library 2.0 tools. Keeping current on technological innovations and developments is critical to meeting the needs of library users. Annual library association conferences feature a range of workshops and presentations covering new technologies and their uses within the library world. Professional journals, Web sites, and blogs publish articles on the current state of the art. The tools included in this chapter are ones that have direct applicability to readers' advisory services, though many more could be discussed.

Blogs

First used in 1999, *Merriam-Webster's Collegiate Dictionary* (11th edition) defines a blog as "a Web site that contains an online personal journal with reflections, comments, and often hyperlinks provided by the writer," but today blogs are so much more, incorporating commentary, events, graphics, audio, and video. Blogs, or more formally Weblogs as we know them today, are content-rich Web sites that are easily updated and edited. They offer users the ability to not only edit content, but to allow comments and contributions by others. Technorati, an online service that tracks blogs, reported that they had indexed more than 133 million blogs since 2002, and that as of May 2008 more than 94.1 million people in the United States read blogs (Technorati, 2008), and use of blogs continues to grow. Most frequently blogs will contain news and events, commentary from blog readers, tags and keywords, navigational links, and the ability to provide RSS feeds. Blogs are also cost-efficient means of communication in that many blog resources are freely available and hosted by online blog services. Some hosting organizations offer open-source applications that can be downloaded and installed on the library's own server; these are more complex and flexible than the free resources, but they do often involve fees for hosting and require more expertise to install and modify.

A library blog is an elegant, simple way to provide information to the community while inviting participation in the form of commentary and feedback. Using blogs for the library offers an advantage in the ease and speed of updating information because blogs require little or no expertise in Web development and design (most blog resources provide templates and easy-to-follow instructions) or experience in HTML coding. This allows the IT staff to concentrate on other mission-critical operations of the library's Web site and systems while allowing a free flow of communication between the library and library users. Among other features, public libraries use their blogs to promote and market programs and activities, highlight new books and materials or portions of the library's collection, and disseminate announcements about upcoming events.

Select Free Sources for Blog Applications
(hosted on the blog provider's site)

Blogger: www.blogger.com
LiveJournal: www.livejournal.com
WordPress: www.wordpress.com
Xanga: www.xanga.com

Selected Resources for Blogging and Content Management
(typically requires a Web host)

Drupal: http://drupal.com
Movable Type: www.movabletype.com
WordPress: www.wordpress.org

Numerous examples illustrate the power of blogs. An extensive list of links to pub-lic library blogs is available at The Blogging Libraries Wiki (www.blogwithoutalibrary .net/links/index.php?title=Public_libraries). Blogging Libraries features sev-eral international libraries along with public libraries across the United States and Canada. Among some of the wide-ranging uses, public libraries promote in-formation and activities for children and teens; announcements of new titles, music, and movies; and book reviews—both those appearing in *New York Times Review of Books* and others as well as those written by patrons and librarians. These blogs tend to be visually appealing and offer search and tagging features to aid in finding information on the blog site.

Readers' advisory blogs provide excellent information both for the library staff and the bibliophile. They bring a wealth of information about authors, books, and book events. RA blogs frequently feature book reviews and provide access to other resources of interest, including resources for writers. Strengths of the RA and book blogs are the availability of plot summaries, reader reviews, and booklists as well as author updates, profiles, and even author chats. Blogs pro-vide far-reaching access to what people are currently reading and discussing, which also keeps the readers' advisor current and in the know.

Wikis

Closely related to blogs, a wiki is another option for encouraging user participa-tion and feedback. Frequently called a social Web site, a wiki is a collaborative Web site for which pages are created and edited by a community of users (think Wikipedia or the ALA wikis). Like blogs, this tool does not require knowledge of HTML coding or advanced Web design techniques, facilitating ease of content creation. By nature wikis allow ongoing and continual editing, making them "works in progress" (Farkas, 2006). The caveat, however, is that wikis and blogs must be maintained in order for them to remain relevant. They serve many pur-

Reading and Book Blogs Worth More Than a Passing Glance

A Work in Progress: http://www.danitorres.typepad.com/
Blogging for a Good Book: http://bfgb.wordpress.com
Book Beast: www.thedailybeast.com/newsmaker/book-beast
Book Group Buzz: http://bookgroupbuzz.booklistonline.com/
Bookninja: www.bookninja.com/ (Canadian literary magazine and blog)
Bookslut: www.bookslut.org/blog/
Citizen Reader: www.citizenreader.com/ (for nonfiction reading interests)
Early Word: www.earlyword.com
Paper Cuts: http://papercuts.blogs.nytimes.com/ (from the *New York Times*)
Pierce County Library System:
   www.piercecountylibrary.org/blogs.aspx?id=1
The Reader's Advisor Online: www.readersadvisoronline.com/blog
Readers in the Mist: www.readersinthemist.blogspot.com (Australian library blog)
Shelf Talk: http://shelftalk.spl.org/about

poses for libraries, both internally as collaborative tools for work groups and externally as communication tools to reach library users and other community members.

Wikis come in two options: hosted on external sites or installed on the library's server. Depending upon the features desired, wikis can be freely obtained or premium packages can be negotiated with modest fee structures and plans, especially for academic institutions, libraries, and community organizations. In general, most wiki applications allow multimedia plug-ins for embedding images, audio and video, RSS feeds, and tagging, not unlike blogs and HTML-scripted Web sites. Because it is a collaborative tool, one critical feature of the wiki is accountability, making it possible to see who made changes, when those changes were made, and having the ability to reverse changes quickly. (To be used effectively, wikis require participants to register a login; participants also need to be granted editing privileges.)

Among other features, the wikis provide access to community information (local education, sports and recreation, news, etc.), local announcements, and community resources. Because wikis promote two-way communication, community organizations can post announcements and upcoming event notices on the library's wiki as a way to disseminate information. This type of collaboration facilitates relationships among community organizations and allows the library to play a prominent role.

Public libraries and readers' advisors have put wikis to good use in reaching out to readers. Through their wiki sites libraries offer links to booklists, genealogy resources, homework help, and research guides along with other resources

Sample Resources for Wiki Applications

Google Sites: http://sites.google.com
MediaWiki: www.mediawiki.org/wiki/MediaWiki
PBwiki: www.pbwiki.com
Wetpaint: www.wetpaint.com

WikiMatrix (www.wikimatrix.org/index.php) is a resource for tracking and comparing wikis in a side-by-side display. It lists more than 100 different wiki engines available in open-source and commercial products. WikiMatrix offers detailed information about features, development, support, and system requirements.

that readers want. State affiliate Centers for the Book have created wikis to promote reading within the state by featuring local authors. The Wyoming Authors Wiki (http://wiki.wyomingauthors.org/) and the Illinois Authors Wiki (www.illinoisauthors.org/), for example, can be browsed by author and provide biographies and profiles along with title lists and external links to more information. Nancy Pearl's Book Lust Wiki (http://booklust.wetpaint.com/), a popular and well-developed wiki, offers access to resources appealing to every reader, and it complements Pearl's *Book Lust* series of readers' advisory books.

From a reader's point of view, wikis come in a range of varieties, covering everything from individual authors and titles to specific genres. These wikis often include booklists and resources for reading in specific genres and subgenres. The content provides links to book reviews, booksellers, and publishers as well as general articles. One strength of wikis lies in the ability to communicate information about emerging genres not readily available in mainstream and traditional readers' advisory tools. For example, Library Success: A Best Practices Wiki (www.libsuccess.org/index.php) includes an extensive resource for urban fiction with links to popular titles, authors, and publishers, and reading lists suitable for different types of libraries; RUSA Wiki: Chick Lit (http://wikis.ala.org/rusa/readersadvisory/index.php/Chick_Lit) features a comprehensive look at chick lit, including titles, authors, and subgenres, and a discussion about selecting titles for the library collection.

RSS Feeds

RSS makes using blogs, wikis, and other Web 2.0 technologies efficient and easy for the end user. Stephens defines it clearly, saying "RSS lets you create content in one place and display it in other places, such as in RSS aggregators (also called "readers"), which pull in various subscribed feeds to let you read them in one place" (2006: 36). More simply, Dave Winer, creator of RSS, calls it "automated web surfing" (O'Reilly, 2005: n.p.). In order to use RSS feeds, the user must in-

Examples of Wikis in the Library World

Chick Lit:
   http://wikis.ala.org/rusa/readersadvisory/index.php/Chick_Lit
Illinois Authors Wiki:
   www.illinoisauthors.org/
Nancy Pearl's Book Lust Wiki:
   http://booklust.wetpaint.com/
Provo City Library Readers' Resources:
   http://readersresources.pbwiki.com/
Urban Fiction/Street Lit/Hip Hop Fiction Resources for Librarians:
   www.libsuccess.org/index.php?title=Urban_Fiction/Street_Lit/Hip_Hop_
   Fiction_Resources_for_Librarians
Wyoming Authors Wiki:
   http://wiki.wyomingauthors.org/

stall a reader or aggregator onto his or her computer and then subscribe to blogs, wikis, and other sources of interest. Whenever the content of the sites is updated, notification is sent to the aggregators about the new updates.

For libraries RSS feeds serve two purposes. First, library users can subscribe to the library's RSS feeds to keep up with library events, content updates, and new materials added to the catalog. Libraries can also display feeds from other resources on the library's site, such as the day's top headlines from local and state newspapers and media resources, booklists and recommendations, and podcasts. Combined, this keeps library sites dynamic with information that meets the needs of the local community and the library staff.

RSS feed aggregators are the key to managing the RSS feeds. The aggregators post the various feeds in a single location, making it easy for the user to read and access news and information efficiently. RSS aggregators are available in two varieties: Web-based, which do not require any software downloads, and desktop-based, which require users to download and install applications on their computers. Not only do aggregators provide access to blogs and news, they also

A Few Resources for RSS Feeds and Aggregators

Blogbridge: www.blogbridge.com
Bloglines: www.bloglines.com
Blogpulse: www.blogpulse.com
Google Reader: www.google.com/reader
Hennepin County Library, Bookspace: www.hclib.org/pub/bookspace/
Illinois Clicks!, Illinois News: www.illinoisclicks.org

provide access to video and podcasts. Other features included in some aggregators are trends and statistics. Trends, in particular, provide information about current events, latest scandals, and subjects that people are talking about here and now. (What better way to keep up with the topics library users are likely to be asking about?)

Podcasting

Podcasting, a blending of the terms broadcasting and iPod, allows creators to distribute audio content on the Web, or audio on demand. It ranges from music to audio to video or combinations of all three, requiring the use of a playback mechanism (i.e., MP3 player, media player, etc.). Podcasting is yet another method for either distributing original internal content to users (recordings of programs, library tours, instructional recordings) or providing access to external content (author interviews, booktalks, news broadcasts). Podcasts are disseminated in episodes, resembling the old-time radio shows. Like blogs and wikis, podcasts are easily accessible through syndication and automatic dissemination (RSS aggregators).

Numerous libraries have taken advantage of the popularity of podcasts by linking their library users to audio content. While many of the public libraries focus their podcast efforts on reaching children and teens, an equal number have included a variety of resources of interest to adult readers. (See Library Success: A Best Practices Wiki: Podcasts at www.librarysuccess.org/index.php?title= podcasting for an extensive list of libraries of all types that are using podcasts to reach and engage readers.) For example, the Public Library of Charlotte and Mecklenburg County (NC) offers Reader's Club Podcasts: Your Guide to Enjoyable Books (www.plcmc.org/readers_club/podcasts.asp). Patrons can download mp3 files of monthly summaries, including featured booklists, reviews, and author spotlights. In addition, PLCMC includes author podcasts that allow patrons to listen to brief readings and discussions by authors on their books. These podcasts range from one-and-a-half minutes to just over five minutes, providing a very brief teaser of the featured authors' works. Finally, the Library of Congress (www.loc.gov/podcasts/bookfest/index.html) features podcasts from the annual National Book Festival with author readings and interviews.

Beyond podcasts related to books and authors, libraries use these as public service opportunities to meet the needs of their communities. The Wadsworth Public Library (OH; www.wadsworthlibrary.com/main/podcasts.cfm) includes episodes on the digital TV transition, Medicare updates, local history, and a candidates' forum for local elections. Sunnyvale Public Library (CA; www .librarypodcasts.org) offers informational podcasts on managing money, developing business plans, and historical patents along with selections from a Business Workshop Series. The Orange County Library System (FL; http:// oclspodcast.libsyn.com/index .php?post_ category= OCLS%20Events) provides podcast downloads of local events from Orlando, Florida, including local parades, holiday concerts, and special events at the library.

Libraries are not the only resource for locating podcasts that will engage the adult reader. National Public Radio (NPR) offers an array of podcasts and audio downloads from their talk shows, including NPR's "Book Tour," "Books We Like," and "You Must Read This" (www.npr.org/templates/topics/topic.php ?topicId=1032). Publishers often provide podcasts, offering readers the opportunity to listen to favorite authors discuss their books, the writing process, and their experiences as writers. Booksellers, such as Tattered Cover Book Store (CO; http://authorsontourlive.com/) or Barnes & Noble (www.barnesandnoble .com/bn-studio/videos-podcasts/index.asp) provide similar access. C-SPAN's Book TV includes "After Words" podcasts (www.c-span.org/Podcasts.aspx), featuring authors of recently published nonfiction books. Podcasts abound, covering fiction and nonfiction for adults as well as children's and teen authors and illustrators. The hardest part is not finding them, but limiting them to resources that are useful to the library's own clientele.

THE SOCIAL SIDE OF LIBRARY 2.0

At its core, networking is a way of connecting with others who have similar interests, either socially or professionally. Networking is nothing new to the library profession. The first professional networking opportunity for librarians was established in October 1876, with the formation of the American Library Association (ALA), culminating each summer with the ALA Annual Conference. The annual conference gathers librarians, library staff, educators, and library users for professional development and socializing. Collaboration and sharing are hallmarks of the annual conference, bringing together diverse individuals and ideas. What *is* new is the speed and enthusiasm with which librarians have embraced social networking and social content management along with inviting user participation in the library world.

Social Cataloging

One phenomenon that has engaged both readers and librarians is social cataloging. Social cataloging Web sites combine the ability to catalog personal libraries and collections by linking to known bibliographic resources such as Library of Congress, WorldCat, or Amazon.com with the ability to tag books with personal descriptions, and the ability to make connections with other individuals having similar libraries and/or similar tagging. Social cataloging offers the user a way to organize collections of books. The most well-known of the social cataloging sites include LibraryThing.com, GoodReads.com and Shelfari.com (see Table 4-1 for a side-by-side comparison).

Table 4-1: Comparison of Online Cataloging/Book Resources			
	LibraryThing	GoodReads	Shelfari
Web Address	www.librarything.com	www.goodreads.com	www.shelfari.com
Number of Books Cataloged	36,004,426	42,000,000	No information available on Web site
Number of Members	613,990	1,800,000	No information available on Web site
Discussion Groups	Standing Groups for LibraryThing; Member Projects; Member Groups	General Book Discussion; Author Groups; Local Groups; Official GoodReads Groups for GoodReads Feedback and GoodReads Librarians	Member Groups (currently 21,155 groups)
Special Features	Author Pages; Author Chat; Early Reviewers Program; Member Giveaways Program; Widgets for Blogs; Book Covers	Book Covers; Popular Lists; Giveaways; Videos; GoodReads Authors	Book Covers; Author Profiles; Blogs; Wish List and Reading List; Widgets for Blogs
Number of Tags	46,487,525		Lists Top 200 tags
Tagging/Organizing	Personal Tags; Library of Congress; Dewey	Arranged by Tagged Shelves	Personal Tags; Broad Subject Browsing
Search Functions	Own Library; Site Search (works/authors/tags); Talk Messages; Groups; Members	Books by Title or Author	Books; Members; Groups; Discussions
Recommendations	Automatic and Member Recommendations	Member Ratings	Member Comments
Registration/Account Required	Yes. Free for basic, $10/year for unlimited additions, or $25 donation for lifetime membership/ unlimited cataloging	Yes. Free	Yes. Free
RSS Feeds	Yes	Yes	Yes
Member Reviews/Rankings	Yes	Yes	Yes
Other			Advertisements; Acquired by Amazon.com (8/2008); FAQ including section for librarians

For the individual, social cataloging Web sites offer ways to track personal collections, find recommendations, and participate in online book discussions. Readers can link to authors and get involved in early reviewing of new book releases. Because they are social sites, users can *befriend* others, making connections with fellow readers and seeing other personal collections and find ideas for other books to read based upon entries in the personal library as well as through comparisons of books commonly shared among community members. Because these are Web-based resources, social cataloging sites can be accessed from anywhere, and users have the ability to download their libraries to mobile devices, such as PDAs and cell phones (check out your personal collection when you're browsing the bookstore to avoid duplicate purchases).

"To Friend"

Unlike the traditional definition (relationship between individuals based on affection and esteem; acquaintances) *friend* takes on entire new connotations in social networks. On MySpace and Facebook, friends are social connections with whom there may be no prior relationships—in essence, strangers. The action of *friending* someone means that an invitation to join a social network has been issued and accepted.

Librarians can also use the social cataloging sites to their advantage. LibraryThing in particular is a powerful tool for libraries, integrating social data into the library online public access catalog (OPAC). This facilitates the inclusion of tag-based browsing, recommendations, and reviews into the OPAC, creating a more user-friendly and user-defined experience. Because of the ability to generate lists of popular titles, the social catalogs provide additional resources for finding authors and titles that readers are currently enjoying. Shelfari and GoodReads share similar functionality, especially in generating popular reading lists along with biographical information about authors and access to online reading groups. Combined, these help readers' advisors keep abreast of popular trends and the books most likely to be requested by readers.

By far the most powerful feature of the social cataloging sites is the ability to tag books. Found on all types of social networking and social content management Web sites, tagging enables users to add personal keywords to digital objects (books, images, blog entries, etc.) for later search and retrieval. The user describes the digital object in personal, descriptive language. Social cataloging sites allow users to search by tags to find books and authors through common language usage. The premise suggests that individuals will use similar tags to describe the same item and as the number of tags per item increase the greater the likelihood that it will be commonly described by a community. Tagging is not intended to replace traditional cataloging and classification functions, but to add a layer of access for retrieval by using terminology established by the end user, or everyday reader.

Tag clouds, an associative function of tagging, generate a visual display of tags applied to individual digital objects (see Figure 4-1 for an illustration). The most common or popular tags will appear in large fonts while the least common or least used tags will appear in small fonts. The phrases in the tag cloud are active links, which retrieve all books with similar tags. For example, in LibraryThing, the tag "book history" is used by 294 unique members for a total of 2,517 times, and using the link makes it possible to see all editions that have been described, adding a little serendipity to finding something new to read. In addition, tag clouds allow retrieval of titles with the similar or related tags.

Author clouds (see Figure 4-2) are generated in the same manner as the tag clouds, providing access to lists of the book by any given author along with variant name spellings, pseudonyms, and all related tags. (Individual users describe books in different ways; some may use character name and place name while others describe elements of the plot or genre). Lists of book awards, series, characters, and places also can be displayed within the social catalogs through the tagging process. In order to avoid some of the confusion between authors with the same name, several of the social catalogs also include a feature called

---

Figure 4-1: Tag Cloud

Acknowledgments Adult Learners Africa ALA Notable Book American History Archaeology Barnaby Baseball Bibliomystery Book Collecting Book Obsession Book Storage Book to Film Books Cats Charleston Chicago Cubs Chick lit China Cigar industry Commodities Cookbooks Cooking Cotton Malone Cultural History Dead-End Job Series Drama Fiction Finance Florida Food Food Science Football Fortune Cookies Genre Fiction Good for a Laugh Harry Fairsteen Harry Potter History of Baseball History of Books History of Mysteries History of Reading Horseracing Hurricane Katrina Influential Women Inscribed by Author Investing Iran Italy Jane Austen Jim Qwilleran Koko Lara McClintoch Legal Thriller Librarianship Libraries Libraries/Archives Library at Alexandria Library philosophy Library Science Lifelong Reading Literacy Literary Classics Literary Fiction Literary Theory Literature Madeleine Albright Manuscripts Memoir Mrs. Murphy Murder Mysteries Mystery Mystery/Detective Mystery/Detective Fiction Mystery/Fiction National Book Awards New Orleans Nonfiction Old Time Radio Poetry Popular Fiction Print Culture Professional Ethics Pulitzer Prize Winner Readers Advisory Reading Reading Groups Reading Lists Reading/Literary Societies Research Romance Sense and Sensibility Series Shoeless Joe Short Stories Sid Halley Signed by Author Southern Fiction Stephanie Plum Suspense T.S. Eliot Tea Theodosia Browning Translation/Spanish Travel UK/England Virginia Wizard of Oz Women Women in Baseball Young Adult Fiction Yum-Yum

Source: Tag cloud generated through author's personal catalog on LibraryThing.com.

Figure 4-2: Author Cloud

Madeleine Albright Jeffrey Archer Jean Hastings Ardell Nicholas Basbanes Pierre Bayard Steve Berry Lilian Jackson Braun Rita Mae Brown Ian Caldwell Scott E. Casper Guglielmo Cavallo John Charles Laura Childs Martha Cooley Bill Cope Nilo Cruz Robert Darnton Cathy N. Davidson Michael Dirda John Dunning T.S. Eliot Janet Evanovich Barbara Fairchild Steven Roger Fischer Kathleen Flinn Karen Joy Fowler Dick Francis Dorothea Benton Frank Gerard Genette Larry & Nancy Goldstone Lawrence Goldstone Michael Gorman Melissa Fay Greene John Grisham Lev Grossman Lyn Hamilton Diana Tixier Herald Tony Hillerman Jed Horne H.J. Jackson Holbrook Jackson Shirley Jackson Syrie James Cynthia Lee Katona W.P. Kinsella Jayne Ann Krentz Allen Kurzweil Jennifer 8 Lee Gregory Maguire Alberto Manguel Nancy Kalikow Maxwell Harold McGee Larry McMurtry Bob Mitchell Heather Murray Azar Nafisi National Book Foundation Arturo Perez-Reverte Henry Petroski Lawrence Clark Powell Cokie Roberts Jim Rogers Betty Rosenberg Nadine Rosenthal Catherine Sheldrick Ross J.K. Rowling Barbara Ryan Dorothy L. Sayers Laura Schenone Mary Ann Shaffer Ronald B. Schwartz Amy Tan Elaine Viets Marguerite Crowley Weibel Gene Wojciechowski Carlos Ruiz Zafon

Source: Author cloud generated through author's personal catalog on LibraryThing.com.

"disambiguation," which includes notes about how to distinguish between the authors. For example, LibraryThing identifies three John Dunnings: a contemporary American writer of detective fiction (Cliff Janeway, Bookman series); a British writer of business and economic works, who died in early 2009; and a true crime writer who lived from 1918 to 1990. Disambiguation allows users to select the correct author or title they were seeking.

Virtual Worlds and Second Life

Virtual worlds represent a growing phenomenon in social computing, not only for the general public but for libraries as well. These are three-dimensional, Web-based worlds that are created and inhabited by members (also called residents). They are multi-user virtual environments, or MUVEs, where the users create digital personas, or avatars, build landscapes, invent objects, and interact with other avatars. In the range of library communications and activities, Second Life dominates the 3-D library community. (For a comprehensive listing of virtual worlds by category, check out www.virtualworldsreview.com/info/categories .shtml.)

Virtual worlds can be described as either open worlds or closed worlds. Open worlds, such as Second Life, are viewed as extensions of the real world. According to the Pew Internet and American Life Project (2008), a developer creates the building blocks of code and an operating platform for the world, but the users (residents) have the freedom to use and manipulate the code to build or invent anything they choose within the world. Closed worlds, on the other hand, are entirely created and controlled by the developers; users may have the ability to make minor modifications within the world, but it is very limited. Most of the multiplayer online games, such as World of Warcraft (WOW), are closed worlds.

Second Life (SL) was created by Linden Labs in 2003 and started with several thousand residents, and it grew to almost 200,000 by April 2006. Since then it has experienced a tremendous growth spurt, with an estimated 5 million residents from around the world, but not all of whom are active. Americans outpace all other users in the total number of hours spent in Second Life (39.38 percent, according to Todd Borst of Virtual World Business). Gartner, Inc., an IT research and advisory company, predicts that by the end of 2011, approximately 80 percent of active Internet users will participate in a virtual world. Surprisingly, Second Life appeals more to the 30- and 40-somethings than it does to the teens, though teens have an exclusive version of Second Life specific to their interests.

Libraries entered Second Life in 2006 when the Alliance Library System (ALS) began investigating whether there was an interest or need for a library in SL, and in early 2007 it created the Information Archipelago with ten library islands. As of February 2009, over 120 libraries and library organizations are reported to have space in Second Life, including Cleveland Public Library (OH), Glenview Public Library (IL), Monroe County Library System (NY), and Public Library of Charlotte and Mecklenburg County (NC) (Stimpson, 2009).

From a library point of view, Second Life and other virtual worlds provide yet another method to reach users and nonusers alike and to attract a new global audience to the library. Not only can the library promote traditional services, such as book discussion groups, but they can showcase special collections and resources that patrons may not be able to interact with physically, such as rare or special photographic collections or documents that have been digitized. Among other opportunities, libraries in Second Life can provide education (tutorials on how to build objects and avatars, how to navigate in-world), entertainment (discussions, events, games, and competitions), and a place to gather and interact (not unlike the bricks-and-mortar library).

Numerous resources are available in Second Life for readers' advisory services, including portals for science fiction and fantasy, mysteries, and historical time periods. While impossible to discuss them all, The Mystery Manor is an excellent example of how SL can be used effectively with readers. Mystery Manor devotes itself to mystery, crime, and horror fiction. Recently relaunched, it currently has an Edgar Allen Poe exhibit on display in the galleries in honor of 200 years of mysteries. As part of the celebration, Mystery Manor sponsored a Gothic Costume Ball and a Poe Scavenger Hunt. (Remember, this is all 3-D and virtual.) Other activities include Poe readings and discussions.

Readers' advisory can be handled in a number of ways within Mystery Manor. To facilitate self-service and self-exploration, volunteers have posted links to off-world resources on the Web to support different mystery reading interests, such as blogs, wikis, and organizations devoted to the mystery genre. Objects related to mysteries have associated note cards that pop up and provide information about the object or the mystery story related to it. Posters announcing various events appear outside of Mystery Manor, much like a theater billboard. Volunteers staff Mystery Manor and engage with visitors, answering questions and providing access to information. Reading lists and bibliographies are readily available. It feels very much like an actual library, offering services that are familiar. Mystery Manor sponsors regular book discussion groups, not unlike the book discussion groups held in the physical library.

Second Life, as do the other virtual worlds, comes with drawbacks along with the array of possibilities. The learning curve for building avatars, landscapes, and objects and for learning to navigate and use the virtual world is significant. It also requires commitments of time and effort to initially build and then maintain the Second Life presence. Outreach to the community—physical and virtual—is crucial to a successful Second Life project. Not only does the staff need to maintain SL, but they need to be proactive in posting announcements about events and activities in Second Life as well as on the library's Web site, blog, and Facebook and MySpace accounts.

The other issue with Second Life—both for the library and for the user—is the need for a high-end computer. Second Life requires a high-speed connection, fast CPU processor speed, large amounts of memory, and high-end video card. The computer must be able to use streaming audio and video. Without the high-end capabilities, the user will experience poor performance and frustration. For users who have firewalls, many of the Second Life functions may be blocked, compounding performance issues.

Social Networks

Do you "friend" other people, some who you know and some strangers who share similar interests? Social networking creates an online community by which individuals and organizations can connect with one another. Members share personal information about their lives, interests, and activities as well as participate in discussions, view video, and listen to music. According to Pew Internet and American Life reports, approximately 35 percent of adults in the United States have a profile on one social network site (Lenhart, 2009). Social networking sites, such as MySpace, Facebook, LinkedIn, or Ning, are used for both personal and professional activities and even educational ones. Social networks extend opportunities for communication and social interaction as well as meet a need for entertainment.

Social networks offer wide ranges of functions, from adding user profiles to joining groups to creative opportunities to add music, images, and video. To join a social network, users register for free accounts and then create personal profiles. Social networks vary in the degree of self-revelation, allowing users to select how much or how little personal information they divulge and make publicly available to others in the network. Once the profile is created then other members are invited to become friends in the creator's network. Search and browse functions facilitate finding others with similar interests or people already known, groups and organizations to join, music and videos to "pimp" (in everyday language: to enhance or spruce up) your profile, and a variety of other features and applications to incorporate into the personal profile (e.g., games, stickers, flair, widgets).

Different social networks appeal to different types of individuals. For example, MySpace generally draws a younger membership—teens to young adults, though it is not limited to only the younger crowd. Facebook appeals to people who are looking for ways to connect with family members and friends (someone said the other day, "the old people" use Facebook). LinkedIn is intended to be a professional networking resource by which individuals can connect with others in a particular business or industry, much like business networks that meet face-to-face for social and professional purposes. Other popular social networking sites include LiveJournal and Friendster, both of which appeal to younger adults. Choice depends upon purely personal preferences, but regardless of choice the purpose is to connect with others in a collaborative environment.

Popular Social Networking Sites

Facebook: www.facebook.com
Friendster: www.friendster.com
LinkedIn: www.linkedin.com
LiveJournal: www.livejournal.com
MySpace: www.myspace.com
Ning: www.ning.com

A growing number of libraries are developing social networking spaces in order to reach potential library users outside of the physical library (those individuals who may never come into the library, assuming it has nothing to offer them). They focus on the "coolness" factor to reach their younger constituents, while promoting and extending library services through multiple vehicles (bricks-and-mortar library, library Web site, and library social network space). Along with creative freedom of expression, MySpace, Facebook, and the others offer two-way communication between library user and library staff through the use of blogs, walls, and comment features.

For many, the library's social network space provides a vehicle to announce events, post images from library events, and make information available about new books, music, and DVDs in the collection. The Denver Public Library on MySpace, for example, is designed to appeal to teens. When accessing the site,

Public Libraries in Social Networks

Brooklyn Public Library (NY):
   www.facebook.com/profile.php?id=8544515249
Chicago Public Library (IL):
   www.facebook.com/profile.php?id=35447572453
The Denver Public Library (CO):
   www.myspace.com/denver_evolver
Hennepin County Library (MN):
   www.facebook.com/profile.php?id=7223112325
Lancaster Library (UK):
   www.myspace.com/getitloudinlibraries
The Public Library of Charlotte & Mecklenburg County (NC):
   www.facebook. com/profile.php?id=8155960271
Stoneham Public Library (MA):
   www.myspace.com/stonehamlibrary
Toronto Public Library (Canada):
   www.facebook.com/profile.php?id=17572765228

Many libraries maintain profiles on multiple social networking services.

music blares; the screen fills with graphic art from popular graphic novels; and links to numerous videos appear. It is glitzy and brash and very appealing to the library's teen population. The Hennepin County Library by comparison is low-key but offers live chat with a librarian, access to the library catalog, and a link to the library's Web site. Some libraries have taken advantage of teens' interest in social networking to provide educational information about using the online environment safely. The sites frequently offer access to library-created video for instruction. Combined, all of these options create a collaborative and dynamic resource to conduct library business through forums in which users actively participate.

Libraries are not the only entity to embrace social networking in order to reach readers. Many authors have found homes in MySpace and Facebook through which members can reach them. In some social networks, authors (or their publicists) have created "fan" pages. The fan pages include a wide variety of information. For example, the Official John Grisham Page on Facebook includes brief reviews of his latest novel, links to Grisham's favorites (authors, books, etc.), a complete list of his publications (in reverse chronological order), and video trailers from YouTube promoting *The Associate* (2009). By comparison, Dean Koontz has an extensive profile on MySpace for his character Odd Thomas, including video Webisodes of Odd's encounters with dead people. Much of this is unique content that adds depth to the reading experience.

Joining groups in the social networks offers yet another way to connect with readers. (LibraryThing, Shelfari, and GoodReads, discussed previously, also offer similar discussion groups.) Fan clubs are a common type of online group on MySpace, Facebook, and others. For example, both Grisham and Koontz maintain extensive fan pages on both MySpace and Facebook, with downloadable materials, video, and their personal recommendations for reading. Clubs and groups related to specific authors, series, or characters abound in social network spaces, though they can be less developed than the official author pages. These are geared to discussion and sharing a common interest, and sometimes author- or title-bashing. Another form of groups is the online book discussion version. The groups operate as threaded discussion with member contributions. Discussions range from simple reports of what members are currently reading to complex critical analysis of titles or authors.

The Caveat Emptor

Participation in social networks is not without some controversy and concern. Safety and trustworthiness of elements in the networks are key components for dissention and discouraging the use of social networks. Because profiles are self-created and content is unregulated, it is possible to disguise one's real identity in the online environment. This prompts concerns about online predators having access to potential victims as well as identity theft and online stalking. Many libraries, due to these concerns, block access to MySpace and Facebook on public computers and do not engage in creating social network accounts. However, this could also been construed as an opportunity to educate the user about protecting his or her personal information and not trusting everything that is posted in an online environment. Other issues include time management and distractions from the job at hand during working hours. Creating, maintaining, and using social networks does take time and effort.

GETTING STARTED WITH LIBRARY 2.0

From a readers' advisory perspective, participatory technologies and social networks offer new possibilities to connect readers with books and authors. Library 2.0 creates a powerful vehicle for reaching library users. Incorporating participatory technologies into library services does not need to be all or nothing. The availability of options that can be used separately or in tandem adds great flexibility to the online services, and librarians can select only those technologies that best suit the interests and needs of their users.

Begin by exploring available options and resources. Start with one or two personal accounts to compare features and get a feel for functionality. Talk with colleagues and library users about their experiences with different social content management systems and networks. Read blogs and message boards, try out the multimedia resources, and observe how members actually use the space. Spend time looking at and comparing the ways in which other libraries are using Library 2.0 tools, and talk to librarians from other libraries about their experience. Consider how these technologies will enhance existing services and the library's Web presence, and determine what is best for your individual library's needs.

Once appropriate tools have been selected, set the ground rules for maintaining the library's online presence. The greatest challenge may be obtaining buy-in from other staff members (too time-consuming; too invasive; not appropriate for the library, users, or community). Be prepared to spend time demonstrating and explaining the functions and goals of the tools. Determine what the content will be and for whom it is intended—there will be significant differences between teen space and adult reader space. Establish a mutual understanding among the staff about expectations. Questions of who, when, and what content will need to be addressed.

After creating the framework for the project, it is time to add content. The library's online profile should be engaging and not simply a mirror of the library's official Web site. It should also invite the user to participate and collaborate in the library's social network. Remember the "coolness" factor—casual, fun, and creative. Because this is an online presence, it should be highly visual, including photos and images. Incorporate calendars of upcoming events, such as "One Book, One Community" reading events and book festivals. These can be linked later to video, audio, and images from the event. Use music and audio to entice users (how about downloading podcasts of author interviews or book readings?). Above all, highlight the features of the library that are distinctive and will be attractive to a digital community.

While Shoeless Joe's advice, "If you build it, he will come," may ring true for Ray Kinsella, it does not hold for the library's social network. Simply establishing a profile on MySpace or Facebook does not guarantee that users will find it or participate. It will take advertising and promotion to ensure that the profile is seen and used. First use the social network's own search and browse functions (zip code, school affiliations, and other characteristics) to identify and invite users into the library's network. Promote the library's new face through traditional channels, such as newsletters, public service announcements, and flyers/posters in the library, and through digital resources, such as listservs, podcasts, and the library's official Web site.

Ongoing maintenance and updating are critical to a dynamic network. There is nothing worse than finding a resource only to have it be two years out of date. This, of course, means a commitment from the library staff (buy-in again) to provide content and make consistent contributions. Post blog entries or comments regularly. Provide access to updated booklists, promote upcoming events, and advertise new materials in the library's collection (physical and digital). Because social networks, blogs, and wikis require little experience with HTML coding, it is an easy process to keep materials updated and fresh.

Finally, remember that social networking can introduce the library to a new audience. If the site offers good content and plenty of options for participation, the library becomes relevant to a new user group, especially younger audiences. That person who enjoys reading e-books may discover that the library has downloadable books for his or her e-reader or multimedia player. Individuals who prefer movies may discover a new resource for locating DVDs outside of Blockbuster and Netflix. The digital community becomes engaged with the library and uses its resources regardless of physical location.

CONCLUSION

It is impossible to enumerate all of the technologies, applications, and resources available to support user participation in the library. And not all Library 2.0 tools will be appropriate for every library. However, incorporating just a few into existing library services can truly enhance the connections between library and patron. One of the best strategies for identifying new technologies and resources is to examine what other libraries have done already. Throughout this section a number of examples are mentioned as starting points. Begin by looking at the examples and then exploring the technologies behind the sites to find which will work best for the library and its staff.

All forays into new technologies involve trade-offs. If applications are selected that need to be downloaded and installed on a server, then time and staff are required to maintain the technical components of content management. Because content and applications are pulled from external resources, if the external site goes offline, then the site's content goes offline, leaving gaping holes on the library's own Web site. In addition, content remains viable only through maintenance; someone must update and contribute new materials in order to keep the users' interests. Instituting even the simplest of Library 2.0 tools into the library's Web site requires a commitment of time, people, and occasional funding.

Ultimately, however, the library extends its reach into the community. Social networking, blogs, and wikis invite the user and potential user to become engaged with the library and use its resources. Limitations of time and space are lifted for those unable to enjoy the library resources otherwise. Above all, Library 2.0 offers new tools to remain accessible and relevant to contemporary users.

WORKS CONSULTED

Borst, Todd. 2009. "Know Your Customers: Second Life Demographics." Virtual World Business. Available: http://virtualworldbusiness.com/2009/04/30/know-your-customers (accessed September 10, 2009).

Casey, Michael E., and Laura C. Savastinuk. 2007. *Library 2.0: A Guide to Participatory Library Service*. Medford, NJ: Information Today.

Farkas, Meredith. 2006. "Wiki." TechEssence.info. Available: http://techessence.info/socialsoftware/wiki (accessed September 10, 2009).

"Gartner Says 80 Percent of Active Internet Users Will Have a 'Second Life' in the Virtual World by the End of 2011." Gartner, Inc. Available: www.gartner.com/it/page.jsp ?id=503861 (accessed September 10, 2009).

Kinsella, W. P. 1982. *Shoeless Joe.* New York: Mariner Books.

Lenhart, Amanda. 2009. "Adults and Social Network Websites." Pew Internet & American Life Project. Available: www.pewinternet.org/PPF/r/272/report_display.asp (accessed September 10, 2009).

O'Reilly, Tim. 2005. "What Is Web 2.0: Design Patterns and Business Models for the Next Generation of Software?" Available: http://tim.oreilly.com/pub/a/oreilly/tim/news/2005/09/30/what-is-web-20.html?page=1 (accessed September 10, 2009).

Pew Internet & American Life Project. 2008. "Internet Activities." Available: www.pewinternet.org/trends/Internet_Activities_7.22.08.htm (accessed September 10, 2009).

"State of the Blogosphere." 2008. Technorati. Available: http://technorati.com/blogging/state-of-the-blogosphere (accessed September 10, 2009).

Stephens, Michael. 2006. "Web 2.0 & Libraries: Best Practices for Social Software." *Library Technology Reports* 42, no. 4. Available: www.techsource.ala.org/ltr/ (accessed September 10, 2009).

Stimpson, Jane D. 2009. "Public Libraries in Second Life: Expanding Service to the Virtual Environment." *Library Technology Reports* 45, no. 2 (February/March). Available: www.techsource.ala.org/ltr/ (accessed September 10, 2009).

FURTHER READING

Arrington, Michael, and Erick Schonfeld, eds. 2009. TechCrunch. Available: www.techcrunch.com (accessed September 10, 2009). This is an excellent resource for keeping up with what's new in technology and gadgets.

Bell, Lori, and Rhonda B. Trueman, eds. 2008. *Virtual Worlds, Real Libraries: Librarians and Educators in Second Life and Other Multi-user Virtual Environments.* Medford, NJ: Information Today.

The Blogging Libraries Wiki. Available: www.blogwithoutalibrary.net/links/index.php ?title=Public_libraries (accessed September 10, 2009).

Casey, Michael. 2008. "LibraryCrunch: Service for the Next Generation Library—A Library 2.0 Perspective." Available: www.librarycrunch.com (accessed September 10, 2009).

Courtney, Nancy, ed. 2007. *Library 2.0 and Beyond: Innovative Technologies and Tomorrow's User.* Westport, CT: Libraries Unlimited.

Eisenberg, Mike. 2008. "The Parallel Information Universe." *Library Journal* 133, no. 8 (May): 22–25.

Jones, Steve, et al. 2008. "Whose Space Is MySpace? A Content Analysis of MySpace Profiles." *First Monday* 13, no. 9 (September 1). Available: www.uic.edu/htbin/cgiwrap/bin/ojs/index.php/fm/rt/printerFriendly/2202/2024 (accessed September 10, 2009).

Macgill, Alexandra. 2008. "Virtual World Continuum." Pew Internet & American Life Project. Available: www.pewinternet.org/Commentary/February/Virtual-World (accessed September 10, 2009).

Winer, Dave. (2009) "Scripting News." Available: http://scripting.com (accessed September 10, 2009). An excellent resource for keeping current on Web 2.0 technologies, especially RSS.

Chapter 5

Reading Electronically through Sight and Sound

Leila Martini and Stephanie Maatta

The first matter was to settle the seemingly easy but really difficult question, What is a book? This they solved by defining it as "a literary work substantial in amount and homogeneous in character."

—from May 1, 1886, *Boston Literary World*, vol. 17, p. 150

In 1886 a book resembled the monographs that we locate on library shelves and in bookstores today, printed on paper or vellum and bound in hard or soft covers of leather, buckram, or paper, and intended to be read silently. The book as a physical artifact retains its original design with pages turned by hand as the reader takes in the words printed on paper. In the same breath, the *book* has evolved into both a physical and a virtual object that can be seen, heard, and manipulated in many more ways than the old-fashioned "page turner." In 1886 books were expensive and available to those few who could afford to purchase them or who had access to library services. Today, on the other hand, books, while still expensive, are more affordable to the average family and readily available through libraries in schools, local communities, and local and online bookstores. More importantly, the format of the contemporary book does not limit the preferences of the reader for engaging with the written word (print, electronic, or sound).

Although alternatives to the traditional book have been in existence for decades, in the form of braille and talking books, for example, current technological changes allow readers to choose from multiple formats in order to read. In a series of early articles about technological advances and the library, Kurzweil suggests that just as the vinyl records and cassette tapes gave way to CDs, and by extension to MP3 players and iPods, book technologies now follow suit (Kurzweil, 1992a: 80, 82). With improved technologies come new products. Ten years ago a reader could select from print books, books on tape (cassettes), or the occasional electronic book to be read online or downloaded to a personal digital assistant (PDA) or printed from a personal computer. Today the variety of options feature downloadable books in MP3 and .wav files to be used with iPods and other media players, electronic readers that are the shape and size of a paperback, and digitized books for print-on-demand (POD) or for electronic reading devices (e-book readers).

EVOLUTION OF READING TECHNOLOGIES BEYOND THE BOOK

Alternative reading technologies date to the late nineteenth and early twentieth centuries with the invention of Edison's phonograph and its application for reading services for the blind. In 1931 the Library of Congress, an early adopter of audiobooks (books recorded and replayed on vinyl discs), created the National Library Services for the Blind and Physically Handicapped (NLS) to make braille and recorded books available to a previously underserved population. Early recordings of written text were made, first, for phonographs on vinyl records and then subsequently for cassettes and CDs. Today these recordings emerge as digitized audiobooks that can be downloaded as MP3, .wav, and .AAC files (see the sidebar for descriptions of file extensions) or distributed in self-contained playback units, such as Playaways.

Similarly, the idea of the electronic book has been around for decades. Project Gutenberg, generally considered the first producer of truly electronic texts, was created in 1971 "with the goal of making available for free, and electronically, literary works belonging in the public domain" (Lebert, 2008: n.p.). Discussions of reference books produced on CD-ROM appear in the professional literature in the 1980s (Hawkins, 2000a: 16). The argument can be made that the idea of portable, electronic-type books is much older than the 1970s and 1980s. Octave Uzanne and Albert Robida, in their book *Contes pour les Bibliophiles* ("Stories of Bibliophiles," published in France), suggested in 1895 that printed books would give way to *phonographoteques*, or gramophones (a cylinder on which sound is recorded à la Thomas Edison), and that libraries would forego book collections and begin to house the sound recordings (Uzanne and Robida, 1895: n.p.). They conclude their story, suggesting that "Books must disappear" and saying: "How happy we will be not to have to read any more; to be able finally to close our eyes! Hamlet, of our beloved Will, could not have said it any better . . . *Words! Words! Words!* . . . words which will pass and which no one will read any more" (Uzanne and Robida, 1895: n.p.).

The challenge for electronic books in the mid-twentieth century was the availability of affordable, portable components to mimic the reading of traditional

Understanding File Extensions for Audio and E-books

Sites like Computer Hope.Com (www.computerhope.com) and Dot What? (http://dotwhat.net/) explain various file extensions. You can search for an extension alphabetically on either site. More extensions than you probably even knew existed are listed on these sites.

File Extensions: Put in layman's terms, a file extension is a way for the computer to recognize file types, or rather, to distinguish a picture from a video from text. It is the lettering (suffix) that comes after the name of the file. Some common file types that relate to audio and electronic book technologies are:

- .AAC: Advanced Audio Coding file. According to http://dotwhat.net/, the .AAC file type "produces better quality audio at the same bitrate" and is the file type "used by iPod/iTunes and Sony Playstation 3."
- .AZW: The e-book file type Amazon uses with its Kindle product.
- .DOC: This is the file extension for Microsoft Word documents. You'll also see .docx for Microsoft Office 2007.
- .JPG: File type used for photographic images.
- .LIT: This is an e-book file read with a Microsoft Reader.
- .MP3: "MPEG audio stream, layer III; High compressed audio files generally used to record audio tracks and store them in a decent sized file available for playback" (www.computerhope.com).
- .PDF: Stands for Portable Document Format. This can be read with the Adobe Reader.
- .TXT: text, or .RTF: rich text (with formatting)
- .WAV: A standard audio format for Windows operating systems for storing high-quality, uncompressed sound. Typically files are large and require large amounts of memory.
- .WMV: This designation is used when a file is audiovisual in format. This type of file is usually played through Windows Media Player.

books, with readability and legibility being two critical issues for consumers. Alan Kaye and his DynaBook (an early facsimile of today's laptop and notebook computers intended primarily for children) represent one of the first theoretical prototypes of the e-book. Beverly Harrison describes Kaye's design as one "that captures [the] notion of today's e-books—a portable, wireless networked device that could act as a notebook and reading device while maintaining many useful affordances of a book" (Harrison, 2000: 35). Although prototypes of the portable interactive personal computer emerged in the late 1960s, the technology able to support such a product in the marketplace did not evolve until the late 1980s (Wilson, 2001).

In 1998 the first PDA was released from Apple, although Casio developed an earlier digital diary, called the PF-3000, in 1983. As handheld electronic devices became marketable (priced for the consumer market) and technologies improved, new uses for these devices also developed. Once used specifically as pocket organizers with features such as calculators, calendars, and address books, handheld devices evolved to include portable music players, cell phones, smart phones, and portable e-book readers (think about today's Apple iPhone). In 2001 Ruth Wilson and others predicted that as technology improves, hybrid personal electronics with multiple functions will likely win out in the marketplace, although the possibility exists that single-purpose e-book readers may hold their own if the user's need for a "unique reading experience" overrides his or her desire for an all-purpose device (Wilson, 2001: n.p.).

The first electronic reader to be widely marketed was the Sony Bookman released in 1992 (Coburn et al., 2001: 146). At a whopping $1,800, the device was neither user friendly nor affordable for the average reader. According to Coburn, the Sony Bookman was bulky and had a screen that was difficult to read due to its size and electronic print quality. While early e-book readers were heavy, expensive, and hard on the eyes, today's portable electronic readers weigh less than a pound (Amazon's Kindle is 10.3 ounces; Sony Reader weighs approximately 12 ounces) and are thin (about the size of a mass-market paperback), relatively inexpensive (averaging between $250 and $359), and employ new technologies enabling user-friendly displays.

Current audiobook and e-book technology has improved immensely, and with improved technology comes wider functionality and marketability. For instance, today's electronic books have internal dictionaries, are compact and lightweight, are less expensive, and use electronic paper and e-ink technologies, all of which creates added value and appeal for the consumer. Audiobooks produced on CD-ROMs have extra features such as printable lesson plans and worksheets for teachers and students. Wireless technology allows the reader to purchase and download books quickly and easily for immediate access. Because they are a form of personal computer, e-book readers provide the ability to mark text, make notes, and place bookmarks, similarly to the reader using a print book with a highlighter or sticky tabs to annotate the text.

Early industry predictions indicated the e-book would overtake print books within a few years. According to Richard Guthrie, in 2000 following the release and ensuing download frenzy of Stephen King's novella *Riding the Bullet* as an e-book, Forrester Research predicted sales of e-books "could reach $436 million by 2004" (Guthrie, 2006: 128), while Accenture (formerly Andersen Consulting) "forecasted that by 2005 twenty-eight million people would be using e-readers, and the total market for consumer e-books would have reached $2.3 billion" (Crawford, 2006: 44). However, by 2005 neither prediction was a reality. In actuality the total market for consumer e-books reached less than $12 million in 2005 ("Industry Statistics," International Digital Publishing Forum, 2008). In March 2008, the Association of American Publishers (AAP) reported an annual estimate of sales of $18 million for audiobooks, which was an increase of 19.8

percent per year, and annual estimated sales of $67 million (or 23.6 percent increase) for e-books (AAP, 2008), far below the earlier enthusiastic predictions.

HEARING, SEEING, READING: ALTERNATIVE FORMS OF THE BOOK

Audiobooks

An audiobook is defined as an "audio representation of a written book" (Egidi and Furini, 2006: 1). A professional narrator records the book to an audio medium which can then be played back by the listener on an appropriate device. Audiobooks come in many formats to appeal to the needs of different consumers. According to the Audio Publishers Association (APA), formats include abridged and unabridged audiobooks (or edited versions and complete, unaltered works); CD for playback on computers and other CD players; CD-ROMs, which include added text and visual features; digital/audio downloads, which are compressed files that are transmitted to compatible media players; and MP3/CD formats, which are played on MP3 players and are capable of storing large files in small amounts of space (APA, 2007b). Many audiobooks now offer searchable text options, and titles produced in a CD-ROM format often contain supplemental materials. Some publishers offer additional enhancements in the form of author interviews and commentaries along with images and nonverbal sound (music, sounds of nature, etc.).

Audiobook Trends

Sales of audiobooks appear to be on the rise, though the popularity of some formats have waxed and waned. (While still used in some libraries, cassettes and cassette players are almost extinct.) Estimated net sales of audiobooks in all formats have increased approximately 8.8 percent annually from 2002 to 2007 (APA, 2008) to approximately $218 million. According to Egidi and Furini, cassette revenues decreased from 2002 to 2003 by almost 10 percent while CD revenues increased by 10 percent within the same time frame. Although CD revenues increased, the revenue of "down-loadable digital formats" increased even more, 112 percent from 2001 to 2002 and 69 percent from 2002 to 2003 (Egidi and Furini, 2006: 2).

In an annual consumer survey, the Audio Publishers Association reported that 28 percent of American adults who responded were avid audiobook listeners in 2008. So who is listening to audiobooks? Comparing audiobook users with nonaudiobook users, the APA surveys conducted in 2006 and 2008 found that audiobook users are slightly younger (44.7 versus 46.9 years old), have higher household income, have larger households (most with children), and tend to read more print books than their nonaudiobook users. The characterization goes on to say "Audiobook listeners also have more education and buy and read more printed books than non-audiobook listeners" (APA, 2006; APA, 2008).

People listen to their audiobooks on long trips, while commuting, and during other activities, such as exercising. Of particular interest to librarians and readers' advisors, audiobook consumers reported that the top five favorite genres in 2008 were as follows:

1.   Mystery/thriller/suspense
2.   General fiction
3.   Science fiction/fantasy
4.   Biography/memoir
5.   Classic fiction (APA, 2008)

In addition, their preferred source of audiobooks is the library (43 percent of listeners looked for their titles at the public library).

Playaways

Playaways are a relatively new phenomenon in digital audiobooks. Developed in 2006 by Findaway World, Playaways are audiobooks loaded on flash memory players (Findaway World, 2009). According to the *Elements of Internet Style* (EEI, 2007), Playaways have been sold to public school districts for use in the classroom and are on loan at more than 11,000 schools and libraries nationwide. *USA Today* reports that the U.S. Army has purchased 150,000 Playaways for troops in Iraq (Baig, 2008). The two-ounce Playaway comes with headphones and one AAA battery. Each self-contained unit plays one book with a capacity of up to 80 hours of recording and can be replayed.

The Playaway Web site (www.playawaylibrary.com/libraryProgram.cfm) offers a program for libraries that includes "ready to circulate packaging," a one-year warranty on all products, marketing support, free shipping, and pre-created MARC records for cataloging. Currently more than 1,600 Playaway titles are available to libraries, with more titles added monthly; the company also offers a small number of bundled starter sets for different reader groups (general adult fiction, young adult fiction, children's, etc.).

The benefits of the Playaway are similar to those of other audiobooks. Print-impaired users may find Playaways preferable because the device allows the user to listen to the story rather than read it and includes easy-to-use functionality. Warren Buckleitner of the *New York Times* notes "there are no USB cables, CDs to rip or burn, downloads, online stores or batteries to recharge" (2007: n.p.). While simple to use, Playaways have an automatic bookmark function to mark one's place and a universal headphone jack that allows the user to plug it into a speaker. The Playaway can also be recycled. For the individual listener Playaway offers a program called RePlay, which allows the listener to return the used unit (without battery or headphones) to be loaded with a new title.

Obvious drawbacks of the Playaways come to light when comparing them with their more technologically advanced competitors. E-book readers such as the Kindle or the Sony Reader feature audio capabilities (text to speech). Unlike Playaways, these types of readers allow for the storage of multiple books and provide a multitude of features from internal dictionaries to annotation functions. Even compared with their audiocassette/audio CD counterparts, Playaways are difficult to listen to in the car since they require the use of earphones. In addition, Playaways cannot accommodate images or text. One final drawback for the individual consumer is price; Playaways can be very costly, ranging from $25 to $185 each.

OverDrive

OverDrive, Inc., has been in the business of providing digital media content since 1986 with development and innovation of interactive diskettes and CD-ROM products, and in 2002 extending access to downloadable audiobooks and other media. Among other products, OverDrive features bestselling digital audiobooks, e-books, music, and video, allowing libraries of all types to expand digital collections to popular materials along with the classics. Current figures from OverDrive estimate that they provide access to more than 100,000 titles from more than 500 suppliers, including HarperCollins, BBC Audiobooks America, PBS, McGraw-Hill, and Harlequin (OverDrive, 2008).

For libraries, OverDrive offers many advantages. As mentioned, the extensive collections of titles and variety of available formats are very attractive. OverDrive creates and hosts customized Web sites for individual libraries, library systems, and consortium, which look and feel like the library's own site, providing access to the library's digital media collection around the clock. For library users, Over-Drive offers easy-to-navigate platforms and popular types of files, such as Over-Drive MP3 Audiobooks. Users may download a free Windows®-compatible media console for playing and transferring MP3, .wma, and .wmv files.

Some of the challenges with OverDrive products include the need to download files to a PC first before transferring them to a mobile device. This is fine for tech-savvy users, but for the library user who does not have a computer at home, or even for libraries whose computer security systems do not allow downloading from external sources, accessibility becomes a problem. The OverDrive Media Console is a Windows-compatible application and therefore not available to Mac users.

ELECTRONIC BOOKS (E-BOOKS)

The general agreement of the definition of an electronic book (or an e-book) suggests that in its simplest form an e-book is disseminated electronically through digital media (no paper involved unless the end user chooses to print the book). More formally, an e-book, according to Siriginidi Subba Rao, is "text in digital form, or a book converted into digital form, or digital reading material, or a book in a computer file format, or an electronic file of words and images displayed on a desktop, note-book computer, or portable device formatted for display on dedicated e-book readers" (Rao, 2003: 86–87). Palm, Inc., a maker of handheld devices such as the Palm Pilot, says, "eBooks are real books. Books aren't paper, print and binding. They're the inspiration and perspiration; the ideas and concepts; the love and labor of people who have to communicate with others. Paper is nothing more than the way many of those books are packaged and delivered" ("An eBook Primer," 2008). Regardless of the description, an e-book replicates a traditional book in that it is intended to be read by the user in a similar manner as one would read a hand-operated book.

However, this is where the similarity ends. According to Donald T. Hawkins, four types or implementations of e-books exist:

1.   downloadable books available on the Web for downloading to a personal computer;
2.   dedicated e-book readers (or specialized hardware);
3.   Web-accessible e-books that remain on the provider's Web site and require purchase or fee payment for access; and
4.   print-on-demand books, which are stored in a system connected to a printer and from which copies can be printed and bound—from as little as one chapter of the book to the book in its entirety (Hawkins, 2000a: 16).

With advances in technology, proprietary e-books and nonproprietary ones further complicate the issue, and then throw in open e-books and public domain e-books for added confusion.

Proprietary books are those that have usage restrictions and require payment (in the form of outright purchase or lease) for access. These proprietary books can be either locked or open. Locked proprietary electronic books are electronic books that can be read only on a dedicated device, such as Amazon's Kindle or the Sony Reader (see Table 5-1 for an e-reader comparison). These books cannot be printed and cannot be downloaded to other devices, even though the user may have "purchased" the book; no sharing of e-books among friends and family is permitted. (However, Amazon's Kindle allows up to six units to share books on one account.) Open e-books are still proprietary (have restrictions and must be paid for or circulated through the library); however, these e-books can be downloaded onto any reader type (e.g., laptops, PCs, or PDAs), and the e-book vendors frequently provide access to free digital media software to facilitate downloading and transferring files.

Nonproprietary e-books, on the other hand, allow the end user to download and transfer files between devices. Open e-books use an open standard (.epub and XML) in the publishing process. The open standard makes the file compati-

Table 5-1: Comparison of Portable Electronic Readers

	Kindle 2.0	Sony Portable Reader PRS 505SC	ECTACO E-Book Reader
Approximate Cost	$359.00 includes shipping	$320.99 includes shipping; also available in retail locations	$339.95 includes shipping
Other Costs	Just the cost of the books. Typically new releases and New York Times bestsellers are $9.99. No monthly wireless bills, service plans, or commitments.	Internet service fees. Cost to purchase books.	
Included in the Box	Electronic reader, book cover, power adapter, USB 2.0 cable, manual	Tan book cover, USB Cable Quick Start Guide CD-ROM	Power adapter, USB 2.0 cable, storage pouch, user's manual, bonus CD
System Requirements/ Technology	Does not require a computer. Uses Whispernet—"utilizes Amazon's technology plus Sprint's national high-speed (EVDO) data network." Electronic paper display technology reduces glare and eye strain.	Operating System—Windows XP (Home Edition/Professional, Media Center Edition, Media Center Edition 2004, Media Center Edition 2005) & Windows Vista (Home Basic, Home Premium, Business, Ultimate).	Compatible with Mac and Windows-based PCs.
Internal Memory	256MB internal (approx. 180MB available for user content). Holds over 200 books.	Holds 160 books.	128MB internal
Content Formats	Kindle (AZW), TXT, Audible (formats 2, 3, and 4), MP3, unprotected MOBI, PRC natively; HTML, DOC, JPEG, GIF, PNG, BMP through conversion	Unsecured audio: MP3 and AAC; Image: JPEG, GIF, PNG, and BMP; Unsecured Text: BBeB Book, TXT, RTF, Adobe PDF, Microsoft Word (conversion to the Reader requires Word installed on your PC); DRM txt; BBeB Book (Marlin)	.TXT, .PDF, .JPG, .GIF, .MP3

(continued)

Table 5-1: Comparison of Portable Electronic Readers *(continued)*

	Kindle 2.0	Sony Portable Reader PRS 505SC	ECTACO E-Book Reader
Display	6" diagonal E-Ink electronic paper display, 600 x 800 pixel resolution at 167 ppi, 4-level gray scale. No screen rotation.	6-inch E-Ink technology display. 180-degree viewing angle. Pixel resolution at 170 ppi, 8-level gray scale. Screen rotation landscape or portrait.	Reflectivve TFT, high contrast with eye-friendly background, 180-degree viewing area. Screen rotation landscape or portrait.
Size (inch)	7.5" x 5.3" x 0.7"	6.9" x 4.8" x 0.3"	6" x 4.2 x 0.4"
Weight	10.3 ounces	9.0 ounces	7.5 ounces
Battery Life	Varies depending on wireless usage.	Up to 7,500 continuous page turns with a single full charge on internal rechargeable battery. Actual battery life will vary based on usage patterns, settings, and battery conditions.	11,500 pages turned on a single charge. More than 20 hours of active use.
Recharge Time	Charges within 2 hours. Need to recharge every other day with wireless on; weekly with wireless off.	Charges within approx. 4 hours with USB charging from powered computer or approx. 2 hours when using optional AC wall charger.	Charges within approx. 4 hours from supplied power adapter, 4 hours on accessory double USB cable from PC, 5 hours from car adapter.
Number of Titles to Select From	More than 140,000	More than 20,000	More than 500,000 from free-access resources
Limitations	Wireless delivery and other Kindle features using wireless connectivity will not function outside of the Sprint high-speed data network coverage area and are subject to Sprint network service outages.	Requires Internet connection (broadband recommended). Internet service may require a fee.	Requires Internet connection, which requires service fee.

(continued)

Table 5-1: Comparison of Portable Electronic Readers *(continued)*

	Kindle 2.0	Sony Portable Reader PRS 505SC	ECTACO E-Book Reader
Special Features	Built-in dictionary; encyclopedia access; book-mark capability; annotation capability. Search content.	Bookmark feature; Web site did not highlight other features.	Built-in dictionary in several languages. Supports books in a variety of languages. Bookmark. Auto page turn. Search content.
Text Size	1 font, adjustable—6 sizes	1 font–adjustable–3 sizes	2 fonts, adjustable—6 sizes
Other Notable Information	"A copy of every book downloaded is backed up online in a 'Media Library'"—allows the user to make room for new titles or re download. The Web site for this product is the most user friendly of all the products listed on this table.	"Using the included eBook Library 2.0 PC Software, you can easily transfer Adobe PDF documents, Microsoft Word documents, BBeB Book, and other text file formats to the Reader, allowing you the flexibility to access and view multiple files at any time."	MP3 player, picture viewer, AudioBooks player, language learning tool.
Warranty	1-year limited warranty and service	Limited Warranty: Labor—90 days from the date of purchase. Parts–1 year from the date of purchase. See actual warranty for details.	12-month limited warranty (international)

Source: Information in this table was adapted from the product Web sites: www.amazon.com; www.sonystyle.com; and www.ectaco.com/ECTACO-jetBook-Burgundy/.

ble with multiple systems, and thus readable from whatever device the reader happens to be using at the time and then transferable to another one to continue reading at a later time. Open standards also allow the publisher to produce print books (for those of us with that predilection) at the same time as producing e-books.

Public domain e-books (also called "freebooks" by Walt Crawford, 2000) are books and other text that have been deliberately placed in the public domain and may be accessed freely by anyone. Project Gutenberg and Bartleby.com are among several resources for obtaining and downloading public domain e-books. These digitized books may be downloaded to various e-readers and personal computers that are compatible with plain text and PDF documents, including the Sony Reader; the public domain e-books may be printed by the user and stored for long-term usage. Making older and out-of-print books available may be the true advantage of the public domain e-books.

E-book Trends and Issues

Electronic books constitute a rapidly expanding area of publishing. A 2008 International Digital Publishing Forum report on U.S. retail e-book sales shows a dramatic increase in net sales from less than $4 million in revenue in the fourth quarter of 2004 to just over $10 million in revenue for the first quarter of 2008. The Association of American Publishers' most recent survey (March 2008) shows a growth in e-book sales of 55.7 percent annually between 2002 and 2007. In a February 2008 *Publishers Weekly* article, Jim Milliot discusses the increase in popularity of e-books, indicating that a recent survey of consumers showed 17 percent would be willing to buy a digitally formatted book. He also suggests that it is likely these e-book sales would represent new sales for publishers rather than supplanting print books (Milliot, 2008). However, Shatzkin and others predict that despite the increase in popularity of e-books, the format will "still make up a tiny share of the market—no more than 2 percent of sales for most titles" (Shatzkin, 2008: 22).

On the positive side, many benefits exist for the use of e-books. For the end user, benefits include better usability among users with disabilities (for example, the ability to change text size and easy-to-operate buttons and page-advancing functions), convenience and portability, and instant access. With many e-readers comes wireless access, providing availability of titles, searchability, and links to dictionaries and encyclopedias along with instant gratification. Storage comprises another advantage for end users and libraries; most current e-book readers hold approximately 160 to 200 titles, allowing the end user to have great portability and choice, while libraries are able to conserve space and offer greater access to titles through e-collections. From the publisher's point of view, cost benefits due to savings during production and stocking of materials is a key component of e-book publishing.

A number of other arguments in favor of e-book readers suggest that they are environmentally friendly to produce and purchase books, "eliminating the need to cut down trees for paper and use fuel to produce the books and to transport them" (Poremba, 2008: 36). The retail price of e-books also suggests some positives for consumers: the average price of e-books runs around $10 per book download compared to $25 for a bestselling hardcover.

Highlights of the negative aspects of alternative reading formats include lack of interoperability due to software dependency (Rao, 2005). In particular this impacts proprietary devices; users are not able to download books and other reading materials from outside providers (e.g., Amazon's Kindle users can acquire only texts published for Kindle's proprietary interface), thus eliminating the use of many library-provided resources. Many publishers and vendors prohibit downloading to print and multiple downloads, limiting the ability to share and transfer e-books (Poremba, 2008).

One final consideration focuses on aesthetics. Many readers feel passionate about their books and simply do not feel that e-book readers can replace the original, physical object in feel, look, and essence. In his article "Electronic Books: A Major Publishing Revolution," Donald T. Hawkins makes a compelling argument for all of the other purposes of books and bookstores, such as family outings, the book as art for display, and satisfying the needs of bibliophiles to collect and display rare, old, and first editions (Hawkins, 2000a,b). Finally, Walt Crawford turns a critical eye on the e-book market and the suggestion that tech-savvy, wired young adults will flock to reading electronically, saying "One thing you don't see mentioned very often: Ebooks are for *book readers*, not for vidiots or gamers. If someone's not interested in reading a book-length text, putting that long text on an electronic device won't make it more palatable" (Crawford, 2006: 44).

ELECTRONIC BOOKS IN THE LIBRARY SETTING

Although some libraries are experimenting with portable e-reader technology, even purchasing a limited number of proprietary e-book readers for circulation, reports suggest that their use continues to be limited. Some of the issues facing libraries that want to incorporate electronic books into their collection include identification of titles, selection, circulation, maintenance, quality assurance, pricing, fair use, and electronic standards for e-books. Among the prime reasons for incorporating electronic books into libraries is cost savings. E-books eliminate or at least reduce the need to purchase books in hardcover, paperback, and large-print versions as well as provide a more durable format that does not have to be replaced over time, unless software evolves or changes. In addition, libraries that incorporate electronic books into their collections can better serve disabled or homebound patrons, can easily expand their collections according to user demand, and can increase staff efficiency.

Conversely, developing systems for selecting, acquiring, cataloging, and managing electronic books will take time and resources. Proprietary issues will make incorporation of e-books into a library's collection difficult. For instance, current proprietary electronic reading devices, such as the Kindle or the Sony Reader, do not lend themselves to checking out e-books from the library. Library patrons with portable devices hoping to download an electronic book from the library, either while visiting the library or accessing resources remotely, may be disappointed. (Patrons may be able to download books remotely to their home computers, but not to their proprietary reading device due to compatibility issues.)

Locating e-book resources and online depositories can be challenging. However, many of the library vendors and publishers have expanded their catalogs as they ride the wave of demand for electronic books and audiobooks, obtaining or producing more titles. Several public library vendors actively sell or lease electronic books, including Ingram's MyiLibrary (www.myilibrary.com), NetLibrary (www.netlibrary.com/), and OverDrive (www.overdrive.com). Numerous resources for e-books in the public domain exist, which adds richness to a library's collection in an economically feasible manner (see Table 5-2 for links to a variety of e-book and audiobook providers).

However, the real challenge for libraries remains in the fact that e-books and e-book technologies are still in their infancy. Inflexible and proprietary applications and devices make it less desirable for libraries to obtain electronic books when their mission is to provide access to all. Several national and international organizations, such as the International Digital Publishing Forum (formerly Open eBook Forum), are currently working toward standards in digital publishing to allow interoperability between consumer products and enhance digital publishing for multiple products (traditional print, large print, and digital from the same file).

WHAT IS A BOOK?

Can we safely say that the definition of a book has changed, or more accurately has the definition been expanded? The quote from the beginning of the chapter still rings true as does the description from Palm: "Books aren't paper, print and binding. They're the inspiration and the perspiration; the ideas and concepts" ("An eBook Primer," 2008). Alternative reading formats expand access to the written word and allow more people to engage with and enjoy the pleasure of reading. As technology continues to evolve, the savvy librarian will stay on the front edge, stay current with the literature, and learn to adapt to user demand. Ultimately, recommending alternative reading formats to a reader will depend on the needs and preferences of the individual patron with whom you are working and on the capabilities of your individual library system.

Table 5-2: Web Sites and Resources for Audiobooks, E-books, and Other Digital Media	
Company/Provider	**Web Address**
Amazon.com Audiobooks Store	www.amazon.com
Audible	www.audible.com
AudioFile	www.audiofilemagazine.com
Barnes & Noble	www.barnesandnoble.com
Bartleby.com Great Books Online	www.bartleby.com/
Bibliomania	www.bibliomania.com/
Blackstone Audiobooks	www.blackstoneaudio.com
Books on Tape	www.booksontape.com/
Borders	www.audiobooks.borders.com
Ebrary	www.ebrary.com/corp/libraries.jsp
Eserver Accessible Writing	http://eserver.org/
Follett	www.follett.com/
Google Books	http://books.google.com/
Ingram MyiLibrary	www.myilibrary.com/company/library.htm
LibriVox	www.librivox.org
Listening Library	www.randomhouse.com/audio/listeninglibrary/
NetLibrary	www.netlibrary.com/
Online Books Page	http://digital.library.upenn.edu/books/
OverDrive, Inc.	www.overdrive.com
Playaway Library	www.playawaylibrary.com
Project Gutenberg	www.gutenberg.org/wiki/Main_Page or www.promo.net/pg/
Random House Audio	www.randomhouse.com/audio/
Recorded Books	www.recordedbooks.com/

WORKS CONSULTED

"An eBook Primer: What Is an eBook?" Palm, Inc. (2008). Available: http://ebooks
.palm.com/palm/help/intro.htm (accessed September 10, 2009).

Association of American Publishers. 2008. "Industry Statistics 2007." Available: www
.publishers.org/mai/IndustryStats/indStats_02.htm (accessed September 10, 2009).

Audio Publishers Association. 2006. "Audio Publishers Association Releases Major Consumer Survey and Announces Increase in Audiobook Usage." Available: www
.audiopub.org/LinkedFiles/2006ConsumerSurveyCOMPLETEFINAL.pdf (accessed
September 10, 2009).

_____. 2007a. "Americans Are Tuning In to Audio: Audiobook Sales on the Rise Nationally." Available: www.audiopub.org/PDFs/2007SalesSurveyrelease.pdf (accessed September 10, 2009).

_____. 2007b. "APAFAQ." Available: www.audiopub.org/faq.asp (accessed September 10, 2009).

_____. 2008. "More Americans Are All Ears to Audiobooks." Available: www.audiopub .org/pdfs/2008 sales consumer final.pdf (accessed September 15, 2009).

Baig, Edward. C. 2008. "Army Goes by the Book for Boosting Morale." *USA Today*. Available: http://blogs.usatoday.com/technologylive/2008/06/army-goes-by-th.html (accessed September 10, 2009).

Buckleitner, Warren. 2007. "Not an iPod, but It's Child-Friendly and Uses One AAA Battery." *The New York Times* (January 4). Available: www.nytimes.com/2007/01/04/ technology/04player.html (accessed September 10, 2009).

Coburn, Michael et al. 2001. "Chapter 7: Ebook Readers: Directions in Enabling Technology." In *Print and Electronic Text Convergence: Technology Drivers across the Book Production Supply Chain, from Creator to Consumer* (pp. 145–182), edited by B. Cope and D. Kalantzis. Altona, Victoria: Common Ground.

Crawford, Walt. 2000. "Nine Models, One Name: Untangling the E-book Muddle." *American Libraries* 31, no. 8 (September): 56–59.

_____. 2006. "Why Aren't Ebooks More Successful?" *EContent* 29, no. 8 (October): 44.

EEI Press, eds. 2007. *The Elements of Internet Style: The New Rules of Creating Valuable Content for Today's Readers*. New York: Allworth Press.

Egidi, Lavinia, and Marco Furini. 2006. "From Digital Audiobook to Secure Digital Multimedia-book." *ACM Computers in Entertainment* 4, no. 3 (July): 1–19.

Findaway World. 2009. "Playaway FAQ." Available: http://playaway.com/faq/for-libraries/#faqSectionTwo (accessed September 2, 2009).

Guthrie, Richard. 2006. "Riding the E-frenzy of 2000: Stephen King and the E-book." *LOGOS* 17, no. 3: 122–132.

Harrison, Beverly L. 2000. "E-books and the Future of Reading." *Computer Graphics and Applications, IEEE* 20, no. 3 (May/June): 32–39.

Hawkins, Donald. T. 2000a. "Electronic Books: A Major Publishing Revolution: Part 1, General Considerations and Issues." *Online* 24, no. 4 (July/August): 14–28.

_____. 2000b. "Electronic Books: A Major Publishing Revolution: Part 2, The Marketplace." *Online* 24, no. 5 (September/October): 18–36.

"Industry Statistics." International Digital Publishing Forum. (2008). Available: www.openebook.org/doc_library/industrystats.htm (accessed September 10, 2009).

Kaye, Alan L. 2008. "Audio Fixation." *Library Journal* 133, no. 9 (May 15): 34–37.

Kurzweil, Raymond. 1992a. "The Future of Libraries Part 1: The Technology of the Book." *Library Journal* 117, no. 1 (January): 80–82.

_____. 1992b. "The Future of Libraries Part 2: The End of Books." *Library Journal* 117, no. 3 (February 15): 140–141.

_____. 1992c. "The Future of Libraries Part 3: The Virtual Library." *Library Journal* 117, no. 5 (March 15): 63–64.

Lebert, Marie. 2008. *The Project Gutenberg EBook of Project Gutenberg (1971–2008)*. Toronto: NEF, University of Toronto and Project Gutenberg. Available: http://www .gutenberg/org/files/27045/27045.txt (accessed September 10, 2009).

Milliot, Jim. 2008. "Report Finds Growing Acceptance of Digital Books." *Publishers Weekly* 255, no. 7 (February 18): 6.

OverDrive. 2008. "Digital Library Reserve." Available: www.overdrive.com/products/ dlr/ (accessed September 10, 2009).

Poremba, Sue Marquette. 2008. "Take a Look at Today's Vibrant Ebook Market." *EContent* 31, no. 2 (March): 32–37.

Rao, Siriginidi Subba. 2003. "Electronic Books: A Review and Evaluation." *Library Hi Tech* 21, no. 1: 85–93.

_____. 2004. "Electronic Book Technologies: An Overview of the Present Situation." *Library Review* 53, no. 7: 363–371.

_____. 2005. "Electronic Books: Their Integration into Library and Information Centers." *The Electronic Library* 23, no. 1: 116–140.

Saricks, Joyce. 2008. "LA: Essentials of Listening Advisory." *Booklist* 104, no. 21 (July): 16.

Shatzkin, Mike. 2008. "15 Trends to Watch in 2008." *Publishers Weekly* 255, no. 1 (January 7): 22–23.

Uzanne, Octave, and Albert Robida. 1895. "The End of Books: A Prognostication from the Past." *Contes pour les Bibliophiles.* Project Gutenberg. Available: http://www.gutenberg.org (accessed September 10, 2009).

Wilson, Rose. 2001. "Evolution of Portable Electronic Books. *Ariadne,* no. 29. Available: www.ariadne.ac.uk/issue29/ (accessed September 10, 2009).

FURTHER READING

Chu, Heting. 2003. "Electronic Books: Viewpoints from Users and Potential Users." *Library Hi Tech* 21, no. 3: 340–346.

Cope, Bill, and Diana Kalantzis, eds. 2001. *Print and Electronic Text Convergence: Technology Drivers across the Book.* Altona, Victoria: Common Ground.

Gomez, Jeff. 2008. *Print Is Dead: Books in Our Digital Age.* New York: Macmillan.

Herther, Nancy K. 2008. "The Ebook Reader Is Not the Future of Ebooks." *Searcher* 16, no. 8 (September): 26–40.

Hutley, Sue, and Wendy Horwood. 2002. "E-book Readers in Australian Public Libraries: Are They REAL-e Worth It?" Available: www.vala.org.au/vala2002/2002pdf/34HutHor.pdf (accessed September 10, 2009).

Larson, Jeanette. 2006. "Listen up! What's New in Audiobooks." *Library Media Connection* 24, no. 7 (April/May): 24–27.

Oder, Norman. 2004. "Feeling a Squeeze: Audiobooks Are Popular, but Librarians Must Navigate Multiple Options and Tighter Budgets." *Library Journal* 129, no. 19 (November 15): 34–36.

Sontag, Sherry. 2008. "The E-reader Experience: An Inside Look at the Leading E-book Readers in Action." *EContent* 31, no. 6 (July/August): 36–40.

Sottong, Stephen. 2008. "The Elusive E-book: Are E-books Finally Ready for Prime Time?" *American Libraries* 39, no. 5 (May): 44–48.

Part III

The Art and Science of Readers' Advisory

Chapter 6

Beyond the General Reference Interview

The things I want to know are in books; my best friend is the man who'll get me a book I ain't read.

—Abraham Lincoln, 1809–1865

The conversation with the reader is integral to the process of readers' advisory. Yet it is only one part of the total interaction. Much like the other activities in the library, readers' advisory is multifaceted and calls upon many skills and resources to connect readers to a few good books. Skills in engaging the reader in conversation, competency in the manipulating of and using readers' advisory tools, and well-developed and current fiction collections are each an essential component to successful readers' advisory relations. The single most important strategy to success in readers' advisory is getting out from behind the desk and meeting the readers where they are—in the stacks, physically or virtually.

THE READERS' ADVISORY CONVERSATION

Nothing disconcerts a librarian more than the question "Can you recommend a good book to read?" Unlike reference transactions that can be resolved by teasing out the patron's needs through a successful reference interview, suggesting a good book is fraught with nuances, from the reader's mood to a book's appeal and characteristics. What's more is the unspoken expectation that since you work with books, you must obviously know the goods ones from the bad. And the phrase "good book" holds a high level of subjectivity and ambiguity: a good book for *me* may be vastly different from *your* definition of "good book."

The readers' advisory interview, perhaps more aptly called a conversation, mirrors the same steps that a standard reference interview follows (see Table 6-1). The purpose of the RA conversation is to guide both librarian and reader to the books that will best suit the given mood and interests. The difference lies in

Table 6-1: Reference Interview or Readers' Advisory Conversation	
Reference Interview	Readers' Advisory Conversation
Establish rapport with patron	Approachability and establishing the relationship with the reader
General information gathering for the big picture	Gather information about the types of books the reader enjoys
Gathering more specific information to meet the patron's needs	Gather specific information about appeal, characteristics, and mood
Intervention and provision of information	Suggest a range of books that might meet reader's interests
Follow up and encourage feedback	Follow up and encourage feedback

the purposes of the reader's requests. Joyce Saricks identifies four basic questions from patrons that prompt the readers' advisory conversation:

1. Reference or factual information about authors and titles;
2. Books and authors within specific genres;
3. Read-alikes;
4. General recommendations for a good book. (2005: 170)

Ultimately the readers' advisor attempts to determine the experience the reader is seeking and the cost he or she is willing to pay in terms of time and effort (an easy beach read or something with challenging characters and complex plot; fast-paced action or rich in descriptive narrative).

Regardless of the reader's purpose, the RA conversation begins with learning something about the reader's interests—what the reader is in the mood for; what she has read recently that she liked; what he did not like about a particular book or author; what sparked the reader's curiosity about a book. As discussed in earlier chapters, reading is a shared activity, and most readers enjoy talking about the books they have read and the appeal the books held for them (their emotional responses to a particular story), and these conversations help make the leap to new authors or titles. The RA interaction requires careful listening skills to discern those elements that the reader most wants from a reading encounter.

Many readers will be hesitant to ask for reading assistance, assuming that the librarian has a higher, more important purpose than discussing books. The adult librarian's purpose is to, first, put the reader at ease, and then engage in a conversation about the books that suit individual tastes and interests. (See Table 6-2 for a few strategies for eliciting information about reading preferences.) Almost without fail, library staff who work with adult readers suggest that one of the most effective RA conversations starts with a question like, "Tell me about a book you really enjoyed" or "What was the last book that you read that you really

Table 6-2: A Few Dos and Don'ts for a Successful RA Conversation	
DO ...	DON'T ...
Listen carefully for the clues that suggest reading preferences.	Make assumptions about what the reader means. "I'm looking for a beach book" could mean a summer beach read or a book for which the setting is a beach.
Listen carefully for clues about what types of books the reader does not like to read.	Focus only on the types of books patrons like; encourage them to discuss books they did not like.
Ask probing questions to be sure you understand the reader's interests and preferences.	Judge the question or the questioner.
Use the range of RA tools to find books that match mood and appeal factors.	Consult the library's catalog immediately as it only identifies known items (title, author).
Suggest more than one title.	Rely upon your personal reading as your only source for suggestions.
Encourage the reader to return and tell you whether he or she enjoyed the titles you suggested.	Neglect to follow up with the patron.
Be patient. A successful transaction takes time and cultivation.	

Note: All of these suggestions came from working librarians and RA staff who willingly shared their experiences and advice.

enjoyed?" and prompting the reader to describe the elements of the book that most appealed to the reader.

It is important to be patient and carefully listen to the patron's responses as you discuss what he or she liked or did not enjoy about particular books. Many readers will be vague in their initial question, hoping to get a quick answer and be on their way. Similar to the traditional reference interview, the RA conversation probes for clues to help make recommendations. It may take multiple attempts to find the perfect match between reader and book.

Several excellent resources explore the practical aspects of the reference interview. Ross, Nilsen, and Radford's text *Conducting the Reference Interview* (2009) includes a chapter devoted to preparing for and conducting the RA conversation as well as presenting excellent practical instruction for general reference interviews. In her book *Readers' Advisory Service in the Public Library*, Saricks (2005) explores strategies for both passive RA activities and conducting productive conversations with patrons. Herald's *Genreflecting* (2006) includes a brief chapter on the readers' advisory interview that includes a number of excellent open-ended questions to get the conversation started. Across the various texts experts generally agree that the RA conversation is designed to find out what reading experience the patron wants from his or her book.

Mood and Appeal

Mood reflects the reader's emotional response to the environment and the selection of books to read, films to watch, or music for listening. We have all experienced moments when we want something light and funny to help soothe a long and stressful day or something deeper that makes us think and stretch. Ross and Chelton (2001) suggest that addressing emotional responses allows the readers' advisor to look across genres with new perspectives in order to meet the reader's mood and to make new groupings based on other similarities beyond the conventions of specific genres. Focusing on mood allows the readers' advisor to distinguish the reader's preferences for elements such as familiarity versus novelty, safety (authors or titles that are familiar and comfortable) versus risk (trying something new and unfamiliar), or easy reads versus challenging ones.

Likewise, appeal addresses those elements or characteristics that provoke a reader's response. Appeal, like mood, focuses on the reading experience and the feelings the book invokes. Pace, setting, time period, story line, and characterization all make up elements of a book's appeal. Other appeal factors include the level of sexuality or violence, the use of profanity or lack of, and the presentation of philosophical ideas, and length, format, and writing style. However, from an RA point of view, these are not the elements that are described in the library catalog's subject headings. These are all the elements that must be drawn out in conversation in order to make the connection between the reader and the story. More importantly, combined with mood, appeal is the overriding factor that defines "a good book." (*Good,* for most readers, implies that the book has a desired effect or draws a particular response from the reader.)

RA 2.0 Solution for Mood and Appeal

Library 2.0 resources, such as those discussed in previous chapters, provide opportunities to enhance the readers' advisor's abilities to connect to the emotional elements of a book. Tagging, a prominent feature of LibraryThing.com, Amazon.com, and in blogs and other social content management resources, makes use of the reader's definitions and descriptions of stories. These tags are better able to describe the nuances of the books that readers discover than are standardized subject headings. Incorporating tags into the library's catalog, which some systems have initiated, offers alternative methods of identifying the elements of a book. For example, *The Reader* by Bernhard Schlink (1997, 2008), now an Oscar Award–winning movie, is classified in the public library catalog with subject headings that do not describe the deeper elements (first love, passion, sexual awakening), but when combining them with the tags from either Amazon.com or LibraryThing.com adds a richness to describing the book's appeal (see Figure 6-1). In addition, because the tags on LibraryThing and similar tools are hot links, users can make connections to other books with similar elements or that are described in a similar fashion.

Figure 6-1: Examples of Subject Headings and Tags for *The Reader* by Bernhard Schlink

Public Library Catalog Subject Headings

Subjects
- World War, 1939–1945 – Atrocities – Fiction.
- War crime trials – Fiction.
- Germany – Fiction.

Genre:
Love stories.
Psychological fiction.

Amazon.com: Tags Customers Associated with This Product

historical fiction (12)
german literature (9)
concentration camps (7)
fiction (6)
auschwitz (5)
first love (5)
literary (4)
literature (3)
2009movie (1)
4 stars (1)
81st oscar (1)
allegory (1)
bernhard schlink (1)
codependent (1)
contemporary fiction (1)
contemporary literature (1)
emotional muffling (1)
ephebophilia (1)

for all ages (1)
glenn thater (1)
harbinger of doom (1)
holocaust (1)
literary fiction (1)
modern literature (1)
mystery (1)
odyssey (1)
on (1)
passion (1)
schlink (1)
sexual abuse (1)
sexual awakening (1)
the fallen angel (1)
the gateway (1)
this is a great movie (1)
useful (1)

LibraryThing.com: Member Tags

1001 1999 20th century coming of age concentration camps contemporary Contemporary fiction crime Europe fiction german German Fiction german literature Germany guilt historical historical fiction history Holocaust illiteracy library literary fiction literature love nazi Nazis novel oprah Oprah's Book Club own owned paperback read reading relationships roman romance schlink sex tbr translated translation unread war wwii

Recommendations or Suggestions?

Another aspect of the readers' advisory interview that creates some consternation is the notion of giving a recommendation for a book. Recommendation by nature implies judgment about the content or quality of an item. It is an activity we engage in with our family and friends: "You really need to read *The Shadow of the Wind*. It's really good," or "*The Secret Life of Bees* was the best book I've read in a long time and you just have to read it." Recommendations are based on our intimate knowledge of the other person and his or her tastes and our desire to share and discuss books with that individual. (Or in the case of book reviews, recommendations become critical analyses of fiction intended to determine the quality and value of the work.)

The readers' advisor relationship is based not on what the librarian's definition of a good book entails, but it is the process of connecting the reader to books that may appeal to his or her preferences. The interaction becomes one of suggesting books that might meet the reader's needs and allowing the reader to make the decision and final selection. Looking at the process as one of suggestion rather than recommendation facilitates the professional relationship between librarian and reader and puts the reader's tastes and mood at the center of the interaction.

Form-Based RA Activities

Form-based RA harkens back to early readers' advisory services when readers' advisors prepared individual reading plans for patrons. These early reading plans were designed to meet the patron's goals for improving his or her educational levels and improving the taste of the reader. Today, form-based RA builds upon the service of helping meet the reader's goals, but the focus is on fiction and leisure reading, even though, as discussed in earlier chapters, reading does serve many purposes besides pleasure.

With the prevalence of online survey mechanisms and easily created Web-based forms, a number of RA librarians have found opportunities to exploit form-based readers' advisory services. Readers access the forms through the library's Web site, generally the "Find a Good Book" section of the Web site. By completing the form and returning it to the library, readers can obtain personal reading lists specific to their unique combination of interests. For example, the Salt Lake County Library offers readers two different options: (1) Personalized Booklists for Genre or Subject List (www.slco.lib.ut.us/booksnmore/personal_booklist.htm) and (2) Personalized Booklists for Similar Reads (www.slco.lib.ut.us/booksnmore/personal_similar.htm). The forms are easy to use by selecting criteria from a series of predefined topics, and they allow for free responses on questions of elements to avoid, likes and dislikes, and specifics about the individual's reading preferences. The Williamsburg Regional Library (www.wrl.org/

bookweb/RA/index.html) offers a similar service, "A Reader for Every Book, A Book for Every Reader," which attempts to match reader profiles with customized reading lists. Once the form is submitted, readers' are advised that response time will be approximately five to seven days for receiving their customized lists.

STRATEGIES AND RESOURCES FOR SUCCESSFUL READERS' ADVISORY ACTIVITIES

You have spent time with the patron, discovering what type of book she's in the mood for and what elements of books appeal to her. You haven't read chick lit, and the patron is looking for a lighthearted read about women in the South with a little romance and adventure with quirky characters. Now what?

The first step in suggesting books requires the readers' advisor to know a little something about genres and about fiction in general. Given the vast quantity of titles held in a library through print, audio, and electronic resources, the task feels near impossible. How can you possibly recall every title and nuance for one genre, let alone 400 subgenres?

Make a Plan

In order to serve readers effectively, the readers' advisor must have a broad background in genre fiction and readable nonfiction. That means you have to read—a lot—and find ways to make connections between books based upon appeal factors. Many readers tend to stay within their own reading comfort zones, and readers' advisors are no exception. But to be conversant the RA librarian needs to cast a wider net into the fiction collection and even the nonfiction selections.

Discussion about books plays a key role in learning about genres. Being able to share responses to the books and the authors allows the readers' advisor to explore and understand the appeal of the various elements that comprise a genre. It also becomes possible to make the connections between authors and books that are more subtle than simply being included in the same genre. The trick is to talk not only to your colleagues and acquaintances but with your patrons as well. You may respond to the fast-paced action while another person reading the same book may respond to the quirky characters or setting, providing you with additional insight about the genre and its appeal.

Many experienced readers' advisors begin by advising to establish a deliberate personal reading plan and base it upon the library's own popular reading lists. Select representative titles from genres normally not read, including popular authors and titles that patrons request, award-winning titles, and recommendations from colleagues who do read the genre. While the library's own popular reading lists make excellent starting points, resources such as NoveList (an EbscoHost product) or the Adult Reading Round Table of Illinois (ARRT;

www.arrtreads.org) provide access to reading lists by genre as well as more detailed genre studies. Accept the challenges posted on discussion boards, such as LibraryThing's group of Librarians Who LibraryThing, to read 5, 10, 20 new books throughout the year. Above all remember to read broadly within the genres to get a feel for the breadth of subgenres as well as the crossovers between genres.

A more intense version of a reading plan involves genre studies; typically it involves multiple people (e.g., staff and colleagues) as well. Genre studies are purposeful examinations of individual genres. They promote in-depth discovery of appeal factors, subgenres and topics, characters, and representative authors and titles. Genre studies also enhance the readers' advisor's ability to communicate with readers about genres, and they raise the comfort level of feeling prepared to engage in the RA conversation. ARRT established genre study groups as part of their services to members, and their study guides provide useful models for others wanting to establish similar activities (www.arrtreads.org/genrestudy.htm). ARRT genre studies are two-year-long programs that delve into the intimate workings of individual genres. (The most current genre study underway is Romance.) The ultimate goal of genre studies is "reading to discover the book, author, and genre's appeal to fans" (Saricks, 2005: 127).

The purpose of a reading plan or genre study, however, is not to read anything and everything, but to learn to discern the characteristics of a genre. Personal RA reading plans and genre studies should be purposeful and approached with intent. Calling upon all of the available tools to explore books becomes as essential as the act of reading itself. These strategies become the foundation from which to grow expertise in a range of genres and to serve the patron well.

Annotations 1.0 and 2.0

One strategy for keeping track of reading and a book's relationship to the universe of genre fiction focuses on the preparation of annotations. Writing annotations about the books you have read has many useful results. First, they provide a way to think about the elements of a book and its relationship to a genre. Second, annotations can be used as an aide-mémoire to recall information about books for suggestions. Finally, annotations can be posted on the library's Web site, blog, or wiki to help save the time of the reader in locating a good read, and to provide opportunities for user interaction and participation. For example, Ann Arbor District Library (www.aadl.org) has incorporated user-defined tags along with summaries, annotations, reviews, and author notes into the library catalog. Likewise, other public libraries such as Hennepin County Library (www.hclib.org/pub/bookspace) and Skokie Public Library (www .skokielibrary .info/s_read/rd_find/index.asp), while decidedly different in approach, offer access to extensive reading lists arranged by genre and subgenre and include book descriptions and annotations along with read-alike lists (see Figure 6-2 for comparisons of annotations).

Figure 6-2: Examples of Annotations	
Carl Hiaasen Read-a-Likes	*Historian, The* by Kostova, Elizabeth
Fans of Carl Hiaasen's zany crime capers set in the steamy South will enjoy these authors who mix humor and suspense in stories filled with outlandish characters and wacky plot twists. All of these titles are located in the Adult Mystery section of the library unless otherwise noted.	*Publisher:* Little, Brown and Co., 2005. *Number of Pages:* 642 **Genres:** Historical Fiction Horror
Barclay, Linwood. *Bad Move.* 2004. Barry, Dave. *Big Trouble.* 1999. (Fiction BAR). Also available: Large Type, Cassette Bartholomew, Nancy. *The Miracle Strip.* 1998. Barton, Dan. *Killer Material.* 2000	**Reviews:** After an unnamed teenage girl finds an unusual book in her father's library in which all of the pages are blank except for a woodcut of a dragon with the word Drakulya under it, she embarks on an odyssey first undertaken by her grandfather and then her parents that leads to the legendary Vlad Tepes (Dracula himself!) and reunites with her mother, who was long thought to be dead (or among the "undead"). An intriguing journey into the history of the legend and of Eastern Europe, told from alternating perspectives of the characters (often through stories and letters written earlier), full of suspense, surprises, and incredibly vivid depictions of time and place, entirely believable, thoroughly chilling, and marred only by a somewhat anticlimactic ending.
	Similar Titles: *Jonathan Strange & Mr. Norrell* by Susanna Clarke *The Gargoyle* by Andrew Davidson *Dracula* by Bram Stoker

Annotations take many forms and include a range of information. Typically the annotations will include author, title, and publication information along with more specific details of geographical setting, time period, and series. They also cover such elements as plot summary, subject headings, and appeal factors. The connections with similar authors and titles present opportunities for suggesting new books to try. Most importantly, annotations provide a method to capture details and impressions of the books being read.

Before the advent of the Web, annotations were maintained by hand, filed in notebooks, or jotted down on index cards. Spreadsheets and homegrown databases filled the void for easily accessible information. Regardless, writing and maintaining annotations was exhausting and time-consuming. With the incorporation of Library 2.0 technologies into library services today, annotations have become much easier to prepare, and the technologies encourage collaboration between colleagues and between library staff and reader.

Services such as Baker and Taylor's Content Café 2 or Bowker's Syndetic Solutions provide integrated options for combining traditional readers' advisory elements with a range of other descriptive features in the library catalog. These options also support the incorporation of Library 2.0 technologies into the catalog. Patrons and staff now have access to tens of thousands of descriptive elements, including book jacket images, author biographies, summaries, annotations, first chapter excerpts, and book reviews, in one place. With the addition of Library 2.0 technologies, readers are empowered to provide descriptive tags, their own reviews, and notes about their reading experiences, making the readers' advisor interaction richer and having the ability to reach further to remote users.

For libraries on tight budgets, online annotations and access can still be accomplished quickly and easily. With Library 2.0 technologies it is now possible to adapt a personal reading list (reading plan) into a resource that is easily shared with others. Many blogs, wikis, and social content management tools are freely available and easy to use. The social cataloging resources, such as LibraryThing, GoodReads, and Shelfari, support the exporting of annotations and tags from the personal catalog to a blog, creating a level of accessibility outside of the traditional library Web site (which frequently requires the intervention of the IT staff for updating and maintenance). Combined with their ease of importing bibliographic details from other bibliographic utilities into the social catalog itself, time and effort can be minimized in creating comprehensive annotations. Citation information will be up-to-date and accurate, allowing the librarian to focus on creating useful annotations and reviews. The social catalogs can also be linked to the library's MySpace or Facebook account to reach library users who may be unlikely to access the library's catalog or come into the library to browse.

Reading Maps, Reading Paths, and Serial Bibliographies

Readers' advisors have suggested and developed many ways to connect titles within and across genres. Among the multiple iterations, common versions include reading maps, reading paths, reading itineraries, and serial bibliographies. Regardless of the name these are yet other methods of not only thinking about book connections yourself, but providing tools to connect readers to the books they want to read. In many ways reading maps or reading paths are intended to visually represent the threads that bind genres together and connect seemingly unrelated titles based on other elements of stories, or "the internal life of the book" (Wyatt, 2006: 38). Not only does the reading map pull in unifying themes between titles, but it offers the ability to extend to related aspects of the book, such as subplots or locations that may intrigue readers. More importantly, reading maps draw on the entire collection within the library, from books to multimedia resources, providing wider access to materials that will enrich the reading experience.

Reading maps and all of the variants aid in making creative connections between readers and books. In many ways they feel like travel itineraries, leading the reader from one experience to the next. Reading maps are not simply read-alikes; in fact they are not lists of read-alikes at all. They are much more eclectic in nature, with unusual twists and turns that look to other pathways and commonalities. Several examples of reading paths can be located at http://wordsworthyreadingpaths.pbwiki.com/, encompassing fiction, nonfiction, poetry, and young adult interests. Nancy Pearl's Book Lust Wiki: A Community for Book Lovers also features a range of reading itineraries that illustrate the paths that can be followed through books (http://booklust.wetpaint.com/page/Reading+Itineraries). Reading maps take many forms, from the highly complex, incorporating bibliographies of fiction and nonfiction, author biographies, and images, to the unadorned but highly useful annotated reading maps that trace a path through books.

They are easily created in a Web-based forum with links to the library's resources or in blogs and wikis. Because wikis and blogs are social tools, library users can be invited to share their links to the reading maps by providing titles that they followed from first book to last (not series, but rather the connections they made through more subtle relationships). While the linking to other books is key, the reading maps also present opportunities to make connections with other media—for example, discussions or interviews from NPR or C-SPAN, films in the theater, on television, or found on YouTube—, which may lead to additional reading stops along the way.

Commercial Readers' Advisory Databases

Strategies and plans are critical to readers' advisory activities. However, tools for finding the links are equally important. Several commercial databases are readily available and designed specifically to make connections between the reader's interests and possible titles. The most powerful databases include Fiction Connection, NoveList, Readers' Advisor Online, and What Do I Read Next? (See Table 6-3 for a comparison of several products.) Each product requires an annual subscription, though free 30-day trials are available to libraries for evaluation purposes. The strength of these resources lies in their ability to search through thousands of entries to find titles based on a variety of customizable criteria.

The RA databases use traditional searches for title, author, subject, or ISBN, but they also include searches that relate more directly to RA needs as well. For

Table 6-3: Quick Comparison of Subscription Readers' Advisory Databases

	NoveList	Fiction Connection	What Do I Read Next?	Readers' Advisor Online
Database Vendor/Producer	EbscoHost	Bowker	Gale	Libraries Unlimited
Number of Titles	150,000+ fiction titles; 50,000+ readable nonfiction titles		134,300+ titles and 74,500+ plot summaries	400 genres, subgenres, and reading interests
Additional Resources for Librarians	Newsletters for RA; Newsletters for Readers (NextReads: genre, bestsellers lists); Pearl's Picks (reading suggestions from Nancy Pearl with annotations); Book Display Ideas; Marketing and Promotion Materials; RA Training; Getting Started in RA (genre outlines, popular fiction checklists)	Companion resource to Bowker's Books in Print; Customizable Web site materials, product information, product training, blog		Reader's advisor materials, RA blog, Newsletters
Annotations	Read-alike and Thematic annotations; References to series; Appeal factors	Book summaries, Genres, Topics	Plot summaries and book descriptions	Genre and Subgenre definitions, Book and Series descriptions
Search Features	Basic and Advanced Searches, Browsing	Basic (title, author); Topic, Genre, Setting, Character, Location, Time Frame; AquaBrowser Visual Faceted	Author, Title, Series, Custom, Genre, Browsing	Quick and Advanced, Browsing
For Adult Readers	Spotlight; Author Read-Alikes; Award Winners; Book Discussion Guides; Articles (genre; Recommended Reads; What We're Reading	Suggested Reading lists based on selected criteria (Read-alikes, award winners)	"Help Me Find a Book;" Genre Search; Award Winners and Top Picks; "Who? What? Where? When?"	Read-Alike Finder, Themes, Genres, Titles in Series, Reading Lists
Other Features	Remote access with user authentication	Remote access with user authentication	Remote access with user authentication	Remote access with user authentication

example, each database offers genre, subgenre, and related-interest searching. Searches can be further narrowed by additional factors such as time periods, locations, and themes (coming-of-age novels, family sagas, etc.). For those readers seeking titles or characters in series, the databases offer search functionality to accommodate this. Each resource generates lists based on the searches, and the lists include book descriptions, related topics, the occasional book cover images, and the ability to print and e-mail the list for future reference. By integrating the systems, libraries may also offer the option to search the library's own catalog for the selected titles and place holds for later pickup and interlibrary loan requests for items in other libraries. Library users may access the databases remotely through user authentication (library card number and password most frequently), and in some instances the database vendors have created complementary patron versions and professional versions.

Each RA database also offers unique features for the library user. For example, Fiction Connection (a Bowker product) offers AquaBrowser, which uses a visual faceted search feature. It displays topics and subtopics in a visual map made up of links that will connect the searcher to additional titles related to the original selection. For example, searching on the title *Pride and Prejudice* displays links to "Austen," "racism," "class," "Darcy," "prejudice," and "poverty." Each tag or facet then leads to additional titles that are related through the individual terms to *Pride and Prejudice*. The links for "Austen," for example, include *The Lost Memoirs of Jane Austen* and *Mr. Darcy's Diary*. This works similarly to a concept map or reading map, allowing readers to follow the threads tying their interest together. Fiction Connection also uses word clouds to guide the reader through the book selection process, making links to titles with similar tags.

While Readers' Advisor Online (Libraries Unlimited) has excellent functionality and a full range of search features, for readers' advisors one of its real strengths is the available professional material. To support readers' advisory activities, a companion blog, titled "RA Run Down" (www.readersadvisoronline .com/blog/), has been created that includes news, tips, and information for readers' advisors. "RA Run Down" provides a weekly update of RA news and interests gathered from other blogs, newsletters, magazines, newspapers, and other resources. Among its many topics, the blog includes the "Hottest Books of the Week" in fiction and nonfiction, books and publishing news, author information, and all manner of book lists (e.g., Top Ten Funniest Books According to the British), and links to other external blogs related to books and reading.

Reader's Advisor Online, along with the public blog, provides an in-depth selection of RA materials to its subscribers. Within the database users will find a number of genre studies based upon the *Genreflecting* series. The materials include essays on the historical foundations of individual genres along with information for collection development including lists of authors, series, and individual titles that well-rounded collections should include. Each genre also covers a small selection of subgenres with brief essays and author and title lists.

NoveList and "What Do I Read Next?" offer similar services to subscribers. NoveList features their "NextReads Service," which includes exhaustive annotations for books and a branded newsletter for the library. Annotations include read-alikes, themes, appeal factors, and information about series. More importantly, this service is customized, meaning that suggestions are drawn from the library's own collection. The newsletter is sent to subscribers through NoveList, with little intervention needed from the library's staff, but it also provides the option to customize the content with library announcements of upcoming events, book club meetings, and other information for local library users. NoveList also offers online newsletters for readers' advisors on a variety of topics.

Finally, "What Do I Read Next?," while having many features that mirror the other commercial databases, includes a section on "Monthly Highlights" providing seasonal suggestions for reading (February's selections include titles on romance and on Abraham Lincoln and books about dogs and pets in honor of the Westminster Kennel Club Dog Show). The highlights feature award-winning books along with those that are new and noteworthy. "What Do I Read Next?" offers both searching as well as browsing, enabling the user to find books easily. The individual-retrieved records are comprehensive, including book descriptions, major characters, related subjects, settings, time period, information about any bestsellers lists the title appeared on, and recommendations for similar titles.

Web-Based RA Resources

Along with the commercial databases, a number of freely available resources for RA activities have appeared on the Web. While a large number of them are currently accessible, only a few will be considered here (see Table 6-4). The Web RA resources were created with a range of applications, from traditional HTML-coded Web pages to user-participatory services, including blogs and wikis. The fact that many of the Web sites can be updated quickly makes them highly desirable for locating current, popular lists as well as lists of standard titles within genres.

Annotations, plot summaries, and book descriptions make up key features of the Web sites. The more comprehensive resources include search and browse functions similar to those found in the commercial databases along with the ability to generate reading and recommendation lists. These Web sites offer the user multiple options for complex searching based on a number of factors, including character, setting, location, and style as well as genre. Some of the additional features include links to official author Web sites, allowing librarians and readers to remain current about their favorites, tagging functions for user-defined characteristics, and integration with other social content management systems such as LibraryThing.

Table 6-4: Web-Based Resources for Readers' Advisors

	Overbooked	FictionDB	AllReaders.com	Library Booklists
Web Address	www.overbooked.com	www.fictiondb.com	www.allreaders.com	http://librarybooklists.org
Subscription	Not required	Free without login (limited browsing), Free with login (full range of search capabilities), Premium $20/year (ability to swap/sell books, no advertising, analytical information)	Not required	Not required
Coverage	Fiction, readable nonfiction, booklists, starred reviews, hot lists, and notables	Genres: Speculative, Suspense, Western, Romance	Genres: Sci-Fi/Fantasy, Mystery/Thriller, Literature, Romance, Biography, History	Library booklists and bibliographies of fiction, nonfiction, children's and YA fiction
Search Features	Can be browsed only by starred reviews, themed booklists, featured title lists, hot lists	Basic and Advanced Searches, Browsing, Pseudonyms, Series	Title/Author, Detailed search by plot, setting, or character, browsable; The Gordonator Precision Search Engine to use detailed searches on specific appeal factors (main characters, plot, setting, style)	Basic search box, browsable by categories
Annotations	Annotations and reviews including suggestions for series, characters, and other appeal factors	Annotations with genre, series, time periods, etc.	Book descriptions and plot summaries	Brief descriptions and plot summaries; Booklists include detailed descriptions of the covered topic
Additional Features	Author Connections database, Overbooked Wiki, access through MySpace, Facebook, and other social networking resources	Links to author Web sites, links to external reviews, book covers, LibraryThing embedded with recommendations and tag clouds, Link to WorldCat to find titles in libraries, Author bibliographies with publication dates	Message boards, Brief lists of similar books based on user search	Links to other libraries' booklists internationally, Calendar of author birthdates, Resources for reading groups

Managing Web Resource Overload

With the wide range of online tools available, it is incredibly easy to become overwhelmed with the richness of the Web. Using Library 2.0 tools to manage your favorite resources will aid in management and organization. Frequently blogs, wikis, and other resources feature RSS subscriptions and feeds so users are updated when content is added or edited. Subscribing to feeds eliminates the need to check resources frequently for new content and maintains updates in one place for efficient access. Feeds can be quickly scanned to determine if they need to be consulted immediately or wait until a later time.

Social bookmarking also provides an excellent and efficient method for managing all of your favorite Web sites, wikis, and blogs. Social bookmarking serves a similar function as using "My Favorites" on your Web browser, but it offers some advantages. Social bookmarking services, such as Delicious, StumbleUpon, or Twine, allow users to bookmark Web sites, tag them with descriptions for organization, and keep them in one place for portability. The bookmarks are held on an external service from which members can access their links using any computer or some mobile devices. Because these are social tools, members can share their bookmarks and tags with other users.

Resources for Social Bookmarking

Buzz Up: http://buzz.yahoo.com
Delicious: http://delicious.com
Digg: http://digg.com
StumbleUpon: www.stumbleupon.com
Twine: www.twine.com

Along with the sharing and tagging features, users can organize tags into groupings, keeping like tags together for ease of access. For example, more than 3,500 resources have been tagged in Delicious as "readersadvisory." The links also show the other tags that have been applied by individuals to the Web sites, enabling users to find genre-specific resources (e.g., mystery or mysteries). Many of the links direct the user to public libraries, including readers' advisory resources that have been created in-house as well as some of the commercial products.

Other Top-Notch RA Tools

Books and journals to support readers' advisory services abound in the marketplace. One well-known RA series is Libraries Unlimited's (LU) *Genreflecting*. It is a multivolume series devoted to genre fiction and readable nonfiction. LU's hallmark title is *Genreflecting: A Guide to Reading Interests in Genre Fiction,* but the series also includes more than 18 other titles for specific genres, ranging from African-American Literature to Strictly Science Fiction. The Readers' Advisor Online is the companion database for this series. Other useful books include Joyce Saricks' *The Reader's Advisory Guide to Genre Fiction* (2001) and *Readers' Advisory Service in the Public Library* (2005), both published by the American Library Association. Nancy Pearl's *Book Lust* (2003) and *More Book Lust* (2005) provide extensive lists of recommended reading for every mood.

Professional journals including *Booklist* and *Booklist Online, Library Journal, Publishers Weekly,* and *Kirkus* are highly useful for finding book reviews and book blurbs along with news about the publishing industry. In particular *Booklist* features genre lists and read-alike lists with annotations. Different issues of *Booklist* will focus on specific genres or formats, providing extensive coverage of titles, authors, and general trends. *Library Journal* offers similar reviewing columns as well as "best of" genre lists (e.g., Best Romance Titles). Consider the professional journals to be current awareness resources to aid in keeping on top of new releases, award-winning books and authors, and other topics of interest to readers' advisors.

Subscribing to listservs is yet another method for learning about genres as well as requesting assistance for hard-to-answer readers' advisory requests. Fiction_L (www.webrary.org/rs/flmenu.html) is probably the best-known e-mail discussion list for all things fiction—from reading lists to information on book discussion topics, collection development, and genre studies. Created and maintained by the Morton Grove Public Library Readers' Service staff, Fiction_L was established in late 1995. The e-mail discussions are lively and active with a great deal of information exchange. Along with the listserv itself, the MGPL staff provides open access to the complete Fiction_L archives, dating from 1995 to the present, as well as Fiction_L booklists that have been created by list members over the years. The Canadian equivalent, RA-Talk, is accessible through Yahoo! Groups and has been active since 2001, though it does require membership to access the discussion forums and archives. Regional library cooperatives and state library associations also have readers' advisory listservs that are general in nature and provide ways to remain current; much like RA-Talk, membership in the listserv is required, and discussion may be limited to topics of interest to the specific region or state. Finally, many of the individual genres have listservs devoted to genre-specific topics, ranging from fan listservs to genre association lists.

Professional associations provide prime opportunities for connecting with professional development and resources. Already discussed, the ARRT offers workshops and tools to members for preparing to work with readers. In addition, the American Library Association's Reference and User Services Association (RUSA) offers ways to assist librarians in professional development and in identifying potential titles, including an online continuing education course entitled RA-101. Selected by the Collection Development and Evaluation Section (CODES) of RUSA, "The Reading List" is a relatively new resource for genre fiction, established in 2007. According to the CODES description, "The Reading List seeks to highlight outstanding genre fiction that merit special attention" (2009). Inclusions on the lists cover brief read-alike lists along with the Council's short-list selections. The titles on "The Reading List" are selected by librarians and are gathered from a broad array of publishers and authors. Regional, state, and local associations also sponsor similar activities.

CONCLUSION

Like any other reference and user service activity, readers' advisory requires skill and knowledge to connect readers and books. The reference interview and the readers' advisory conversation are not dissimilar. The critical components are the ability to engage in conversation and use the tools to connect patrons to the information and books they want. Readers' advisory is not about suggesting books from a popular fiction list, but about engaging the reader to discover what sparked interest and excitement about reading, and helping the reader move along the path to other books.

WORKS CONSULTED

CODES. 2009. "The Reading List." American Library Association. Available: www.ala .org/mgrps/divs/rusa/awards/readinglist/index.cfm (accessed September 10, 2009).

NoveList Editorial and St. Louis Public Library Staff. 1999. "The Appeal of Books." *RA-101 Training Guide*. Ipswich, MA: EbscoHost Industries.

Ross, Catherine Sheldrick, and Mary K. Chelton. 2001. "Reader's Advisory: Matching Mood and Material." *Library Journal* 126, no. 2 (February 1): 52–55.

Ross, Catherine Sheldrick, Kirsti Nilsen, and Marie L. Radford. 2009. *Conducting the Reference Interview: A How-To-Do-It Manual for Librarians*, 2nd edition. New York: Neal-Schuman Publishers.

Saricks, Joyce G. 2005. *Readers' Advisory Service in the Public Library*, 3rd edition. Chicago, IL: American Library Association.

Wyatt, Neal. 2006. "Reading Maps Remake RA." *Library Journal* 131, no. 18 (November 1): 38–42.

_____. 2007a. "An RA Big Think." *Library Journal* 132, no. 12 (July 1): 40–43.

_____. 2007b. "2.0 for Readers." *Library Journal* 132, no. 18 (November 1): 30–33.

FURTHER READING

Berger, Pam, and Sally Trexler. 2007. "Social Bookmarking: Locate, Tag and Collaborate." *Information Searcher* 17, no. 3: 1–5.

Cassell, Kay, and Uma Hiremath. 2009. *Reference and Information Services in the 21st Century: An Introduction*, 2nd edition. New York: Neal-Schuman Publishers.

Herald, Diana Trixler. 2006. *Genreflecting: A Guide to Popular Reading Interests*, edited by Wayne A. Wiegand. Westport, CT: Libraries Unlimited.

Katona, Cynthia Lee. 2005. *Book Savvy*. Lanham, MD: Scarecrow Press.

Kleckner, Karen. 2007. *ARRT and the ARRT Popular Reading Fiction List*, 3rd edition. Rolling Meadows, IL: ARRT.

Moyer, Jessica. 2008. "Core Collections: Electronic Readers'-Advisory Tools." *Booklist Online* (July). Available: www.booklistonline.com (accessed September 10, 2009).

_____. 2008. *Research-Based Readers' Advisory*. Chicago, IL: American Library Association.

NoveList Editorial and St. Louis Public Library Staff. 1999. "Keys to Building a Background in Fiction." *RA-101 Training Guide*. Ipswich, MA: EbscoHost Industries.

Reference and User Services Association Collection Development and Evaluation Section Readers Advisory Committee. 2004. "Recommended Readers' Advisory Tools." *Reference and User Services Quarterly* 43, no. 4 (Summer): 294–305.

Reference and User Services Division, American Library Association. 1996. *50 Years of Notable Books*. Chicago: American Library Association. Also see "The Notable Books List" (www.ala.org/ala/mgrps/divs/rusa/awards/notablebooks/index.cfm) for current lists from 1997 to the present.

Rethlefsen, Melissa L. 2007. "Tags Help Make Libraries Del.icio.us." *Library Journal* 132, no. 15 (September 15): 26–28.

Ross, Catherine Sheldrick, Lynne (E. F.) McKechnie, and Paulette M. Rothbauer. 2006. *Reading Matters: What the Research Reveals about Reading, Libraries, and Community*. Westport, CT: Libraries Unlimited.

Shearer, Kenneth D., and Robert Burgin, ed. 2001. *The Readers' Advisor's Companion*. Englewood, CO: Libraries Unlimited.

Chapter 7

Knowing a Few Good Books

It is a great thing to start life with a small number of really good books which are your very own.

—Sir Arthur Conan Doyle (1859–1930)

One of the uphill battles in readers' advisory services is keeping current on fiction publishing and specifically with genre fiction. Not only do new authors, series, and titles appear with great regularity, but genres are becoming fuzzier as they cross over and combine elements—paranormal romance, historical fantasy, sci-fi chick lit—into something new and unexplored. Toss in e-books, audiobooks, and print-on-demand and an already complex environment is further confounded. The readers' advisor needs to know what will be the next popular trend, when popular authors will be releasing new titles, and what readers are likely to be requesting.

The flip side of the readers' advisory services is promoting and marketing the RA services to readers. Just because you've built a great collection of genre fiction and readable nonfiction does not mean that readers will rush through the doors to find a few good books. It requires work to entice the readers to talk with the readers' advisors about books and then to act upon suggestions for read-alikes and sure bets for a good read. Not only do readers' advisors need to keep up with the book buzz, but they also have to create their own buzz to promote the library's collection and services.

RECONNAISSANCE AND THE BOOK BUZZ

Environmental scanning is critical to maintaining currency not only for libraries in general but for more narrowly focused activities including readers' advisory. Bowker (2008) reported that in 2007 the total U.S. book publishing output for new titles was 276,649, and of these 50,071 were new fiction titles, and these figures are expected to continue at this level of production. (The *book* certainly isn't dead, nor does it appear to be dying.) Perhaps not all, but at least a good number, of these new titles will make their way into public libraries. So where does the readers' advisor begin to learn about the blockbusters and the sleepers and to keep up with the industry buzz for the local community?

Advanced knowledge about upcoming releases keeps the RA librarian in synch with readers. More importantly, it enables the readers' advisor to be effective and proactive in serving the reader's interests. Being aware of upcoming releases offers opportunities to connect existing titles and authors to new materials, engaging patrons with new possibilities for read-alikes, and ultimately promoting the library as a place to find information about good books.

Professional Resources and Popular Magazines

Numerous strategies and resources present themselves as possibilities for monitoring the book industry. Professional literature, popular magazines, broadcast media, and the Internet provide a range of choices to find prepublication and postpublication information. *Booklist, Library Journal,* and *Publishers Weekly* feature prepublication announcements along with news about the book publishing industry (trends, authors, new products, mergers and acquisitions). For postpublication information, these resources include reviews and commentary about newly released books and information about bestsellers. Experienced readers' advisors recommend paying close attention to the special book announcement issues (usually in the spring or autumn) that highlight the seasonal releases.

Print copies of the library review journals are not the only way to go. *Booklist* (www.booklistonline.com), *Library Journal* (www.libraryjournal.com), and *Publishers Weekly* (*PW*) (www.publishersweekly.com) each have robust Web sites that offer many additional options for keeping current. For example, a late winter feature on *Library Journal's* (*LJ*) site is "Spring Book Buzz," which offers a Webcast of several prominent publishers discussing their new and upcoming fiction and nonfiction titles. In addition, *LJ* maintains an archive of past Webcasts for information you may have missed. *Booklist Online* and *PW* offer similar features. Another important feature of the Web sites is the ability to use RSS feeds for fast updates, eliminating the necessity of trawling multiple Web sites many times a week.

For those seeking additional online access to prepublication information and other tools to help with collection development and readers' advisory services, look to EarlyWord (www.earlyword.com). This is a blog with the intent of providing the earliest information available about books that readers will be requesting and of helping "librarians stay ahead of public demand and identify hidden gems" (EarlyWord, 2009). Along with book reviews, the resource offers links to bestsellers lists, book/movie tie-ins, publisher contacts and catalogs, and weekly news magazines.

Overbooked (www.overbooked.com) is a similar comprehensive resource for finding out about books. This award-winning site (winner of the 2008 Louis Shores-Greenwood Publishing Award) focuses its efforts on book reviewing and other media for libraries. It includes annotated and themed booklists (discussed in previous chapters), starred reviews, and award nominees. The RA section of the site includes an exhaustive set of links to answer the "What should I read next?" question, providing access to libraries and reading lists.

Yet another resource worth bookmarking in your Delicious, StumbleUpon, or Twine account is BookBrowse (www.bookbrowse.com). Much like EarlyWord and Overbooked, the creators and editors of BookBrowse seek out and recommend "exceptional" books for readers. The site covers adult fiction and nonfiction and offers access by genre, setting, time periods, themes, and award winners. Similarly to LibraryThing, BookBrowse gives members access to advanced reading copies of forthcoming books. One of its strengths lies in providing access to information about upcoming releases, including advanced reviews when available. According to the Web site, BookBrowse does not sell books or accept payment to list books; the featured books are included based on merit, not media hype.

Reading popular magazines is essential to keeping current with readers' preferences. Readers frequently consult magazines such as *O: The Oprah Magazine*, *People*, *Entertainment Weekly*, *Essence*, and other popular magazines for book news, reviews, and related feature articles. Readers value the information presented in these resources. Because these magazines are intended for the general adult reading public, the books featured and the reviews are written to be approachable and to appeal to the everyday reader (as in nonspecialist). Popular magazines are a source of valuable information that allows readers' advisors to maintain their connection with the interests of the readers.

Local newspapers form another outlet for tracking books popular in the community. Many local papers will feature a book section (sometimes in the Sunday edition) or a column that reviews new releases and current favorites. In addition, local book and author events will be promoted regularly in the local news. And like many other publishing venues, the local news media has migrated to the Web, making information quickly and conveniently accessible through RSS feeds.

Did You Know?

LibraryThing features local events held in area bookstores and other venues related to books and authors. You'll find links to area libraries, bookstores (chain stores and independent booksellers), book festivals, and other similar events and activities. The "Local Events" page features an interactive Google map showing locations of all events.

Local, Chain, and Online Booksellers

When is the last time you spent an afternoon wandering your local book-stores—and not just the chain store on the corner? Local bookstores hold a wealth of information about the reading public. They sponsor author talks and book signings and other events related to reading and writing. Not only do the bookstores feature the bestsellers and nationally recognized authors, but they frequently sponsor events for local authors as well. Their shelves will display the books that are popular in the local community alongside the big sellers. The in-dependent booksellers, perhaps even more readily than the chain bookstores, will feature many of the readable, delightful titles produced by small presses and local authors. Combined, the chain booksellers and indies offer insight into the tastes of readers and what titles and other resources will appeal to them.

To facilitate finding the hidden jewels among myriad bestsellers and popular books, look to IndieBound (www.indiebound.org), an association of independ-ent booksellers who still hand-sell their books. IndieBound is an excellent source to find less familiar titles, including first-time authors and books that are less publicized by the national media. Not unlike the *New York Times* bestsellers list, IndieBound features their bestsellers of the week, which may or may not be on the *NYT* and other prominent lists, but they also offer lists based on regional divisions (New England, Southern, Mountain and Plains, etc.) and specialty top-ics (e.g., parenting, travel, baseball). Locating less familiar titles and authors adds depth to the fiction collection offered to readers. The readers make amaz-ing discoveries and connections through access to a broader range of options.

The online bookstores, such as Amazon.com, provide yet another resource for keeping up with books and authors. For example, Amazon.com features "Hot New Releases," "Popular Pre-Orders in Books," and links to bestsellers (Amazon bestsellers and *New York Times* bestsellers lists). Barnes & Noble (www.bn.com) also offers access to "New Releases," "Coming Soon," and "Bestsellers." The advantage that these online bookstores have includes the ability to have readers rate and review the books. This provides information about how actual readers respond to individual books and authors. The online systems also incor-porate options for creating tags to describe the books (www.amazon.com) and detailed ratings that allow readers to rate specific elements of the book (www.bn.com), such as characters, plot, writing style, and book cover.

Publishers

Who better than publishers to provide information about upcoming releases? Being in the business to sell books, publishers offer current awareness resources to librarians, and much of this is readily available on publishers' Web sites or through e-mail services. Beyond their catalogs, publishing houses produce sup-port materials for the books they sell, including newsletters for "hot" releases, reading guides for book clubs and discussion groups, printable bookmarks, and advanced reading editions. HarperCollins, for example, sponsors "First Look," a program that invites readers to preview and review books prior to publication, while Random House offers an extensive list of podcasts and blogs related to their books and authors. Macmillan gives readers an opportunity to watch Webisodes (online video) based on their books. These are short teasers that introduce characters and scenes from the books and add another layer of engagement with reading. Newsletters and alerts from the publishers are among the most useful features for readers' advisors, serving as additional tools for current awareness.

A Few Publishers' Web Sites for Current Awareness and Book Buzz

HarperCollins: www.harpercollins.com
Macmillan: http://us.macmillan.com/default.aspx
Penguin: http://us.penguingroup.com/
Random House: www.randomhouse.com
W. W. Norton & Company: www.wwnorton.com/trade/

Conferences and Book Expos

Attending conferences and book expos is crucial to keeping abreast of the book publishing industry. Book publishers flock to library conferences, especially the American Library Association (ALA) annual conference held each summer. Conference participation puts publishers in touch with librarians who are likely to get books into the hands of readers. ALA sponsors an Author's Forum throughout the conference period, offering attendees opportunities to respond to and interact with authors. Authors discuss their books, thoughts on writing, and their responses to their own protagonists and characters. They also sign books and interact with conference attendees after their forum presentations, putting librarians in touch with authors personally. Visiting with the publishers on the exhibit floor also presents opportunities to talk about the industry and upcoming events and releases, including finding the treasures hidden among the mega-releases. A side benefit of talking with publishers is access to advanced readers copies of forthcoming releases; with advanced reader copies comes the benefit of knowing about books before they are released and on the shelves. (A couple of years ago, we were fortunate enough to snag a copy of Stephen King's *Lisey's Story* well before the publication release, and we were able to review it and talk it up with other readers.)

Keeping Up with the Book Buzz

1. Find current awareness resources.
2. Keep up with library review journals.
3. Visit your local bookstore.
4. Attend local book events.
5. Attend conferences and book expos, or at least access publisher resources.
6. Use RSS feeds to keep up with favorite RA Web sites and blogs.
7. Pay attention to broadcast media.
8. Above all, listen to your patrons as they discuss books, series, and authors.

Book Expo America

Book Expo America (BEA) is the "big daddy" of book publishing events. It is held late each spring, and is considered to be the premier publishing event in North America. During the event the autumn releases are launched and the buzz begins about new authors and products. Conference sessions at BEA cover social media, digital technologies, genres, and the latest publishing trends. BEA attendees are a grand mix of authors, publishers, vendors, librarians, and other avid readers. For those unable to attend the event, *Library Journal* and *Publishers Weekly*, among others, will feature articles from and about the conference, and C-SPAN Book TV posts Webcasts from BEA on their site with interviews and "man on the street" experiences.

International Book Fairs

Along with the BEA are numerous international book expos and book fairs that promote and honor books, authors, and reading. For those able to travel, consider the Frankfurt Book Fair (www.frankfurt-book-fair.com/en/fbf/) held each fall in Frankfurt, Germany. It is the largest book fair in the world, featuring more than 7,300 exhibitors from more than 100 nations. Each year the Frankfurt Book Fair offers professional programs on specific themes and focuses. (The 2008 program focused on children's and teen books.)

The London Book Fair (www.londonbookfair.co.uk/) carries equal importance for the book publishing industry, and occurs each spring. Like Frankfurt, the London Book Fair features thousands of exhibits and is global in nature. One of the unique features of the London Book Fair is the English PEN Literary Café, where attendees may listen to live interviews with a wide array of authors. The 2009 English PEN Literary Café included James Patterson alongside Umberto Eco. And for the gourmand, the London Book Fair partners with the Gourmand World Cookbook Awards to host a culinary event that features internationally renowned chefs from around the world. For those unable to travel to the London Book Fair, the Web site includes a broad range of podcasts from events, including author interviews, award ceremonies, and seminars.

Paris, the City of Lights, also hosts an annual book fair each spring. The Salon du Livre (www.salondulivreparis.com/site/GB,I1.htm) is very similar in nature to both the Frankfurt and London Book Fairs. Along with hundreds of exhibitors, the fair also hosts numerous events, book-signing sessions, and seminars and workshops. One of the highlights of the 2009 fair was the "Tomorrow's Re@d" platform where attendees could experience new reading media, including e-books and digital resources. Though presented in French, the Web site offers a variety of Webcasts from the fair.

One advantage of being aware of the international book fairs is the ability to identify foreign publishers of popular reading materials. This aids the readers' advisor in locating books and materials for a multicultural community, especially materials (print, film, and music) published in languages other than English. While traveling to the book fairs is impractical for most, the Web sites do offer lists of publishers and other exhibitors and authors who may be of interest to members of the local reading community.

Paying Attention to Broadcast Media

Television and radio are part of everyday readers' lives. They watch *Oprah*, *Good Morning America*, or the *Today* show. They will catch snippets from NPR and other talk shows. Authors clamor for spots on these programs to tout their latest books, and readers pay attention. For the readers' advisor, missing the buzz due to work schedules and sheer volume of programming creates a hole in knowledge about new, hot trends. To counter this, vendors such as Baker and Taylor provide ways to keep on top of the buzz. Baker and Taylor offers two products of interest: (1) FirstLook, which provides automatic monthly notification of high-visibility new and forthcoming titles and (2) Fast Facts, an e-mail service that provides information on new releases and bestsellers. Ingram Books (www.ingrambooks .com/) also offers similar services to librarians and readers. Ingram Interact is a portion of the company's Web site that features podcasts and blogs related to the book industry, including author interviews, booklists, and advance information about new titles and upcoming author media events.

A similar approach is provided through Fresh Fiction (www.freshfiction .com). Unlike Baker and Taylor or Ingram, which are commercial library vendors, Fresh Fiction is a Web site designed for readers to find information about their favorite genres, authors, and titles. In addition, the Fresh Fiction site includes book descriptions, author bibliographies, and book reviews. The editorial staff produces a daily e-mail newsletter, "Fresh Press," for subscribers highlighting books that received national media coverage the previous day. This enables readers' advisors to maintain current awareness of books likely to be discussed or requested by their patrons.

Podcasting

One final strategy for keeping current is to use podcasting resources to find book reviews and author interviews. These can be quickly and easily downloaded to a media player and listened to at one's leisure. Mentioned previously, many publishers provide podcasts on their Web sites, including excerpts from books and author interviews. One of the highly popular sources for podcast episodes is iTunes, but there are many others available. The iTunes Store has a complete section devoted to "Book Lovers" with links to talk shows, book reviews, interviews, and book readings. The *New York Times* offers a weekly book review podcast that can be downloaded for playback on MP3 media players (www.nytimes.com/ref/books/books-podcast-archive.html). NPR features a similar service from their various talk shows (www.npr.org/templates/topics/topics.php?topicId=1032). These are easy-to-use resources that provide RSS feed subscriptions for convenience.

BOOKS IN ALTERNATIVE FORMATS

Print books are not the only "reading" materials patrons seek out in the libraries. Audiobooks (books on tape, books on CD or DVD, and downloadables) are increasingly popular choices for circulation in public libraries. According to the Audio Publishers Association (www.audiopub.org/), in 2007 approximately 43 percent of audiobook listeners obtained their audiobooks from the public library. Like our beloved print fiction, audiobooks are produced for all genres and from a wide range of bestsellers and authors. Not only does the readers' advisor need to read widely, but he or she now needs to listen widely for a well-rounded approach to books and reading opportunities.

Evaluating and Selecting Audiobooks

Selecting and recommending audiobooks requires additional considerations beyond the traditional ones (genre, pace, reader's preferences, etc.), such as the quality of the narration and the technical production. Joyce Saricks explains that "adding audio brings a new universe of materials to learn. What's more listeners'-advisory conversations must take place on two levels: addressing the appeal of the book and discussing the audio production, particularly the artistic skill of the narrator" (Saricks, 2008: 16). Narration and technical quality encompass key components to excellent audiobooks and listener engagement. Mary Burkey suggests "a truly effective audiobook maintains a perfect balance between meaningful content and faultless production values" (Burkey, 2007: 104). Narration requires a "golden voice," an actor or reader who can bring the book to life through inflection, sound, and rhythm ("Golden Voices," 2003). Audiobooks also require close attention to the production aspects: clear, crisp sound quality; consistent volume levels; unobtrusive background music and sound effects; and accuracy in packaging, including title, author, and narrator names, playing time, and whether abridged or not. The most crucial aspect of selecting audiobooks, however, is listening to a variety of samples of titles and narrators from a range of producers.

Several publishers and vendors of audiobooks stand out among the many who produce print and digital books, including Playaway and OverDrive along with Blackstone Audiobooks, Audible.com (owned by Amazon.com), Random House with its subsidiaries Books on Tape and Listening Library, NetLibrary, and Recorded Books (see Table 7-1 for a more complete listing of vendors and providers). Combined, the audiobook publishers and vendors provide access to hundreds of audio titles for adults, children, and young adults. Information

Table 7-1: Web Sites and Resources for Audiobooks	
Company/Provider	Web Address
Amazon.com Audiobooks Store	www.amazon.com
Audible	www.audible.com
AudioFile	www.audiofilemagazine.com
Barnes & Noble	www.barnesandnoble.com
Bartleby.com Great Books Online	www.bartleby.com/
Bibliomania	www.bibliomania.com/
Blackstone Audiobooks	www.blackstoneaudio.com
Books on Tape	www.booksontape.com/
Borders	www.audiobooks.borders.com
Follett	www.follett.com/
Ingram MyiLibrary	www.myilibrary.com/company/library.htm
LibriVox	www.librivox.org
Listening Library	www.randomhouse.com/audio/listeninglibrary/
NetLibrary	www.netlibrary.com/
OverDrive, Inc.	www.overdrive.com
Playaway Library	www.playawaylibrary.com
Random House Audio	www.randomhouse.com/audio/
Record Books	www.recordedbooks.com/

about narrators, authors, upcoming releases, and award winners is readily available on their respective Web sites. Many of the audiobook providers include continuous order plans, core and specialized collections, and MARC record information.

Not unlike print books, several resources exist for reviewing and evaluating audiobooks. *AudioFile Magazine* devotes itself to reviewing and promoting audiobooks, especially adult popular fiction and family titles. Along with reviews of individual titles, *AudioFile* includes author interviews, narrator profiles, and lists of "best audiobooks." One added feature on the Web site is the AudioFile Podcasts! (available through iTunes), which offers audio clips and excerpts from audiobooks being reviewed and aids critical selection of exceptional titles. *AudioFile* is available in print and electronic versions, and while a subscription is required for full access, the Web site offers a good selection of freely available resources.

Library Journal and *Booklist*, among other professional and industry journals, feature regular columns that review audiobooks as well as the audiobook industry as a whole. Copious articles in both journals suggest that for libraries the circulation of audiobooks is among the fastest-growing component of the public library collection. Listeners demand both audiobooks on CD along with downloadable versions for MP3 and other digital media players. More importantly, for those providing readers' advisory services, *Library Journal*, *Booklist*, and *Library Media Connections* (for school media centers and children's services) feature bibliographic essays devoted to specific genres and the availability of the genres in audio and other formats.

BOOK COVERS, BOOK BLURBS, AND READERS' REVIEWS

The only way to truly know a book is to read it—cover to cover, including the dust jacket. Given that hundreds of new books, fiction and nonfiction combined, will walk through the doors of the library every year, it is impossible to read every title. The immense volume requires finding strategies to become acquainted, if not intimate, with books quickly. Books come with many built-in aids to accomplish this very task, from the book cover to the book's physical structure.

In selecting books for themselves readers respond to clues presented on the books, such as cover art, descriptions on book flaps, and blurbs that tout the finer points of the book. Readers' advisors do well to follow the readers' lead and look to these elements also. Romance novels, for example, can be clearly defined by their covers: handsome heroes and breathtakingly beautiful females locked in a passionate embrace (the publishing industry calls this "the clench"). The romance covers are predictable; they are safe; readers know what they are getting when they look at the cover. The use of colors also suggests something about the book's content. Chick lit tends toward hot pink and bubbly; horror runs to dark and brooding. For series readers, the covers convey consistency and comfort, relaying the information that the same elements will run across the series while still retaining individual uniqueness.

A focus on book covers is a new strategy for many booksellers who have come to realize that the way to sell a book is to show the customer what he or she is getting, and they do this by displaying books cover side out. However, publishers have known for years that covers sell and that they "remain a source of fascination for . . . ordinary readers" (Poynor, 2007: 27). Readers determine if a book looks interesting based upon the cover art, and book publishers respond to that with covers intended to catch the eye. This is especially crucial for promoting new authors and debut novels; it serves as the hook to grab the attention of the reader.

Book jackets carry a wealth of information, from descriptive information to author biographies and photographs. A well-written book description can entice the reader to look a little further into the book, maybe reading a few sample pages. The descriptions on the book flaps provide just enough information to give a feel for plot and characters without giving away anything crucial. Combined with the cover art, a reader can learn a great deal about the book, including plot summary, characterization, and appeal—all elements readers' advisors attempt to discern in conversation with the reader.

Book blurbs are an additional way to learn a little something about the book. While authors may not hold stock in their effectiveness, readers do pay attention to the blurbs. For new authors or genres, the blurbs provide a brief introduction to the book, and who may be reading it (or at least glancing at it). They make connections between known authors who provided a blurb to new authors they want to try. For example, Randy Wayne White, author of the Doc Ford series, wrote a brief description for H. Terrell Griffin's *Blood Island* (Oceanview, 2008), and several authors writing in the same subgenre provided blurbs. Combined, these suggest that Griffin's book may be similar and read like the others. Connections are made.

Beyond the physical and artistic structure of books, reader reviews also carry weight in learning something about the title. While subject to bias and personal reaction rather than critical analysis, reviews on Amazon.com or the Barnes & Noble Web site do offer insight from the real readers. If nothing else these types of reviews explore the readers' expectations and disappointments along with information about what they liked best or what the author does well. Reader reviews are easily balanced by consulting library reviewing resources and book reviews, such as the *New York Times Review of Books* or those appearing in local and national newspapers. Combining reader reviews with critical reviews may provide a well-rounded picture of the book's content with sufficient detail to suggest it to other readers.

PROMOTING AND MARKETING RA SERVICES

Once you know, and continue to learn, what the fiction collection has to offer, you need to promote it to the readers likely to use it and to encourage nonusers to make discoveries about what the library can offer. Librarians have toolkits full of possibilities for reaching out to readers, from book displays to book discussion groups. By incorporating Library 2.0 resources into the toolkit, librarians can extend their reach beyond the physical walls of the library and encourage nonusers to take a second glance at what may be available to meet their tastes.

Lasting Impressions and Book Displays

What are the first things you see when you walk into your neighborhood Barnes & Noble or Borders? You're probably confronted with attractively displayed shelves or rounds of newly released books, comfortable chairs, and a café. While it is unlikely that librarians can do much about the library's physical layout or the installation of a coffee shop, they can greatly influence the displays of materials and the creation of a pleasant environment. Attractive and well-placed signs, appealing displays, and resources that are conveniently placed encourage the patrons to use the space and browse the shelves. The old adage of first impressions being lasting ones holds true for the library as well. If the patrons view the library as welcoming and easy to navigate, they are likely to return.

Book displays with descriptive signage encourage idle browsing. This is a way to highlight particular sections, authors, or themes from the collection. By incorporating related materials, such as film, audio, and music, it becomes possible to make connections with other components of the whole collection. Displays can be small and placed in locations where they catch readers by surprise, or they can be grand and placed in prominent locations within the library. The displays are easily coordinated with materials the library has on hand, such as bookmarks and reading lists (i.e., Sure Bets, or While You're Waiting, or Stop, You're Killing Me). They are also dynamic when changed regularly to pique interest and promote awareness of all that is available.

Book displays are easily highlighted on blogs and Web sites with links to author Web sites, annotated reading lists, and reading maps. Hennepin County Library (www.hclib.org/pub/bookspace/), for example, features several book displays on their Bookspace site, including a variety of featured themes. Some of their recent displays included "Multicultural Mysteries" (stories of detectives from various cultures and countries) and "New and Forthcoming Movies Based on Books." They also feature booklists from their readers, with far-ranging topics including sports, current reads, South African fiction, and female crime fighters. Because integrated library systems can incorporate tags and user contributions, the online displays become richer and more approachable to other everyday readers, encouraging readers to participate and share their own ideas and responses.

Bookmarks and Reading Lists

A mainstay of readers' advisory services incorporates bookmarks and reading lists into the range of resources on hand for readers' convenience. Many of these are staff-prepared and readily available to library browsers. Bookmarks and reading lists take time to prepare, but once completed they are easily reproduced and distributed. Electronic versions can be quickly updated with new titles and authors. For libraries with limited space, these types of printed resources take up little room and can be placed throughout the library within easy reach of the reader. Numerous resources are accessible with templates for creating bookmarks. (Microsoft Office Online, for example, has free downloads; NoveList has bookmark templates in their RA tools for subscribers.) They are quickly customizable for particular themes and require little physical storage space.

Reading lists take more effort in preparation, but like bookmarks once they are created, they can be updated almost effortlessly. Unlike bookmarks, reading lists are generally annotated (see Chapter 6 for more information on annotations) and can be more extensive than brief information on bookmarks. Lists can be generated in a number of ways. First, they can be original creations prepared by the staff, from writing to producing. Topics for the reading lists are selected to reflect readers' interests and the library's collection. Time, effort, and knowledge are required to select, read, annotate, and produce the lists. However, they serve two purposes: (1) providing a tool for readers and (2) serving as a way to familiarize staff with new books in the collection or with new genres. Annotated lists can also be generated through the library's subscription to commercial RA databases, such as Fiction Connection, NoveList, Readers' Advisory Online, or "What Do I Read Next?" In either form, annotated reading lists provide the reader with a resource to use in selecting additional reading materials. Similarly to book displays, bookmarks and reading lists lend themselves nicely to Internet access. They can be converted into blogs or posted as printable documents on the library's Web site. Used in conjunction with social cataloging sites, bibliographic details, book covers, and tags can be incorporated to provide comprehensive information and reactions to the books.

Booktalks

Booktalks are yet another way to promote both readers' advisory services and the library's collection. Most typically a part of children's and young adult services, booktalks also lend themselves to adult fiction discussions. While booktalks take skill and willingness, they can be highly effective in introducing new books, authors, and genres to individuals and groups. Booktalks incorporate the same elements that are found in the RA conversation. Book appeal, descriptions of the books' features, and comparisons to other authors and titles comprise some of the talking points for a booktalk. This should be accomplished in about five minutes. The point is to make a book seem irresistible, but the booktalk must also focus on the reader's tastes and interests rather than the RA's enthusiasm for a particular book or genre.

Like many other RA activities, booktalks are well suited to Web delivery. Podcasts can be quickly and easily created and posted on the library's Web site or social networking account. They require a bit of preplanning and scripting, but podcasts provide an effective way to reach users outside of the library. If already presenting a booktalk, have another staff member record the event. Editing and file conversions can be accomplished through some of the freely available podcast resources, such as Audacity (http://audacity.sourceforge.net/download/). For RA staff not yet ready to create their own on-the-air booktalks, a number of resources are available by which podcasts can be downloaded and posted to the library's site, including publishers' Web sites. Two possible resources for podcasts featuring booktalks and author interviews are Authors on Air (www.blogtalkradio.com/stations/AuthorsOnAir/splash.aspx) and iTunes (www.apple.com/itunes/). Other library Web sites and social networking sites can be an inspiration for ideas and possibilities.

Quick Tip

An array of tutorials and resources are available on the Web for podcasting. A quick and dirty search in your favorite search engine for "podcasting tutorial" retrieves a great selection of popular and easy-to-use Web sites. Resources are readily available for both PC and Mac users.

A FEW OTHER STRATEGIES TO REACH READERS

Building the book buzz does not stop with the creation of reading lists and other resources to support the fiction collection. It is also essential to spread the word that the library offers a wonderful range of services to help connect the reader with good reads. Announcements in the local news and on the library's Web site are among the first considerations. These are two places where library events can be prominently featured. Brochures and flyers placed at service points and on bulletin boards throughout the library provide other outlets for spreading the news. Library users expect to see these types of marketing tools.

With the time and attention of library users and nonusers stretched thin, it becomes critical to reach them where they are—through e-mail and social networking sites. (The Pew Internet and American Life Project of 2008 reports that

35 percent of adults in the United States have social networking accounts and the numbers are increasing; the same Pew report estimates 58 percent of adults send or read e-mail on a daily basis.) Mentioned previously, NoveList and other commercial vendors provide newsletter services for subscribers. NextReads (a product of Ebsco's NoveList) combines annotations with information on read-alikes with customizable content for library events, such as book club meetings or author talks. The newsletters are branded specifically for the individual library, featuring books and materials from the library's own collection. Library users subscribe to the newsletters, which are sent out regularly with updates.

Membership in social networking sites, such as MySpace and Facebook, puts the library in front of the user also. Discussed in detail in Chapter 4, the social networking accounts create ways to link with library users and nonusers alike. These are readily accessible points where libraries can post information about upcoming events, new materials, and general library information. Numerous libraries post lists of new books they received in the previous 30 days as well as new movies and music. These are great forums for posting booktalks and video of library events, making them widely available to the entire community (local and global). It goes back to the "coolness" factor of libraries being hip places to socialize and find unexpected pleasures.

CONCLUSION

Readers approach book selection in a variety of ways. Readers' advisory activities and services are intended to support the needs and interests of readers. This support begins with a readers' advisor who is well versed in genre fiction. Not only does the RA librarian know books, but he or she also has broad awareness of trends, authors, and forthcoming titles. Keeping up with the buzz, while seemingly impossible, is also critical to meeting the needs and interests of readers. It also becomes essential to meet the readers where they are—in the stacks and online.

Many of the common standbys (bookmarks, annotated reading lists) can be remade and extended to Web access. Tapping into the technologies and resources to promote and market the library and its services to readers and others extends the reach of the library into the greater community. Much of the RA activities that take place within the walls of the library can be adapted for electronic delivery. They can also be remade to encourage user participation and contribution.

WORKS CONSULTED

"Bowker Reports U.S. Book Production Flat in 2007." (2008). Available: www.bowker .com/ index.php/press-releases/66-corporate2008/526-bowker-reports-us-book-production-flat-in-2007 (accessed September 10, 2009).

Burkey, Mary. 2007. "Sounds Good to Me: Listening to Audiobooks with a Critical Ear." *Booklist* 103, no. 19/20: 104.

Dyer, Lucinda. 2008. "The Forever Clinch." *Publishers Weekly* 255, no. 46 (November 17): 29.

EarlyWord. 2009. "About Early Word." Available: www.earlyword.com/about (accessed September 10, 2009).

"Golden Voices: What Is a Golden Voice?" 2003. *AudioFile.* Available: www.audiofilemagazine.com/gvpages/what.shtml (accessed September 10, 2009).

Pew Internet & American Life Project. 2008. "Internet Activities." Available: www.pewinternet.org/trends/Internet_Activities_7.22.08.htm (accessed September 10, 2009).

Poynor, Rick. 2007. "Cover Me." *Print* 61, no. 4 (July/August): 27–28.

Saricks, Joyce G. 2008. "LA: Essentials of Listening Advisory." *Booklist* 104, no. 21 (July): 16.

FURTHER READING

Apple. "Making a Podcast." (2008). Available: www.apple.com/itunes/whatson/podcasts/specs.html (accessed September 10, 2009).

Olson, Georgine N., ed. 1998. *Fiction Acquisition/Fiction Management: Education and Training* [co-published simultaneously as *The Acquisitions Librarian*, no. 19]. Binghamton, NY: The Haworth Press.

Saricks, Joyce G. 2005. *Readers' Advisory Service in the Public Library*, 3rd edition. Chicago, IL: American Library Association.

Shearer, Kenneth D., and Robert Burgin, ed. 2001. *The Readers' Advisor's Companion.* Englewood, CO: Libraries Unlimited.

Van Orden, Jason. 2005. "How to Podcast Tutorial." Available: www.how-to-podcast-tutorial.com/17-audacity-tutorial.htm (accessed September 10, 2009).

Chapter 8

Reading in the Genres

The house of fiction has . . . not one window, but a million.

—Henry James, "The Art of Fiction" (1884)

At the beginning of this book, we explored the history of reading from its earliest utterances to the birth of the novel and on to reading in a multimedia world. Stories began as cave paintings, telling tales of life in prehistoric times. As humans acquired language stories were relayed in an oral tradition. These were tales of adventure and heroism, tragedy and comedies, told with verve and delight by bards and storytellers, and handed down across generations. Eventually the stories were recorded in a written format and shared among readers and listeners through scrolls, codices, and, today, electronic reading devices. Contemporary fiction grew from these traditions, becoming a way to entertain us and make sense of our world.

The readers' advisor's stock in trade is stories combined with the ability to match a reader's interests to the range of stories that make up the library's collection. These stories encompass literary fiction, genre fiction, and readable nonfiction. The stories come in a variety of formats, from print to audio to multimedia. The next several chapters will explore the corpus of work we call reading for pleasure and personal enlightenment, and how these stories fulfill the needs of the individual reader.

DEFINING FICTION

Fiction, by definition, is a form of narrative literature that is at its simplest a made-up story, but it is also a story made up of words alone. The words paint a picture in the reader's imagination—not the gestures or actions of performers on a stage or screen, but the simple telling of a tale through carefully selected words. According to the range of definitions, from *The Concise Oxford Dictionary of Literary Terms* (2009) to the popular consensus of Wikipedia, fiction:

117

- is a literary work;
- is written in prose;
- portrays characters and events created in the writer's imagination, and not necessarily based in fact; and
- is an imaginative work whose purpose is to entertain, enlighten, and expand the reader's life experiences through vicarious participation in events.

Fiction is also a compilation of carefully crafted elements—plot, character, setting, and pace—most of which are also the elements that readers' advisors use to describe a book's appeal.

Literary Fiction versus Genre Fiction

Fiction as an oeuvre has been the focus of literary argument and controversy since the first novels appeared and were greedily read by the working class. In looking to the style of fiction, it can be delineated into a hierarchy with literary fiction (or literature) at the pinnacle and genre fiction at the base and popular or mainstream fiction falling somewhere between the extremes (see Table 8-1). Frequently likened to junk food and being flabby entertainment, popular fiction, especially genre fiction, is eschewed and belittled as having no educational or literary value. Literary fiction endeavors to achieve layers of depth and artistry while saying something meaningful about the human condition. Popular fic-

Table 8-1: Literary versus Popular Fiction	
Literary Fiction	**Popular Fiction**
Art	Craft
Elitist distribution	Broad-based distribution
Highbrow	Lowbrow
Fewer works produced over extended periods of time	Prolific in output with multiple novels produced regularly over shorter periods of time
Complex	Simplistic
Intimately connected to life	Gives itself over to fantasy
Cerebral	Sensuous
Restrained or discrete	Excessive and exaggerated
Complete entities	Lends itself to series and continuations
Does not require story or plot	Follows conventions revolving around story and plot
Dull	Exciting
Source: Adapted from Gelder, 2004: 13–19.	

tion, by comparison, is intended to be fun and entertaining and less *important* than literary fiction, but by no means does this suggest it has any less value to the reader than literary fiction has. Fiction—popular or literary—as a whole has the function to entrance and engage, keeping the reader turning the pages. It can be argued that good books are good because they have engaged the reader, whether or not they enlighten or elevate the reader's taste or intellect.

Genre fiction, the stuff of many public library popular collections and readers' advisory activities, is most frequently defined by its relationship to other novels written in a similar style or theme. It is typified by conventions or characteristics that allow it to be categorized as relating to a specific genre—i.e., mystery or romance, horror or science fiction. While criticized for being formulaic and predictable, for many readers it is the very consistency and reliability of expectations that keeps them reading genre fiction. The outcomes are predictable and unambiguous; plots are straightforward and not tangled. Nancy J. Holland, in her confession of being an unpublished genre writer, suggests "genre fiction reveals a world in which the good guys always win, love conquers all, the bad guys always get caught, and humans always prevail" (2002: 222). However, genre fiction does aspire to good writing where every word counts; it just does it with an eye to reader engagement and appeal.

Literary fiction, on the other hand, is considered to be "unclassifiable"; it is the author's unique voice that defines it. (For the sake of classification argument, it falls into Class P—Language and Literature in the Library of Congress Classification Outline, and 800 Literature in the Dewey Decimal System.) Literary fiction relies upon style and elegance of language to provoke the reader's response. Plot is of less importance than the characters and the style. Typically literary novels are densely written with rich narrative descriptions, and their endings are most frequently ambiguous or open to interpretation. Primary along with the secondary characters are multidimensional and do not act in ways that are predictable. Literary fiction, by nature, is multilayered and intends to speak to the reader on many levels. This is not to say that literary fiction is unread and unreadable by fans of genre fiction; it simply tends to appeal to a different mood or need.

Genre fiction finds its roots in what is today considered literary fiction or classics. Without Edgar Allan Poe ("The Murders in the Rue Morgue," 1841), the horror and detective genres would not exist (or at least not in their present-day forms). Jane Austen's *Pride and Prejudice* (1813) gave us the framework for contemporary romance fiction. And the work of H. G. Wells (*The Time Machine*, 1895; *The Island of Doctor Moreau*, 1896) provided a firm base for science fiction. Many of the literary works we celebrate for their message were also written originally as popular forms of entertainment, incorporating brilliantly composed language with a measure of reader's engagement with the story for pleasure. Charles Dickens, for example, published his lengthy works in the "penny dreadfuls" as serials; today his novels are part of the British literary canon.

Genre fiction comprises the preponderance of titles on the bestsellers lists for fiction. In fact, the major names in genre fiction, including James Patterson, Dean Koontz, and Janet Evanovich, among many others, dominate the bestsellers lists, frequently having hardcover and paperback titles on lists simultaneously. Genre fiction also dominates the "Books Most Borrowed in U.S. Libraries" list published biweekly by *Library Journal*. Literary fiction (discounting recommendations from Oprah and Great Britain's Richard and Judy) finds it more difficult to reach and sustain bestseller status unless it has been recognized through major literary awards (which by themselves are no guarantee of bestseller status) or through box office movie tie-in.

It is crucial to keep in mind that fiction—genre and literary—reflects and affects contemporary culture. Culture, by definition, encompasses the characteristics, beliefs, values, behaviors, and material objects of a people. Fiction is an artistic attempt to explore and explain our culture through works of imagination. Looking at popular television, our genre fiction reflects our viewing preferences and vice versa: Kathy Reichs' forensic anthropologist in the Bones fiction series is now a popular television show by the same name; we see our literary fiction on the movie screen (Bernhard Schlink's *The Reader*, for example, or Khaled Hosseini's *The Kite Runner*). The ideas and values of our culture appear across our works of art, literature, music, and performance.

READING CHOICES

Adult reading choices are personal and unique, incorporating choices between fiction and nonfiction and genre fiction and literary fiction. Each reader approaches the selection process carefully and deliberately. Reading selections may even be fraught with danger, from "not being able to get into the book" to making the wrong selection (a book that does not suit mood or does not appeal). However, patterns in adult reading selections can help guide the RA staff in connecting readers with satisfying books across genres. Many of the large-scale studies in the United States, Canada, and United Kingdom suggest that fiction readers tend to lean toward "a few preferred genres and known authors" (Great Britain Library and Information Commission, 2000; Toyne and Usherwood, 2001; NEA, 2004, 2007, 2008; Ross, McKechnie, and Rothbauer, 2006). Readers also selected books based on ease of access to them, whether it was readily available at home, in a library, or through a book retailer. These same studies suggest that experienced readers (avid, voracious, or habitual are all good descriptions) oftentimes are willing to experiment with new authors and genres, offering the RA staff opportunities to broaden the range of suggestions to meet the reader's needs and interests, especially when focusing on mood and appeal as a way to connect across genres.

The choice between genre and literary fiction clearly has a role in the process, but other factors that affect a reader's choice can be applied to all types of fiction. Ross, Nilsen, and Radford (2009) suggest the following factors to consider in a book's appeal and as a basis for the conversation with the reader:

- Subject and theme—or what the book is about
- Setting—or where and when the story takes place
- The kind of reading experience desired—or whether the reader wants to learn something or feel something from the experience
- Accessibility—or the readability, predictability, size/length, or physical aspects of the book

For experienced readers these factors are intertwined. Experience readers have developed successful strategies for identifying good books suited to their tastes, and they build on their success to find others. Perhaps more telling, in Ross's study of adult readers and their reading choices is personal context in which book selection is situated, including the reader's previous experiences, reading preferences developed across time, and the events in the reader's life that support or inhibit reading at a particular time (Ross, 2001; Ross, McKechnie, and Rothbauer, 2006).

THE GENRES ACCORDING TO READERS' ADVISORY

Looking to the tools of readers' advisory, somewhere between 8 and 12 distinct mainstream genres are identified. Then there is a category of emerging genres and thematic topics. The following are included among the most recognizable genres that will be considered: Adventure, Fantasy, Historical Fiction, Horror, Mystery/Crime Fiction, Romance, Science Fiction, Suspense/Thrillers, and Westerns. In a 2005 study of readers, the Romance Writers of America examined the total market share each genre held, with romance comprising 39.3 percent of the market share, mystery/thrillers with 29.6 percent, and science fiction sales at 6.4 percent, while other genre fiction, including horror, historical, and Westerns combined to comprise 11.8 percent (2005: 2). Many ways exist to parse and study the individual genres, but we'll start with a basic overview and then move to the more intricate details.

Each genre has its own framework and conventions under which it works (see Table 8-2). It is also noteworthy that genres cross boundaries and become challenging to distinguish, such as science fiction and fantasy and suspense and thrillers. For a general discussion and understanding of genres it may be useful to consider some of the very basic elements of the individual genres to distinguish between them. Adventure and suspense/thrillers, for example, tend to focus on the action and the resolution of a life-and-death situation. Adventure features dangerous missions in exotic and hostile environments (à la Indiana Jones or James Bond); suspense/thrillers, while also focusing on the action and the protagonist, have a sense of foreboding and apprehension (think Thomas

Table 8-2: Framework for Genre Fiction	
Broad Genre	**Identifying Frame**
Adventure	Hero on a mission; fast paced; action packed; often set in exotic lands; focus on extremes
Fantasy	Magic rules; describes a world that never could exist; emotions and relationships; legends and myths; good versus evil; good triumphs
Historical Fiction	Set in the past; relies on historical accuracy of time, place, events; brings history to life
Horror	Produces fear in the reader; nightmares come to life; surprise is key; good versus evil; evil can be beaten but never really destroyed
Mystery/Crime Fiction	The puzzle; readers are drawn into the story in an attempt to solve it through clues provided by the author
Romance	The love relationship with a happy ending; wide range of settings from historical to contemporary, from gentle to racy
Science Fiction	Speculative; science drives the story; explores future worlds and technologies that could exist
Suspense/Thrillers	Action and danger; sense of foreboding; pacing is important; see both the hero and the villain's point of view
Westerns	Set primarily in the Western United States against backdrop of historical setting from end of Civil War to beginning of twentieth century; struggle to survive against many dangers; not tied to historical accuracy; survival and revenge common themes

Source: Synopsis compiled from NoveList's "Genre Outlines (EBSCOhost, 2008); Saricks, 2001; and Herald, 2006.

Harris or Michael Crichton). In both adventures and suspense/thrillers the protagonist perseveres and in the end the world realigns to its proper order.

One consideration in trends for genre fiction relates to the proliferation of series. Many of the genres lend themselves to the creation of ongoing series. For example, Terry Pratchett has published approximately 32 novels in the popular Discworld series; Agatha Christie produced 39 Hercule Poirot novels and another 15 Miss Marple stories; and Carolyn G. Hart has generated at least 19 novels in her Death on Demand series. Writers make significant investments of time and energy in the process of creating their fictional worlds. In the case of fantasy novels, the author creates very elaborate worlds that develop and evolve over years and across individual stories. To be believable, historical novels (historical romance and historical fictions) require careful research and development, offering many opportunities for novelists to maintain ongoing sagas across multiple titles and even multiple series. By far the more interesting aspect of series fiction are the series that have books contributed by more than one author while still maintaining consistency in setting and character. The James Bond series by Ian Fleming, for example, also includes titles written by Christopher Wood, Raymond Benson, and John Gardner as well as two related series, the James Bond Files by John Peel and Young Bond by Charlie Higson.

Longevity of series makes another intriguing focus. Many series have been ongoing for years with the characters growing and aging across the series. The first book in the Amelia Peabody series by Elizabeth Peters (also known as Barbara Michaels; both are pseudonyms for Barbara G. Mertz), for example, was published in 1975 and the most current in the series was released in 2006—a 31-year span. *Crocodile on the Sandbank*, the first novel, takes place in 1880; the most current novel, *Tomb of the Golden Bird*, is set in 1922. The characters mature, raise a family, and witness the birth of grandchildren and death of friends during the 42 intervening years. Many of the fantasy series, Terry Brooks' Shannara series for example, follow a similar pattern of growth and maturation across time. This approach of time and character creates an entire world for the reader, allowing the reader to immerse herself or himself into the lives of the characters and experience their lives vicariously.

As mentioned previously, genre fiction writers are very productive. Even if they do not produce regular series, they do write multiple titles on particular themes. Dick Francis, for example, is known for his British horseracing (steeplechasing) novels (a total of 36 published or soon to be released). John Grisham, best known for his legal thrillers, has produced 17 legal novels and four other fiction titles as well as one work of nonfiction. Many genre writers will produce as many as three, four, or more new titles each year, frequently writing with pseudonyms; each pseudonym will cover a different genre or subgenre. Nora Roberts, also known as J. D. Robb, covers romance, paranormal romance, and thrillers, with multiple works being released throughout the year.

Further compounding the issue is the subset of subgenres that exists within each of the primary genres. For example, in science fiction the labels of hard SF and soft SF exist, which are differentiated between a focus on technology and the physical sciences (hard SF) and the social sciences (soft SF). This is then further subdivided by a number of narrower themes: classics, adventure (space operas and militaristic), time travel, shared worlds, techno SF, dystopias/utopias, social structures, alternate/parallel worlds, Earth's children, psionic powers, and aliens. Each of these types of stories plays out under the broader heading of science fiction, but with their own unique characteristics as well. Not only do subgenres offer variety, but they open paths for new writers to explore and find their own niches. They also offer a similar function to readers, by allowing them to pick and choose among the many factors that appeal to them.

Subgenres, and even genre blending, add multiple layers to the reading experience. Romantic suspense, for example, takes the "lone wolf" protagonist, frequently a strong male character, and provides a romantic interest (a spouse, a lover, a family) whose presence makes the protagonist vulnerable. It heightens the tension of the story and adds unexpected twists (kidnapping is a particularly well-used device). Catherine Coulter's FBI Thriller series (romantic thriller) and J. D. Robb's Eva Dallas series (futuristic romance with elements of science fiction) are prime examples of this type of blending. The plus to this blending improves the likelihood that it will appeal to a larger audience, female and male, by combining the best of both genres, and it provides more opportunities for expanding the reader's horizons.

Aligning Genres and Collections

With today's contemporary genres comes a current trend of genre blending or genre sliding. The conventions no longer seem to be hard and fast about what constitutes a particular genre. A prime example is Diana Gabaldon's Outlander series. Described as a paranormal romance, the series combines strong elements of historical fiction (British and American) with science fiction (time travel) and romance. Even literary fiction authors have stepped across the lines separating genre fiction from literary fiction. This might be described as taking the best elements from the genres and from literary fiction and combining them into something new and unexplored. For example, Cormac McCarthy's Pulitzer Prize–winning novel *The Road* (Knopf, 2006) can be described as a postapocalyptic thriller complete with elements from horror (zombielike creatures). Richard Price, nominated for a National Book Critics Award for his first novel *The Wanderers* (1974), also crosses between literary fiction and genre fiction (crime fiction or police procedurals).

From a writer's point of view, genre classification can be limiting. Stephen King, Dean Koontz, and James Rollins all question the genre labels, suggesting that their stories, and those of others, transcend the genre profile and offer so much more to the reader. Incorporating multiple elements from multiple genres provides a greater appeal across the sea of readers. It also offers writers opportunities to do something fresh and exciting, different even, and to offer readers other ways to look at a story. While perhaps a double-edged sword, genre blending can offer readers the convention of one genre with a new and challenging twist through the use of elements from another.

Yet for the new writer or the unfamiliar reader with a new book, genre provides a way of describing and understanding what the story intends to tell and how it may progress. Genre also indicates that as a literary form a specific genre has a history, tradition, and a lineage. It provides a framework of common knowledge from which to start writing or reading.

For many readers genre makes stories recognizable, especially when browsing on their own in the stacks. Using conventional descriptions of genres allows readers to see connections between titles; however, it also distorts perceptions of titles that would be equally good reads but fall outside of the genre. From the readers' advisory perspective, genres provide a way to examine the elements of stories that appeal to the reader, but to be effective the RA staff must look beyond the conventions and look to additional access points into the popular fiction collection. This requires knowing not only genres, but authors and their relationship to a broader range of fiction.

GENERAL STRATEGIES FOR DISCOVERING GENRE FICTION

Before examining the individual genres in detail, a number of general strategies can be applied to their discovery. Many genres have associations that celebrate the writers and the fans, which also track trends and emerging subgenres, and sponsor conferences and conventions. The associations are a primary resource for the most current information as well as booklists and popular authors. Associations frequently sponsor a range of book and author awards, from debut novels to lifetime achievements. Genre magazines and fanzines are crucial to remaining current and on top of the genre news. Most frequently the fanzines are produced by and for aficionados of the genre and contain a great deal of information about the genre in general, authors and extensive interviews with them, and book reviews including books in alternate formats (e.g., audiobooks). Web sites, including fan blogs, author sites, and official association Web sites, provide access to a wide range of information about current trends, authors, and popular titles.

Reference resources provide a wide range of options for both the reader and the readers' advisor in discovering more about the individual genres (see Appendix 1 for genre-specific reference resources). Biographical dictionaries and bibliographies aid in discovering authors and reading lists. They are highly useful in developing core collections and supplementing existing collections in specific genres. Genre dictionaries, encyclopedias, and almanacs provide much-needed factual information. Guides to writing in the genre provide excellent information about the standards for the genre and publishing information. Readers' guides and companions along with atlases and manuals aid in exploring specific series, such as Gabaldon's Outlander series (*The Outlandish Companion*, 1999) or Tolkien's Middle-Earth (*The Complete Guide to Middle-Earth: From* The Hobbit *through* The Lord of the Rings *and Beyond*; Robert Foster, 2001). Histories and criticisms explore genres from more scholarly points of view and historical development of genres, series, and authors. Anthologies and collected stories provide a useful way to explore the depth of genres and find a sense of who the authors are and how the genre may be subdivided.

While the primary genres have associations and resources to aid in studying them, emerging genres (e.g., chick lit, street fiction) can be more difficult. These emerging genres lend themselves to good use of electronic resources for discovery. The most current information about hot, new authors and topics will be found on the Web before located in print. Blogs and wikis and fan sites are perfect starting places to find out a little more about emerging genres, or perhaps more accurately described as new reading interests. The challenge, however, is that emerging genres are often ephemeral, disappearing as quickly as appearing, not becoming recognized as part of standard popular reading.

CONCLUSION

The next several chapters will introduce genres in more detail. Each is unique in and of itself, but they also include strong relationships among themselves. Adventures, suspense, and mysteries, for example, share many characteristics and will appeal to many types of readers. Historical romance and historical fiction share the need for in-depth historical research to be effective and authentic. When approaching readers' advisory activities it may be better to consider issues of genre distinctions and of a book's appeal to the reader.

WORKS CONSULTED

Brennan, Allison. 2008. "Genre Blending." Murder She Writes. Available: www .murdershewrites.com/2008/10/16/genre-blending (accessed September 10, 2009).

EBSCOhost. 2008. "Getting Started in RA: Genre Outlines." Available (by subscription): http://web.ebscohost.com/novelist/search?vid=18&hid=38&sid=54b3f674-c71a-493e-bdad-5175ef893819%40sessionmgr10 (accessed September 10, 2009).

Gelder, Ken. 2004. *Popular Fiction: The Logics and Practices of a Literary Field*. London: Routledge.

Great Britain Library and Information Commission. 2000. *Reading the Situation: Book Reading, Buying & Borrowing Habits in Britain*. London: Book Marketing, Ltd.

Herald, Diana Trixler. 2006. *Genreflecting: A Guide to Popular Reading Interests*, edited by Wayne A. Wiegand. Westport, CT: Libraries Unlimited.

Holland, Nancy J. 2002. "Genre Fiction and 'The Origin of the Work of Art.'" *Philosophy and Literature* 26, no. 1 (April): 216–223.

King, Stephen. 1981. *Danse Macabre*. New York: Berkley Books.

National Endowment for the Arts. 2004. *Reading at Risk: A Survey of Literary Reading in America*. Research Division Report #46. Washington, DC: National Endowment for the Arts.

_____. 2007. *To Read or Not to Read: A Question of National Consequence*. Research Report #47. Washington, DC: National Endowment for the Arts.

_____. 2008. *Reading on the Rise: A New Chapter in American Literacy*. Washington, DC: National Endowment for the Arts.

Romance Writers of America. 2005. "Romance Writers of America's 2005 Market Research Study on Romance Readers." Available: https://eweb.rwanational.org/eweb/docs/o5MarketResearch.pdf (accessed September 10, 2009).

Ross, Catherine Sheldrick. 2001. "Making Choices: What Readers Say about Choosing Books." In *Readers, Reading and Librarians* (pp. 5–22), edited by Bill Katz. Binghamton, NY: The Haworth Press.

Ross, Catherine Sheldrick, Lynne (E. F.) McKechnie, and Paulette M. Rothbauer. 2006. *Reading Matters: What the Research Reveals about Reading, Libraries and Communities*. Westport, CT: Libraries Unlimited.

Ross, Catherine Sheldrick, Kirsti Nilsen, and Marie L. Radford. 2009. *Conducting the Reference Interview: A How-To-Do-It Manual for Librarians*, 2nd edition. New York: Neal-Schuman Publishers.

Saricks, Joyce G. 2001. *The Readers' Advisory Guide to Genre Fiction.* Chicago: American Library Association.

Steele, Alexander, ed. 2003. *Gotham Writers Workshop: Writing Fiction, The Practical Guide from New York's Acclaimed Creative Writing School.* New York: Bloomsbury.

Toyne, Jackie and Bob Usherwood. 2001. *Checking the Books: The Value and Impact of Public Library Book Reading.* Sheffield, England: Department of Information Studies, The University of Sheffield. Available: www.shef.ac.uk/content/1/c5/07/01/24/CPLIS%20-%20Checking%20the%20Books.pdf (accessed September 10, 2009).

FURTHER READING

Beard, David, and Kate Vo Thi-Beard. 2008. "Rethinking Books: New Theories for Readers' Advisory." *Reference & User Services Quarterly* 47, no. 4 (Summer): 331–335.

Le Guin, Ursula K. 2005. "Genre: A Word Only a Frenchman Could Love: A Speech Given at the PLA Preconference on Genre, Seattle, February, 2004." *Public Libraries* 44, no. 1 (January/February): 21–23.

Leddy, Chuck. 2008. "Loot vs. Literature: Genre and Literary Fiction." *Writer* 121, no. 1 (January): 8–9.

Moyer, Jessica. 2008. *Research-Based Readers' Advisory.* Chicago, IL: American Library Association.

Nance, Kevin. 2008. "Invasion of the Genre Snatchers." *Poets & Writers* 36, no. 5 (September/October): 12–15.

Trott, Barry, and Vicki Novak. 2006. "A House Divided? Two Views on Genre Separation." *Reference & User Services Quarterly* 46, no. 2 (Winter): 33–38.

Wyatt, Neal. 2007. "An RA Big Think." *Library Journal* 132, no. 12 (July): 40–43.

Chapter 9

Adventure, Suspense, Thrillers, and Mysteries

Crime is common. Logic is rare.

—Sir Arthur Conan Doyle, *The Adventures of the Copper Beeches* (1924)

AN INTRODUCTION TO ADVENTURE

Adventure, suspense, and thrillers share many similar characteristics and are easily blended. What distinguishes the genre is that adventure is filled with fast-paced, action-packed stories featuring a larger-than-life hero on a mission. Frequently set in exotic locations, the hero is placed in dangerous or extreme situations that he must overcome with ingenuity and his own wits and fists. Adventure novels rely upon physical action and violence, and they generally build up to a culminating event that ends in the hero's successful resolution of the situation. They also lend themselves to movie tie-ins with significant appeal at the box office. (*James Bond, The Bourne Identity,* and *The Hunt for Red October* were all highly popular adventure movies based on bestselling novels of the same genre.)

The story line is primary to the genre's appeal. Descriptions that typically come up in discussions of adventure include physical danger, foreign locales, survival against surmounting odds, and the journey or mission. Readers also suggest that adventure novels are like "rollercoaster rides" or adrenalin rushes—page-turners that cannot be put down. To be successful in capturing the adventure reader, the story must end with the hero prevailing and surviving—and often surviving to appear in another story. (Series are a strong component of adventure fiction.) The plot invariably twists and turns, building the suspense and anticipation as the story moves along at a brisk pace.

Without a doubt it is the hero that defines and directs the adventure story. Most frequently the hero is male—a man of strong moral character who is committed to his mission and his own personal code of conduct. Heroes can be described as falling into two types: the accidental hero caught up in unforeseen circumstances, and the one who resembles a superhero with specialized skills and talents and who is world-wise, even world-weary. In either scenario, the protagonist must overcome extreme difficulties by facing down adversaries and obstacles.

While the protagonists in adventure novels are dominated by males, a few series feature strong female protagonists. For example, Peter O'Donnell's Modesty Blaise is a female James Bond, making her first appearance in a comic strip in 1962 and in a novel in 1965. Modesty Blaise appeared in 13 novels between 1965 and 2001. For a lighter approach, Dorothy Gilman's Mrs. Pollifax series features a grandmother who is also a CIA agent. The series began in 1966 and is set in exotic locations around the world. The fourteenth novel appeared in 2000. Female adventure readers may also find some of the romantic suspense novels and even some romance novels fit the bill for adventure, including Suzanne Brockmann's Troubleshooter series or the novels of Elizabeth Lowell (*The Wrong Hostage, The Color of Death,* or The Donovans series).

While not crucial to the story line, love interests occasionally appear in adventure fiction. More typically the male-female relationship is of a sexual nature rather than what may be considered a romantic one, according to the definition of the romance genre. The females in adventure novels are secondary to the plot and to the hero's mission, frequently being the prize for accomplishing the job, or occasionally a confounding factor in the identification of good and evil. The sexual encounters are more graphic than provocative, and are secondary to the overall plot.

Historical Aspects and Trends

Historically the adventure genre has a long and illustrious past. The earliest known adventure, or epic genre, was *The Epic of Gilgamesh* (written in approximately 3000 BC), a tale of the King of Uruk, a superhero vainly searching for immortality. Other historical adventures include *The Odyssey* (an epic poem attributed to Homer), *The Kalevala* (an epic poem of Finnish and Karelian folklore, written down in the late 1600s and compiled in the late 1800s; interestingly some scholars have suggested J. R. R. Tolkien used *The Kalevala* and the Karelian language in the creation of *The Hobbit* and *The Lord of the Rings* trilogy), and *Beowulf* (an Old English epic poem dating to somewhere between the eighth and eleventh centuries; *Beowulf* has experienced a revival in contemporary fiction with the popularity of graphic novels and its translation into film, and the "retelling" of the classic tale in contemporary language). The elements of the adventure genre can also be seen in many of the classic tales of the nineteenth century, including the work of Alexandre Dumas (*The Three Musketeers* and *The Count of*

Monte Cristo), Robert Louis Stevenson (*Treasure Island* and *Kidnapped*) and Mark Twain (*The Adventures of Huckleberry Finn*).

Adventure tales featuring spies and espionage have been overwhelmingly popular since they emerged in the early twentieth century just prior to the start of World War I. World wars and foreign backdrops, such as Russia and China, form the settings for these types of adventure-espionage novels. They frequently feature protagonists who are or were agents for various secret services (CIA, KGB, MI6) and top-secret government agencies. Ian Fleming's James Bond series certainly stands as a benchmark for these types of novels, but Robert Ludlum's Jason Bourne and Tom Clancy's Jack Ryan illustrate the range of heroes, locales, and action as does Clive Cussler's Dirk Pitt.

The popularity of Dan Brown's *The Da Vinci Code* in 2003 started a new trend in adventure-thriller novels: the cipher thriller and the search for hidden treasure and knowledge through the solving of hidden clues. Not quite mysteries, but certainly filled with adventure and thrill rides, the cipher thrillers lead the protagonist on a journey of discovery as he cracks the codes to take him on the next step of his quest. *The Da Vinci Code* is the standard-bearer for the subgenre that includes Steve Berry's *The Amber Room*, *The Templar Legacy*, and *The Alexandria Link* as well as David Baldacci's *The Camel Club* and *The Collectors*. Unequivocally, these types of novels are fodder for film based on their action, ruggedly handsome heroes, and intriguing plots.

Final Thoughts on Adventure Readers

Adventure has many meanings to readers. They enjoy the opportunity to live vicariously through the hero, finding themselves on dangerous missions in exotic lands. For an adventure story to be successful, it must engage the reader in the fast-paced action, pulling the reader through the story as if on a rollercoaster ride, conveying the excitement and danger. It needs a larger-than-life hero ("Bond, James Bond"), challenges to overcome (physical, emotional, or natural), and a degree of complexity.

The genre can be subdivided into several subgenres, ranging from military adventure to adventure on the high seas. Each subgenre offers its own focus, but the general features of plot and character apply (see Table 9-1 for a sampling of titles). Adventure blends well with other genres, especially crime, Westerns, historical fiction, science fiction, and fantasy to create additional new subgenres. No hard and fast rules dictate what encompasses an adventure novel other than the emphasis on action and hero. Many readers of adventure fiction are likely to be comfortable with suspense, thrillers, and mystery. Any number of nonfiction adventures may pique the reader's interest as well, including *Into Thin Air* (Jon Krakauer, 1999), *Into the Wild* (Jon Krakauer, 1996), or *Alive: The Story of the Andes Survivors* (Piers Paul Read, 2006).

Table 9-1: A Few Authors and Titles Not to Miss in Adventure, Suspense, and Thrillers		
Author	Title/Series/Protagonist	Subgenre
David Baldacci	Camel Club series, *Hour Game, Absolute Power*	Political Thrillers
Dale Brown	Patrick McLanahan series	Military Adventure
Lee Child	Jack Reacher series	Private Detective (Rogue PI)
Tom Clancy	Jack Ryan series	Techno-Thrillers, Political Adventure
Mary Higgins Clark	Regan Reilly series, also *Two Little Girls in Blue, Loves Music, Loves to Dance*	Private Investigator and Psychological Suspense
James Clavell	Noble House series, *Shogun, Tai-Pan*	Political Adventure, Exotic Setting
Harlan Coben	*Tell No One*	Psychological Suspense
Robin Cook	*Terminal, Mindbend, Foreign Body*	Medical Thrillers
Stephen Coonts	Jake Grafton	Political Adventure
Bernard Cornwell	Nate Starbuck series	Civil War Adventure, also Arthurian Adventure, Historical Adventure
Patricia Cornwell	Kay Scarpetta series	Forensic Thriller
Clive Cussler	Dirk Pitt series	Exotic Adventure
Jeffery Deaver	Lincoln Rhyme series	Psychological Thriller
Nelson DeMille	John Sutter, Paul Brenner, John Corey	Bio-Thrillers, Techno-Thrillers, Espionage, Political Suspense
Vince Flynn	Mitch Rapp series	Political Thriller
Ken Follett	*Eye of the Needle, Key to Rebecca, The Man from St. Petersburg, The Jackdaws*	Historical Espionage
Frederick Forsyth	*Day of the Jackal*	Espionage
Tess Gerritsen	Jane Rizzoli and Maura Isles	Medical Thrillers
John Grisham	*The Firm, The Appeal, The Associate*	Legal Thrillers
H. Rider Haggard	*King Solomon's Mine* and *She*	Classic Adventure (nineteenth century)
Thomas Harris	Hannibal Lector series	Psychological Thriller
Jack Higgins	*The Eagle Has Landed, Sure Fire, The Killing Ground*	Wartime Adventure
Greg Iles	*24 Hours*	Psychological Suspense
Robert Ludlum	Jason Bourne, *The Bourne Trilogy*	Military and Political Adventure
Eric Lustbader	Nicholas Linear	Political Adventure
Patrick O'Brian	Captain Jack Aubrey, *Master and Commander*	Sea Adventures
Arturo Perez-Reverte	*Club Dumas, The Flanders Panel, Captain Alatriste*	Exotic Adventures, Historical Adventure

Author	Title/Series/Protagonist	Subgenre
Douglas J. Preston and Lincoln Child	*Thunderhead, The Ice Limit, Riptide*	Blend of history, science and adventure along with a little of the supernatural
Kathy Reichs	Temperance Brennan series	Forensic Thriller
Matthew Reilly	Shane Schofield series	Military Adventure, Exotic Locales
James Rollins	Sigma Force series, *Amazonia, Excavation, Ice Hunt*	Military Adventure, Scientific Adventure
Lisa Scottoline	Rosato & Associates series	Legal Thrillers
Randy Wayne White	Doc Ford series	Exotic and Political Adventure

Note: There are a number of excellent and comprehensive resources for finding Author/Title lists. Start with Saricks' *The Readers' Advisory Guide to Genre Fiction*, Herald's *Genreflecting: A Guide to Popular Reading Interests*, or the Adult Reader's Round Table of Illinois' *ARRT Popular Fiction List*. Consult Appendix 1 for additional reference resources that may be of interest for finding more. And, of course, the commercial and online readers' advisory databases will provide additional read-alikes and related lists.

Supporting Associations and Organizations

Until recently the adventure genre did not have an affiliated association that supported or organized authors within the genre. In 2004, International Thriller Writers (www.thrillwriters.org) was established to promote the interests of authors in the suspense, thriller, and adventure genres. Each summer the association hosts a conference called "ThrillFest," which features author readings, presentations, and, since 2006, "Thriller Awards." The Thriller Awards are given for "best novel," "best first novel," "best paperback original," and "best screenplay." The association offers an online Webzine, "The Big Thrill," which has a number of excellent columns and features to aid in collection development and in discovering new authors and debut novels. An interesting feature of "The Big Thrill" are the articles written by adventure, suspense, and thriller writers that define what the genre means to them, from elements of the story to reflections about the authors who are instrumental to the continuance of the genre. For readers looking for something or someone new to read, "The Big Thrill" includes an excellent list of debut authors with author bios and title descriptions.

AN INTRODUCTION TO SUSPENSE AND THRILLERS

The Suspense and Thriller genre is closely aligned with Adventure (see Table 9-1 for a sampling of titles). These genres incorporate many of the same features of excitement and adrenalin-pumping circumstances with psychological twists (or "head games"). The element that distinguishes suspense/thrillers from adventure is the sense of menace and foreboding felt from beginning to end of the story. Novels of suspense consider both the hero's and the villain's points of view, allowing the reader to know more than the hero. Thrillers, on the other hand, allow the reader to become an insider while the story plays out against the protagonist's profession (legal, medical, science). But the real key to thrillers is fear. Apprehension and tension are primary factors in suspense/thrillers, keeping the reader engrossed. As in adventure, elements of good and evil are clearly displayed (either a character is good or a character is evil) and few gray areas exist. And like adventure, suspense and thrillers lend themselves very well to cinematic production and television programming. (John Grisham, Nelson DeMille, and Thomas Harris have had multiple books created into box-office hits in recent years. Kathy Reichs' forensic thrillers based on the character of Temperance Brennan have been made into television programs in both the United States and Canada.)

Suspense in particular carries a great deal of ambiguity. It makes up a significant element in other genres, including romance, horror, science fiction, and mystery, frequently used to heighten the story's appeal. Unlike other genres, suspense relies on the human element to provide a frame—often a very evil human—and the protagonist does not always know who his or her pursuer may be. Suspense, compared to mystery, ensures that the reader knows all and is not required to unravel a puzzle; the reader watches the action unfold, anticipating the actions and reactions of protagonist and antagonist, though not necessarily knowing who is who until well into the story, hearing the villain's voice but not always seeing him or her clearly.

Fast-paced action is critical to suspense/thrillers; however, the action takes place in narrow time frames, such as a day or a week rather than across months or years. Another necessary element is danger. The protagonist faces danger at every step and must overcome the dangers in order to move forward. In the end, however, the protagonist overcomes all odds to win the day, and justice is served.

The story line plays a crucial role in suspense/thrillers. The more complex and twisted the story lines, the better for engaging the reader. Conspiracy and intrigue are prime elements in the genre, and corruption is a favored theme. For example, John Grisham's first legal thriller, *The Firm*, features a very secretive and corrupt law firm whose partners are exposed by a young, ambitious attorney. Grisham's subsequent legal thrillers offer similar scenarios, ranging from corrupt individuals to organized syndicates and corporations. In his later novels, such as *The Last Juror* and *The Appeal*, manipulation of events and of people (jurors and judges) heightens the feelings of foreboding and inevitability. Graphic violence and elements of horror (or at least horrific descriptions of events) provide common ground among the suspense and thriller novels. Tess Gerritsen's medical thrillers, such as *Surgeon* (the first novel in the Jane Rizzoli series), use graphic description of crime scenes and surgical procedures to both horrify and engage, pulling the reader further into the story.

Suspense/thriller novels intend to provoke empathy from the reader by offering multiple points of view—hero and villain. In fact, it is this very manipulation of the reader that adds to the feelings of anticipatory fear and peril. The reader can be led by a skillful writer to feel sympathy for the antagonists, almost against the reader's will. Unlike adventure novels, the protagonist in suspense/thrillers may be male or female. The heroes or heroines typically portray morally strong characters with a sense of right and wrong while the villains may be amoral or just plain evil. Characters also need to be believable in their portrayal of professions; they need to sound and act like the attorneys, doctors, and scientists with whom the reader is already familiar (either from personal knowledge or as seen in film and television).

Other elements that help bind suspense/thrillers include the setting. Suspense and thrillers take place in the present. It is the abuse of technology, medicine, and science in contemporary society that aids in building tension. This may be an unspoken attitude of "this could really happen" or "torn from the newspaper headlines." Suspense and thrillers rely upon extensive details in the telling of the story. The details are interwoven and involved with the story line and the action, and many readers may see the intricacies as the foundation for the story.

Historical Aspects and Trends

Because suspense and thrillers rely on the contemporary, the genre continuously evolves. Stories follow current technology and science, which make for a wide range of subgenres. Current subgenres include novels featuring computers, terrorism (biological and psychological), medicine and forensics (including genetics, cloning, and medical research), politics, and the law (including the courts and legal practice). Disasters, both man-made and natural, are highly featured in suspense and thrillers. In addition, contemporary military themes frequently appear in suspense and thrillers.

Historically, suspense and thrillers have been popular for generations. While more appropriately categorized as horror, Mary Shelley's *Frankenstein* (published in 1818) contains elements of suspense and thrillers in its exploration of the abuse of science and medicine. However, the earliest recognizable forms of suspense and thrillers appeared in the mid- to late-nineteenth century with the high seas adventures. Espionage made its debut with James Fenimore Cooper's *The Spy* (1821), but it was not until the publication of John Buchan's 1915 novel *The Thirty-Nine Steps* (made into a film of the same name by Alfred Hitchcock in 1935) that the espionage novel came into its own. Spy novels have been highly popular, and have a large following of readers and writers.

Politics have provided significant seed for suspense and thrillers. Major war and enemy conflict present opportunities for espionage, terrorism, and suspenseful thrill rides. The Cold War was a useful backdrop for many suspense novels, such as *The Spy Who Came in from the Cold* (John Le Carré, 1963) and *The*

Russia House (John Le Carré, 1989). Jeffrey Archer, David Baldacci, and Vince Flynn are strongly represented in political suspense/thrillers. Global thrillers are closely related to political thrillers, frequently considering the overthrowing of major political powers, especially in Asia, the USSR and Russia, and the Middle East.

Bio-thrillers, cyber thrillers, medical thrillers, and techno-thrillers form an intricately woven relationship focusing on the sciences that dominate the headlines. (See Table 9-1 for a few authors and titles that fall into these subgenres.) Michael Crichton's *The Andromeda Strain* (1969) forms the roots for the thrillers based upon biological accidents, ultimately leading to the work of authors such as Robin Cook and Dean Koontz, who frequently become classed as horror. Not only was Cook prominent in bio-thrillers, he laid the foundation for the development of the related medical thrillers with *Brain* (1981) and *Godplayer* (1983). Medical thrillers follow similar paths, using medicine for evil, forgetting the rules of the Hippocratic oath "to do no harm."

In techno-thrillers the inventions, innovations, and gadgets are as elemental to the story line as are the characters. Techno-thrillers typically focus on armed conflict, using high-tech gadgets and weaponry, such as the tales of Tom Clancy. Cyber-thrillers, on the other hand, while technology oriented, focus on computers as either the villain (think HAL in *2001: A Space Odyssey*, by Arthur C. Clarke) or as the tool to conduct villainy. In contemporary cyber-thrillers the Internet is prominently featured as a source to gather victims or to pass or steal information. Dan Brown uses computers as the lynch pin for *Digital Fortress*. Interestingly, cyber-thrillers saw the height of their popularity in the mid to late 1990s.

Final Thoughts on Suspense and Thriller Readers

Individuals who enjoy suspense and thrillers expect many of the same elements that adventure readers enjoy: larger-than-life heroes, fast-paced action, and high levels of suspense. More importantly, these readers expect sympathetic heroes and clearly defined elements of good and evil. In particular, suspense and thriller readers enjoy highly complex conspiracies and scheming villains. What differentiates thrillers from adventure stories is that the reader believes he or she has learned something about a profession or industry or current events and hot topics in the news media.

Suspense and thrillers have a broad appeal among both men and women. They read the genre for the pace of the story and the inevitable twists. Readers expect to be pulled into the book within the first few pages of the story and expect to be held captive throughout the telling. The elements of suspense and thrillers move easily through many other genres, pointing to other possibilities for satisfying reads. This is also a genre that makes it easy to expand reading horizons outside of the genre itself and into science fiction, mystery, fantasy, and adventure.

For suspense and thriller novels, the cover art is an important feature of the books. It provides strong clues about the content. The reader can indeed "judge a book by its cover." For example, legal thrillers will often feature the scales of justice, gavels, or the statue of "Blind Justice." Cyber thrillers are identified by their computer-like fonts (remember old DOS scripts?), while espionage and spy novels will incorporate flags, dark colors, and shadowy figures. For suspense/thrillers the covers are all about symbolism, both overt and covert.

Supporting Organizations, Associations, and Other Resources

As with adventure, it has been only in the past few years that suspense and thriller authors and readers have been supported by their own focused organization. They share International Thrill Writers with adventure authors and readers (see Adventure discussion). Because suspense and thrillers are subject to significant genre blending, resources for mysteries and crime fiction are also appropriate points for consultation. For example, Reviewing the Evidence (www .reviewingtheevidence.com) provides extensive reviews of mysteries and thriller titles. Stop, You're Killing Me! (www.stopyourekillingme.com), a murder and suspense novel site, is an extensive resource to identify authors, titles, and series, and offers a list of characters' names. One of the highly useful features of Stop, You're Killing Me! is the linking of authors with their pseudonyms. An extensive list of reference resources for the Suspense/Thriller genre is included in Appendix 1.

MYSTERIES AND CRIME FICTION

Mystery stories are among the most popular novels requested in libraries or purchased in bookstores, making up about 30 percent of books acquired by readers (Romance Writers of America, 2005: 2). These novels generally make up between 45 and 60 percent of the titles featured on the weekly bestsellers lists, including the *New York Times* and *Publishers Weekly* (Maatta, 2007). They come in a wide range of types, from the cozy mysteries of Britain to the hard-boiled detectives of contemporary novels. Series occur commonly in the mystery genre, and mystery writers are industrious in churning out mystery after mystery with great regularity and with more than a few pseudonyms. While closely aligned with the suspense/thriller genre, mysteries revolve around solving the crime, and thrillers revolve around preventing crime (Braver, 2009: 24).

At the heart of a mystery is the puzzle, and this aspect is a serious consideration for readers. Many readers enjoy the quest for the answers to "whodunit," and particularly enjoy resolving the puzzle before the perpetrator is revealed by the detective. Patrick Anderson, quoting S. S. Van Dine's 1928 article "Twenty Rules for Writing Detective Stories," describes mysteries as an "intellectual game . . . where the reader has the same opportunity as the detective to solve the crime

(2007: 25). Readers derive great pleasure from solving the author's puzzle, especially if it is well-crafted and cleverly plotted.

A number of elements define the mystery genre. On the whole, they involve a crime, usually that of a murder and resulting body. Even those that involve theft and other types of criminal activities will have the required dead body. Along with the necessary victim, mysteries include an investigator, either professional or amateur, to solve the crime. Readers follow the investigator from the discovery of the victim through the clues to the revelation of "whodunit" and the restoration of order. While justice may be served, it may be outside of the law and administered at the hands of the protagonist. Additional elements that play into the story include the setting and location, and the historical time period. All of these are critical in the appeal of mysteries.

Readers engage in mysteries for a number of reasons. As already mentioned, some readers want to solve the crime before the investigator. They have specific expectations of the writer to play fair with them, allowing readers to solve the mystery from the presentation of clues. The structure of the mystery itself can be critical to many mystery readers, having a beginning, middle, and a conclusion. A crime is committed, an investigation ensues, and the guilty party is revealed. The reader finds reaching a successful conclusion to the story very satisfying.

For others, the ability to participate in the investigation and in the life of the investigator is tantamount. This preference gives life to many mystery series, allowing the readers to participate in the investigator's life across time and place. Prime examples of this include Elizabeth Peters' character, Amelia Peabody, or John Dunning's Cliff Janeway character. Readers have been with Peabody from her first adventure in Egypt when she meets her future husband (*The Crocodile on the Sandbank*, 1975) through the adventures of her son and birth of her grandchildren (*Tomb of the Golden Bird*, 2006). In the Dunning mysteries, readers follow the evolution of Cliff Janeway from jaded Denver cop (*Booked to Die*, 1992) to talented bookman (*The Bookwoman's Last Fling*, 2006). The protagonists in mystery series become comfortable, much like old friends. Mystery readers deliberately seek out and read everything that is written featuring these characters.

Characterization plays an important role in the success of mysteries. The personality of the protagonist—from curmudgeon to comic—becomes a way to identify with the story and knowing how the investigation will advance. One of the features that readers seek in read-alikes is characters who have similar appeal or behave in similar ways, not just the type of detective (police detective, amateur sleuth). Protagonists in many of the mystery series become unforgettable. Even Sir Arthur Conan Doyle was unable to kill off his character, Sherlock Holmes, when Doyle became tired of him. (Holmes has lived on through other mystery series, including Laurie King's Mary Russell and Sherlock Holmes series.)

Secondary characters are equally as important to the mystery as the protagonists. They have lives of their own, and the reader knows the secondaries almost as well as the investigators. These secondary characters, both supporting ones and nemeses, frequently reappear in other books within series, contributing to or confounding the investigation. They even return in dreams and as supernatural beings, having died or been eliminated in earlier novels. (Amelia Peabody's former foreman and old friend Abdullah continues to appear in the series, though dead and buried many novels previously.)

What mysteries offer readers is variety, from character to plot. Many mysteries are multilayered and complex, exploring social and cultural issues that frame the mystery. Details of setting and location are important to some stories, and often contain clues to solving the mystery; in other instances they offer a secondary function of simply giving a frame of place and time to the mystery. The setting is more critical to series than to stand-alone mysteries. Tone also plays a role in the variety of mysteries, ranging from dark and moody novels (James Lee Burke, Dave Robicheaux series) to laugh-out-loud antics of the protagonists and supporting cast (Janet Evanovich's Stephanie Plum or Alexandra Barnaby series).

Unlike adventure stories and suspense/thrillers, the pace of action is less critical in mysteries. The complexity of the novel drives the pacing. The complex, multilayered mysteries, such as those of P. D. James and Elizabeth George, will develop at a much slower pace than the mysteries of Janet Evanovich and Carolyn G. Hart, which use the pace to get the story on its way. Other factors pull in the reader to keep reading, especially that of character.

Historical Aspects and Trends

Mysteries and detective novels as a genre have a real history. The genre can be traced back to its roots of *Murders in the Rue Morgue* and the primary character of C. Auguste Dupin (Edgar Allan Poe, 1841). Dupin served as the prototype of many contemporary detectives. Poe also offered the foundations for the detective series with the second Dupin story ("The Mystery of Marie Roget," 1842), of plotting and following of clues in "The Purloined Letter," and the basis for contemporary cipher-thrillers in "The Gold Bug."

If Poe and Doyle gave mysteries the foundation for the detective and the use of deductive reasoning, then Agatha Christie supplied the complex, carefully plotted puzzle. With her Hercule Poirot (detective) and Miss Marple (snoop) novels, Christie introduced elements of false clues and proverbial red herrings designed to deceive and manipulate the reader with the intent that the detective should reveal the solution before the reader has discovered it. She also provided what could be called the culminating scene where all is revealed (*Death on the Nile, Murder on the Orient Express, Evil Under the Sun*).

The harsh realities of the Great Depression and the influences of writers such as Hemingway gave birth to the hard-boiled detective. Sparse, gritty language was the hallmark of detective fiction during the early part of the twentieth century, along with a dash of realism or at least realistic settings. Dashiell Hammett's

Classic Mystery Authors to Know

Raymond Chandler	Edgar Allan Poe
Agatha Christie	Mary Roberts Rinehart
Wilkie Collins	Dorothy L. Sayers
Arthur Conan Doyle	Josephine Tey
Dashiell Hammett	

Sam Spade and Raymond Chandler's Philip Marlowe epitomized the hard-drinking, hard-talking detective. Sexual encounters became overt elements in the detective novels, though perhaps not quite as graphic as contemporary novels.

Beginning in the 1970s, a period of significant cultural and societal changes and challenges, cultural and social elements were ingrained into mystery fiction. Regionalism and multiculturalism added new locales to mystery fiction, such as Tony Hillerman's Southwestern mysteries that also introduced Native American protagonists. An increasing number of women as private eyes and protagonists appeared in mystery series, including P. D. James' Cordelia Gray, Marcia Muller's Sharon McCone, Sue Grafton's Kinsey Millhone, and Sara Paretsky's V. I. Warshawski. Issues of race and faith began to creep into mysteries, including protagonists who were "men of the cloth" or who were people of color. Joseph Hansen was the first author to introduce a gay private eye with his character Dave Brandstetter.

This was also a period in which specialization became a key element in mystery fiction. The focus became the detective's occupation, which added a much broader depth to the array of mystery novels. Dick Francis was the standard-bearer for occupation with his British horseracing novels. A long list of occupational mysteries have since developed, including food and catering (Diane Mott Davidson, Joanna Fluke), forensics (Patricia Cornwell, Kathy Reichs), cats (Lilian Jackson Braun, Rita Mae Brown and Sneaky Pie), bookstores/libraries/publishers (Jo Dereske, Julie Kaewert, John Dunning), and sports (Harlan Coben).

Subgenres are critical to contemporary mysteries (see Table 9-2). They offer a range of options to suit the different needs of individual readers. Subgenres also open the possibilities for more publishing opportunities through additional series and pseudonyms for the writers. A number of ways may be used to look at subgenres, including by type of mystery (cozy to hard-boiled), type of detective (amateur to professional), type of setting (historical to contemporary), or genre-blending aspects (romantic mystery, paranormal mystery). The subject of mysteries, like many other genres, draws on contemporary cultural and societal issues. Today an increasing number of mystery series feature detectives representing numerous racial and ethnic backgrounds, detectives who are gay or les-

Table 9-2: A Few Key Authors and Titles for Contemporary Mystery		
Author	Title/Series	Subcategory
Nevada Barr	Anna Pigeon series	Amateur Detective
M. C. Beaton	Hamish Macbeth series	Humorous Mystery
Cara Black	Aimee Leduc	International Mystery—France
Lilian Jackson Braun	James Qwilleran series	Cozy Mystery
Rita Mae Brown & Sneaky Pie	Mrs. Murphy series	Humorous Mystery
James Lee Burke	Robicheaux series	Private Investigator
Jan Burke	Irene Kelly series	Amateur Detective
Michael Connelly	Harry Bosch series	Police
Robert Crais	Elvis Cole series	Private Investigator
Diane Mott Davidson	Goldy Schulz series	Cozy Mystery
Tim Dorsey	Serge Storms series	Crime/Caper Mystery
John Dunning	Cliff Janeway series	Professional Detective—Bookman
Janet Evanovich	Stephanie Plum series	Amateur Detective—Humor
Joanna Fluke	Hannah Swenson series	Cozy Mystery
Earlene Fowler	Benni Harper series	Cozy Mystery
Dick Francis	*Dead Cert to Silks*	Amateur Detectives, Private Eye
Elizabeth George	Inspector Lynley series	Police
Sue Grafton	Kinsey Millhone series	Private Investigator
Kerry Greenwood	Phryne Fisher series	International Mystery—Australia
Martha Grimes	Richard Jury series	Police
Carolyn G. Hart	Death on Demand series	Cozy Mystery
Joan Hess	Claire Malloy series, Maggody series	Humorous Mystery
Carl Hiassen	*Powder Burn, Sick Puppy, Skinny Dip, Flush, Nature Girl, Scat*	Crime/Caper
Tony Hillerman	Joe Leaphorn and Jim Chee series	Police—Native American
P. D. James	Adam Dalgleish series	Police
J. A. Jance	J. P. Beaumont, Joanna Brady, Alison Reynolds series	Police
Roderic Jeffries	Inspector Alvarez series	International Mystery—Majorca
Faye Kellerman	Peter Decker and Rina Lazarus series	Police
Jonathan Kellerman	Alex Delaware series	Amateur Detective—Psychological Suspense
Donna Leon	Guido Brunetti series	International Mystery—Italy
Elmore Leonard	Carl Webster series, *Cuba Libre, Rum Punch*	Crime/Caper
Henning Mankell	Kurt Wallender	International Crime

(continued)

Table 9-2: A Few Key Authors and Titles for Contemporary Mystery *(continued)*		
Author	Title/Series	Subcategory
Walter Mosley	Easy Rawlins series	Private Eye
Sara Paretsky	V. I. Warshawski	Private Eye
Robert B. Parker	Spenser series	Private Eye
Anne Perry	Thomas Pitt series, William Monk series	Historical
Elizabeth Peters	Amelia Peabody series	Historical
Charles Todd	Ian Rutledge series	Historical
Jacqueline Winspear	Maisi Dobbs series	Historical
Stuart Woods	Stone Barrington series	Amateur Detective

Note: There are a number of excellent and comprehensive resources for finding Author/Title lists. Start with Saricks' *The Readers' Advisory Guide to Genre Fiction*, Herald's *Genreflecting: A Guide to Popular Reading Interests*, or the Adult Reader's Round Table of Illinois' *ARRT Popular Fiction List*. Consult Appendix 1 for additional reference resources that may be of interest for finding more. And, of course, the commercial and online readers' advisory databases will provide additional read-alikes and related lists.

bian, and a significant trend in genre blending, especially with horror and fantasy.

Final Thoughts on Mystery and Crime Readers

Readers of mystery and crime novels enjoy these stories for a number of reasons. For some it is the challenge of solving a case before the detective; others enjoy participating in the investigation. Most important for the reader of mystery and crime novels is the sense of order and justice served, and good and evil are easily distinguished. Ultimately, however, it is the character (the detective—professional and amateur alike) that holds the greatest appeal for mystery readers, and they frequently identify with the protagonist (gender, education, background, occupation, or life situation, for example).

Any well-written and crafted story will entertain as well as educate. Mysteries are no exception. We have discussed many of the reasons for the mystery's appeal, but the final factor for many readers is that the mystery can also provide a way to acquire knowledge along the way. Readers are introduced to forensic anthropology and forensic science through the works of Patricia Cornwell and Kathy Reichs; the international mysteries explore foreign and exotic locations; historical mysteries pay careful attention to the verisimilitude of time and place.

Readers' advisory in the mystery genre may be more complex than with others. Not only does the readers' advisor require knowledge about pacing, characters, and setting, he or she must also be able to sort out other more subtle differences between the subgenres. Mysteries have varying degrees of violence, from no violence at all to highly graphic descriptions. Does the reader prefer cozy mysteries without graphic details or hard-boiled detectives with gritty, even realistic, examination of murder and violence? This applies to language and sexual content as well: profanity acceptable, no profanity at all; suggestions of sexual relationships are okay, sexual content as electrically charged as the violence is acceptable. Theme is also a focal point in mysteries with plots structured around specific elements, such as art/museum mysteries or biblio-mysteries. These types of distinctions require the readers' advisor to be well acquainted with the intricacies of the genre along with knowledge about the reader's interests.

Supporting Organizations, Associations, and Other Resources

Mystery novels probably have one of the largest fan bases among the genres, and some of the most extensive, comprehensive range of resources for consultation. So many resources exist that they cannot all be covered here. Mystery magazines are prolific, with many dedicated to publishing original mystery fiction (short stories and novellas). Published by associations and organizations dedicated to furthering and supporting mystery authors, these journals hold a wealth of information for readers as well as would-be authors. In particular *Mystery Readers Journal: The Journal of Mystery Readers International* is a must to know. In the "Mystery Periodicals" section is an extensive international list of mystery fanzines, magazines, and periodicals. Other periodicals to be aware of include *Mystery Scene, The Strand, Crime Time Magazine* (a British publication, which is going entirely online), and *Deadly Pleasures.*

Several mystery reader and writer associations can be consulted for both contemporary and historical information. The first is Mystery Readers International, a fan-based organization that is open to readers, critics, editors, publishers, and writers. Sisters in Crime (SinC) supports the interests and needs of women mystery writers. It is an advocacy group that offers a range of services to paid members, including a quarterly newsletter, listserv, and Books in Print online listing of books by members. SinC was founded by Sara Paretsky and a group of women writers.

While many additional resources are listed in Appendix 1, several other useful Web sites should be bookmarked in your social bookmarking account. In Reference to Murder (www.inreferencetomurder.com/index.html) is an extensive online reference resource that provides links to bibliographies, biographies, blogs, book clubs, publishers, libraries, and a host of other sites that focus on murder and mystery. Reviewing the Evidence (www.reviewingtheevidence.com) and Stop, You're Killing Me! (www.stopyourekillingme.com) both feature book reviews, including books in other formats. Stop, You're Killing Me! includes a very useful "Diversity Index" that provides details about the diversity of series characters, including age, sexual orientation, and race/ethnicity.

Conventions and conferences are an important adjunct to the mystery genre. Several annual events are musts for mystery writers—events to see and be seen. Bouchercon, the World Mystery Convention, is a fan convention held each fall, traveling between cities. (Bouchercon 2010 takes place in San Francisco, CA.) The convention features panel discussions, lectures, and presentations by mystery writers and experts. The Left Coast Crime Conference is an annual conference held during the first quarter of each year. It takes place in locations in Western North America, including Hawaii in 2009. As with Bouchercon, this convention is for fans and authors, featuring speakers, panels, discussions, and a variety of social activities. Malice Domestic is a fan convention held annually in Washington, DC, each spring. It salutes the traditional mystery (in the style of Agatha Christie and Dorothy L. Sayers, for example). The prestigious Agatha Award for mysteries is awarded during this convention. Finally, Magna cum Murder is sponsored by Ball State University and offers an annual conference and crime-writing festival. One of the interesting side notes about Magna cum Murder is their sponsorship of a "One Festival, One Book" program in which all participants are invited to read the same book. The selected book serves as a touchstone or point of common discussion throughout the festival activities.

CONCLUSION

Adventure, suspense, thrillers, and mysteries comprise some of the most popular of the genres. Adventure and suspense, in particular, share many commonalities, from characterization to plot, making them difficult to distinguish at times. Along with mysteries, these genres share elements of excitement and emotional response. Individually and combined, these genres lend themselves to a range of genre blending with the other genres. Due to this flexible nature, they appeal to a wide cross-section of readers, adding unique twists to history and romance. This also makes it easier to meet the needs of adventure, suspense, and mystery readers when they are seeking something new and untried.

WORKS CONSULTED

Anderson, Patrick. 2007. *The Triumph of the Thriller: How Cops, Crooks, and Cannibals Captured Popular Fiction.* New York: Random House.

Braver, Gary. 2009. "How to Write a Successful Thriller." *The Writer Magazine* 122, no. 4 (April): 24–26.

Charles, John, Joanna Morrison, and Candace Clark. 2002. *The Mystery Reader's Advisory: The Librarian's Clues to Murder and Mayhem.* ALA Reader's Advisory Series. Chicago: American Library Association.

Gelder, Ken. 2004. *Popular Fiction: The Logics and Practices of a Literary Field.* London: Routledge.

Herald, Diana Trixler. 2006. *Genreflecting: A Guide to Popular Reading Interests,* edited by Wayne A. Wiegand. Westport, CT: Libraries Unlimited.

Maatta, Stephanie L. 2007. "Murder, Mayhem & America's Bestselling Fiction." Paper presented at the Popular Culture/American Culture Association Joint Conference, Boston, MA, April 4–7, 2007.

Morrell, David. 2008. "Defining a Thriller by David Morrell." *The Big Thrill.* Available: www.thrillerwriters.org/2008/02/what-defines-a-thriller-by-david-morrell.html#more (accessed September 10, 2009).

Romance Writers of America. 2005. "Romance Writers of America's 2005 Market Research Study on Romance Readers." Available: https://eweb.rwanational.org/eweb/docs/05MarketResearch.pdf (accessed September 10, 2009).

Saricks, Joyce G. 2001. *The Readers' Advisory Guide to Genre Fiction.* Chicago: American Library Association.

FURTHER READING

Cawelti, John G. 2004. *Mystery, Violence, and Popular Culture: Essays.* Madison, WI: Popular Press.

Donahue, Dick. 2006. "Upping the Body Count." *Publishers Weekly* 253, no. 48 (December 4): 22–23.

Foster, Jordan. 2008. "The Cozy Gets the Hard-Boil." *Publishers Weekly* 255, no. 16 (April 21): 22.

Garfield, Brian. 2008. "Ten Rules for Suspense Fiction by Brian Garfield." *The Big Thrill.* Available: www.thrillerwriters.org/2008/03/ten-rules-for-suspense-fiction-by-brian.html#more (accessed September 10, 2009).

Williams, Wilda W. 2007. "The Killer Genre." *Library Journal* 132, no. 7 (April 15): 38–41.

_____. 2008. "The Sound of Crime Fiction." *Library Journal* 133, no. 7 (April 15): 36–39.

Winston, Kimberly. 2008. "Keeping Us in Suspense." *Publishers Weekly* 255, no. 22 (June 2): S6.

Chapter 10

Science Fiction, Fantasy, and Horror

Bruce G. Smith and Stephanie L. Maatta

Fantasy is the impossible made probable. Science fiction is the improbable made possible.

—Rod Serling, creator of *The Twilight Zone* (1924–1975)

AN INTRODUCTION TO SCIENCE FICTION OR SPECULATIVE FICTION

Nonreaders of science fiction and fantasy have a hard time distinguishing between the two genres. While the two genres do have a number of crossover and overlapping titles, they have one distinct difference. The alternative worlds designed by science fiction authors are grounded in scientific theory and technology, while the worlds of fantasy are built upon enchantment, mystery, and faerie. Science fiction worlds provide plausible predictions of the future incorporating robotics, space travel, nanotechnology, psychology, biology, engineering, chemistry, and physics. Science fiction stories often include intricate technological minutiae. Authors of fantasy novels include magic, elves, sorcery, the paranormal, ghosts, and nonhuman characters. Fantasy stories may be based on myths, fables, and folktales. In fantasy anything goes as long as rules remain consistent within the story, while science fiction worlds follow the same rules as our own. Science fiction questions the use of technology and deals with philosophical questions of "why." Is cloning, nuclear power, biotechnology, etc., a good thing? Ben Bova, author of the Voyagers series and others, stated that another goal of science fiction is to show how technology can improve the world in which we live as well as to predict the unintended consequences of that technology (*Finding the Future*, 2006). Fantasy, by comparison, pits good against evil; poses religious confrontation; and sets technology versus faerie.

Science fiction and fantasy exhibit similarities. The author creates alternative worlds and universes which require in-depth development and highly visual description. Because the worlds are excruciatingly intricate and take so long to develop, many authors choose to write multiple books in a series. Since the story settings require intricate detail to develop, science fiction writers exhibit cooperation and collaboration on works not often seen in other genres. They may co-author or grant permission for others to use their settings. Both genres tend to challenge the norms and ethics of society, including racial and gender issues.

Unlike other genres, science fiction focuses on the story line and the setting or frame of the story. While detailed, the scientific and technological aspects of the story line must be approachable by novice readers as well as the longtime fan. Readers have to be able to understand the questions at hand and how the writer approaches these questions. Characterization is less critical in appealing to the reader, though the questions considered by the genre are approached through the actions of the characters. Much like mysteries, the pacing of science fiction novels depends upon the story itself. Some move at a very brisk pace, such as David Weber's Honor Harrington series, while others explore philosophical questions through complex ideas and actions.

Science fiction lends itself extremely well to the production of series. In many ways this is similar to the interests of mystery readers who follow characters across time and place. Like mystery authors, sci-fi authors are prolific and tend to release multiple books each year in several different series. Of particular note, many science fiction writers produce in several genres, including fantasy and horror. Orson Scott Card is well-known for genre crossing in science fiction, fantasy, and horror, and for his multiple pseudonyms, including Dinah Karkham, Scott Richards, and Byron Walley.

Historical Aspects and Trends

Classical Science Fiction

Three nineteenth-century authors, Mary Shelley, H. G. Wells, and Jules Verne, could be considered the frontier authors of science fiction. While Mary Shelley's *Frankenstein* traditionally falls under literary classic and horror classifications, the argument can be made that she utilizes a science foundation in the book. H. G. Wells penned *The Island of Dr. Moreau, War of the Worlds,* and *The Time Machine* beginning in 1895 at a time when space exploration as we know it today was unheard of. All three are inarguably science fiction, and their themes have been used numerous times by other authors and by Hollywood. Jules Verne has captured the interests of readers for more than 200 years with his science fiction masterpieces *Journey to the Center of the Earth* (1864); *Begum's Millions* (also known as *The Begum's Fortune,* 1879); *From the Earth to the Moon* (1865); and *20,000 Leagues Under the Sea* (1869). Hollywood has liberally borrowed ideas from *Jour-*

ney to the Center of the Earth and the others to entertain modern moviegoers. While space travel and submarines were a figment of the imagination when these books were written, they are now existing technology.

Classic Science Fiction Authors to Know

Isaac Asimov	Ursula K. Le Guin
Ray Bradbury	Andre Norton
Octavia Butler	Theodore Sturgeion
Arthur C. Clarke	Jules Verne
Robert Heinlein	H. G. Wells
Frank Herbert	

In the early twentieth century, several science fiction authors come to mind. Edgar Rice Burroughs, among other things, wrote the Mars series and *The Land That Time Forgot*. In the Mars series an astral phenomenon transports Captain John Carter from the Civil War to Mars. The method of transport could place this series in fantasy, but since it deals with aliens on a real planet generally it gets labeled as science fiction. In the *Land That Time Forgot* British soldiers become stranded on an island in the Pacific. The soldiers must fight for their survival against prehistoric monsters. Sir Arthur Conan Doyle, more widely known for his Sherlock Holmes books, wrote *The Lost World*, which depicts a plateau in South America where dinosaurs still live. Aldous Huxley's *Brave New World* tells about a strictly controlled dysfunctional society. E. E. Doc Smith wrote the Skylark series and the Chronicles of Lensman series.

Contemporary Science Fiction

Science fiction as a genre blossomed after World War II. The war had driven technological advances, including the atom bomb. The Cold War began between Russia and the United States. Authors questioned the seemingly uncontrolled development of weapons and technology. A number of books dealt with atomic war, robotics, and space travel. Apocalyptic or dystopian stories became the norm. Authors appearing during the post–World War II to 1970 time frame include Isaac Asimov, Robert Heinlein, Arthur C. Clarke, Frank Herbert, Ray Bradbury, Andre Norton, Kurt Vonnegut, Jack Finney, George Orwell, George R. Stewart, Richard Matheson, and Philip K. Dick. (See Table 10-1 for a sampling of authors and titles.)

Isaac Asimov, one of the most influential authors in the field, wrote on a broad number of topics. His accomplishments include short stories and essays of both fiction and nonfiction and well over 300 books. Several biographical lists appear on the Web, including on LibraryThing. Asimov deals extensively with

Table 10-1: A Sampling of Popular Science Fiction Authors and Titles to Know		
Author	Title/Series	Subgenre
Catherine Asaro	Skolian Empire, Lost Continent	Sci-fi Adventure
Kage Baker	Company series	Society
John Barnes	Century Next Door, Timeraider, Million Open Doors, Timeline Wars, Jak Jinnaka series	Society
Greg Bear	Songs of Earth and Power, Eon, Forge of God, Darwin series	Society
Orson Scott Card	Worthing Chronicles, Ender Wiggin, Alvin Maker, Maps in a Mirror, Homecoming, Shadow Saga, Women of Genesis, Mithermages series	Society
C. J. Cherryh	Hanan Rebellion, Morgaine, Faded Sun, Arafel, Company Wars, Compact Space, Merovingen Nights series	Sci-fi Adventure
William C. Dietz	Sam McCade, Pik Lando, Legion of the Damned, Jak Rebo, Hitman, Resistance	Sci-fi Adventure
Peter Hamilton	Greg Mandel, Night's Dawn, Commonwealth Saga, Void Trilogy	Technology
Nancy Kress	Sleepless, Probability, Crossfire series	Technology
Sharon Lee & Steve Miller	Liaden, Gem ser'Edreth, Great Migration, Beneath Strange Skies series	Sci-fi Adventure
Anne McCaffrey	Catteni, Brainship, Doona	Society
Jack McDevitt	Alex Benedict, Engines of God series	Society
Elizabeth Moon	Deed of Paksenarrion, Planet Pirates, Legacy of Gird, Serrano Legacy, Vata's War series	Sci-fi Adventure
Larry Niven	Ringworld, Moties, Inferno, Dream Park, Known Space	Technology
Robert Reed	Veil of Stars, Marrow series	Technology
Alastair Reynolds	Revelation Space series, *Century Rain, Pushing Ice, House of Suns, Terminal World*	Technology
John Ringo	Posleen War, Empire of Man, Council Wars, Looking Glass, Paladin of Shadows series	Sci-fi Adventure
Kim Stanley Robinson	Mars, Captial Code series	Society
Robert J. Sawyer	Quintaglio Ascension, Neanderthal Parallax series	Society
Dan Simmons	Hyperion, Joe Kurtz, Ilium series	Sci-fi Adventure
Neal Stephenson	Baroque Cycle series, *The Big U, Interface, Cryptonomicon, Anathem*	Society
Bruce Sterling	Mechanist Shapers, series, *Zeitgeist, The Zenith Angle, The Caryatids*	Technology
Charles Stross	Singularity Sky, Merchant Princes series	Society
Harry Turtledove	Gerin the Fox, Videssos, Krispos, Worldwar, Times of Troubles, Great War, Darkness, Atlantis series	Sci-fi Adventure
John Varley	Eight Worlds, Gaea, Red series, *Mammoth, Rolling Thunder*	Technology

Author	Title/Series	Subgenre
Vernor Vinge	Across Real Time, Quen Ho series, *Rainbows End*	Technology
David Weber	Starfire, Dahak, Honor Harrington, Oath of Swords, Empire of Man, Assiti Shards series	Sci-fi Adventure
Connie Willis	*All Seated on the Ground, D.A., Passage, To Say Nothing of the Dog*	Society

Note: There are a number of excellent and comprehensive resources for finding Author/Title lists. Start with Saricks' *The Readers' Advisory Guide to Genre Fiction*, Herald's *Genreflecting: A Guide to Popular Reading Interests*, or the Adult Reader's Round Table of Illinois' *ARRT Popular Fiction List*. Consult Appendix 1 for additional reference resources that may be of interest for finding more. And, of course, the commercial and online readers' advisory databases will provide additional read-alikes and related lists.

societal issues and technology. His Foundation series won a special Hugo Award in 1966 for best all-time series. It is the only series to do so, and competed that year with *Lord of the Rings*. His other series, such as *I, Robot*, merge with the Foundation series, creating a story en masse.

Heinlein, Clarke, Norton, Herbert, and Bradbury write across a wide array of topics and have a large published collection. Robert A. Heinlein's writings include *Have Spacesuit Will Travel*; *Starship Troopers*; *Stranger in a Strange Land*; and *Job*. Among Arthur C. Clarke works are *Childhood's End* and *The Fountains of Paradise*. His best-known work was the short story *2001: A Space Odyssey*. He collaboratively worked on this with Stanley Kubrick for the screen (released in 1968, and winning an Oscar in 1969); it has since become a science fiction cult classic. Readers know Frank Herbert best for his Dune series. Some of Ray Bradbury's better-known works include *Fahrenheit 451*; *Something Wicked This Way Comes*; and *The Martian Chronicles*.

Andre Norton (also known as Andrew North) works in both science fiction and fantasy. She has also published a number of works with other authors, including Pauline Griffin, Lyn McConchie, and Mercedes Lackey. Her story *Daybreak 2250 AD*, originally published as *Star Man's Son* (1952) looks at competing civilizations generations after a nuclear holocaust. Her books also relate stories of space travel as in the Solar Queen series. She also has a series dealing with time travel called Time Trader.

Kurt Vonnegut, Jack Finney, and Philip K. Dick write edgy science fiction. Kurt Vonnegut's books challenge the reader with social and moral questions. Among his works are *Slaughterhouse Five* and *Welcome to the Monkey House*. Jack Finney's better-known works are *Time and Again* and *Invasion of the Body Snatchers*. Philip K. Dick's most famous novel is *Do Androids Dream of Electric Sheep?*, which served as the basis for the movie *Blade Runner*.

Two works greatly influenced the genres of science fiction and fantasy. In George R. Stewart's *Earth Abides*, the protagonist describes civilization's survival after a plague. This is one of the first books pertaining to life after civilization collapses. Stewart does not judge in this book; he merely narrates the breakdown and regrowth of civilization. On the other hand, Richard Matheson's *I Am Legend* also describes life after a plague, but in this story some of those infected live on as zombies. Matheson receives the credit for being the first work to use zombies or the living dead. This concept has been used ad infinitum by other authors and by filmmakers. The theme of Matheson's story grapples with social bias, and a topic of importance to science fiction fans: What is normal? Who defines normal?

In the late 1970s the third generation of science fiction writers began to emerge. They were influenced by the earlier authors and in some cases have worked with the earlier authors. The genre still discusses social attitudes, questions the use of technology, and incorporates cataclysmic events, but the technology begins to change. Stories begin to involve wormholes, chaos theory, string theory, bioengineering, and nanotechnology. Among this generation of authors are David Brin, Lois McMaster Bujold, Orson Scott Card, Michael Crichton, C. J. Cherryh, William C. Dietz, L. Ron Hubbard, Larry Niven, David Weber, and Anne McCaffrey.

Space operas enjoyed a new emergence and popularity with George Lucas's *Star Wars* saga. Space operas provide epic tales with romance and adventure in deep space. *Space Opera Renaissance*, edited by David Hartwell and Kathryn Cramer, provides a compilation of space opera stories. Other examples of space operas would be any of the many books of the *Star Trek: Deep Space Nine* collection or Alastair Reynolds' *Revelation Space* adventures.

When readers think of Michael Crichton, science fiction may not be the first thing that jumps to their mind, but several of his books definitely fit in the science fiction genre. His very first book, *The Andromeda Strain*, which also laid the groundwork for contemporary bio- and medical thrillers, portrays classic science fiction. It utilizes scientific principles, threatens dystopia, and questions government activities. *Jurassic Park* questions genetic engineering. *Timeline* looks at corporate greed and time travel, and in *Prey* he uses nanotechnology.

Science fiction readers know Larry Niven best for his Ringworld series, which incorporates heavy technology. Intelligent beings have created a flat planet that encircles a sun, but it is falling apart. Over the breadth of the series, the reader learns about the technology behind the system and culture that lives on the system. He has also written a humorous collection of short stories, *Draco Tavern*, about a galactic bar, and a militaristic series, Man-Kzin Wars, which pits humans against aliens.

Three popular contemporary female authors include Anne McCaffrey, Lois McMaster Bujold, and C. J. Cherryh. Anne McCaffrey is best known for her *Dragonriders of Pern* collection. Bujold writes both science fiction and fantasy. In science fiction, she is best known for her Vorkosigan series. Cherryh also writes in both fantasy and science fiction and bridges the two genres. She has built an elaborate world for her Alliance/Union Universe, and she is also known for her Faded Sun Trilogy and Foreigner series.

An area of science fiction not yet addressed concerns militaristic science fiction. This category features futuristic wars using spaceships rather than sailing ships, and battles fought by cyborgs, androids, and robots. These books tend to focus more on action and less on philosophy, exploring themes such as the appropriateness of war. Some militaristic science fiction includes Robert A. Heinlein's *Starship Troopers* and L. Ron Hubbard's *Battlefield Earth*. Some militaristic series include David Weber's Honor Harrington, William C. Dietz's The Legion, and Orson Scott Card's Ender's Game sequence of stories.

Not all science fiction uses violence or depicts apocalyptic stories. Some works actually use humor to argue for social change. Douglas Adams' Hitchhiker's Guide to the Galaxy series originally began as a BBC radio program and has morphed into many different formats. Other humorous science fiction authors include Robert Asprin's Phule series and Terry Pratchett's Bromeliad series.

David Brin is probably best known for his work *The Postman*, which was made into a movie starring Kevin Costner (1997). In addition to *The Postman*, he has written a group of six books, the Uplift Saga and the Uplift Trilogy, which share a common history. Brin exemplifies a recent phenomenon among authors with the embracing of interactive technology. Most authors have Web sites and fan sites, but more authors are actively involved in creating interactive Web sites with constant updates. Brin's Web site, www.davidbrin.com, provides a highly interactive approach to science fiction. He posts podcasts, updates, links to interesting online articles, and political commentary. He also has a Facebook page. These are all technologies that contemporary readers of science fiction have embraced.

Final Thoughts on Science Fiction Readers

Science fiction serves multiple purposes for the reader. First, sci-fi readers appreciate the genre's ability to raise thought-provoking issues that may be social, political, intellectual, or moral. They also like to examine "what if" situations, including time travel, aliens, and alternate histories/alternate endings, and engaging in opportunities for the willing suspension of disbelief. The theme of "other worlds" comprises an important element in science fiction, appealing to questions of "what if" and to the importance of imagination. Notions of unlimited possibilities and the exploration of the effects of science and technology also dominate among readers' preferences.

Science fiction is not limited to adults. Robert A. Heinlein's 13 juvenile novels formed the basis for many a youthful introduction to science fiction. Aficionados of this genre begin reading at an early age, as older children and young adults. They are prodigious readers with in-depth knowledge of science and technology, and they expect that the novels for adults will be equally engrossing as what they experienced as young readers. "Age appropriateness" is not a term typically applied to science fiction, as teens and adults find many of the same titles engaging and popular. For these readers, young and old, the appeal comes down to questioning and speculating the norms and the unintended consequences of actions.

Anthologies, magazines, and the Web provide good sources of short stories and information about the science fiction industry. For example the anthology *The Year's Best Science Fiction: Twenty-Fifth Annual Collection* (2008) provides a compilation of award-winning short stories written by new and existing authors for the year 2007. More importantly, the summation in the beginning of the book provides an update on the health of the science fiction industry, such as which publishers have been bought or gone out of business and the number of science fiction books published that year. The summation also provides the latest news on magazine publishers and their online counterparts.

Supporting Organizations, Associations, and Other Resources

Numerous organizations support the work of science fiction writers and the interests of sci-fi fans through publication and conventions. In fact, the conventions are highly popular events for serious science fiction aficionados, replete with costuming, characters, gaming, and toys to intrigue conventioneers. (Being a reader of mysteries and suspense, I was amazed the day that several of my staid, quiet students were overwhelmed by the thought that a Star Trek convention was being held in the same facility as our class meeting. I was even more amazed when they returned from lunch in Star Trek costuming they purchased at the convention and then rushed back to the convention after class adjourned for the day.) The granddaddy of science fiction conventions, Worldcon (www .anticipationsf.ca/English/Home; the site is also available in French) was first held in 1939 and has occurred annually since then. Much like conventions for the other genres, Worldcon hosts authors, special events, programming with multiple tracks of interest, and workshops. It draws thousands of attendees worldwide. Worldcon has accounts on numerous social networking sites, including Facebook, LiveJournal, and Twitter.

The British Science Fiction Association (BSFA; www.bsfa.co.uk/) is a group of authors, publishers, booksellers, and fans in Britain who encourage the creation and dissemination of science fiction in every form. The association sponsors annual awards for science fiction in the categories of "best novel," "best short fiction," "best artwork," and "best nonfiction." The short lists, nominees, and past awards are posted on their Web site. An equivalent European Science Fiction Society (www.esfs.info/index.html) for science fiction professionals and fans is dedicated to promotion science fiction in Europe and worldwide. ESFS also promotes fantasy and horror as part of the overarching umbrella of Science Fiction. Like BSFA, they also have a selection of annual awards and conventions. Both the United States and Canada also have their own associations. Science Fiction & Fantasy Writers of America (www.swfa.org) is open only to writers of published science fiction and fantasy. They sponsor the prestigious Nebula Awards for science fiction and fantasy. SF Canada is a similar organization, open only to published authors. The SF Canada Web site (www.sfcanada.ca) offers access to online articles and short stories as well as lists of members' books.

AN INTRODUCTION TO FANTASY

Fantasy fiction appeals to readers of all ages. Many fantasy titles fall in the young adult category. These include *The Hobbit, Chronicles of Narnia,* and the Harry Potter series, but adults enjoy reading them as well. In genre classification, fantasy titles are sometimes confused with science fiction and horror, and some titles slide between the various genres. For the purposes of this section, fantasy does not involve science (as does science fiction), and it is not intended to evoke fear in the reader (as does horror).

What does classify a story as fantasy? The story takes place in another world that does not necessarily follow the same rules as our reality. The story will involve magic, wizards, and witches. Animals can act like humans. Fantasy stories have enchantment and belong to the world of faerie. They may have elves, ogres, unicorns, gnomes, pixies, and faeries. Witches and warlocks battle with magic in fantasy, while mortals battle with swords and shields. The protagonist has limited powers and must grow more powerful or rely on allies in order to defeat a much stronger evil opponent. Fantasy pits good against evil. The main character appears naive at first and must grow morally through experiences. The reluctant protagonist must go on a quest to stop a momentous event that threatens society. The protagonist confronts an evil dangerous foe that will be difficult to overcome, but does so with an optimistic outlook regardless of the odds.

There is no one simple way to describe fantasy or the elements that appeal to readers. For some, fantasy involves magic and Merlin and dragons; for others it is the Arthurian tales of chivalry retold. But regardless of the subgenre, fantasy considers the quest at its heart as well as the battle between good and evil, with good achieving the ultimate victory. This theme of good being triumphant distinguishes fantasy from horror, where the possibility of evil continues. Finally, political intrigue (and even political opinion) is a frequent theme in fantasy novels. Fantasy, unlike science fiction, tells a continuous story, and this story is separated across novels within a series, following a single (or several closely related) themes.

Unlike science fiction, characters play an important role in fantasy fiction. Similarly to thrillers, characters are either good or evil; however, in fantasy the characters are much more multilayered, with underlying traits that will win in the end. The protagonists are much more complex in fantasy than some of the other genres, and the characters grow and change as they travel across the series, using their special powers of magic. These may be considered "coming of age" stories where the protagonist must make a spiritual voyage of discovery as well as a physical journey. Finally, characters in fantasy stories are not always human; they take many forms and guides, including that of animals, though exhibiting human behavior.

Historical Aspects and Trends

Classic Fantasy

The early works of fantasy occurred around the end of the nineteenth century. Two of the earliest authors of fantasy include L. Frank Baum and Mark Twain. Some may argue against classifying Twain's *A Connecticut Yankee in King Arthur's Court* as fantasy genre, but it fits into fantasy via nontechnological time travel, and it has an Arthurian theme. In Twain's story, Hank Morgan finds himself transported back to King Arthur's court from nineteenth-century New England. In L. Frank Baum's and W. W. Denslow's *The Wonderful Wizard of Oz*, a cyclone transports Dorothy to another land. In this new land she finds that rules of her reality no longer exist. The Land of Oz has munchkins, witches, wizards, and flying monkeys. It also has a Scarecrow, Tin Man, and Cowardly Lion that take on human characteristics. Dorothy is a naive, reluctant protagonist who only wants to get home, but must fight the wicked witch to succeed. (The Oz tales have spun off a series of adult fantasy novels by Gregory Maguire, including *Wicked: The Life and Times of the Wicked Witch of the West*.)

Classic Fantasy Authors Not to Be Missed

Marion Zimmer Bradley	J. R. R. Tolkien
Edgar Rice Burroughs	T. H. White

Middle Years

In the 1920s and 1930s fantasy fans would have been reading Lord Dunsany and J. R. R. Tolkien. *The Hobbit* and the *Lord of the Rings* trilogy were written and published after World War I and through World War II. The story takes place in a magical enchanted land (Middle Earth), and naive reluctant protagonists Bilbo and Frodo must save society. They find themselves befriended and aided by a strong wizard, Gandalf. J. R. R. Tolkien's stories have thrilled readers for more than 80 years. His trilogy experienced resurgence in popularity with the release of Peter Jackson's *Lord of the Rings* movie trilogy in 2001–2003. Edward Plunkett, aka Lord Dunsany, the eighteenth Baron of Dunsany, Ireland, was one of the earliest authors of fantasy. His most famous work is *The King of Elfland's Daughter*. This work was originally published in 1924, and republished in 1999. Neil Gaiman wrote the introduction for the 1999 version. Other authors in this time period are C. S. Lewis and T. H. White. In *The Chronicles of Narnia* Lewis writes seven books detailing the history of Narnia. Individuals from our world are transported to Narnia to help Prince Caspian and a talking lion, Anslan, save the lands of Narnia in times of conflict. The transport occurs magically through inanimate objects like a painting or a wardrobe. The story has nonhuman characters and magic. T. H. White, in *The Once and Future King*, revisits the realm of King Arthur, and includes the story of *The Sword and the Stone*.

In the 1970s the fantasy field began to grow. Andre Norton was crossing over from science fiction with her Witch World series. Richard Adams wrote *Watership Down*, which follows the adventures of a band of talking rabbits that have been displaced by a land development project. Mary Stewart penned the Merlin sequence of novels that looked at King Arthur's Court through the eyes of the wizard Merlin. Christopher Stasheff wrote several stories and series concerning reluctant protagonists who must save various kingdoms through the use of magic. He wrote *Her Majesty's Wizard*, which starts the A Wizard in Rhyme series. He also wrote the series The Warlock of Gramarye, which contains aspects of science fiction and fantasy.

Contemporary Fantasy

In the late 1980s and early 1990s, the fantasy genre blossomed with multiple and varied subgenres and themes. This corresponded with the advent of role-playing games such as Dungeons and Dragons. Authors such as Margaret Weiss and Tracy Hickman, Stephen Donaldson, Marion Zimmer Bradley, Ursula LeGuin, Terry Brooks, and David and Leigh Eddings created worlds of fantasy in epic proportions. Stephen Donaldson's protagonist Thomas Covenant finds himself in The Land, which is being destroyed by evil. He refuses to believe in this alternate reality. In his own reality Covenant suffers from leprosy, but in the alternate land he is healthy. His sliding back and forth challenges his reality. This epic fantasy is titled *The Chronicles of Thomas Covenant, the Unbeliever*. Marion Zimmer Bradley wrote and co-authored the Arthurian novels, starting *Mists of Avalon*. (She also wrote a science fiction series titled the Darkover series.)

This time frame saw the beginning of the fantasies even bigger and more elaborate in scope than *Lord of the Rings*. Authors began writing three-to-five-volume series that took place in a larger epic setting that might be comprised of several related series. Margaret Weiss and Tracy Hickman are some of the most prolific fantasy writers. They created the *Dragonlance Chronicle, The Death Gate Cycle, The Dragonlance Legends Trilogy*, and *The Sovereign Stone Trilogy* as well as many others, both together and individually. Ursula LeGuin penned The Earthsea Cycle series. David Eddings and Leigh Eddings authored multiple series such as Tamuli,

Belgardia, Elenium, Malloreon, and The Dreamers. All of these stories and series display the classic fantasy structure with a reluctant protagonist who must learn magic and/or seek the aid of wizards to save the world. The stories pit good versus evil, and even when things are darkest the characters remain optimistic.

Terry Brooks sets his stories in Shannara and tells the saga of the Ohmsford family. The Ohmsford heirs find themselves entwined in the history of Shannara, and fated to save the land whenever evil threatens. This epic story starts with the *Sword of Shannara Trilogy* and proceeds through several generations of Ohmsfords and their corresponding trilogies. In the current series, The Genesis of Shannara, and the previous series The Word and the Void Trilogy, Terry Brooks takes the reader back to the beginning when magic and technology fought for control—good versus evil.

Three more authors fit into this mold of genre fantasy. George R. R. Martin's A Song of Ice and Fire setting is based on medieval England and the War of the Roses. It includes supernatural creatures such as ice vampires and dire wolves. Robert Jordan's Wheel of Time series contains 11 books and is based on Nordic mythology. Twelve books were planned, but he died before the last book could be completed. Rumors say the final installment is scheduled to be out in 2009 and that it will be written by Brandon Sanderson using notes from Robert Jordan. (This rumor has not been confirmed.) Terry Goodkind's The Sword of Truth series contains about 11 novels that for the most part stand alone. However, these differ from most of the previous epics discussed because they need to be read in order of publication.

Not all fantasy involves epic sagas, nor do they all involve dire consequences should the protagonist fail to save the world. Robert Asprin provides comic relief in the fantasy genre with his MYTH Inc stories. Skeeve the bumbling magician finds himself leading a gang of misfit faerie-land characters that try to operate as a private investigation company. The ten stories in this collection are riddled with puns, and are a quick, fun read. Piers Anthony's Xanth novels involve a non-human protagonist, Bink. The Xanth stories contain interesting characters, and use puns. Terry Pratchett's Discworld books poke fun at just about everything, and are not concerned with formality. Jasper Fforde in the Thursday Next series also provides fun fantasy reading. Special Operative Thursday Next solves crimes of literary mystery by actually becoming entrenched in the literary story.

A current trend in fantasy fiction is the development of urban fantasy. Originally starting as an adjunct to horror, urban fantasy combines the supernatural with urban settings. Charles de Lint writes about urban fantasy in his North American make-believe town of Newford, where faerie meets modern day. He has several books in this collection, with *Onion Girl* being the first. Other authors currently identified with urban fantasy include Emma Bull, Neil Gaiman, and Mercedes Lackey. As with many of the other subgenres, urban fantasy contains significant genre blending, encompassing romance and mystery. Two popular series in which urban fantasy merges with mystery include Jim Butcher's Dresden Files (also made into a television program) and Charlaine Harris's Southern Vampire novels. These two series are as far apart on the spectrum as possible, but both combine elements of the supernatural (a wizard in Dresden Files; a telepathic cocktail waitress with a vampire for a boyfriend in Southern Vampires) with urban life (Chicago and small-town Louisiana).

Two of the more popular current authors are J. K. Rowling and Neil Gaiman. Rowling's young adult literary success, the Harry Potter series has proven to be a popular read with the young crowd as well as adults. The books are being turned into movies and video games. The Harry Potter series is also generating spin-offs, such as *The Tales of Beedle the Bard*, which are also highly popular. Neil Gaiman also enjoys popularity among adults and young adults. His stories tend toward stand-alone novels rather than epics. His works include *American Gods*; *Stardust*; *Coraline*; *M Is for Magic*; and *Graveyard Book*. In *Stardust*, Tristan Thorn crosses the wall between his town and the land of faerie in search of a fallen star in order to win the heart of his true love. Once he finds the star, he discovers it has turned into a beautiful young girl. In *American Gods*, the protagonist Shadow falls under the control of Wednesday, who turns out to be the Norse god Odin. Together they round up the remaining pagan gods who traveled to America with their immigrants only to be forgotten. *American Gods* is a satirical look at modern society.

Several other authors and series should be considered for other forms of genre blending and just plain popular fantasy reads (see Table 10-2). Brian Jacques' The Redwall series has no human characters, only animals that take on human characteristics. These books are not consecutive, and can be read in any order. Philip Pullman's *His Dark Materials* is comprised of three books, and his protagonists travel through different worlds with daemons as their cohorts. Pullman's *The Golden Compass* was released as a popular movie in 2007. Diane Gabaldon's The Outlander series provides a crossover between historical romance and fantasy; a new title in the series continuing the saga of Jamie and Claire Fraser was released late in 2009.

Final Thoughts on Fantasy Readers

Fantasy offers unique appeal to readers. As with science fiction, fantasy stories are filled with other worlds and characters that are believable; the reader becomes a part of the world and through the imagination lives the story. Characters in fantasy grow and mature through experience, allowing the reader to recognize the characters as human with the foibles, fears, and phobias common to all other humans. Fantasy is about finding one's place and celebrating both the joys and the sorrows of life. Ultimately the appeal of fantasy lies in its optimism for the future, offering the reader hope.

Readers have specific expectations about fantasy books. They expect to see densely written, thick books and long series. Much like mystery series readers,

Table 10-2: A Sampling of Popular Fantasy Authors and Series to Know		
Author	**Title/Series**	**Subgenre**
Piers Anthony	Xanth series	Humorous Fantasy
Anne Bishop	Black Jewels, Tir Alainn, Ephemera series	Dark Fantasy
Terry Brooks	Shannara series	Epic Fantasy
Steven Brust	Vlad Taltos series	Urban Fantasy
Lois McMaster Bujold	Cordelia Naismith, Miles Vorkosigan, Curse of Chalion, Sharing Knife series	Quest/Adventure Fantasy
Charles De Lint	Moonheart, Cerin Songweaver, Jack of Kinrowan, Newford series	Urban Fantasy
David & Leigh Eddings	Belgariad, Malloreon, Elenium, Tamuli, Dreamers	Epic Fantasy
Jasper Fforde	Thursday Next series	Humorous Fantasy
Neil Gaiman	*Anansi Boys, Coraline, Stardust, American Gods*	Urban Fantasy
Terry Goodkind	Sword of Truth series	Epic Fantasy
Laurell K. Hamilton	Anita Blake, Vampire Hunter	Dark Fantasy
Kim Harrison	Rachel Morgan series	Urban Fantasy
Robin Hobb	Farseer, Liveship Traders, Tawny Man, Soldier Son series	Quest/Adventure Fantasy
Robert Jordan	Wheel of Time series	Epic Fantasy
Guy Gavriel Kay	Fionavar Tapestry, Sarantine Mosaic series	Quest/Adventure Fantasy
Greg Keyes	Children of the Changeling, Age of Unreason, Kingdoms of Thorn and Bone series	Legends
Mercedes Lackey	Valdemar, Bedlam's Bard, Elemental Masters	Urban Fantasy
Steve Lawhead	Dragon King, Empyrion, Pendragon, Celtic Crusades series	Legends
Gregory Maguire	Hamlet Chronicles, Wicked Years series	Legends
George R. R. Martin	Song of Ice and Fire series	Epic Fantasy
Anne McCaffrey	Dragonriders of Pern series	Dragons
Dennis McKiernan	Mithgar series	Quest/Adventure Fantasy
Patricia McKillip	Quest of the Riddle-Master, Kyreol, Cygnet series	Legends
Rosalind Miles	Guenevere, Tristan and Isolde series	Legends
Terry Pratchett	Discworld	Humorous Fantasy
Mickey Zucker Reichert	Bifrost Guardians, Renshai, Legend of Nightfall, Books of Barakhai series	Quest/Adventure Fantasy
R. A. Salvatore	Chronicles of Ynis Aielle, Spearwielder's Tales, Crimson Shadow, Saga of the First King series	Quest/Adventure Fantasy

Author	Title/Series	Subgenre
Sharon Shinn	Samaria, Safe Keepers, Twelve Houses series	Quest/Adventure Fantasy
Margaret Weis	Death Gate, Dragonvarld, Dragonships of Vindras series	Dragons
Jack Whyte	Camulod, Templar Trilogy series	Legends
Tad Williams	Memory, Sorrow and Thorn, To Green Angel Tower, Otherland, Shadowmarch series	Epic Fantasy

Note: There are a number of excellent and comprehensive resources for finding Author/Title lists. Start with Saricks' *The Readers' Advisory Guide to Genre Fiction*, Herald's *Genreflecting: A Guide to Popular Reading Interests*, Herald and Kunzel's *Fluent in Fantasy*, or the Adult Reader's Round Table of Illinois' *ARRT Popular Fiction List*. Consult Appendix 1 for additional reference resources that may be of interest for finding more. And, of course, the commercial and online readers' advisory databases will provide additional read-alikes and related lists.

fantasy readers follow the characters across the series, and even across multiple series. Readers expect that good will triumph in the end and that the characters will somehow grow. They also expect to find highly developed worlds and landscapes. Fantasy asks readers to revisit the myths and tales that have been handed down across time, from tales of the Greek and Norse gods to the Arthurian legends, and build these myths and tales into the fabric of the fantasy world.

Genre blending, and even genre crossing, is a significant factor in the popularity of fantasy fiction. Writers cross easily among fantasy, horror, and science fiction. They also combine elements of historical fiction, mystery, romance, and certainly adventure with fantasy. Fantasy ranges from dark to humorous. Satire and parody are common elements. A contemporary theme, taking its lead from street fiction or urban fiction, considers urban fantasy with issues of drugs, gangs, racism, and other current social issues. Dark fantasy, the worlds of Laurell K. Hamilton for example, is linked to horror, but unlike horror the purpose is to explore good versus evil. Few limits exist in what might constitute a good tale of fantasy as long as it includes elements of magic and the conflict between good and evil.

Much like science fiction, anthologies are of particular importance to the fantasy genre. The anthologies showcase the broad range of types and styles of stories likely to appear in the fantasy literature. *The Year's Best Fantasy and Horror*, for example, offers a summation of the year in review, including the trends, emerging subgenres, and new authors. Anthologies will also include compilations of short stories and essays useful for discovering the breadth and depth of fantasy fiction. Collections by comparison are compilations of the works of an individual author, serving a similar purpose to anthologies. Appendix 1 identifies a small selection of anthologies and collections.

Supporting Organizations, Associations, and Other Resources

As with science fiction and mysteries, several organizations and associations support the interests of fans and writers alike. The British Fantasy Society (www .britishfantasysociety.org.uk/) was established in 1971 to meet the needs of both writer and fan. The society hosts the annual FantasyCon, an event similar to sci-fi's WorldCon, featuring speakers, authors, and events related to the writing, publishing, and reading of fantasy. The Society's Web site offers access to articles and short fiction as well as a Webzine with interviews, reviews, and articles. They also give an array of awards to fantasy authors, artists, and publishers, and they provide access to the list of "Best Novels 2000–2008" on their Web site.

A similar agency is the Mythopoeic Society (www.mythsoc.org), whose intention is to promote the study and discussion of fantasy and mythical literature. The California-based society sponsors publications, awards, and the annual Mythcon. Mythcon, however, is much smaller and more intimate than many of the science fiction conventions that attract thousands. Finally, a similar organization, World Fantasy Convention (www.worldfantasy.org), celebrates fantasy and horror with an annual convention with a unifying theme for panel discussions and events. Like the others, the World Fantasy Convention sponsors a number of awards for best novels, novellas, short stories, art, etc. The complete list of winners from 1975 to the present is available on the Web site.

AN INTRODUCTION TO HORROR

In the nonfiction work *Danse Macabre*, Stephen King discusses the history, scope, and pop culture of horror. While he does not like to define or categorize horror, for him the distinguishing factor of horror is the intent of the author to entertain and scare. When King writes, he wants to horrify, terrify, and/or gross out the reader. A story may contain all three of these aspects or only one depending on what it takes for the author to get the desired response from the reader.

In a talk at the American Library Association annual convention in Anaheim, CA (June 2008), Dean Koontz said that he dislikes being classified as an author of horror stories because his stories contain so much more. Indeed, many of his stories contain aspects of other genres. In *the Darkest Evening of the Year*, he has two nasty, villainous child molesters and a supernatural golden retriever. While the two antagonists in this story are incredibly, deeply evil, and the book has been classified as horror, the supernatural golden retriever provides aspects of fantasy. The book would also be a really good fit for the suspense/thriller genre. In Koontz's Odd Thomas series the protagonist, Odd Thomas, sees dead people and comes to their aid. The third segment of this series, *Brother Odd*, contains aspects of horror, science fiction, and a good dose of humor.

What is horror fiction then? At its simplest level, horror fiction intends to scare the reader. In *Danse Macabre*, King says that horror occurs at two levels. The first level consists of the obvious scare—the grossing out of the reader through vividly described torture and infliction of bodily harm in unexpected circumstances. The subtler scare reaches down into the reader's most primitive level and yanks at his or her darkest secrets. It grabs at the reader's phobias. The author must determine what that phobia is and how to best illicit a response from the reader. The horror author discusses social taboos, and brings to the forefront items that have been hidden away in the closet because they are too scary to discuss in the light of day. These phobias may manifest as monsters and things that go bump in the night.

Horror fiction authors have many tools to call on in scaring the reader. They may use natural or supernatural monsters—witches, ghosts, aliens, vampires, werewolves, and many other nonhuman creatures that threaten to devour you or your soul or steal your virginity. They may take ordinary creatures and turn them into giants. Authors have used giant spiders, snakes, and lizards just to name a few. Douglas Preston and Lincoln Child use a genetic mutation between a supernatural creature and a research scientist in *Relic*. The purpose is to play upon the fears, phobias, and anxieties of the reader regardless of the device.

Some of the characteristics of a good horror story include a sense of menace that is intended to provoke an emotional response and a dark and foreboding atmosphere. Horror authors often set their stories in an eerie, dark, and dank location, such as a crypt or a haunted castle. The setting could be an abandoned summer camp, a closed mine, or a ghost town. Soul-gripping horror stories tend toward graphic violence and sex and a high degree of graphic, profane language. The stories rarely boast a happy ending. The antagonist may be defeated, but it lives in the background waiting to grow strong again and can come back when you least expect it. (Think of the many incarnations of Jason in *Friday the Thirteenth* or Freddy in *Nightmare on Elm Street*).

The characters themselves in horror stories are unique. Frequently haunted and shattered, the protagonist is almost always susceptible or vulnerable in some way. The villain, on the other hand, is always seriously, wickedly evil. These stories are not the classic battles between good and evil, as occur in fantasy and science fiction. Point of view is critical in horror stories because it guides the reader's response. Unlike suspense/thrillers, however, the reader does not experience the protagonist's and antagonist's point of view, but only one or the other. This heightens the effect of the horror and ultimate surprise or twist.

Two distinct streams of horror stories exist: the storyteller horror and the visceral horror. In the storyteller horror anticipation and response builds slowly, drawing in the reader. Typically the menace builds over time in these stories, creating an atmosphere of foreboding and anticipation and playing on the normal, mundane world in which the reader lives. Among authors who best represent the storytelling aspects are Stephen King (*The Shining* is the benchmark for this subgenre), Dean Koontz, John Saul, and Peter Straub.

Visceral horror, by comparison, intends to shock and frighten from the onset of the story. Intense violence is introduced right from the beginning and never lets up. This will frequently include graphic sex (no love or romance here) and dark, profane, explicit language. The reader is intentionally disoriented from the start. Many authors writing in a visceral tone place the reader in worlds and environments that are unknown, altering perspective and presenting the reader with actions that are not part of the normal, everyday world. Like King does for the storytellers, Anne Rice sets the standard for the visceral horror with *Interview with the Vampire*. However, Clive Barker and Brian Lumley are also masters of the blood-curdling chill.

Historical Aspects and Trends

Classic Horror Stories

Horace Walpole wrote one of the earliest works of gothic horror, *The Castle of Otranto*, in 1764. It is not a very memorable story except for its claim to being the first of its kind and for introducing aspects that provide a foundation for the genre. A talisman, a giant helmet, falls out of the sky, killing Conrad, the prince of the castle, on his wedding day. The lord of the castle, Manfred, divorces the queen and seeks to wed the widowed bride-to-be Isabelle. A series of supernatural events hinder the wedding.

The next addition to the horror genre, Mary Shelley' *Frankenstein: Or, the Modern Prometheus*, written in 1818, tells the tale of Dr. Frankenstein and his creation of life. This novel contains both aspects of science fiction and horror. It uses technology to create life and horror to exploit it. This is a theme that has occurred many times since, including Michael Crichton's *Jurassic Park* and Dean Koontz's *Brother Odd*.

Edgar Allan Poe in the early to mid-1800s became well-known for his short stories of the macabre. His short story "The Fall of the House of Usher" introduces the psychological horror story. He revisits the psychological horror story with "The Tell-Tale Heart". In "The Fall of the House of Usher" the protagonist's demise occurs because of his own mental failings and anxieties. The protagonist/narrator in "The Tell-Tale Heart "is the killer. He dismembers the body and buries the heart below the floorboards, but it continues to beat in his mind.

Toward the end of the 1800s, a trio of horror stories were published that continue to entrance readers and provide the scaffolding for contemporary horror: Robert Louis Stevenson's *The Strange Case of Dr. Jekyll and Mr. Hyde*; Bram Stoker's *Dracula*; and Henry James' *The Turn of the Screw*. In *The Strange Case of Dr. Jekyll and Mr. Hyde*, once again the story deals with internal horror. The good doctor must deal with his desires for societal taboos. Two horror themes are introduced at this point. Henry James introduces one of the first ghost stories, and Bram

Classic Horror Authors Not to Be Missed

Robert Bloch	H. P. Lovecraft
Ray Bradbury	Richard Matheson
Emily Brontë (*Wuthering Heights*)	Robert R. McCammon
Daphne Du Maurier (*Rebecca*)	Edgar Allan Poe
Charles Grant	Mary Shelley
Nathaniel Hawthorne (*The House of the Seven Gables*)	Bram Stoker
	Whitley Strieber
Shirley Jackson	Oscar Wilde (*The Picture of Dorian Gray*)
Henry James	

Stoker sets the groundwork for vampire stories, leading eventually to the stories of Stephen King, Dean Koontz, and Anne Rice among others.

Contemporary Horror

The next generation of horror story authors includes H. P. Lovecraft, Ray Bradbury, Robert Bloch, Shirley Jackson, and Ira Levin. Although they wrote a number of books across the horror, science fiction, and fantasy genres, only those stories that best represent horror will be considered. H. P. Lovecraft's work borders on the extremely strange. Two works to check out are *The Dunwich Horror and Others* and *At the Mountains of Madness and Other Macabre Tales.* Ray Bradbury's *Something Wicked This Way Comes, October Country,* and *Illustrated Man* provide interesting, weird, and scary tales. Robert Bloch wrote *Psycho,* another psychological horror story. Alfred Hitchcock popularized this story with a Hollywood adaptation in 1960 (and as the story goes Janet Leigh was unable to use a shower after starring in the film). Shirley Jackson's writings in addition to being tales of horror also show the 1960s influence and contain social commentary. Her best-known stories are *The Lottery and Other Short Stories, We Have Always Lived in the Castle,* and *The Haunting of Hill House* (also a film adaptation titled *The Haunting* in 1963). Ira Levin wrote *Rosemary's Baby,* which is about demonic possession. William Peter Blatty also wrote about demonic possession in his book *The Exorcist.* And like many of the other horror novels, Levin's and Blatty's novels were adapted for the box office, with great success.

The 1970s and 1980s saw an increase in the popularity of horror. Many of those authors are still popular today and going strong. They include Stephen King, Peter Straub, Dean Koontz, Anne Rice, and Clive Barker. Stephen King's works probably cover most of the subgenres of horror except romantic horror. He features vampires, the horror from without, and the horror from within. He has used aliens, psychological horror, haunted houses, haunted cars, psychic powers, demonic possession, and zombies. His works include *Salem's Lot, It, The Shining, The Tommyknockers, Christine, The Stand, Firestarter, Pet Sematary,* and *Duma*

Key. This only begins to list King's works. Peter Straub and Stephen King worked on a pair of books, *The Talisman* and *Black House.* In *The Talisman,* 12-year-old Jack Sawyer travels between parallel worlds to find a magical device to save his mother's life. *Black House* is the sequel, and this time Jack is a 30-year-old retired detective. He travels between worlds to save a child and stop the Crimson King from destroying both worlds. The main distinction that keeps these two books in horror rather than fantasy is the authors' intent to create terror in the reader. Both of these authors are masters of creating terror. Peter Straub also wrote *Ghost Story* and *Shadowland,* both of which are very scary and highly complex reads.

Dean Koontz's stories genre blend easily. He is generally classified as horror, but his stories could just as easily be suspense/thriller. Unlike Stephen King and Peter Straub, he does not intend to provide the reader with nightmares, but oftentimes he does. His works include *Phantom, Intensity,* and *Watchers.* He also has the humorous Odd Thomas series in which the protagonist Odd Thomas sees the dead. Koontz contributes to a Frankenstein series with various authors, including Kevin J. Anderson and Ed Gorman. Interestingly, Koontz also writes under close to a dozen pseudonyms.

Other popular authors include Anne Rice, Clive Barker, and John Updike (see Table 10-3 for a sampling of authors and titles). Anne Rice wrote the Vampire Chronicles from 1976 to 2003, a collection of vampire stories beginning with *Interview with the Vampire.* These volumes are extremely popular with vampire fans. Her books tend to discuss sexual and bisexual content. She has since returned to Catholicism and only writes Christian works today. In *The Witches of Eastwick,* John Updike looks at witches living in 1960s suburbia, rounding out the story with demonic possession and graphic sex. Clive Barker's works delve into parallel worlds and sensual pleasures/pain. His works could be construed as fantasy, if not for the pure evil of his characters. His works include *Mister B. Gone, The Hellbound Heart,* and *Clive Barker's Books of Blood 1–3.* Laurell K. Hamilton also writes a vampire series called Anita Blake, Vampire Hunter. This series also possesses elements of horror, fantasy, romance, and adventure.

Final Thoughts on Horror Readers

Readers enjoy horror stories for the pure chills and fright they induce. They expect to be drawn into a dark and frightening atmosphere that moves quickly. Horror stories are our individual nightmares come alive, allowing us to face down personal monsters in a safe environment (huddled under the covers of our beds). Whether it is grisly descriptions of horrific events, manifestations of evil in the form of vampires or demons, or deeply psychological mind games, horror stories allow the reader to explore the dark side of human nature.

Authors use many devices in horror fiction to create stories of unforgettable fear. These devices lend themselves to a variety of subgenres, ranging from

Table 10-3: A Sampling of Tales to Horrify Your Readers		
Author	**Title/Series**	**Subgenre**
Kingsley Amis	*The Green Man*	Modern Classic Horror
Kelley Armstrong	Women of the Otherworld, Nadia Stafford, Darkest Powers	Occult and Supernatural
Clive Barker	*Coldheart Canyon, Mister B. Gone, Galilee*	Occult and Supernatural
William Peter Blatty	*The Exorcist*	Occult and Supernatural
Ramsey Campbell	*The Darkest Part of the Woods, The Overnight, Secret Story, The Grin of the Dark, Thieving Fear*	Occult and Supernatural
Simon Clark	*Blood Crazy, Darkness Demands, Darker*	Monsters
Douglas Clegg	Harrow Academy, Vampyricon Trilogy, Mordred Trilogy	Occult and Supernatural
Nancy A. Collins	Sonja Blue series	Monsters and Vampires
Tananarive Due	My Soul to Keep series	Occult and Supernatural
John Farris	*Elvisland, Phantom Nights, You Don't Scare Me, High Bloods*	Occult and Supernatural
Laurell K. Hamilton	Anita Blake, Vampire Hunter series	Occult and Supernatural
Charlaine Harris	Southern Vampire series	Occult and Supernatural
Thomas Harris	*Silence of the Lambs, Hannibal*	Psychological Horror
Tom Holland	The Lord of the Dead series	Monsters and Vampires
Stephen King	*Salem's Lot, Carrie, Bag of Bones, The Cell, Insomnia, It, Pet Sematary, Lisey's Story, Just After Sunset, etc.*	Occult and Supernatural, Techno-Horror and More
Dean Koontz	*Demon Seed, Dragon's Tears, Hideaway, Watchers, Your Heart Belongs to Me*	Psychological Horror and More
Bentley Little	*Dispatch, The Burning, The Vanishing, The Academy*	Occult and Supernatural
Brian Lumley	Necroscope series	Occult and Supernatural
Barbara Michaels	*Other Worlds, Ammie, Come Home*	Ghosts and Hauntings
Kim Newman	The Anno Dracula series	Vampires
Joyce Carol Oates	*Zombie*	Psychological Horror
Douglas Preston and Lincoln Child	*Relic*	Monsters
Anne Rice	Vampire Chronicles, *The Mayfair Witches*	Occult and Supernatural
John Saul	*Black Creek Crossing, The Manhattan Hunt Club, Midnight Voices*	Occult and Supernatural, Psychological Horror
Dan Simmons	*Carrion Comfort, Children of the Night, A Winter Haunting, The Terror*	Occult and Supernatural, Haunted Houses

(continued)

Table 10-3: A Sampling of Tales to Horrify Your Readers *(continued)*		
Author	Title/Series	Subgenre
Peter Straub	*Ghost Story, The Blue Rose Trilogy, Shadowland, In the Night Room*	Ghosts, Occult, and Supernatural
Chelsea Quinn Yarbro	Saint-Germain series	Monsters
Note: There are a number of excellent and comprehensive resources for finding Author/Title lists. Start with Saricks' *The Readers' Advisory Guide to Genre Fiction*, Herald's *Genreflecting: A Guide to Popular Reading Interests*, or the Adult Reader's Round Table of Illinois' *ARRT Popular Fiction List*. Consult Appendix 1 for additional reference resources that may be of interest for finding more. And, of course, the commercial and online readers' advisory databases will provide additional read-alikes and related lists.		

gothic horror to the apocalypse. Horror contains a fair amount of genre blending, combining elements of dark fantasy, psychological thrillers, and romance. As long as the reader likes evil twists and not a little gore, a broad range of titles is available, sure to gross and engross. Horror readers also tend to be very willing to cross over into other genres, such as vampire romances and medical or scientific thrillers.

Much like science fiction and fantasy, horror fiction appeals to teens and young adults. In fact, they flock to the box office for screenings of *Friday the Thirteenth* and *Nightmare on Elm Street*. They also read many of the same authors that the adult readers enjoy, from Stephen King to V. C. Andrews. Many horror stories feature young protagonists battling evil, and these protagonists appeal to young readers. They also enjoy the dark humor presented in many of the horror stories.

Supporting Organizations, Associations, and Other Resources

Not surprisingly, conventions exist for horror aficionados as well as magazines, anthologies, and collections. The World Horror Society (www.worldhorrorsociety .org) is international in participation, representing authors, publishers, critics, and fans of horror. They sponsor an annual convention, World Horror Convention (www.worldhorrorconvention.com), similar in nature and intent to those for science fiction and fantasy. Held each spring, the convention is billed as a weekend to celebrate "All Things Scary."

The Horror Writers Association (HWA) (www.horror.org) is geared specifically to horror writers. Features of the Web site include tips for writers, lists of new releases, and information about publishing in the horror genre. The association sponsors the annual Bram Stoker Awards for outstanding horror writing. They also present an HWA Librarian of the Year Award to a librarian who has done an outstanding job of promoting reading within the horror genres.

Anthologies and collections of short stories are crucial to examining the range and depth of the genre. This is especially helpful for readers' advisors who may not read the genre; anthologies and collections provide excellent introductions. Two particularly useful titles include *The Year's Best Fantasy and Horror* and *The Mammoth Book of Best New Horror.* Both are published annually and include the year's best in short stories as well as summaries of the industry specifics. One of the positive features of anthologies and collections is that they never go out of style and even older editions remain in constant demand and circulation.

CONCLUSION

Combined, these three genres are incredibly popular among readers. They test the boundaries of our willingness to believe. Not only are they generally popular, but science fiction, fantasy, and horror appeal to a broad range of readers from preteens and teens to older adults. The genres have been the subject of in-depth study and critical analysis, and an array of guides, encyclopedias, and bibliographies exist to further explore and understand the nature of each genre. Because the genres embrace science and technology, authors and fans are great users of technological innovation. Online resources, social networks, and online groups abound and make excellent resources to consult for current information. Be sure to check resources such as Facebook, MySpace, LiveJournal, Ning, and Twitter for genre-related book clubs and discussion groups.

WORKS CONSULTED

Datlow, Ellen, Kelly Link, and Gavin J. Grant. 2008. *The Year's Best Fantasy & Horror: 2008,* 21st edition. New York: St. Martin's Griffin.

Dozois, Gardner, ed. 2008. *The Year's Best Science Fiction: Twenty-Fifth Annual Collection.* New York: St. Martin's Griffin.

Finding the Future: A Science Fiction Conversation. 2006. DVD. Directed by Casey Moore. Phoenix, AZ: Anomalous Entertainment.

Fonesca, Anthony J., and June Michele Pulliam. 2003. *Hooked on Horror: A Guide to Reading Interests in Horror Fiction.* Englewood, CO: Libraries Unlimited.

Gelder, Ken. 2004. *Popular Fiction: The Logics and Practices of a Literary Field.* London: Routledge.

Herald, Diana Trixler. 2006. *Genreflecting: A Guide to Popular Reading Interests,* edited by Wayne A. Wiegand. Westport, CT: Libraries Unlimited.

_____, and Bonnie Kunzel. 2008. *Fluent in Fantasy: The Next Generation.* Genreflecting Advisory Series. Westport, CT: Libraries Unlimited.

King, Stephen. 1981. *Danse Macabre.* New York: Berkley Books.

Saricks, Joyce G. 2001. *The Readers' Advisory Guide to Genre Fiction.* Chicago: American Library Association.

FURTHER READING

Burcher, Charlotte, Neil Hollands, Andrew Smith, Barry Trott, and Jessica Zellers. 2009. "Core Collections in Genre Studies: Fantasy Fiction 101." *Reference & User Services Quarterly* 48, no. 3 (Spring): 226–231.

Connors, Scott. 2008. "The Politics of Military SF." *Publishers Weekly* 254, no. 22 (April 7): 34–35.

Crawford, Philip Charles. 2008. "A New Era of Gothic Horror." *School Library Journal* 54, no. 10 (October): 32–33.

Donohue, Nanette Wargo. 2008. "The City Fantastic." *Library Journal* 133, no. 10 (June 1): 64–67.

Freitas, Donna. 2008. "The Next Dead Thing." *Publishers Weekly* 255, no. 46 (November 17): 23–24.

Richards, Michael. 2006. "Bring Out Your Undead: The Children of Lestat." *Publishers Weekly* 253, no. 23 (June 5): 22–24.

Wyatt, Neal. 2007. "Dark and Stormy Reads: The Pleasure of Gothic Novels." *Library Journal* 132, no. 5 (March 15): 105.

Chapter 11

Romance, Historical Fiction, and Westerns

Stephanie L. Maatta and Bruce G. Smith

Has not romance been penned with history in view?

—Arsène Houssaye, 1815–1896

It may seem strange to combine Romance, Historical Fiction, and Westerns in a single chapter. Yet at the heart, these three genres are closely aligned. Romance makes strong use of historical settings while history is filled with romance. Likewise, many a Western story includes strong elements of romance, and certainly when we look to traditional Westerns set against the Great Plains and the Rocky Mountains we are also experiencing a tremendous sense of history.

AN INTRODUCTION TO ROMANCE FICTION

In literary terms, "romance" refers to "a fictional story in verse or prose that relates improbable adventures of idealized characters in some remote or enchanted setting" (Baldick, 2008: 291). According to this definition the works of Sir Thomas Malory (*Le Morte D'Arthur*), Sir Philip Sidney (*Arcadia*) and Edmund Spenser (*The Faerie Queene*) can all be described as romances, involving elements of chivalry, fantasy, and magic. This same definition could also be applied to many of the contemporary genres (e.g., science fiction, horror, fantasy, and mystery), especially when they use illusion and enchantment to provide momentum for the story.

However, romance has come to mean something different in contemporary genre fiction. While its harshest critics label it "trash," romance fiction is defined by two elements: a central love story, which is the main focus of the work, and an optimistic ending—a sense of hope for the future (Romance Writers of America [RWA], 2008). Other genres may include romantic relationships in their stories as subplots, but it is the love story that is the central focus of the romance. A romance is a story of two individuals finding each other, falling in love, struggling to make the relationship work despite difficult odds, and ultimately triumphing—the fairy-tale ending.

On the whole, women read romance fiction. This does not mean that men don't read romance fiction; they are just less likely to. Romance fiction appeals to women in very particular ways. First, and perhaps foremost, romance appeals to the emotions. Readers respond to the characters—both heroine and hero— and become emotionally involved with the fantasy lives being played out on the page. (Women's fiction and chick lit, which will be discussed in Chapter 12, have a similar effect on the reader.) Romance readers invest pieces of themselves in the story, recognizing a personal fantasy or struggle within the details and responding to it. Romance readers participate vicariously in the unfolding story. The story gives the reader permission to laugh and cry with the heroine and to become a part of the tale.

Romance is also about empowerment—finding oneself and discovering the depths of honor and courage, intelligence and determination that dwell within the female soul. The lead character in romance fiction is a woman, generally an emotionally strong woman. She is imbued with the power to bring down the male, not to damage or emasculate him but to make him whole. It also showcases the struggles of finding independence and success through one's own efforts. More importantly, the discovery of honor and courage and many other admirable traits are reflected in the relationship between heroine and hero, who find the best of themselves mirrored in the other.

Readers find pleasure in the predictable nature of romances. They can count on the happy ending. It is the interaction of characters and ensuing process of resolution that makes each romance different and engaging. Despite the inherent formulaic approach of romances, every romantic relationship has its own unique way of entwining the characters, facing and confronting obstacles, and finding the fairy tale. The unique qualities of the individual story are part of the reason romance readers return time and again to these types of stories.

Story lines and plotting are secondary to the developing love relationship. But it is the story line that makes each tale unique. Like other genres, romance does have significant crossover between mystery, adventure, even science fiction and fantasy. These other genre elements add interest and provide a way for the romance to unfold, allowing romance to appeal to a broader range of readers. Many of these genres and story lines bring in other elements that enlighten or educate, revolving around such disparate topics as paleontology, gems, or antiques. At the heart, however, is the courtship and winning of love between the heroine and hero.

Important to the genre is the range of historical settings that are used as the backdrop for the story. Like the other genres, history adds an interest of time and place to the story. Regency romances and other historical romances must be accurate in time, place, and events. History also provides a way to engage in social commentary about the role of women and their efforts to improve their lot in life. Starting with the earliest romances, social issues have been a strong underlying theme, including those of alcoholism, domestic abuse and violence, and birth control.

Romance stories are all about the style of language. The reader must be drawn into the story in order for the romance to be effective. These are carefully crafted stories that use highly descriptive language that intends to evoke visual and visceral responses. The reader needs to feel the action and respond to it with emotions, sighing with the first kiss, cheering on the heroine as she fights for her place and her man. Language sets the tone and the pacing, and it must also accurately reflect the time and place of the setting. (Contemporary slang has no place in a historical novel set in the nineteenth century.)

Romance fiction has enjoyed a long and illustrious history. It has been instrumental in the firm establishment of other genres, including historical fiction. Among the genres romance has retained its continued popularity through genre blending and by evolving with cultural and societal changes to reflect the interests and lifestyles of the readers. Today romance fiction comprises almost 40 percent of the market share compared to all of the other genres. It is a multi-billion-dollar industry, generating approximately $1.375 billion in sales and publishing almost 8,100 romance titles annually. According to the Romance Writers of America, more than 64.5 million Americans read at least one romance novel in the past year (RWA, 2008). This is not an insignificant population, and many of these readers obtain their books through their public library.

Historical Aspects and Trends

Love stories have a very long history, receding thousands of years to Greek mythology and poetry (poems of Sappho, for example, exalting love and suffering unrequited love). Love relationships are threaded throughout biblical stories, including the Song of David and Samson and Delilah. Love and other similar relationships appear in the works of Shakespeare and his contemporaries. However, the focus of these early tales was uniquely different from contemporary romances; while including elements of amorous relationships, they focused on adventure and war or other elements of the story rather than the love relationship.

The real foundation of contemporary romance is generally attributed to Samuel Richardson's *Pamela: Or Virtue Rewarded* (written in 1740), which details the story of a servant girl who preserves her virtue (virginity) from the cajoling of the master of the house to end up marrying him and having a happy life of luxury, as opposed to Richardson's equally popular *Clarissa Harlowe* (1747), whose protagonist succumbs to temptation and in the end dies. (An underlying current of eighteenth-century morality of reward and punishment for one's behavior exists here.) A number of similar novels appeared around the same time, giving birth not only to the romance novel but to the beginnings of popular reading in general and its controversies over value and morality. During this time period, the rise of Gothic novels, including the work of Horace Walpole (*The Caste of Otranto*) and Ann Radcliffe (*The Mysteries of Udolpho*), occurred. This provided another thread in the evolution of romance fiction: Gothic romances, leading to the work of the Brontë sisters (*Wuthering Heights* and *Jane Eyre*) and many others, including Victoria Holt and her *Mistress of Mellyn* and *Bride of Pendorric*.

Historical romances and sentimental romance were among the earliest forms of modern romances, combining elements of the Gothic, adventures, and even religion. But the unifying theme of all of these early romances was the focus on the romantic, often sentimental relationship between women and men. Today's romance structure and language was established in these novels. Interestingly, many of these same Gothic and sentimental novels laid the foundation for other contemporary genres as well (Walpole for gothic horror, Austen and the Brontë sisters for women's fiction, Alexandre Dumas for adventure and suspense).

A Sampling of Early Romance Classics to Know

Jane Austen, *Sense and Sensibility, Pride and Prejudice*, and others
Charlotte Brontë, *Jane Eyre*
Emily Brontë, *Wuthering Heights*
Alexandre Dumas, *The Three Musketeers, The Count of Monte Cristo*
Caroline Lee Hentz, *Linda: Or the Young Pilot of the Belle Creole, The Planter's Northern Bride*
Ann Radcliffe, *The Mysteries of Udolpho*
Samuel Richardson, *Pamela: Or Virtue Rewarded*
E.D.E.N. Southworth, *The Hidden Hand*
Horace Walpole, *The Castle of Otranto* (also horror genre)

At the start of the twentieth century, many of the romantic subgenres emerged to become established in the romantic canon. Historic romance reestablished its popularity, especially those set in more romantic times and places (*Gone with the Wind* by Margaret Mitchell, for example, or *Forever Amber* by Kathleen Winsor); romantic sagas stretching across multivolume works became a norm. The Gothic romance fully emerged with *Rebecca* by Daphne Du Maurier, who led the way for Victoria Holt, Barbara Michaels, and Phyllis Whitney. During this same time many of the contemporary romance publishers were beginning to establish themselves firmly in the romance marketplace, including Mills and Boon (Great Britain) and Harlequin (Canada). (Mills and Boon merged with Harlequin in 1971, forming Harlequin Mills & Boon Enterprises; HMB is now the world's leading publisher of romance fiction.)

Other significant moments in the history of romance novels included a surge in popularity of the saga romance and in gay romance in the 1960s and 1970s. This was quickly followed by a resurgence of historical romances, including the sensual, hot historicals of Kathleen Woodiwiss (*The Flame and the Flower, The Wolf and the Dove*) and Rosemary Rogers (*Sweet Savage Love*). This also triggered new interest in nonromance historical fiction. Light, gentle romances published by Harlequin, Dell, and Silhouette continued to be and still are popular, publishing typically contemporary stories rather than ones with historical settings and themes. (Harlequin does have a series of historical romances, Harlequin Historicals, as does their imprint Steeple Hill.)

Contemporary romance has undergone more changes. Female protagonists have careers; they are highly independent; and sexuality and sensuality are common. These novels reflect current society in attitude and action (see Table 11-1 for a sampling of authors and titles). The works of Jennifer Crusie (*Fast Women, Bet Me*), Susan Elizabeth Phillips (*Natural Born Charmer, What I Did for Love*) and Nora Roberts (*Gabriel's Angel, First Impressions*) fall among some of the most popular of the contemporary romances, often combining a touch of humor with the struggle to find love. A range of ethnic and multicultural romances have appeared in recent years, again reflecting contemporary trends, becoming more inclusive and attentive to the needs of women, including Donna Hill (*Sex and Lies*) and Sandra Kitt (*The Color of Love, Celluloid Endings*).

Contemporary romance has experienced significant genre blending, especially between contemporary romance, women's fiction, and general popular fiction. Combining romance with mystery, science fiction, and fantasy occurs commonly in today's romance fiction. (Interestingly, RWA reports 48 percent of romance readers enjoy mystery, thriller, and action plots entwined with the romance; 2005 Market Research Study.) Paranormal romance combines romance with suspense and speculative fiction. Unique twists are added to the stories with these elements of mystery and psychic abilities, and a few ghost stories (Nora Roberts' *Key Trilogy*, J. D. Robb's Eve Dallas series, for example). Historical romance (Elizabeth Chadwick's medieval tales or Stephanie Lauren's Regency romances) and sagas, especially with American settings (e.g., Diana Gabaldon's Outlander series), are highly popular and appeal to a larger segment of the population besides romance readers.

Final Thoughts on Romance Readers

Romance appeals to the emotions. Readers invest themselves emotionally in the lives of the protagonists, and they expect a satisfactory outcome for the lovers

Table 11-1: A Sampling of Romance Authors and Titles to Know		
Author	Title	Subgenre
Susan Andersen	*All Shook Up, Just for Kicks, Coming Undone*	Contemporary
Suzanne Brockmann	Troubleshooter series	Romantic Suspense
Sandra Brown	*Chill Factor, Ricochet, Smoke Screen*	Romantic Suspense
Jennifer Crusie	*Bet Me*	Contemporary
Christine Feehan	Dark series, GhostWalkers series, Drake Sisters	Paranormal Romance
Diana Gabaldon	*The Outlander*	Paranormal Time Travel
Julie Garwood	Crown's Spies, Highlands' Lairds series	Historical
Rachel Gibson	*See Jane Score, Tangled Up in Love, Not Another Bad Date*	Contemporary
Jennifer Greene	*Blame It on Cupid*	Contemporary
Candice Herne	*A Garden Folly*	Regency
Georgette Heyer	*The Grand Sophy*	Regency
Linda Howard	*Up Close and Dangerous, Death Angel, Burn*	Romantic Suspense
Madeline Hunter	*Lessons of Desire*	RITA Award Winner
Carla Kelly	*Mrs. Drew Plays Her Hand*	Regency
Sherrilyn Kenyon	Dark-Hunter series	Paranormal Romance
Jayne Ann Krentz	Arcane Society series (writing as Amanda Quick)	Paranormal Romance
Allison Lane	*The Rake's Rainbow*	Regency
Stephanie Laurens	*The Taste of Innocence, Where the Heart Leads, Temptation and Surrender*	Historical
Elizabeth Lowell	*Always Time to Die, The Wrong Hostage, Blue Smoke and Murder*	Romantic Suspense
Debbie Macomber	*Twenty Wishes*	Contemporary
Judith McNaught	*Almost Heaven*	Historical
Barbara Metzger	*A Debt to Delia*	Regency
Constance O'Day-Flannery	*Best Laid Plans, Old Friends*	Paranormal Romance
Robin D. Owens	Celta series	Paranormal Romance
Susan Elizabeth Phillips	*Ain't She Sweet, Natural Born Charmer, What I Did for Love*	Contemporary
Mary Jo Putney	Bride Trilogy, *Loving a Lost Lord*	Historical
Julia Quinn	Bridgerton series: *The Duke and I, Two Dukes of Wyndham, What Happens in London*	Historical
Evelyn Richardson	*Lady Alex's Gamble*	Regency
Nora Roberts	*Born in Fire*	Contemporary

Author	Title	Subgenre
Robin Schone	*Scandalous Lovers*	Historical Erotic
Linnea Sinclair	Gabriel's Ghost series	Paranormal Romance
Bertrice Small	Skye O'Malley Saga, Border Chronicles, *The Shadow Queen*	Historical Erotic
Anne Stewart	*Ice Blue*	Romantic Suspense
J. R. Ward	*Lover Revealed*	RITA Award
Susan Wiggs	*The Lightkeeper, At the King's Command:* Tudor Rose Trilogy	Historical

Note: Author/Title list was compiled from Adult Reader's Round Table of Illinois' *ARRT Popular Fiction List*, Fantastic Fiction, Romance Writers of America Web site, and numerous articles on Romance fiction. Consult Appendix 1 for additional reference resources that may be of interest for finding more. And, of course, the commercial and online readers' advisory databases will provide additional read-alikes and related lists.

(specifically the happy ending). Romance also holds other appeals for the reader, including the upholding of positive story lines (love wins the day; empowerment), the belief in the woman as a strong and capable person, and predictability. The reader knows how the story will end; it's the path to the ending that changes with each story and each character.

Much like science fiction and fantasy, the reader can judge the content of romance novels by the cover. Walk through the romance section of your local bookstore and it is easy to identify the elements of the individual stories and even the focus of specific authors. Historically speaking, the covers of the "bodice rippers" suggested a certain level of steamy reading (couples in seemingly impossible positions and barely dressed, bodice often ripped open), inducing readers to either hide their books from view or hesitate about purchasing them at all; some readers did not want to announce that they enjoyed "trash" or were scintillated by the racy stories. Yet, the clench covers, as they are called by the publishing industry, tell the reader what they can expect from the novel: the novel will be predictable in its happy ending and provocative in its content and, depending upon the style of dress (or undress), set in a particular historical setting.

Many publishers began experimenting with covers to determine if they could achieve the same effect of knowing without telling all. Some of the new styles include "real estate" covers with evocative scenes (castles in the mist, mansions), and perhaps a discreet inset of the couple locked in an embrace. What might be called "trinket" covers with items representing the story (Scottish plaids, boxes of gems or jewelry, horse and carriage) present visual illustrations about the story without the sexual overtones of the clench. Many romance covers include blooming flowers, especially roses, suggesting the blooming of love and passion without revealing the more sensuous nature of the story. Even contemporary romance novels have distinctive covers with caricature drawings of women, light breezy colors (pale yellow, pinks, aqua), and titles set in stylish script. The covers of romances truly serve as advertisements for the book's content; what you see is what you get.

For romance readers, size matters. The length of the novel is an important decision when appealing to mood. Does the reader want a quick, fast-paced read, or will a deep, historical novel satisfy? Length tends to indicate the level of detail the reader can expect, such as the slow unraveling of the love story with multilayered conflict and struggle and perhaps a historical or social lesson. Harlequins and Silhouettes, for example, tend toward quick snapshot stories; the action takes place quickly with the struggle between male and female reaching a fast climax and resolution. Gabaldon's *Outlander* and *Dragonfly in Amber*, on the other hand, are a slow unfolding of the struggle with a richly detailed historical backdrop that confounds the lovers.

Finally, the romance novel follows one of two distinct formats. Short series romances (also known as category romances) come in monthly releases and they are numbered. For example, the Harlequin Presents or the Silhouette Desire series feature glamorous settings and passionate wealthy men who are brought to their knees by young, beautiful women. These novels frequently include a secret liaison and hidden passion, maybe an unexpected pregnancy. Single-title romances, on the other hand, are longer novels released individually and not as part of numbered series. Many of the single-title romances lend themselves to series, more specifically historical sagas, but they tend to stand alone as individual novels.

Series or Saga?

A series is a group of separately published works related in subject, such J. K. Rowling's Harry Potter series or Harlequin Presents with regularly released editions. In the case of Harlequin, they are published monthly.

Saga comes from the Norse meaning a prose tale or translated as "thing said." These are typically lengthy tales of feuds and family histories stretching across multiple volumes, such as the Skye O'Malley stories by Bertrice Small. Historical fiction and Westerns make full use of sagas to keep the story going.

Supporting Organizations, Associations, and Other Resources

Similarly to some of the other genres, romance writers and readers are well supported by organizations. The Romance Writers of America (www.rwanational .org) very actively supports and advocates for romance writers and readers. They have a comprehensive Web site that includes reading lists, statistical information, and information for booksellers and librarians and other industry professionals. Each year RWA hosts a romance writers' conference featuring workshops, roundtables, and panel discussions, opportunities to make a pitch to an editor or literary agent, and book signings. The showcase event at the conference is the annual RITA Award (for published romance novels) and Golden Heart Award (for unpublished romance manuscripts) along with Lifetime Achievements and Librarian of the Year. RWA publishes a monthly trade magazine, *Romance Writers Report*, for members, covering all aspects of the craft and business of romance writing.

RWA includes a variety of chapters, including state and regional chapters. They also have seven chapters in Canada. For those with more narrow interests, RWA includes special-interest chapters (much like special-interest groups for library associations). The special-interest chapters range from those interested in Regency romances to networks for electronic and small-press authors.

The Romantic Novelists' Association (www.rna-uk.org) is the British version of the RWA. Their annual highlight is the Awards Lunch, held each April, to celebrate the Romantic Novel of the Year Award and the Love Story of the Year Award. Throughout the year the association sponsors workshops and events that support the needs of established romance novelists as well as the interests of new writers. They also publish a quarterly magazine titled *Romance Matters* for members, featuring articles, news, and market information.

Romance in Color (RIC) (www.romanceincolor.com) is a Web site devoted to the African-American romance novel. The site promotes romance novels written by authors of color with protagonists of color. The Web site provides reviews of current and new releases, news for and about authors, and special features on publishing. The Web site includes lists of romance novels released since 1994 by and about people of color. RIC sponsors two awards for books that touch readers and reviewers, including an Award of Excellence, which is granted to only those books that go beyond the telling of a love story and touch the souls of reviewers and readers alike. They also sponsor annual Reviewers' Choice Awards and Readers' Favorites Awards. All of the award lists are available on the Web site.

The Internet has been a very productive and prolific resource for the romance reader. Blogs, reading groups, associations, and reading lists are readily available. (See Appendix 1 for an extensive listing of Internet resources for romance readers and writers.) Among other things, each of these resources includes book reviews, author information, and links to reading lists and romance publishers and literary agents. Several of them offer newsletters and e-mail newsletters along with online discussion groups and blogs. An active and indispensable source for all things romantic was the Romance Readers Anonymous (RRA) listserv. While RRA ceased in 2007, a new site has been established in Yahoo! Groups to continue the conversation (http://groups.yahoo.com/group/rra-l). The current Yahoo! group averages 155 messages each month related to romance readers and authors. Similar to the functions of Fiction-l and Dorothy-l, the group is comprised of librarians, authors, and readers of romance fiction with the intent of discussing reading romance. Membership is required, and the message threads are not available to nonmembers.

AN INTRODUCTION TO HISTORICAL FICTION

History by definition is the study of the past, including people, places, and events. By extension historical novels or historical fiction are stories that occur in the past, using the settings, events, and people of distant times and places to create and drive the story. Historical fiction can take place in prehistoric times, such as Jane Auel's *The Clan of the Cave Bear,* or in the recent past of World War II, such as Michael Ondaatje's *The English Patient.* For children born in the 1990s and 2000s, however, the 1950s and 1960s are historical time periods to be studied. Certainly, a definition of history can be challenging and dependent upon the view of the reader. Most readers' advisors and other library specialists agree that historical novels are set in the past before the author's lifetime and experiences; some go as far as saying "historical" begins in the middle of the previous century around 1950.

The characteristic that makes historical fiction unique is that it combines fiction—made-up stories—with historical fact to both entertain and enlighten the reader. Unlike mysteries and romances, for example, that use historical settings as a backdrop for the main story, history *is* the main story in historical fiction. One of the rules of historical fiction writing is that it must make use of historical research, and not the author's personal experience, to develop the story. History allows the reader to explore time and place in story rather than textbook facts. In fact, readers use historical fiction to learn about past events and lives through well-constructed, richly detailed stories. Readers rely upon the author to faithfully and accurately depict the customs, behaviors, and culture of the time period in which the story takes place.

One of the hallmarks of the finest historical fiction is the carefully researched details. Historical novelists pay serious homage to historical accuracy of time, place, people, and events. Cultural artifacts and language are re-created with authenticity, though with an eye for the knowledge of the contemporary reader. (It is unlikely that an entire novel will be written in Old English to create the historically accurate patterns and rhythms of the language, but the influences and nuances will be there to help frame the story.) Authors use the story to bring history to life for the reader. James Michener's novels represent the standard-bearer for the genre with the richly detailed, in-depth examinations of culture and customs (e.g., *Hawaii* or *Chesapeake*) as do the novels of Philippa Gregory (*The Queen's Fool, The Virgin's Lover, The Other Boleyn Girl*) and Michael Shaara (*The Killer Angels*).

The appeal of historical fiction lies in its accurate depiction of historical elements and its wealth of details. Many readers, both male and female, read historical fiction in order to learn about events from the perspective of the individuals steeped in the time and places of the past. For these readers, historical fiction offers an insider's view and encourages them to engage with the past. They seek the accurate, historical detail related to the setting, including geography, dress, customs, and even dwellings, and they want to be immersed in the time and lives portrayed. As the saying goes, the devil is in the details, and it is the details that make the historical novel. Fans of historical fiction expect the novel to be interesting, rich in detail, and believable—from the characters to the politics of the time.

Not only do time and place need to be accurate, but historical fiction readers expect that characters will be presented accurately. Characters do not need to be well-known historical figures, but the protagonists and secondary characters must fit appropriately into the historical framework. Real historical figures themselves must be authentic, though historical fiction writers can and do take liberties with the characters in order to make them believable and to embellish the story. (Josephine Tey's *The Daughter of Time* bends history to her will to tell the story of the murder of Richard III's young nephews, even though the evidence suggests otherwise.) Their words and actions must reflect the historical period, and the reader must believe that the characters are real and may truly have lived. Above all, the key for characterization is consistency. The characters must play their roles consistently across the novel.

Story line varies across the range of historical fiction. The emphasis of historical fiction falls either to time and event or to the lives of the characters in a particular time. For example, Jeff Shaara in his novels about the American Revolution, the Civil War, and World War I focuses on the conflicts and the emotions of events that devastated and strengthened the American people as a nation. John Jakes and Max Byrd by comparison use the lives of people (real and fictional) to explore the same or similar stories. None of these authors present strict biographies or histories, but rather they use the details of place or person to create provocative, accurate representations and reinterpretations of history that are reachable by the common reader.

By nature historical fiction cannot be considered quick reads. Novels tend to be longer and more slowly paced. That does not mean the novels lack excitement; they simply unfold more carefully with attention to detail that provides verisimilitude and authenticity. However, in order to retain the reader's interest, historical fiction must draw in the reader quickly and keep him or her enthralled to the end. This requires historical fiction to be carefully crafted with language selected to engage the reader's mind and create visual and instinctual responses to the story.

Historical Trends and Aspects

The antecedents of historical fiction can be seen in the tales that were handed down from generation to generation to celebrate a people's ancestors and to explain one's place in time. Most frequently these were oral histories of adventure, lineage, and war told as stories. Greek and Norse mythology and Arthurian legends all formed the base for what has become to be known as historical fiction.

These were epic tales retold, and even embellished, to each succeeding generation to help situate them and define their relationship to the order of the world.

Sir Walter Scott's novel *Waverley* is commonly considered to be the seminal
work of published historical fiction. Published in 1814, it was a popularized story
of eighteenth-century Scottish history. It established the first of the historical sagas in its three-volume series, which attempted to accurately explore life during
the Jacobite Rebellion of 1745 through a fictional hero, Edward Waverley. (For a
synopsis and access to the e-text, consult the Edinburgh University Library, Walter Scott Digital Archive at www.walterscott.lib.ed.ac.uk/home.html.) This work
established the pattern for the generations of historical fiction that followed.

James Fenimore Cooper, a contemporary of Scott's, is credited with the cre-
ation of the American historical novel, starting with *The Spy: A Tale of the Neutral
Ground* (published in 1821). It was quickly followed by the first volume of the
Leatherstocking novels (an American saga) and *The Pioneers: or, The Sources of the
Susquehanna* (published in 1823), which is considered to be the first American
frontier and environmental novel. The most popular and beloved of Cooper's
novels that firmly established historical fiction as a genre was published in 1826:
The Last of the Mohicans: A Narrative of 1757.

Early Works of Historical Fiction

James Fenimore Cooper, *The Leatherstocking Tales*
Charles Dickens, *A Tale of Two Cities*
Alexandre Dumas, *The Three Musketeers*
Gustave Flaubert, *Salammbô*
Nathaniel Hawthorne, *The Scarlet Letter*
Victor Hugo, *Les Misérables, Notre-Dame de Paris* (*The Hunchback of
Notre Dame*)
Leo Tolstoy, *War and Peace*

Many of these novels, now part of the literary canon, were popular bestsellers
of their time.

The early twentieth century saw the proliferation of historical novels (see Table 11-2 for a sample of authors and titles). Several of these were considered
among the finest of fictional works in detailing accurate portrayals of historical
life and figures. Along with the expanded interest in and publishing of historical
fiction in general, several other genres and subgenres became firmly established
with the advent of historical fiction's popularity. Already closely aligned, romantic and historical fiction fed off each other to create a robust and popular
subgenre. Historical romances, while the love story was central, used history as a
backdrop to create new and exciting novels, throbbing with passion; and historical fiction, while the love story was secondary, made use of romantic elements to

Table 11-2: A Few Popular Authors of Historical Fiction		
Author	**Title/Series/Saga**	**Historical Era/Geographic Setting**
Jean Auel	*Earth's Children*	Prehistory
James Clavell	Asian Saga	17th-century Asia—Japan, China, and Hong Kong
Sara Donai	Wilderness series	Late 18th-century American Frontier
Sarah Dunant	*The Birth of Venus, In the Company of the Courtesan*	14th and 15th centuries
Dorothy Dunnett	The Lymond Chronicles	16th-century Scotland
Umberto Eco	*The Name of the Rose*	14th-century Italy
Diana Gabaldon	Outlander series	18th-century Scotland and America
W. Michael and Kathleen O'Neal Gear	*First North American*	Prehistory
Margaret George	*Mary, Called Magdalene, The Memoirs of Cleopatra*	Ancient civilizations
Philippa Gregory	Wideacre Trilogy, Boleyn series	Tudor Era
Robert Harris	*Pompeii*	Ancient civilizations
Cecelia Holland	*Pillar of the Sky, Valley of the Kings, The Kings in Winter*	Ancient civilizations, 11th-century British Isles
John Jakes	The Kent Family Chronicles, North and South Trilogy	American Revolution, American Civil War
Ross King	*Ex-Libris*	17th-century England—Stuart Era
Morgan Llywelyn	*Lion of Ireland, Pride of Lions, Grania, The Irish Century*	British Isles and Ireland
Colleen McCullough	*The Song of Troy, The Masters of Rome, The Thorn Birds*	Trojan Wars, Ancient Rome, 1940s Australia
David Nevin	*American Story*	Early 1800s United States
Iain Pears	*The Instance of the Fingerpost*	17th-century England—Stuart Era
Sharon Kay Penman	Plantagenet Trilogy, Welsh Trilogy	Medieval England
Ellis Peters	Brother Cadfael series	12th-century England
Jean Plaidy	The Norman Trilogy, the Plantagenet Saga, Mary Queen of Scots, the Tudor novels	British Isles
Steven Pressfield	*Gates of Fire: An Epic Novel of the Battle of Thermopylae, Tides of War, Alexander: The Virtues of War*	Ancient Greece
Mary Renault	*The King Must Die*	Ancient Greece
Edward Rutherfurd	*The Dublin Saga*	England and Ireland from prehistory to contemporary
Anya Seton	*Katherine*	14th-century England

(continued)

Table 11-2: A Few Popular Authors of Historical Fiction *(continued)*		
Author	**Title/Series/Saga**	**Historical Era/Geographic Setting**
Jeff Shaara	*Gods & Generals, The Last Full Measure,* Revolutionary War series	American Revolution, American Civil War, World War I, and World War II
Michael Shaara	*The Killer Angels*	American Civil War
James Alexander Thom	*The Red Heart, Warrior Woman*	American Revolution
Susan Vreeland	*Girl in Hyacinth Blue, The Passion of Artemisia*	17th-century Europe

Note: Author/Title list was compiled from Adult Reader's Round Table of Illinois' *ARRT Popular Fiction List,* Fantastic Fiction, Historical Novel society Web site, Johnson's *Historical Fiction: A Guide to the Genre,* and numerous articles on historical fiction. Consult Appendix 1 for additional reference resources that may be of interest for finding more. And, of course, the commercial and online readers' advisory databases will provide additional read-alikes and related lists.

appeal to a broader range of readers. During this same period historical fiction also gave birth to the traditional Western and today's historical and contemporary novels set in the American West.

Historical fiction lends itself readily to genre blending. Romance, already discussed, combines with history to create highly popular, richly in-depth historically framed novels. Mysteries and women's fiction also have highly popular subgenres that incorporate historical settings and characters. Ellis Peters' Brother Cadfael series is set in England along the Welsh border in 1137; this series set off an interest in medieval mysteries. Umberto Eco's literary thriller *The Name of the Rose* also combines mystery with medieval history. M. M. Kaye's romance *The Far Pavilions,* set in nineteenth-century India, is frequently described as India's *Gone with the Wind,* combining romance, history, and suspense.

Most currently, historical fiction has shown a trend of blending multiple genres into effective, entertaining stories. Diana Gabaldon's Outlander series blends history (American and British with the Jacobite Rebellion and the American Revolution) with adventure, romance, and time travel (an element of fantasy); David Liss combines adventure, suspense, and mystery in *A Conspiracy of Paper* and its sequel, *A Spectacle of Corruption.* Two novels that have successfully combined fantasy, horror, and history include *Jonathan Strange & Mr. Norrell* by Susanna Clarke and *The Historian* by Elizabeth Kostova.

For many readers, historical fiction provides new angles on existing topics. The accounts of the life of Queen Elizabeth I of England are vastly different when comparing the work of Philippa Gregory (*The Virgin's Lover*), Jean Plaidy (*Queen of the Realm*), and Rosalind Miles (*I, Elizabeth*). These novels look at the historical record and historical figures in very different ways to construct stories that intrigue the reader and provide additional food for thought about what history really means—truth versus fiction.

Benchmarks of Historical Fiction

Jean Auel, Earth's Children series
Geraldine Brooks, *Year of Wonders: A Novel of the Plague*
James Clavell, *Shôgun*
Sarah Dunant, *The Birth of Venus*, *In the Company of the Courtesan*
Dorothy Dunnett, *Lymond Chronicles*
Howard Fast, *Spartacus*, Lavette Family series
Philippa Gregory, Boleyn series
Cecelia Holland, *An Ordinary Woman*, *The Story of Anna and the King*
James Michener, *Chesapeake*
Margaret Mitchell, *Gone with the Wind*
Sena Jeter Naslund, *Ahab's Wife*, *Abundance: A Novel of Marie Antoinette*
Sharon Kay Penman, *Welsh Princes*, *Eleanor of Aquitaine*, *Justin de Quincey*
Jean Plaidy (aka Philippa Carr and Victoria Holt), Tudor Saga, Mary Stuart Queen of Scots Saga, Stuart Saga
Mary Renault, *The King Must Die*
Edward Rutherfurd, *Sarum*, *Russka*
Anya Seton, *Katherine*
Jeff Shaara, *Gods and Generals*, *The Last Full Measure*
Irving Stone, *The Origin: A Biographical Novel of Charles Darwin*

Historical fiction is not without detractors and is subject to much literary snobbery. Frequently criticized for fantasized and hackneyed accounts of history and lack of good research, historical fiction is frequently decried as either bad history (inaccurate, modern-day characters pretending to be historical figures) or bad fiction (the amount of historical fact and research overwhelm the story, leaving out the fictional part). The consensus among these authors and critics appears to be that historical fiction is rarely done well or satisfactorily.

While many of today's outstanding historical novels include the characteristics of genre fiction, they most often carry the label of literary fiction set in the past and held above the lowly bad history novels. The element that distinguishes the literary from the genre is the perspective that while the fiction occurs in the past it emphasizes themes that pertain to the present (Johnson, 2002). Literary historical fiction transcends time and place to speak to the reader here and now. A few of the contemporary examples of this include *Girl with a Pearl Earring* (Tracy Chevalier), *Memoirs of a Geisha* (Arthur Golden), and *Cold Mountain* (Charles Frazier).

Final Thoughts on Historical Novel Readers

One of the best explanations about why people enjoy reading historical fiction was given by Philippa Gregory in an interview for a reading guide to *The Other Boleyn Girl* (2001). She says, "I think people want to know where they came from and where they are going, and stories about the past satisfy that" (Gregory, 2003: n.p.). Ultimately historical fiction allows the reader to become an insider to events and times that still impact our world today. Readers come to know the characters and understand the perspectives of those individuals caught up in historical events. Historical fiction readers expect that these novels will be large and rich and that they will move at a slower pace than other genres.

Because historical fiction relies upon accuracy of details, for which it is frequently criticized as lacking, one of the roles of the readers' advisor is to discern the level of historical authenticity of novels. This is much easier to say than it may be to do. The first step requires a familiarity with those authors and novels that are benchmarks of historical fiction; in other words, read broadly in the genre and read the best of the genre. It also requires reading unfamiliar works with a critical eye for obvious errors or blunders compared to minor slips in the historical record. Making use of the author-provided tools, such as bibliographies, notes, and genealogical tables, gives an indication of the level of research that went into the preparation of the story. The inclusion of epilogues allows the reader to know what happens after the story ends, and epilogues wrap up any necessary historical details about historical events and characters. Glossaries of unfamiliar and foreign words provide evidence of the author's research and authenticity to the dialogue and language.

One challenge in serving historical fiction readers is the range of time periods and geographical settings available. As mentioned previously, the two threads of historical fiction are either historical event or historical figure both bound by some level of realism. Traditional historical novels can be classified by their historical time period: prehistoric Europe, Asia, and North America; biblical times; ancient civilizations (Egypt, Greece, Roman Empire); the British Isles from the early Middle Ages to the twentieth century (Europe and the United States have similar designations as do Canada and Latin America). Historical fiction will focus on a particular event or geographic setting within the specific time or era. Historical figures further complicate the search for historical novels. Figures range from ancient kings and queens to modern war heroes and fit within the frame of historical events and settings.

Historical fiction is well suited to the format of sagas and chronicles. While much of historical fiction can stand alone as single-title novels, a significant body of work encompasses both single-title sagas (*Roots* by Alex Haley) and multi-volume works, such as those by John Jakes (The Kent Family Chronicles or the North and South Trilogy). The intricately written stories leave readers wanting to know what happened next, and much like the sagas of historical romance, the reader builds a relationship over time with the characters. While the characters in the sagas are not necessarily instruments of change, they do feel the impact of change all around. These stories give a sense of continuity across time and a feel of how events impact and change life and people with the passage of time.

Supporting Organizations, Associations, and Other Resources

Unlike mysteries, science fiction/fantasy, and romance, historical fiction does not have a wide range of organizations or associations that support authors and fans. One of the primary organizations is the Historical Novel Society (HNS) (www.historicalnovelsociety.org), whose purpose is to promote all aspects of historical fiction. The society publishes a quarterly magazine titled *Historical Novels Review* and reviews new works of fiction released in the United States and the United Kingdom along with selected titles from Canada and Australia. Members also receive a semi-annual magazine called *Solander*, featuring interviews with current authors of historical fiction along with retrospective essays on the standard-bearers. HNS hosts two conferences each year, one in the United Kingdom and one in North America. The conferences include workshops, panel discussions, speakers, and events with authors and industry professionals.

While there are no major awards for adult historical fiction, a number of historical fiction novels have been recipients of national and international awards, including American Book Award, Man Booker Prize, National Book Award, National Book Critic's Circle, Orange Prize for Fiction, Pulitzer Prize for Fiction, and, of course, the Nobel Prize in Literature. In addition, several of the genre organizations recognize historical novels placed within the specific genre, such as Romance Writers of America's RITA Award for Best Historical Romance and Best Regency Historical Romance (Madeline Hunter, *Lessons of Desire*, and Julie Quinn, *The Secret Diaries of Miss Miranda Cheever*, respectively, in 2008). A number of historical novels received Spur Awards, sponsored by the Western Writers of America, for distinguished writing about the American West, and WILLA Literary Awards, sponsored by Women Writing the West for literature featuring women's stories set in the American West.

AN INTRODUCTION TO WESTERNS

Much like historical fiction, Westerns are a complex lot that follow many paths and appeal to many different types of readers. At the heart of Westerns are two distinct threads: the traditional Western novel filled with stories of revenge, rivalry, and range wars, and novels set in the West more closely resembling historical fiction, using historical characters and events to tell the story. Interestingly, Westerns are both a genre of their own and a subgenre of historical fiction and historical romance. They can also be compared to adventure novels, sharing many similar characteristics of the lone male protagonist and a lot of action, especially traditional Westerns.

The traditional Western features a hero who is a loner, traveling the range to administer justice and right the wrongs done to the weak and unprotected. The protagonist resembles the heroes of Arthurian legends, the knight-errant held to a code of chivalry. While attempting to use reason and fairness to find resolution, the protagonist (almost always male) in the end may resort to fists and guns to achieve his ends. He also closely mirrors the protagonists in Adventure (the accidental hero) and in Mysteries (private detectives) who work alone and follow their own code of conduct and morality. The Westerns of Zane Grey and Louis L'Amour share the strong male protagonist who is self-reliant and willing to fight for what is right and just. The protagonists of Westerns take many forms, not just cowboys. They may be explorers, trail riders, settlers, mountain men, or soldiers.

A small selection of Westerns features female protagonists, or women pioneers, who help to settle the West against all odds. The women include young, orphaned girls who take up with a strong male protagonist for protection and security as well as women suddenly widowed and responsible for guiding fellow settlers and pioneers across harsh and unforgiving lands or making a go of the ranch alone. She may be the stereotypical prostitute with a heart of gold, or the good woman who stands at the side of her man to overcome the odds against them. Much like the male protagonists, the heroine is strong and not afraid of hard work, and frequently she is a woman seeking justice in a man's world.

Strong Females and Exceptional Stories

Lenore Carroll, *One Hundred Girls' Mother*
Sandra Dallas, *The Chili Queen*
Molly Gloss, *The Jump-Off Creek*
Jane Kirkpatrick, *A Sweetness to the Soul*
Susan Lang, *Small Rocks Rising*
Joann Levy, *For California's Gold*
Ellen Recknor, *Leaving Missouri, Prophet Annie*
Barbara Riefe, *Westward Hearts*
Jane Smiley, *The All-True Travels and Adventures of Liddie Newton*
Gladys Smith, *Deliverance Valley*
Glendon Swarthout, *The Homesman*

The setting is as important to the Western as the hero. The exterior landscape (e.g., Rocky Mountains, Sonora Desert, or the Great Plains) gives a sense of history and timelessness to the stories, offering readers a nostalgic illusion of another time and place. Stories most typically occur west of the Mississippi River, ranging from the Southwestern United States to the northernmost Plains and into Alaska (or historically the Northwest Territories). While traditionally set in the American West, this genre also encompasses the Canadian West as a setting as well as the Mexican-American border. In many Westerns it is the battle between man (or woman) and the harsh elements of the natural environment that frame the story. Many traditional Westerns are elusive in exact location, but the general feel is that of the frontier or the Western wilderness.

The recurring themes of traditional Westerns include justice, survival, and redemption. This is seen in the setting (comparison between the wilderness and civilization), the protagonist and secondary characters (clash between the individual and society), and conflict that is resolved clearly and decisively through action. As in adventure and suspense novels, good always prevails, though the protagonist may not survive. These themes make the traditional Westerns exciting and engaging, though not necessarily fast-paced.

Historical Aspects and Trends

Just as James Fenimore Cooper lent his stories to the foundation of historical fiction, he is also attributed with the establishment of the Western tradition. Cooper's *Leatherstocking* novels occurred on what was then the American Frontier. More specifically, *The Last of the Mohicans* and *The Prairie* illustrated the conflict and confrontation of two societies, white man and Indian (Native American in today's language), which appears repeatedly in what we know today as Westerns. Among the other elements Cooper introduced the frontier hero (Natty Bumppo, aka "Hawkeye"), the noble savage (Chingachgook and Uncas), kidnapping and white captives, lots of action, and a violent climax (Mort, 2006: 3).

Other popular American writers contributed to the development of the Western. Mark Twain's travelogue *Roughing It* included outlaws and rough mining towns, which are recurring themes in Western fiction. The short stories of Bret Harte ("The Luck of Roaring Camp") and Stephen Crane ("The Bride Comes to Yellow Sky" and "The Blue Hotel"), and even Twain's "The Celebrated Jumping Frog of Calaveras County," gave life to stories set in California and to the harsh natural landscape that frame Westerns. Willa Cather, a beloved American novelist, immortalized life on the prairie and the settling of the prairie by immigrants with *O! Pioneers* and *My Antonia*.

Some of the earliest paperbacks published, known as dime novels, had significant influence on the future of Westerns. Beadle's Dime Novels series is credited with originating the concept of action-packed adventures with the publication of *Maleaska, the Indian Wife of the White Hunter* by Ann S. Stephens in 1860. Many of the dime novels glorified and celebrated the men we now know as frontier heroes. Highly stereotypical in the portrayal of characters, the dime novels established some of the characterizations found in modern Westerns, both as novels and in film. It is quite likely that many of the Western writers grew up reading the dime novels and eventually emulating the excitement and adrenalin rushes in their own stories.

Traditional Westerns

The traditional Western genre includes stories of the old West dealing with the settlement of the Western frontier. The stories tell of cattle rustlers, cattle drives, range wars, gunfighters, Indian (Native American) fights, mountain men, lawless mining towns, and the lawmen who tamed them. The traditional Western genre also includes stories about the settling of Texas and the Texas Rangers. Western stories turned men such as Wyatt Earp, Buffalo Bill, Wild Bill Hickok, Kit Carson, and Doc Holiday into mythological heroes. Native Americans such as Crazy Horse, Geronimo, Cochise, Sitting Bull, and Red Cloud were demonized and created the stereotype of the red-skinned savage. These novels were highly prejudiced and male dominated.

In the early 1900s, right at the turn of the century, a number of books were published that established American Western lore. They established the mythical cowboy who rode into town, guns blazing, to kill the evildoer and save the rancher's daughter. Owen Wister wrote the first cowboy book, *The Virginian*, in 1902, and it enjoyed long-lived popularity, culminating in the creation of a television show and several film adaptations. *The Virginian* takes place in Wyoming, and tells the story of a range war along with the story of the daily life of being a cowboy, and continues to serve as a standard for cowboy stories.

B. M. (Bertha Muzzy) Bower, a prolific author of Westerns, established the format for the romantic Western with the publication of her 1906 novel *Chip of the Flying U*. It featured a female protagonist who falls in love with a Montana cowboy. Equally popular, Bower's contemporary, Clarence Mulford, invented the familiar character of Hopalong Cassidy in 1907 with the publication of *Bar-20*. His works as well as those of Bower remained popular well into the 1940s, spawning film and television adaptations.

Key Western Writers to Know

Max Brand	Elmer Kelton
Benjamin Capps	Louis L'Amour
Zane Grey	Larry McMurtry
Ernest Haycox	Luke Short
Will Henry	Owen Wister

Zane Grey, whose very name is synonymous with traditional Westerns, was among the most successful of Western writers. His work remained on the bestsellers lists from 1914 through the 1930s. Modeling his novels on the work of Wister, his books are best known for their descriptive ability in allowing the reader to visualize the setting. His first bestselling book was *Riders of the Purple Sage*. Some of his other works include *The Code of the West*; *The Border Region*; and

The Lone Star Ranger. His books continue to be reprinted and sold. (In a recent visit to my favorite bookstore, Westerns took up about 20 linear feet; about 40 percent were Zane Grey titles, 40 percent Louis L'Amour, and the remaining were other authors with the most current publication date of 1989.)

One of the most prolific Western authors, Louis L'Amour published more than 86 novels and short story collections. His protagonists were knights in shining armor that fought evil and did only good because it was the right thing to do. Protagonists lived the "code of the West." They rescued the damsel in distress and preferred a chocolate chip cookie to sex. He called himself a frontier writer rather than a Western writer. At least 16 of his novels told the story of the Sackett family from Clinch Mountain in Tennessee. William Tell, Tyrel, and Orrin Sackett, three brothers, were the mainstay of the stories, but a number of cousins existed to aid them in time of need. Cap Rountree was always available to bail them out of trouble as well. They did everything, including cattle driving, ranching, mining, and taming towns as sheriffs. Some of his Sackett titles include *Sackett; The Sky-liners;* and the *Daybreakers.* Some of his other titles include *Flint; The Quick and the Dead; How the West Was Won;* and *Hondo.* Like Zane Grey's works, many of L'Amour's novels are being reprinted and released and continue to be popular among Western readers.

Some other traditional Western authors include A. B. Guthrie, Dorothy M. Johnson, Luke Short, and Jack Schaefer (see Table 11-3 for a list of authors and titles). A. B. Guthrie's *Big Sky* follows the travels of Boone Caudell and his friends on the Mississippi River. Dorothy M. Johnson wrote the short stories *A Man Called Horse* and *The Man Who Shot Liberty Valance,* both of which were made into popular film adaptations. Jack Schaefer wrote *Shane,* a classic Western about a range war that was adapted into a popular cult film. Luke Short wrote many Westerns over 40 years, covering all of the subgenres. Some of his titles include *The Branded Man; The Man from Two Rivers; Ramrod;* and *Raiders of the Rimrock.* Frederick Schiller Faust, also known as Max Brand, has a tremendous number of Westerns, including *Destry Rides Again; The Black Rider;* and *Luck.* Many of these traditional Westerns are out of print, though some may be available through Project Gutenberg and other e-book resources.

Contemporary Westerns

In the 1970s the popularity of Westerns waned. For many the urbanization of the United States and the death of the frontier made tales of the West unfamiliar and unapproachable. Readers were no longer able to relate to the broad expanses of harsh landscape and the clash of the wilderness with society. The wilderness did not exist anymore. The rise of the women's movement and civil rights for Native Americans and blacks resulted in a lack of interest in novels that were clearly biased and prejudiced. Yet, interestingly, a small number of Western

Table 11-3: A Brief Sampling of Western Authors and Novels		
Author	Title/Series	Description
Edward Abbey	The Fool's Progress, The Monkey Wrench Gang	Contemporary West
Thomas Berger	Little Big Man	Native Americans
Michael Blake	Dances with Wolves	Native American
Max Brand	The Trap at Comanche Bend	The Southwest
Willa Cather	O! Pioneers, My Antonia	Great Plains and Prairies
Don Coldsmith	Spanish Bit Saga	Native American
Robert J. Conley	Real People series	Native American
Janet Daily	The Calder series	Montana
Annie Dillard	The Living	Frontier and Pioneer Life
Ivan Doig	The Whistling Season	Ranching
Loren D. Estleman	Aces and Eights, Journey of the Dead	Legends
Vardis Fisher	Mountain Man	Explorers
Kathleen O'Neal Gear and Michael Gear	The Anasazi Mysteries	Native Americans
A. B. Guthrie	The Big Sky Trilogy	Mountain Men
Stephen M. Harrigan	The Gates of the Alamo	Texas and Mexico
Ernest Haycox	Canyon Passage, Bugles in the Afternoon	Business of the West, Indian Wars
Will Henry	From Where the Sun Now Stands, Yellowstone Kelly, The Gates of the Mountains	Mountain Men, Explorers, Native Americans
James D. Houston	Snow Mountain Passage	Trail Stories
Dorothy M. Johnson	Buffalo Woman	Native American Women
Terry C. Johnston	Titus Bass series	Explorers
Elmer Kelton	The Wolf and the Buffalo, Dark Thicket, The Good Old Boys	Buffalo Soldiers, Cowboys
Louis L'Amour	The Burning Hills, The Californios, To Tame a Land, Hondo, Flint, Hopalong Cassidy	Gunfighters, Cowboys, Range Wars, Border Stories
Cormac McCarthy	All the Pretty Horses, No Country for Old Men	Literary
Michael McGarrity	Kevin Kerney series	Mysteries
Larry McMurtry	Buffalo Girls, Boone's Lick, Lonesome Dove series	Legends, Settlers, Texas Rangers
James A. Michener	The Eagle and the Raven	Soldiers
David Nevin	Meriwether	Explorers
Jack Schaefer	Monte Walsh, Shane	Cowboys, Range Wars

Author	Title/Series	Description
Jeff Shaara	Gone for Soldiers	Mexican War
Jane Smiley	The All-True Travels and Adventures of Liddie Newton	Women Pioneers
Glendon Swarthout	The Homesman, They Came to Cordura, The Shootist	Women Pioneers, Mexican Revolution
James Alexander Thom	From Sea to Shining Sea	Explorers
Anna Lee Waldo	Sacajawea	Women Pioneers

Note: Author/Title list was compiled from, Fantastic Fiction, Historical Novel society Web site, Mort's *Riding the High Country*, Western Writers of America, and Women Writing the West, along with articles on Western fiction. Consult Appendix 1 for additional reference resources that may be of interest for finding more. And, of course, the commercial and online readers' advisory databases will provide additional read-alikes and related lists.

writers achieved significant prominence as the overall popularity of Westerns declined, including Larry McMurtry and Cormac McCarthy.

Westerns started to receive new labels as "frontier novels," "Western historical novels," and "romantic historical fiction." They were aimed at a different readership from in the past. While Westerns most typically drew their readerships from men, the new Westerns (contemporary Westerns) began to attract women. The novels moved away from the traditional cowboys and range wars and entered mainstream fiction with history and romance being the driving momentum.

One of the better-known contemporary Western authors is Larry McMurtry. *Lonesome Dove* won the Pulitzer Prize and Spur Award. The Lonesome Dove series is more traditional in nature, following life on the range as two former Texas Rangers take a cattle drive from Texas to Montana. This book, along with some of his others, was made into a miniseries for television, which helped spread its popularity. He has also written the Berrybender series, *Leaving Cheyenne*, and *Horseman, Pass By*, which are contemporary Westerns. The popularity of his novels may be attributed more to the film and television adaptations rather than the novels themselves.

Cormac McCarthy's Border Trilogy expresses two changes in the evolution of the Western genre. McCarthy tends to take a darker look at society than traditional Western genre fiction. He has also moved the time point of the Western from frontier to modern-day activities. *All the Pretty Horses, The Crossing,* and *Cities of the Plain* take place pre– and post–World War II. Unlike McMurtry, who is truly a popular fiction writer, McCarthy follows a much higher literary tradition with multilayered, complex stories set in the West. McCarthy was nominated for the Pulitzer Prize for Fiction for *All the Pretty Horses*, which did receive a National Book Award, but he did not receive a Pulitzer until the publication of his more contemporary work, *The Road*, a postapocalyptic novel.

Other changes came to the Westerns. Historical Westerns, or stories set in the West, began emerging. These gained a much broader appeal than the traditional Westerns, often generating bestsellers. Jeff Shaara's *Gone for Soldiers*, for example, focused on the Mexican War, but it certainly is not a traditional Western of cowboys and range wars. Another bestselling author that demonstrates the changes in the Western genre is Barbara Kingsolver. In her novels *Bean Trees* and *Pigs in Heaven*, which take place in Arizona and Oklahoma, the protagonist Taylor Greer has a Cherokee infant placed in her care. The Cherokee tribe has discovered that Taylor has not legally adopted the infant of Cherokee descent, and they want the infant returned to the tribe to be raised in her own culture.

Nontraditional, or contemporary, Westerns contain an element of social critique, such as in Kingsolver's novels. They focus on the clash of societies, which was seen in early Westerns, but they do not typically include the traditional protagonists. The contemporaries also consider the loss of ideology and identity as the cowboy finds it harder to hold onto the romantic dreams of the West and must face a changing social and environmental world. Edward Abbey best epitomizes this social critique and changing world in his works such as *The Brave Cowboy* and *Fire on the Mountain*.

Today the genre has morphed to include current Native American tribal life. Sherman Alexie writes about life growing up on the "rez" and treats it in a humorous fashion. Some of his titles include *Lone Ranger & Tonto Fistfight in Heaven*; *Reservation Blues*; *Absolute True Diary of a Part Time Indian*; and *Smoke Signals*. His book *Serial Killer* is a more serious look at the societal problems Native Americans face. In this case the Native American is a disenfranchised Native American-turned-serial killer.

Louise Erdrich's novels, while only marginally Western, are set in North Dakota on the Ojibway reservation. She examines Native American life and the attempts of Native American characters to assimilate into urban life while holding onto their old traditions and ways of life. *The Antelope Wife*, *Tracks*, *Four Souls*, and *The Painted Drum* are among Erdrich's many contemporary Western novels. Much of her work also blends with women's fiction and can certainly be considered strong contenders in multicultural and ethnic fiction.

Final Thoughts on Western Readers

Great diversity in reading experiences exists within the Western genre, from the formulaic Western novels of the early periods to the rich, literary novels about the West. At the heart, Western novels appeal to deep-seated feelings about the land and the settling of the range. Much like other genres, Westerns also appeal to the reader's sense of order and prevailing justice. These novels incorporate many of the appeal elements of adventure and of historical fiction with strong protagonists, fast-paced action, and a feeling or nostalgia for a time past.

Genre blending is common in contemporary Westerns. They lend themselves not only to historical fiction but to mysteries as well. Native American detectives are increasingly popular among readers of Western literature and among mystery aficionados. Two authors classified as mystery writers, but who cross over into Westerns, are Tony Hillerman and James D. Doss. Both authors have protagonists who are Native American. Hillerman, who died in late 2008, wrote about crime on the Navajo (Diné) reservation. His Navajo tribal policeman Jim Chee teams up with Detective Joe Leaphorn to solve tribal crimes. Chee often finds himself caught between tribal spiritual beliefs and modern scientific crime fighting. Some of Hillerman's books include *The First Eagle*, *Skinwalkers*, *Dance Hall of the Dead*, and *The Blessing Way*. His last work was *The Shape Shifter*.

James D. Doss is of the same ilk as Hillerman in that he writes modern-day mysteries set on Native American tribal lands. Charlie Moon, a Ute tribal policeman, works with detective Scott Parris to solve crimes that span tribal and nontribal lands. Moon's aunt Daisy Perika, a shaman, gains insights into the crimes through her dreams of a dwarflike character, *pitukupf*. Doss combines Native American spirituality with contemporary mysteries set in the West. Some of Doss's works include *The Shaman's Bones*; *The Shaman Sings*; *Grandmother Spider*; and *White Shell Women*.

Westerns have adapted very well to the mystery genre. Along with Hillerman and Doss, a number of other authors have created mysteries set in the West with ethnic protagonists. Rudolfo Anaya published the Sonny Baca series, which is set in Albuquerque and features a Latino private eye. C. J. Box's Joe Pickett series is set in Saddlestring, Wyoming. And Paula Boyd's character, Jolene Jackson, is a "good ol' girl" from Texas.

Romance, historical fiction, and mainstream fiction all provide homes to Western literature readers. They have all appropriated the setting of the West as a backdrop for the larger story. They frequently include the adventure and action that appeals to Western readers. Western fiction, much like historical fiction, lends itself to the creation of sagas that explore the families and feuds of the frontier or of the West. Popular or mainstream fiction borrows characters from Western models. For example, Nicholas Evans' *The Horse Whisperer* certainly plays on the model of the lone protagonist and the unforgiving landscape of the West.

Supporting Organizations, Associations, and Other Resources

Western Writers of America (WWA) (www.westernwriters.org) is the premier organization for Western writers and readers. Like the associations for other genres, WWA hosts an annual convention to celebrate the writing and reading of Western novels. Among the oldest of the genre associations, it was founded in 1953 to promote the literature of the American West. The association annually honors the best in Western writing through the Spur Awards, including the Best Western Novel, the Best Historical Novel, and the Best Short Story. Their magazine, *Roundup*, features regular reviews of Western fiction, nonfiction, and poetry. The association includes film and screen writing along with fiction and nonfiction.

Women Writing the West (WWW) (www.womenwritingthewest.org) is an association of writers, editors, publishers, agents, booksellers, and other professionals who write about and promote the Women's West. They sponsor an annual conference for members to explore women, writing, and the West. Among other events, the conference features discussion panels, networking opportunities, and workshops. Women Writing the West sponsors the annual WILLA Award, honoring outstanding literature featuring women's stories set in the West. The award panel consists of professional librarians. Awards are bestowed for contemporary fiction, creative nonfiction, historical fiction, poetry, original softcover fiction, and children's and young adult materials. Their online newsletter features articles of interest about publishing and writing within the genre. WWW also has a listserv for members.

CONCLUSION

Romance, historical fiction, and Westerns, while being popular reading genres, have experienced great success on the screen—both film and television. The novels from these genres have been readily adapted and provide another form of popular entertainment. In particular, the historical novels adapted for film are rich tapestries of the lives and times presented in fiction. They are visual feasts for the eyes. Histories and Westerns on the screen are regularly honored with not only literary awards but with film awards (Oscars and Sundance, for example). This synergy between book and film fuels readers' interests.

The lines have blurred among many of the genres of popular fiction. This can be readily seen in romance and historical and Western fiction. While distinctly different in focus, appeal, and approach, they each contain many of the elements of the other. The combination of elements makes each of the genres rich in character and setting and evocative of other times and places. Perhaps more than the other genres, romance, historical fiction, and Westerns share significant foundations in the literary canon, and many classic tales are equally at home in any of the three.

WORKS CONSULTED

Baldick, Chris. 2008. "Romance." *Oxford Dictionary of Literary Terms*. Oxford: Oxford University Press.
"Checklist of Cooper's Works." 2001. James Fenimore Cooper Society. Available: http://external.oneonta.edu/cooper/bibliography/works.html (accessed September 10, 2009).
Gregory, Philippa. 2003. *The Other Boleyn Girl*. New York: Touchstone.
Herald, Diana Trixler. 2006. *Genreflecting: A Guide to Popular Reading Interests*, edited by Wayne A. Wiegand. Westport, CT: Libraries Unlimited.

Johnson, Sarah L. 2002. "What Are the Rules for Historical Fiction?" Historical Novel Society. Available: www2.historicalnovelsocity.org/historyic.htm (accessed September 10, 2009).
———. 2005. *Historical Fiction: A Guide to the Genre.* Genreflecting Advisory Series, edited by Diana T. Herald. Westport, CT: Libraries Unlimited.
Krentz, Jayne Ann, ed. 1992. *Dangerous Men & Adventurous Women: Romance Writers on the Appeal of the Romance.* Philadelphia: University of Pennsylvania Press.
Mort, John. 2006. *Reading the High Country: Guide to Western Books and Films.* Genreflecting Advisory Series, Diana T. Herald, ed. Westport, CT: Libraries Unlimited.
"Our History." 2008. Mills and Boon. Available: www.millsandboon.co.uk/history.asp (accessed September 10, 2009).
Ramsdell, Kristin. 1999. *Romance Fiction: A Guide to the Genre.* Englewood, CO Libraries Unlimited.
Romance Writers of America. 2005. "Romance Writers of America's 2005 Market Research Study on Romance Readers." Available: https://eweb.rwanational.org/eweb/docs/05MarketResearch.pdf (accessed September 10, 2009).
———. 2008. "About the Romance Genre." Available: www.rwanational.org/cs/the_romance_genre (accessed September 10, 2009).
Saricks, Joyce G. 2001. *The Readers' Advisory Guide to Genre Fiction.* Chicago: American Library Association.
Wyatt, Neal, et al. 2007. "Core Collections in Genre Studies: Romance Fiction 101." *Reference & User Services Quarterly* 47, no. 2 (Winter): 120–126.

FURTHER READING

Allen, Tracy. 2004. "Mystery and the Romance Reader." *Collection Management* 29, no. 3/4: 161–178. (Includes an extensive reading list.)
Johnson, Sarah L. 2008. "Masters of the Past: Historical Fiction, Volume II." *Bookmarks* 37 (November/December). Available: www.bookmarksmagazine.com/37-nov-dec-2008 (accessed September 10, 2009).
Lee, Richard. 2000. "History Is but a Fable Agreed Upon: The Problem of Truth in History and Fiction." Historical Novel Society. Available: www.historicalnovelsociety.orgnhistoryis.htm (accessed September 10, 2009).
Radway, Janice A. 1984. *Reading the Romance: Women, Patriarchy, and Popular Literature.* Chapel Hill, NC: The University of North Carolina Press.
Taylor, Rhonda Harris. 2004. "The Native American Detective." *Collection Management* 29, no. 3/4: 101–105.

Chapter 12

Merging, Emerging, and Re-emerging Genres

The proper stuff of fiction does not exist; everything is the proper stuff of fiction.

—Virginia Woolf, "Modern Fiction," 1925

Indeed, "everything is the proper stuff of fiction," and it is this everything that allows genres to grow and change. Culture and society and our responses to them form the basis for emerging genres and the merging of genres from old into new. Genres take on new shapes and forms as readership changes. The stories our parents read were different from those we read, and certainly different from those our children enjoy today. However, many of the same themes remain identifiable (triumph of good over evil, questioning of societal norms); they are simply presented in ways that we can respond to with our own schemas and points of reference.

Reading within genres provides particular challenges for contemporary readers. Genre blending, which has been discussed, makes it much more difficult to provide precise definitions of genres. Emerging genres, growing out of the blending of elements and changing interests of readers, create new bodies of literature that must be incorporated into the library. And with the changing demographics of society, a greater demand for multicultural fiction prompts new approaches to developing libraries' leisure reading collections.

Emerging genres evolve through several instances. First, they may be reactions to a particular cultural or social phenomenon. Emerging genres encompass stories that explore situations and circumstances not well described by mainstream fiction. For example, street fiction grew out of street culture (rappers, drugs, violence) as a way to both explore and explain life on the street for young adults, often black or Hispanic. Emerging genres are also components of subgenres that simply outgrew the confines of standard convention. Chick lit, a subgenre of both women's literature and romance, has given rise to an entire new class of fun, sexy reading for women. Finally, emerging genres, or what may be better defined as topical or thematic fiction, responds to the needs of individual groups of people and a multicultural society.

The important factor of all of the emerging genres is that they are speaking to a need expressed by their individual readers. As discussed previously, fiction provides a way for readers to relate to others in similar circumstances and to explore their own identities. It will be impossible to explore every variation, but the resources provided in the reading lists and appendixes will help you find more information on a range of emerging genres and multicultural fiction.

WOMEN'S FICTION AND CHICK LIT

Women comprise a significant portion of the reading public. According to the National Endowment for the Arts, nearly 60 percent of adult readers are women (NEH, 2002). Content Connections explored the book-buying habits of women and found that on average women spent approximately $500 per year on book purchases, and that approximately 37 percent of women purchased 11 or more fiction books during the year (Content Connections, 2007). As a group, women have major influence over the types of books being published and on content that suits their tastes, interests, and needs.

Women's fiction seems to be a misnomer for a rich body of literature that focuses on women's lives and relationships. First, it is not written just for women, as it appeals to both female and male readers, nor is women's fiction written only by women. (Nicholas Sparks is a best-selling author of romance and relationship stories, which are told from the male protagonist's point of view.) It also cannot be called a genre in the way that genres have been discussed and described in earlier chapters; women's fiction encompasses romance, science fiction, suspense, and mystery along with other classifications. In addition, women's fiction, while including issues related to feminism, cannot be defined solely as feminist literature.

We might point to the writing of Jane Austen and her contemporaries as the beginning of women's literature, as women tested the boundaries of their lives and freedom, or to the work of Virginia Woolf and others who examined the working lives and careers of women against the backdrop of a male-dominated society. Historically we may even say that women's fiction grew out of the traditions of romance—the ultimate stories of relationships. And, indeed, women's fiction contains all of these elements.

Without a doubt, Oprah Winfrey has greatly influenced the choices women make about reading. In the early years of her television book club, many of Oprah's selections were issue-driven and considered the ways in which women reconciled and resolved the challenges in their lives. Her selections consisted of literary fiction as opposed to genre and tended toward the dark side of dysfunction and danger. But she also selected novels with which women could identify and grow. Oprah's range of women's fiction, including that of Toni Morrison, Anita Shreve, and Chris Bohjalian, has enticed many women readers to seek out stories with similar themes but lighter tones from their local libraries and bookstores.

Women's fiction is an umbrella term that focuses on issues of interest to women, including family, friends, careers, empowerment, and aging (see Table 12-1 for a sample of authors and titles). Stories range from the quickly paced easy read to complex, multidimensional stories. Regardless of the setting or other genre elements, women's fiction focuses on the protagonist's familial and professional relationships and experiences. On the whole, women's fiction examines the unique ways in which women confront issues in their lives. Of note, women's fiction is usually contemporary, taking place in today's society, though many historical works and family sagas examine these same issues from multiple viewpoints across time and place.

Women's fiction is always character centered. The protagonist in women's fiction is almost without fail a female, and the novels generally have secondary characters who are also important to the unfolding of the story. Secondary characters typically comprise a small group of female family members and friends (sisters, girlfriends, co-workers) who may have portions of their stories revealed along with the protagonist's. No age restrictions are placed on characters; they range from the mature women of Haywood Smith's *The Red Hat Club*, to Dorothea Benton Frank's middle-aged Southern women, to the young professionals of Jennifer Weiner and Sophie Kinsella.

Story lines run the gamut along with the protagonists. However, themes are contemporary. Early women's fiction from the 1980s and 1990s focused on a woman's struggle to find success in a man's world. The novels of the late 1990s and today focus on topics such as caring for aging parents, juggling careers, and motherhood, marriage, and divorce, or dealing with breast cancer and other catastrophic illnesses. The real appeal is in the protagonist's ability to find resolution and reconciliation. These stories may not have a fairy-tale ending, but the protagonist emerges resilient and strong and able to handle whatever challenges the future holds.

Women's fiction is broadly multicultural. It crosses racial and ethnic lines in ways that other genres may not be able. Some of it is the appeal of everyday

A Sampling of Multicultural Women's Fiction

Julia Alvarez, *How the Garcia Girls Lost Their Accents*
Edwidge Danticat, *Breath, Eyes, Memory*
Arthur Golden, *Memoirs of a Geisha*
Terry McMillan, *Waiting to Exhale*
Gloria Naylor, *The Women of Brewster Place*
Susan Power, *Grass Dancer*
Amy Tan, *The Joy Luck Club*

Table 12-1: A Sampling of Popular Women's Fiction	
Author	**Title**
Mary Kay Andrews	*Savannah Breeze, Savannah Blues, Hissy Fit, Deep Dish*
Elizabeth Berg	*Open House, Never Change, The Year of Pleasures, Home Safe*
Maeve Binchy	*Heart and Soul*
Chris Bohjalian	*Midwives, The Law of Similars, Trans-Sister Radio, The Double Bind*
Jennifer Chiaverini	Elm Creek Quilters series
Barbara Delinksy	*The Vineyard, The Woman Next Door, Flirting with Pete, Family Tree*
Katie Fforde	*Going Dutch, Wedding Season, Love Letters*
Dorothea Benton Frank	*Sullivan's Island, Bulls Island*
Patricia Gaffney	*Flight Lessons, The Goodbye Summer, Mad Dash*
Jane Hamilton	*The Book of Ruth, A Map of the World, When Madeline Was Young*
Kristin Hannah	*Magic Hour, Firefly Lane, True Colors*
Jane Heller	*Cha Cha Cha, Lucky Stars, An Ex to Grind, Some Nerve*
Lorna Landvik	*Oh My Stars, The View from Mount Joy, 'Tis the Season*
Elinor Lipman	*The Dearly Departed, The Pursuit of Alice Thrift, My Latest Grievance, The Family Man*
Debbie Macomber	*Wednesdays at Four, His Winter Bride, Be My Angel*
Sue Miller	*The Good Mother, The World Below, Lost in the Forest, The Senator's Wife*
Jodi Picoult	*The Tenth Circle, Nineteen Minutes, Change of Heart, Handle with Care*
Anna Quindlen	*Blessings, Being Perfect, Rise and Shine*
Luanne Rice	*The Edge of Winter, The Geometry of Sisters, The Deep Blue Sea for Beginners*
Anita Shreve	*Light on Snow, A Wedding in December, Body Surfing, Testimony*
Anne Rivers Siddons	*Nora Nora, Island, Sweetwater Creek, Off Season*
Lee Smith	*Saving Grace, The Last Girls, On Agate Hill*
Nancy Thayer	*Custody, Moon Shell Beach, Summer House*
Adriana Trigiani	*The Queen of the Big Time, Rococco, Very Valentine*
Joanna Trollope	*Girl from the South, Brother and Sister, Second Honeymoon, Friday Nights*

Note: Author/Title list was compiled from Adult Reader's Round Table of Illinois' *ARRT Popular Fiction List,* Fantastic Fiction, and numerous articles on chick lit and women's fiction. Consult Appendix 1 for additional reference resources that may be of interest for finding more. And, of course, the commercial and online readers' advisory databases will provide additional read-alikes and related lists.

women facing issues and overcoming obstacles that are common to all women. Readers also appreciate how these same issues of family, career, and marriage play out against the backdrop of other cultures. The issues of women's lives are universal and touch readers at multiple levels.

Chick Lit

A subgenre of both women's fiction and romance, chick lit forms a highly popular and very contemporary selection of reading. What distinguish chick lit from other categories of women's fiction are the level of humor, especially the witty, tongue-in-cheek variety, the heavy focus on popular culture (brand names, designer clothing, trendy lifestyles), and urban settings. While not exclusively so, protagonists and secondary characters tend toward 20- and 30-somethings, on their own for the first time, grappling new careers and new relationships.

Did You Know?

Chick Lit also goes by another name: the "sex 'n' shopping novel." The characteristic features of these novels include detailed discussion of expensive designer clothing, hot cars, jewelry, perfume, and other brand-name accessories of the nouveau riche. Judith Michaels' *Scruples* is credited with founding the trend.

Chick lit was born with the publication of Helen Fielding's *Bridget Jones's Diary* in 1998 (also a popular box office hit starring Renée Zellweger in 2001). Bridget Jones burst into the women's fiction scene juggling a career, boyfriends, and a bad-habit-filled life. She appealed to the young women who knew exactly where Bridget Jones was in her life, personally identifying with the daily challenges Bridget encounters. The chick lit phenomenon expanded rapidly with the infusion of similar quirky, witty, fast-paced novels. Major romance publishers and some small presses, including Avon, Harlequin, and Warner Books, quickly created chick lit imprints to keep the success going(see Table 12-2 for a sample of chick lit authors and titles). Unlike women's literature, while contemporary in nature, chick lit takes place "right here and right now" and has a tremendous ephemeral quality, changing focus as quickly as the protagonists change their Manolo Blahnik knockoffs.

Chick lit evolves at the same pace as the women who read it, or the protagonists. The freewheeling career girls found love and marriage in the early 2000s and are now giving birth to children; this throws a whole new light on chick lit, called mommy lit or the yummy mummy. The genre has turned from the freewheeling life of "singletons" (the British term for the young, single career woman) to examining the struggle to balance a career with children and a home

Table 12-2: A Sampling of Current Chick Lit Authors	
Author	**Title**
Elizabeth Buchan	*Wives Behaving Badly, The Second Wife, Chiara's Book*
Meg Cabot	Queen of Babble series, *Size 12 Is Not Fat, Big Boned*
Claire Cook	*Must Love Dogs, Life's a Beach, Summer Blowout*
Helen Fielding	*Bridget Jones's Diary*
Jane Green	*The Other Woman*
Kim Wong Keltner	*The Dim Sum of All Things, I Want Candy*
Marian Keyes	*Watermelon*
Sophie Kinsella	The Shopaholic series
Tonya Lewis Lee and Crystal McCrary	*The Gotham Diaries*
Emma McLaughlin and Nicola Kraus	*The Nanny Diaries*
Terry McMillan	*Waiting to Exhale*
Alison Pearson	*I Don't Know How She Does It*
Jeanne Ray	*Julie and Romeo, Eat Cake, Julie and Romeo Get Lucky*
Haywood Smith	The Red Hat Club series, *Queen Bee of Mimosa Branch, Wedding Belles*
Alisa Valdes-Rodriguez	*The Dirty Girls Social Club*
Jennifer Weiner	*Good in Bed, In Her Shoes, Little Earthquakes, Goodnight Nobody*
Lauren Weisberger	*The Devil Wears Prada, Chasing Harry Winston*
Lolly Winston	*Good Grief*
Laura Wolf	*Diary of a Mad Mom-to-Be*

Note: Author/Title list was compiled from Adult Reader's Round Table of Illinois' *ARRT Popular Fiction List*, Fantastic Fiction, and numerous articles on chick lit and women's fiction. Consult Appendix 1 for additional reference resources that may be of interest for finding more. And, of course, the commercial and online readers' advisory databases will provide additional read-alikes and related lists.

life. These stories continue to be told in the same fast, witty way, but they are now addressing the changing needs and interests of their readers.

This phenomenon of aging with the protagonists illustrates one of the overall patterns in women's fiction in general. Authors of women's fiction tend to write about women close to them in age and lifestyle. This adds the veneer of realism and the elements of knowing what the readers are experiencing. Popularity of chick lit has increased for more mature women (matron lit or hen lit). This particular chick lit appeals to the 40- to 60-year-olds, with themes related to this age group's interests but still written in the same breezy, light style.

Resources for Women's Fiction and Chick Lit

No single readers' guides for women's fiction and chick lit exist. In fact, you'll find these novels dispersed through the general fiction collection in most libraries and bookstores. However, Joyce G. Saricks and Diana Trixler Herald include chapters in their general guides to genre literature, focusing on women's literature and some of the subgenres of women's literature. In addition, several writing manuals and collections of essays provide excellent introductions to chick lit. (See Appendix 1 for additional resources for women's literature and chick lit.) A number of useful articles have been published in the past few years that review current titles and authors. However, the best place to find reading lists and resources is the Web.

Starting with social cataloging sites, such as LibraryThing.com, provides access to a number of authors and ways in which this type of literature is described outside of the formal cataloging classifications (women's lives). This will include tags such as "friendship," "relationship," "chick lit," and "women's fiction," as well as "domestic fiction" and "young women fiction." This will also lead to a list

Did You Know?

Black chick lit and women's fiction is frequently called "sisterfriend" literature, focusing on the unique familial and communal relationships between black women.

of titles cataloged in the social networking tools and links to related titles and authors. GoodReads and LibraryThing offer access to discussion groups that focus on women's fiction and chick lit and information about the authors contributing to this genre. Women's writers frequently participate in the discussion groups, giving firsthand access to their audience.

The commercial databases, including NoveList and Reader's Advisor Online, offer multiple options for locating authors, read-alikes, and genre possibilities. Reader's Advisor Online, for example, identifies approximately 215 individual titles described as "women's lives." The resource also points to other authors and other genres that will offer similar appeal characteristics. The commercial databases are excellent for finding subgenres in women's fiction and chick lit, such as chick lit mysteries or science fiction.

While it does not offer extensive lists or recommendations, Book Reporter (www.bookreporter.com/womens_fiction/index.asp) regularly features different women's fiction authors. The Web site includes biographical information about the featured authors, interviews, information about featured books, and excerpts along with readers' comments. Book Reporter also has a separate spotlight for chick lit with similar features of interviews, biographical information, and excerpts. Links are provided to other Web sites that offer related information on romance, chick lit, and women's fiction.

Candy Covered Books (www.candycoveredbooks.com/) provides book reviews and more for chick lit and, more broadly, women's fiction. The books section features reviews on approximately 1,350 titles in a wide range of topics, from lighthearted chick lit to women's literary fiction. While some of the sections of the Web site are not current, the authors and titles include currently released new titles.

ChickLitWriters (www.chicklitwriters.com) is a chapter of Romance Writers of America. The site is devoted to supporting, encouraging, and promoting the writing of chick lit as opposed to traditional romance. Upcoming book releases of chapter members are featured, and links to author Web sites can be accessed for additional information. For new writers who have yet to publish their novels, ChickLitWriters sponsors the "Get Your Stiletto in the Door Contest." In order to receive newsletters and participate in listservs, membership in both Romance Writers of America National Organization and ChickLitWriters is required.

Another good source for author biographies and reading lists is ChickLitClub (www.chicklitclub.com). The site has active links to titles and authors, sneak peeks, and awards. ChickLitClub features interviews with writers and an extensive archive of materials. Some of the titles featured here would be more broadly described as women's fiction, dealing with many of the everyday issues and encounters in women's lives (death, breast cancer, infidelity, birth and babies).

Finally, a useful, all-purpose resource for multiple genres is "Pop Goes Fiction" (http://popgoesfiction.blogspot.com/). This is a blog maintained by Lora Bruggeman, a former readers' advisory librarian. The blog features reviews of popular fiction that she has read and enjoyed along with suggestions for related titles and read-alikes. It is possible to browse the blog by genre, and separate links are offered for chicklit, family relationships, and women's lives and relationships.

SERVING A MULTICULTURAL COMMUNITY

Women do not comprise the only special-interest group seeking stories to which they can relate. A number of other populations exist within the library community, including those who speak languages other than English, the elderly, or racial and ethnic groups, each with their own unique interests and reading preferences. While it may be impossible to fully serve every group through the fiction collection, the RA staff can make significant in-roads in meeting the needs of a diverse community. What might have once been called "mainstream fiction" has exploded with genre fiction that includes new voices addressing the interests of racial and ethnic communities, including Latinos and African Americans, as well as fiction for the LGBTQ (lesbian, gay, bisexual, transgendered, queer/questioning) community and a variety of religious and spiritual communities (Christian, Jewish, Muslim, etc.).

Not unlike women's fiction, multicultural fiction is not a genre in and of itself, though it has distinct groups of readers who follow it. Contemporary genre fiction is rich in the diversity of writers looking at common issues among all people, and more specifically at life within their own culture. Multicultural genre fiction encompasses mystery, suspense, science fiction, and fantasy along with many other elements of fiction. What makes multicultural fiction unique is not simply the inclusion of characters in the story representing people of color or other diverse groups, but the celebration of the culture, social and political values and beliefs, material culture (food, music, dress), and the authenticity of the expression of that culture. More importantly, authentic multicultural literature is written by an insider, a member of the culture about which he or she is writing.

Two titles in particular have been credited with the growing popularity and emphasis on multicultural fiction: Terry McMillan's *Waiting to Exhale* (1992) and Amy Tan's *The Joy Luck Club* (1989). These two novels appealed to a much wider cross-section of the reading public beyond African Americans and Asian-Americans through the quality of the stories and the characters, whose stories were the stories of every woman. The financial success of these novels and bestseller status lent credibility to multicultural literature in general and demonstrated their appeal to a wide range of readers. Their success bred not only more success for McMillan (including paperback and movie rights) and Tan but led to an increasing interest by other writers to continue the trend that McMillan and Tan began.

African-American Fiction

In recent years extensive study has been made of the elements that constitute multicultural fiction (see Table 12-3 for the range of multicultural fiction that is available). The most comprehensive of these studies focuses on African-American fiction. Not only has African-American literature grown in richness and depth, but in general genre fiction is burgeoning with titles and authors aiming to meet the specific needs and interests of African Americans. Significant demand exists for fiction that tells authentic stories of the everyday issues and challenges that African Americans encounter. Publishers responded to this need with the development of a number of imprints at the large houses and the growth of small presses that publish high-quality books for and about African Americans, and by adding an emphasis to editing and publishing priorities for multicultural literature.

In terms of genre fiction, detective novels and romance fiction are growing in popularity with an increasing number of books featuring African-American protagonists (Latino and Native American detectives are experiencing a similar growth and popularity). In the past several years, an increasing number of inspi-

Table 12-3: Selected African-American Fiction	
Author	**Title/Series**
James Baldwin	Go Tell It on the Mountain, If Beale Street Could Talk, Giovanni's Room
Connie Briscoe	Sisters and Lovers, Big Girls Don't Cry, Can't Get Enough
Bebe Moore Campbell	What You Owe Me, Brothers and Sisters, Your Blue Eyes Ain't Like Mine
Stephen Carter	The Emperor of Ocean Park
Pearl Cleage	What Looks Like Crazy on an Ordinary Day
Gina Cox	Mortal Verdict
Virginia DeBerry and Donna Grant	What Doesn't Kill You
Eric Jerome Dickey	Liar's Game, Milk in My Coffee, Sister Sister, Friends and Lovers
Candice Dow and Daaimah S. Poole	We Take This Man
Larry Duplechan	Got 'Til It's Gone
Ernest J. Gaines	A Lesson Before Dying, The Autobiography of Miss Jane Pittman
E. Lynn Harris	Not a Day Goes By, Invisible Life, Any Way the Wind Blows
David Haynes	Live at Five
Beverly Jenkins	Bring on the Blessings
Yolanda Joe	He Say, She Say, The Hatwearer's Lesson, Bebe's by Golly Wow, This Just In
Benilde Little	The Itch
Bernice McFadden	This Bitter Earth, The Warmest December, Camilla's Rose
Diane McKinney-Whetstone	Blues Dancing, Tumbling, Tempest Rising, Leaving Cecil Street
Terry McMillan	Waiting to Exhale, How Stella Got Her Groove Back
Meesha Mink and De'neshan Diamond	The Hood Life
Toni Morrison	The Bluest Eye, Sula, Beloved, Jazz, A Mercy
Darryl Pinckney	High Cotton
Kimberla Lawson Roby	The Best of Everything
Omar Tyree	For the Love of Money, A Do Right Man
Alice Walker	The Color Purple
Tiffany Warren	The Bishop's Daughter
Carl Weber	Lookin' for LUV, So You Call Yourself a Man, She Ain't the One
Valerie Wilson Wesley	Ain't Nobody's Business If I Do
Colson Whitehead	The Intuitionist, John Henry Days
John Edgar Wideman	Two Cities, Sent for You Yesterday
Bil Wright	Sunday You Learn How to Box

Note: Author/Title list was compiled from Adult Reader's Round Table of Illinois' *ARRT Popular Fiction List*, Fantastic Fiction, and Nancy Pearl's *Book Lust* and *More Book Lust*. Consult Appendix 1 for additional reference resources that may be of interest for finding more. And, of course, the commercial and online readers' advisory databases will provide additional read-alikes and related lists.

rational and Christian fiction titles based on black faith appeared in the marketplace. At the heart of the genres is the dichotomy of remaining true to the genre's conventions while upholding the ethnicity of the characters and authentic representation of their culture as central to the story. These genres are frequently used as a forum for social and political commentary and for exploring the racial divide between minority and dominant cultures.

The appeal elements that are applied to other genres can easily be applied to African-American fiction as well. The difference is that these elements need to also consider the relationship to a multicultural society. A particularly crucial appeal factor is characterization and the degree of development of protagonists and secondary characters in regard to race and ethnicity. Many African-American writers will use the story line to explore being black in America; they will also use story line to explore the past's impact on today and the future. For many, fiction is a voyage of discovery and a way to explore their roles in contemporary society. Perhaps even more so than other genre fiction, setting provides both emotional and physical boundaries for the story, including a sense of community or of entrapment.

Urban Fiction, Street Fiction, or Hip-Hop Fiction

A growing subgenre within African-American fiction considers street culture: life in the ghettos and on the streets; drugs; violence. Called street lit, hip-hop lit, and ghetto lit, this genre explores contemporary urban life. Not without significant controversy over language, graphic violence and sex, and heavy focus on drugs, urban fiction appeals to teens and young adults, especially African Americans. Street fiction portrays the hard-core, violent life on the streets, written in explicit raw language. Crime and hustling are seen as the only means for survival in urban fiction. Novels are fast-paced, graphic in violence, and use sex as a form of power and control over others. And like thrillers and suspense novels, street fiction opens with action that never stops. The appeal for many readers is that street fiction questions dominant cultural norms.

Historically, street fiction arose in the early 1970s with the publication of Donald Goines' novel *Dopefiend*. (We could say that urban fiction is spiritually older than that, evolving from the work of Charles Dickens, including *The Adventures of Oliver Twist*, who described the life on the mean streets of London.) Goines' work is credited with the creative foundations for contemporary street fiction. His novels, including *Black Gangster*, *Whoreson*, *Black Girl Lost*, and *Never Die Alone*, depict the life of gangsters, drug addicts, and pimps. Equally as important, his novels laid the groundwork for contemporary hip-hop culture and rap.

Contemporary street fiction made its appearance in the late 1990s with the publication of Omar Tyree's *Flyy Girl* and Sister Souljah's *The Coldest Winter Ever*. These are cautionary tales of life on the streets, and they have struck a chord among young African-American readers, especially young men (an often neglected reading demographic). Interestingly, African-American young adults, mostly women, comprise the majority of street fiction authors. Perhaps more telling, a large component of the male street lit authors is incarcerated. Proverbially speaking, they've done the crime, they're doing the time, and now they want to write about it in graphic, raw detail.

A Sampling of Street Lit Authors

Al-Saadiq Banks	Shannon Holmes
Robert "Iceberg Slim" Beck	Solomon Jones
Tracy Brown	K'wan
Chunichi	Sister Souljah
Wahida Clark	Vickie Stringer
Keisha Ervin	Nikki Turner
Donald Goines	Teri Woods

While the demand for street lit is high in public libraries, it is not without challenge. First, of course, it must face issues of street fiction's "appropriateness" for public libraries and their communities. Many individuals believe that street lit has no place in the library, that it has no educational value, and that it celebrates violence, drugs, and sex. Another critical issue considers the availability of the novels. Street fiction, until recently, has flourished with self-publishing and print-on-demand, making it near impossible to acquire through mainstream channels and distributors. It wasn't until small and independent presses saw the demand for and value of producing street fiction that the works became more identifiable in the marketplace.

The task of locating reading lists and reviews can be difficult. No formal guides to the literature that focus on street fiction exist. However, a number of excellent essays and articles provide names of authors, publishers, and titles. The Web, of course, is an extremely important tool for this subgenre. For example, Library Success: A Best Practices Wiki, offers links to booklists, publishers, reviewing resources, and bookseller lists for street fiction. Numerous discussion and review sites exist that provide guidance to learning about the genre. (See Appendix 1 for links and resources.)

Library Journal runs a column featuring street literature titled "The Word on the Street," in *LJ Booksmack*, an online newsletter. The column features book reviews and current information about the genre. It is written alternately by Rollie Welch and Vanessa J. Morris. Each issue of the column takes on a different topic, including themes in street lit, such as revenge or second chances. Perhaps the most interesting feature of the column overall is the comparison of male and female perspectives between the column authors. Information about young adult titles and collection development issues are included in the column.

Other places to consult for information, titles, and authors are the independent presses, small presses, and major publisher for street lit. Triple Crown Publications is an independent publisher specializing in street lit. It was founded by Vickie Stringer, a well-known street lit author. Carl Weber, another street lit author, founded Urban Books. Kensington Books, St. Martin's Griffin, Simon and Schuster, and Random House have aggressively acquired new talent in street fiction writers.

FINDING MULTICULTURAL FICTION

Multicultural fiction does not limit itself to the interests of African-American readers. It also considers Latino, Asian-American, and Native American cultures and others (see Table 12-4 for suggested authors and titles). Many of the same appeal elements that encompass other forms of genre fiction, including setting and protagonists, appear in multicultural fiction. Latinos want characters who look like them, act like them, and hold the same cultural beliefs and values, as do Asians and Native Americans. Attention must be paid to the interests and needs of the cultural communities. The first step is to ask readers what they want and what their fiction must include. Once that is established, it becomes a matter of identifying the right books.

Among the most useful sources of finding multicultural fiction and nonfiction are the cultural and ethnic affiliates of the American Library Association (ALA). Each of the affiliate agencies sponsors annual book awards that honor the best of the year's books by people of color and about their culture (see Chapter 15, "Book Awards and Award-Winning Books," for more information). The booklists are available on the association Web sites and provide a good starting point for building collections. Many of the associations create bibliographies and reading lists, which are readily available on their Web sites. Association journals and newsletters also provide sources of information about authors and titles and the occasional review.

Many of the professional publications, including *Library Journal* and *Publishers Weekly*, will feature articles and reviews of multicultural fiction. *Publishers Weekly*, in particular, publishes articles on the book industry as it relates to specific genres and multicultural groups. Articles on publishing trends, industry surveys, and author interviews are highly useful in keeping up with emerging trends as well as contemporary titles and authors.

A search through public library Web sites tends to be a fruitful activity. For example, a search for Native American fiction gave access to the Madison Public Library (WI) and the Harris County Public Library (TX). Both Web sites included well-organized lists of fiction and short story collections written by and about Native Americans. (Sherman Alexie is prominently featured on both.) The online social cataloging sites, such as LibraryThing, offer similar lists, using tags such as

Table 12-4: A Multicultural Sampler		
Author	**Selected Title**	**Multicultural Group**
Kathleen Alcala	*Spirits of the Ordinary*	Latino Fiction
Sherman Alexie	*Ten Little Indians, Indian Killer, Lone Ranger and Tonto Fistfight in Heaven*	Native American Fiction
Paula Gunn Allen	*The Women Who Owned the Shadows*	Native American Fiction
Julia Alvarez	*How the Garcia Girls Lost Their Accents, Yo!*	Latino Fiction
Rudolfo A. Anaya	*Bless Me Ultima, Zia Summer*	Latino Fiction
Richard Bertematti	*Project Death*	Latino Fiction
Ana Castillo	*Peel My Love Like an Onion*	Latino Fiction
Frank Chin	*Donald Duk*	Asian-American Fiction
Wayson Choy	*The Jade Peony*	Asian-American Fiction
Lucha Corpi	*Black Widow's Wardrobe*	Latino Fiction
Louise Erdrich	*The Last Report on the Miracles at Little No Horse, The Painted Drum*	Native American Fiction
Maria Amparo Escandon	*Esperanza's Box of Saints*	Latino Fiction
Cristina Garcia	*The Aguero Sisters*	Latino Fiction
Carolina Garcia-Aguilera	*Bloody Waters*	Latino Fiction
Diane Glancy	*Pushing the Bear, The Man Who Heard the Land, Stone Heart, Flutie*	Native American Fiction
Genaro Gonzalez	*The Quixote Cult*	Latino Fiction
Oscar Hijuelos	*Empress of the Splendid Season*	Latino Fiction
Rolando Hinojosa	*Ask a Policeman*	Latino Fiction
Thomas King	*Truth & Bright Water*	Native American Fiction
Andrea Louie	*Moon Cakes*	Asian-American Fiction
Manuel Luis Martinez	*Crossing*	Latino Fiction
Elias Miguel Munoz	*Brand New Memory*	Latino Fiction
Michael Nava	*The Burning Plain*	Latino Fiction
Fae Myenne Ng	*Bone*	Asian-American Fiction
Himilce Novas	*Mangos, Bananas, and Coconuts: A Cuban Love Story*	Latino Fiction
Louis Owens	*The Sharpest Sight*	Native American Fiction
Manuel Ramos	*Blues for the Buffalo*	Latino Fiction
Rick P. Rivera	*A Fabricated Mexican*	Latino Fiction
Benjamin Alire Saenz	*Carry Me Like Water, House of Forgetting*	Latino Fiction
Esmeralda Santiago	*America's Dream*	Latino Fiction
Leslie Marmon Silko	*Gardens in the Dunes*	Native American Fiction
Amy Tan	*The Joy Luck Club*	Asian-American Fiction

Author	Selected Title	Multicultural Group
Alfredo Vea	The Silver Cloud Café, Gods Go Begging	Latino Fiction
Ana Veciana-Suarez	The Chin Kiss King	Latino Fiction
Marcos McPeek Villatoro	The Holy Spirit of My Uncle's Cojones	Latino Fiction
Helena Maria Viramontes	Under the Feet of Jesus	Latino Fiction
James Welch	The Indian Lawyer, The Heartsong of Charging Elk	Native American Fiction
Shawn Wong	Homebase, American Knees	Asian-American Fiction
Lois-Ann Yamanaka	Blu's Hanging, Wild Meat and the Bully Burgers	Asian-American Fiction
Note: Author/Title list was compiled from Sherry York's "What's New in Latino Literature?", Fantastic Fiction, and Nancy Pearl's Book Lust and More Book Lust. Consult Appendix 1 for additional reference resources that may be of interest for finding more. And, of course, the commercial and online readers' advisory databases will provide additional read-alikes and related lists.		

"Native American fiction" and the names of individual Native American peoples (e.g., Cherokee or Ojibway).

Libros en Español

Multiculturalism means more than having a collection of adult fiction in English with characters and plots that appeal to people of color. It also demands that public libraries offer collections of materials in languages other than English, including the adult fiction collection. According to the most currently released American Community Survey data, approximately 19.5 percent of the U.S. population speaks a language other than English, and approximately 12 percent speak Spanish or Spanish Creole (U.S. Census, 2007). With this sizeable population comes the increased likelihood that patrons will request fiction titles and other materials in languages other than English.

Recognizing the needs of this diverse population, the Reference and User Services Association of the ALA revised its "Guidelines for Library Services to Spanish-Speaking Library Users" (www.ala.org/ala/mgrps/divs/rusa/resources/guidelines/guidespanish.cfm) in 2006. The guidelines provide a comprehensive approach to supporting both the educational and recreational needs of library users whose first language is not English. Focusing on both collections and services, the guidelines promote an understanding of the complex nature of a highly diverse community. At the core of the guidelines is the advice to provide a collection of foreign-language materials that is relevant to the users' interests; that includes titles from publishers in the countries of the majority of foreign-language speakers (e.g., Mexico, Puerto Rico, Cuba); and that the collection represent materials in all formats, including print and nonprint (audio and film, for example). The guidelines also promote programming and resources that support an "intercultural understanding" within the community. More importantly, while the guidelines focus on Spanish-speaking library users, the guidelines can be applied more broadly to develop collections and to serve other non-English-speaking communities.

However, is this easier to espouse than it is to accomplish, especially for readers' advisory services? One of the first challenges many libraries face is one of general knowledge about the purpose and availability of public libraries. Unlike the public library system in the United States, many countries do not provide free access to library materials, including libraries in Latin America. It becomes crucial to reach out to this population through the agencies (social welfare, faith-based, and educational) that support their needs and by forming community partnerships. Providing general information and reading lists in the predominant language of the non-English speakers will help illustrate that the public library does indeed support their needs and interests. For those libraries that have the financial and personnel support, providing access points in the library's online catalog encourages potential library patrons to use the resources available to them.

Developing well-rounded, appropriate collections of bilingual materials requires a depth of knowledge about not only the users, but of the availability of resources. Until it ceased publication in early 2009, *Críticas* (a sister publication of *Library Journal*, *School Library Journal*, and *Publishers Weekly*) was the most comprehensive resource for reviews of adult and children's materials in Spanish. The Web site, with its archives, is currently available (http://www.criticasmagazine .com) and includes a number of very current articles and material reviews (adult fiction, children's and young adult materials, and Spanish-language films). One of the features still available is the bestsellers lists, which include a number of popular fiction titles translated into Spanish from English as well as titles in their original Spanish language. The caveat for Spanish-language materials—and

Brief List of Contemporary Bestselling Books in Spanish

Rhonda Byrne, *El Secreto*
Paulo Coelho, *El Alquimista*
Junot Diaz, *La Breve y Maravillosa Vida de Óscar Wao*
Laura Esquivel, *Como Aqua para Chocolate*
Andrés López-López, *El Cartel de los Sapos*
Gabriel Garcia Márquez, *Cien Años de Soledad, Amor en los Tiempos del Cólera*
Stephanie Meyer, *El Huésped*
William Paul Young, *La Cabaña*
Carlos Ruiz Zafón, *El Juego del Ángel*

those in other languages—is that translations from English into Spanish must be carefully undertaken to retain the original intent and meaning of the story.

Publishers are an excellent resource for obtaining catalogs and book descriptions. The U.S. publishing houses, such as Random House and HarperCollins, regularly include Spanish-language materials, including fiction, in their catalog of publications. Rayo, an imprint of HarperCollins, provides comprehensive materials to support the Latino community. As part of their services, Rayo produces reading guides in Spanish and lists of upcoming releases available in Spanish. Not only do these tools provide advanced intelligence about upcoming releases, they also present opportunities to provide programming in the library for non-English-speaking patrons, for example, book discussion groups. At both the mid-winter and annual ALA conferences, a number of foreign publishers and foreign book dealers exhibit their products and have representatives available to discuss needs and interests for materials in a variety of foreign languages. Also consider wandering the floor of your local bookstore to see what they have on the shelves; many of the major chains have a section specific to "Libros en Español." Amazon.com and Barnes & Noble also feature similar sections in their online bookstores, which also include professional and reader reviews in Spanish.

A Sampling of Publishers and Providers of Foreign-Language Materials

Anaconda Books	Farrar, Strauss, and Giroux
Aux Amateurs de Livres	Follett Library Resources
Baker & Taylor	Pan Asian Publications
Bilingual Publications Company	Puvill Libros S.A.
China Sprout	Santillana USA Publishing Co.
Cinco Puntos Press	Tsai Fong Press

A number of writers and illustrators are honored annually through literary awards for materials written for and by non-English-speaking authors, including the Pura Belpré Awards, celebrating books written or illustrated by Latinos. Several of the State Book Awards (see Chapter 15, "Book Awards and Award-Winning Books") present separate awards for foreign-language books. The Florida Book Awards (FBA), for example, honor books written in Spanish. Entries in the FBA Spanish Language Book include nonfiction, novels, young adult literature, children's literature, and poetry.

To support the need for more publications in Spanish, the Association of American Publishers formed the Publishing Latino Voices for America Task Force. As part of their endeavors, the PLVA produces an annual summer reading list that includes adult fiction and nonfiction as well as materials for children and young adults. PLVA also supports and helps sponsor festivities held nationwide for "El Día de los Niños/El Día de los Libros." In conjunction with Las Comadres, a national Latina organization, PLVA launched the National Latino Book Club, which is hosted at selected Borders bookstores nationwide. The selected titles for the book club are written in English by Latina or Latino authors. Among other resources, PLVA offers access to a recommended reading list for Hispanic Heritage Month (September 15 through October 15), information for starting Latino reading groups (in Spanish and English), and information for scheduling appearances at events by Latino authors (www.publishers.org/main/Latino/Latino_02.htm).

CONCLUSION

Women's fiction and multicultural fiction are simply two more opportunities to look at the way in which fiction evolves and develops. They are unique in that they do not fit any specific genre, but yet they exhibit many of the same elements of genre fiction, including devoted readers. However, many other special-interest populations abound in library communities with their own unique interests and followers. While not discussed in any detail in this chapter, materials to meet the needs of these groups are included in Appendix 1 in the section on Multicultural Fiction. Genre fiction is rich with good reads to meet the tastes of everyone who asks. As with the mainstream (or perhaps mature) genres, the key becomes knowing what is available and how to match the interests of the reader with the body of literature that is available.

WORKS CONSULTED

Burns, Ann. 2008. "For Black History Month, 40 Exciting Titles: African American Views." *Library Journal* 133, no. 18 (November 1): 78–84.

Chavers, Linda, and Calvin Reid. 2005. "Five Figures: Black Book Publishing Today." *Publishers Weekly* 252, no. 49 (December 12): 26–31.

Content Connections. 2007. *Women and Books 2007: The Survey.* Available: www .womenandbooks2007.com (accessed September 10, 2009).

Craig, Lisa. 2000. "Women's Fiction vs. Romance: A Tale of Two Genres." Writing World. Available: www.writing-world.com/romance/craig.shtml (accessed September 10, 2009).

Hall-Ellis, Sylvia D. 2008. "Subject Access for Reader's Advisory Services: Their Impact on Contemporary Spanish Fiction in Selected Public Library Collections." *Public Library Quarterly* 27, no. 1: 1–18.

Herald, Diana Trixler. 2006. *Genreflecting: A Guide to Popular Reading Interests,* edited by Wayne A. Wiegand. Westport, CT: Libraries Unlimited.

Hill, Marc Lamont, Biany Pérez, and Decoteau J. Irby. 2008. "Street Fiction: What Is It and What Does It Mean for English Teachers?" *English Journal* 97, no. 3 (January): 76–81.

Labbé, Theola. 2000. "Black Books in the House." *Publishers Weekly* 247, no. 50 (December 11): 36–42.

National Endowment for the Arts. 2002. *Reading at Risk: A Survey of Literary Reading in America.* Research Division Report #46. Washington, DC: National Endowment for the Arts.

Pearl, Nancy. 2003. *Book Lust: Recommended Reading for Every Mood, Moment, and Reason.* Seattle, WA: Sasquatch Books.

———. 2005. *More Book Lust: 1,000 New Reading Recommendations for Every Mood, Moment, and Reason.* Seattle, WA: Sasquatch Books.

Pride, Felicia. 2007. "Buyers Aware: Inside the Black Book Market." *Publishers Weekly* 254, no. 49 (December 10): 22–26.

Reference and User Services Association. 2008. "Guidelines for Library Services to Spanish-speaking Library Users." American Library Association. Available: www.ala.org/ala/mgrps/divs/rusa/resources/guidelines/guidespanish.cfm (accessed September 10, 2009).

Saricks, Joyce G. 2001. *Readers' Advisory Guide to Genre Fiction.* Chicago, IL: American Library Association.

Shearer, Kenneth D., and Robert Burgin, eds. 2001. *The Readers' Advisor's Companion.* Englewood, CO: Libraries Unlimited.

"Urban Fiction/Street Lit/Hip Hop Fictions Resources for Librarians." 2009. Library Success: A Best Practices Wiki. Available: www.libsuccess.org/index.php?title=Urban_Fiction/Street_Lit/Hip_Hop_Fiction_Resources_for_Librarians (accessed September 10, 2009).

U.S. Census. 2007. "American Fact Finder Subject Tables: S1601 Language Spoken at Home." Available: http://factfinder.census.gov/servlet/STTable?_bm+y&-geo_id=01000US&-qr_name=ACS_2007_3YR-G00_S1601&-ds_name=ACS_2007)3YR_G00_ (accessed September 10, 2009).

Vnuk, Rebecca. 2005. "Hip Lit for Hip Chicks." *Library Journal* 130, no. 12 (July 15): 42–45.

FURTHER READING

Ferriss, Suzanne, and Mallory Young. 2005. *Chick Lit: The New Woman's Fiction.* New York: Routledge.

Moharram, Jehanne. 2005. "Book Publishing for Minorities in the United States: The Arab-American Conundrum." *Logos* 16, no. 3: 140–147.

Skurnick, Lizzie. 2006. "Chick Lit, the Sequel: Yummy Mummy." *The New York Times Online* (December 17, 2006). Available: www.nytimes.com/2006/12/17/fashion/17MomLit.html?pagewanted=1&_r=1 (accessed September 10, 2009).

Taylor, Rhonda Harris. 2004. "The Native American Detective." *Collection Management* 29, no. 3/4: 101–105.

Van Fleet, Connie. 2004. "African-American Mysteries." *Collection Management* 29, no. 3/4: 83–99.

Wright, David. 2006. "Collection Development: 'Urban Fiction': Streetwise Urban Fiction." *Library Journal* 131, no. 12 (July): 42–45.

———. 2008. "Culturally Speaking: Booktalking Authentic Multicultural Literature." *Library Media Connection* 27, no. 1 (August/September): 16–18.

York, Sherry. 2001. "What's New in Latino Literature?" *The Book Report* 19, no. 4 (January/February): 19–24.

Chapter 13

Readers' Advisory Services for Special Populations

To me, not reading is like having the spirit imprisoned.

—Isabel Allende (1942–)

SETTING THE STAGE

Reading for pleasure is not an activity in which all adults engage. In 2003 the National Assessment of Adult Literacy estimated that 14 percent of the adult population (approximately 30 million adults) in the United States had less than basic literacy skills, able to accomplish only the most simple and concrete of literacy activities, and approximately 11 million adults were nonliterate in English. In 2005 the U.S. Department of Education reported more than 2 million adults were enrolled in adult basic education programs or English-literacy programs. The last survey conducted of programs for adults in public libraries estimated that 17 percent of public library outlets offered some form of adult literacy program, ranging from adult basic literacy to GED preparation and English as a second language. While libraries and library programs may be of great benefit to these individuals, it is unlikely that many of them have visited a public library or that they are aware that the library may have something to offer them.

A number of specialized populations—or underserved populations—can benefit from their public library. Besides adult new readers, adults learning to speak English (ESL or ESOL) make up significant portions of potential library user groups in most communities. It could be said that a triumvirate of nonreaders exists: (1) reluctant readers who struggle to read; (2) individuals who cannot read due to literacy or language barriers; and (3) aliterate individuals who can read but choose not to do so. Other factors to examine regarding user groups within public libraries include individuals with disabilities and issues raised by multiculturalism (race and ethnicity, sexual orientation, and religious orientation, even gender). Not only do libraries need to welcome these individuals with unique interests, but librarians need to recognize that they can serve these populations by preparing reading lists, providing services, and offering resources and programs in an open and supportive atmosphere.

When looking to the studies about why adults read, one of the common threads suggests that adults read to discover their identities to know themselves and to know others. In their study of adult readers, Ross, McKechnie, and Rothbauer suggest readers believe "reading about other lives helps them try out possible roles or helps them give shape to inarticulate feelings or yearnings" (2006: 166). This voyage of self-discovery through reading lends itself to individuals who are trying to assimilate into American life or who are trying to identify with others who face similar challenges.

While there are many groups for whom the library could provide support through reading and resources, this chapter will focus on only a few. Many of the strategies and resources discussed can be applied to any number of users with specialized needs. The purpose of readers' advisory services to adult learners and individuals with disabilities illustrates the range of opportunities for librarians to meet the needs of all within their community.

THE ROLE OF THE READERS' ADVISOR

Already discussed in some detail in earlier chapters, the readers' advisory conversation is intended to understand what the reader is seeking and to help the reader make connections with books and other resources through the library's collection. This is even more critical for adults who are newly literate or learning literacy and language skills. Strategies to use with readers are equally effective with nonreader populations with a few modifications. It may be unlikely that an adult new reader will reveal that he or she has limited reading skills. The readers' advisor will need to look for additional clues in body language and through careful listening. The readers' advisor needs to identify books with high interest for adults but with low vocabulary for novice readers. Not unlike interactions with avid readers, the readers' advisor must determine the elements of reading that create a pleasurable experience, whether for leisure or education, and then match the new reader to titles that will be of interest.

The most important element of connecting readers, especially new readers, to books requires identifying material that captures their interests and imagination. This will encompass fiction and nonfiction, poetry, and short stories. For new readers and ESL students, the language of the reading material—the flow and rhythm as well as meaning—is equally as critical as interest. Similarly to guiding everyday readers to books, the readers' advisor must know the breadth and depth of the library's collection—what books may be appealing and appropriate to new readers.

Readers' advisors in public libraries can assist in many ways that are already familiar. Reading lists and bibliographies, booktalks, and knowledge of resources

Reaching Out to Special Populations

- Find out about the needs and interests of the specialized populations
- Develop relationships with community agencies that serve adult learners and patrons with disabilities
- Distribute brochures and information kits that detail the services and collections available to specialized populations
- Create reading lists and annotated booklists that appeal to the specialized populations
- Repeat finding out about the needs and interests of the specialized populations
- Provide materials in a range of formats, from traditional print to audio-enhanced
- Create materials in alternate formats that can be used with assistive technologies
- Create and maintain Web and other electronic resources that are accessible and meet Section 508 standards of the Rehabilitation Act of 1973
- Market and promote readers' advisory services widely to schools, agencies, and other programs that serve adult learners and individuals with disabilities
- Maintain an environment that is accessible to all

are practical applications of services for new readers. Talking with new readers or with literacy and language tutors provides opportunities to discover what elements excite curiosity in new readers. Preparing an annotated booklist of titles with high interest and easy reading levels requires nothing different from preparing thematic booklists for genre fiction—just a wealth of knowledge about the library's collection. Well-prepared and well-implemented booktalks can drive enthusiasm to read and to discover books of value and interest. Just as many librarians identify individual genres within the collection with spine labels, it is equally possible to provide labeling that identifies books appropriate for new readers throughout the collection. Finally, a number of public libraries have established book discussion groups for their new readers that mirror the library's other adult book discussion groups, offering new readers opportunities to explore the ideas presented in fiction and through illustration.

Using the Web to inform the community about services for groups with specialized needs is as effective as it is for other library users. The library's Web site becomes a consultation source for reading lists and information for supporting all members of the community who have specialized needs. In many instances it will be the adult's family members or caregivers who will access the information on their behalf. The readers' advisory sections of the library Web site can be designed to include sections for specific needs, including adult new readers and their families and tutors, ESL needs, patrons with disabilities, senior patrons, etc. This may serve as a way to reach out to individuals who are unaware that the public library can support their educational and recreational needs.

Books comprise only one part of the collection. Audiobooks and CDs provide access to the written word that enables new readers to develop language skills. Well-told stories read by accomplished narrators add an element of interpretation of language through listening. (This is not unlike the process many children experience when adults read stories to them, and which many adult new readers may have missed as youngsters.) Audiobooks also serve patrons with vision impairment or who are blind, offering them options for engaging with written text through voice. A number of narrators have been recognized for the quality of their achievements in spoken-word recordings; these narrators make the written word come alive for the individuals engaged with the words (check out *AudioFile Magazine*'s "Golden Voices" for profiles and information about their award-winning narrators; www.audiofilemagazine.com/gvpages/index .shtml). Audiobooks should be selected with an eye (or in this case ear) for the quality of the narration and its ability to engage the listener.

Public libraries and RA services must become part of the larger learning community if they are to be effective in meeting the needs of adult new readers and other specialized populations. As a public agency, the library makes space available to literacy and ESL programs that provide more than just a place to study. It offers access to resources in print and audio/video, access to public computers, and a welcoming and nonthreatening environment with a staff that is supportive and nonjudgmental. Providing collections that suit the needs of adult learners and other library users not only creates a welcoming environment but also upholds the ethics and ideals of the library and information profession.

SERVING ADULT NEW READERS AND ESL LEARNERS

The library is a place full of stories, in fiction and in readable nonfiction. However, much of the library's adult resources may be out of the reading reach of the newly English literate. Thus begins the search for materials that will engage those acquiring new literacy and language skills. Consider first the collection of genre fiction, such as tales of romance or mystery. Much of it is written in a predictable, formulaic style with simple, engaging language that can be easily followed. Genre fiction carries adult themes of relationships, work life, and health that appeal to adult learners. Fiction stories written in short chapters with vivid descriptions and intended for a general reading audience may be very readable for intermediate and advanced new readers. (Poetry, such as that of Langston Hughes or Maya Angelou, will serve a similar purpose.) Using the fiction collection in conjunction with the DVD collection through book and movie tie-ins offers adult new readers opportunities to make connections between visual representations of written works and the books themselves.

Readers' advisors need to look to the entire collection within the library. A number of young adult titles and even picture books will provide excellent resources for introducing adult learners to books. Young adult fiction, in particular, frequently includes strong adult characters with whom adult readers can identify. The adage "a picture is worth a thousand words" reflects opportunities to reach adult learners through picture books and even photographic "coffee table" books. Many picture books provide limited text that is rich in description but at an achievable reading level. When selecting young adult or children's books for adult learners, we should keep a few points in mind:

- Select books that address topics and interests of adults.
- Select books that treat these themes in complex ways.
- Select book that provide high quality illustration or photography that is not childish. (Bloem and Padak, 1996)

Picture books and young adult books frequently present complex issues and raise questions that are sophisticated and appeal to adults—issues of racism, family relationships, and new cultures. (See Table 13-1 for a small selection of titles for adult new readers.)

A number of topics lend themselves to the interests of adult learners, and they will also have broader appeal to the general adult readers in the library. Consider including series and individual titles that cover job skills and job searching, books on parenting skills, pregnancy and child development, and science. Scientific topics are well suited to illustration, appealing to all levels and ages of readers. Stories of new immigrants and attaining citizenship add depth to the collection and serve not only adult new readers but ESL students as well. Health information and women's issues are also highly popular topics that appeal to a range of adult readers.

Readers' advisory outreach can be highly beneficial for local adult literacy and language programs. RA services for adult learners should include the promotion of materials specifically for adult new readers and ESL students, including information about books and resources within the library for tutors and adult learners. Provide agencies that support adult learners with brochures and flyers about the library's services. Make personal presentations or visits to these agencies to introduce them to the services available. Like any other library user, adult learners should be offered library tours and orientation sessions to help familiarize them with the library's layout and where they can find appropriate materials as well as the services that are available. The same can be said of workshops; while they need to be tailored to the needs and abilities of adult learners, workshops can help improve self-confidence in finding and using materials.

A number of resources are available that provide extensive lists of books and resources for adult learners. Several books by Marguerite Weibel—*Choosing and*

Table 13-1: A Sampling of Titles for Adult New Readers*		
Author	Title	Brief Description
Tom Feelings	Soul Looks Back in Wonder	Children's illustrated book; combines full-color illustration with poetry of Langston Hughes and Maya Angelou
Jane Yolen and David Shannon (illustrator)	Encounter	Thought-provoking look at the voyages of Christopher Columbus; illustrated
Jacob Lawrence	The Great Migration: An American Story	An illustrated chronicle of the migration of blacks from the American South to the North from 1916 to 1919
Cynthia Rylant and Barry Moser (illustrator)	Appalachia: The Voices of Sleeping Birds	Illustrated essay of the people who live in Appalachia
Cynthia Voigt	Dicey's Song	Developing family relationships as narrated by 16-year-old Dicey. Strong, central adult characters
Mildred D. Taylor	Roll of Thunder, Hear My Cry	Complexities of an African-American family life in a time of racial tensions during the Great Depression
Karen Hesse	Out of the Dust	Written in free-form verse; enduring the personal and economic hardships of the Dust Bowl
Sandra Cisneros	House on Mango Street	Coming of age in the Hispanic Quarter of Chicago
Ernest J. Gaines	A Lesson before Dying	Story of two African-American men struggling to attain manhood in 1940s Louisiana
Joan Lowery Nixon and Kathleen Nixon Bush	Champagne with a Corpse	Thumbprint Mysteries series; high interest, low vocabulary
Ellen Godfrey	Murder in the Shadows	Thumbprint Mysteries series; high interest, low vocabulary
Antoinette Moses	The Girl at the Window	Ghost fiction
J. K. Rowling	Harry Potter and the Sorcerer's Stone	Young adult fantasy; magic and the struggle between good and evil
Marilyn Reynolds	Baby Help	Issues of spousal abuse and shelter living; fiction
*Arranged in order of reading difficulty.		

Using Books with Adult New Readers (1996), *Joining the Conversation: An Anthology for Developing Readers* (2003), and *Adult Learners Welcome Here* (2007)— offer a variety of titles and readings appropriate to the interests of adult new readers, from beginning readers to advanced. Rosemarie Riechel's book *Easy Information Sources for ESL, Adult Learners and New Readers* (2009) includes an extensive annotated bibliography of recommended juvenile nonfiction to meet the interests of adult new readers and ESL students. *Accessing the Classics: Great Reads for Adults, Teens, and English Language Learners* (2006), by LaVergne Rosow, considers the use of classics to improve reading skills. Rosow includes annotated lists of some of the world's most renowned literature to foster language and literacy skills for adults and teens. Several titles specific to the needs of ESL adult learners are available, including Rosow's *Light 'n Lively Reads for ESL, Adult, and Teen Readers: A Thematic Bibliography* (1996) and Laura Hibbets McCaffery's book *Building an ESL Collection for Young Adults: A Bibliography of Recommended Fiction and Nonfiction for Schools and Public Libraries* (1998).

Searching the Internet for adult learner resources provides access to numerous public and academic libraries and adult literacy agencies that support adult learners. Many of them either provide lists of resources or provide access to searchable databases and catalogs of fiction and nonfiction. For example, the Chicago Public Library features a section on its Web site devoted to the needs and interests of adult new readers, including access to focused searches in the catalog and links to "helpful Web sites" for literacy learners and literacy tutors (www.chipublib.org/cplbooksmovies/espfor/adultnewreaders.php). Salt Lake City Public Library and the New York Public Library also provide access to literacy resources for adult new readers, as do many others. The American Library Association's Office of Literacy and Outreach Services (OLOS) offers an exhaustive compilation of resources for libraries in supporting the needs and interests of adult learners (www.ala.org/ala/aboutala/offices/olos/index.cfm). In addition, the Center for Adult English Language Acquisition (CAELA) (www.cal.org/caela/index.html) provides access to ESL resources, tools, and research specific to English-language acquisition for adults; some materials on the Web site are available in Spanish.

A number of companies prepare and publish materials for adult learners, many of whom are not mainstream, big-name publishing houses. New Readers Press (www.newreaderspress.com) has a wide range of resources for adult new readers and ESL students and their tutors. New Readers Press materials for ESL students are divided between learning English as a second language and resources for acculturation and citizenship. Oxford University Press, a department of the University of Oxford, (www.oup.com/elt/catalogue/teachersites/bookworms/?cc=global) has prepared a complete reading program to support new readers across all levels of experience. The titles from OUP Bookworms include easy-reader versions of many classic works of fiction as well as topic-specific nonfiction titles. Proliteracy Worldwide (www.proliteracy.org/NetCommunity/Page.aspx?pid=181&srcid=-2) is one of the preeminent agencies supporting adult learning and literacy internationally. They provide a wide range of resources, workshops, and publications for both literacy tutors and adult learners. Finally, Peppercorn Books (www.peppercornbooks.com/catalog) and Grassroots Press (http://grassrootsbooks.net/us/) provide an extensive range of materials for adult literacy and ESL learners and tutors. Included in their catalog are easy readers and chapter books, biographies, "page-turner" collections, and materials related to health, employment, and other topics of interest to adult learners.

Differentiating between Adult New Readers and ESL Students

Many agencies lump adult literacy and ESL together, and, indeed, they share many of the same issues and concerns. However, for ESL students, an additional barrier of language exists. ESL students typically fall into one of two categories: (1) they are literate in their native language but cannot read or speak English, or (2) they are not literate in their native tongue or in English. The language barriers are compounded in many instances by additional social and cultural considerations. ESL learners are further differentiated from adult literacy learners by their personal experiences; many experienced significant trauma (war, poverty, displacement) due to events in their native countries and subsequent resettlement, immigration, and asylum in the United States and Canada (Florez and Terrill, 2003).

Chapter 3 explored the process of reading, including schema theory. Schema theory suggests that individuals have frameworks built on their own experience and knowledge, which they use to give meaning to their reading. But schemas are also related to cultural knowledge. Those with a common language share a common worldview or common experiences. Individuals in the early stages of acquiring new literacy skills may find it difficult to process descriptions of places, events, etc., presented in the schema of the new language. This will also impact their comprehension of written texts. It is in these instances that it is critical for the readers' advisor to build bridges between the library's book collections and the adult learner's cultural knowledge.

READING MENTORS

Reluctant or frustrated readers and new readers benefit greatly from having someone mentor them. Reluctant readers, however, unlike adult literacy learners, do have the ability to read, but they read at a very slow pace with poor comprehension. While much of the research has focused on reading mentors for children, adults can also be greatly influenced through this same type of activity. One of the premises is that readers enjoy sharing their reading experiences and the books they loved, and they can relay that enthusiasm for the written word to others. Readers' advisors are in the prime position to both formally and informally mentor readers and literacy learners. Unlike literacy and ESL tutoring, the focus of the relationship is on individual books and titles and on sharing reactions to those books.

In her book *Speaking of Reading* (1995), Nadine Rosenthal outlines a number of strategies for mentoring. Some of these echo the same strategies RA librarians employ in suggesting books to readers.

1. Suggest books with fast-paced plots and dialogue that will grab and keep the reader's attention (in RA speak—appeal factors);
2. Choose books with topics of interest to the individual;
3. Suggest books with characters that are in situations similar to those of your mentoring partner;
4. Choose books that you can read together and discuss. This is not intended to be a teacher-student relationship, but one of mutual benefit and pleasure;
5. Be aware of potential sensitivities and self-image of the mentoring partner. Many reluctant readers are embarrassed and frustrated by their inability to read well;
6. Encourage your reading partner and build mutual trust in the relationship. (Rosenthal, 1995: 204–205)

Part of the mentoring process is to model your own reading comprehension strategies for your reading partner. Many reluctant readers and adults with limited literacy skills never learned the reading strategies that avid readers employ. Encourage your protégé to monitor his or her comprehension through provocative questions, summarizing, and exploring the texts.

If the readers' advisor has neither the time nor the ability to mentor, it is possible to make use of RA tools and strategies to engage the reluctant reader with books. Maintain a list of sure bets and engaging reads that can be used to introduce reluctant and new readers to genre fiction, readable nonfiction, and poetry. Use the whole collection, from books to film, for encouraging adults to read for pleasure, focusing on interest-driven reading. Reluctant readers and new readers need help in making the connections between their interests and written materials that will support and foster their interests.

READERS' ADVISORY SERVICES FOR PATRONS WITH DISABILITIES

Today more than 40 million residents in the United States over the age of 16 report having at least one disability that limits one or more of their major life activities. This comes with significant legal connotations and implications, especially for public libraries that provide services and access to the local community. Beginning with the Rehabilitation Act of 1973, the U.S. government began enacting legislation to protect the rights of Americans with disabilities, ensuring equal access to education, employment, public agencies, and information technologies, and protection from discrimination. Section 504 of the Rehabilitation Act underscores reasonable accommodations and "prohibits discrimination against persons with disabilities by any program or activity that receives federal financial assistance" (ALA, 2006), and by extension it requires libraries that receive federal funding to make reasonable accommodations for patrons with disabilities through modifications of the physical building and environs and adaptation of materials, including online catalogs and Internet resources. Section 508 of the Rehabilitation Act of 1973 (amended and enacted in 1998), while specific to federal agencies and departments, requires that electronic and information technology be accessible to all members of the public who seek information by these means; this also has implications for agencies who receive federal grant funding with the requirement to meet federal accessibility standards.

But what does this all mean for providing readers' advisory services? By law, all library staff is required to provide reasonable accommodation for patrons with disabilities. Ultimately, patrons with disabilities comprise a special population who will benefit greatly from readers' advisory services and access to a knowledgeable RA librarian. As in serving other specialized populations, it requires knowing what their interests are and matching interests to collections. The RA conversation must take into account the formats in which the patron with a disability requires materials and books as well as the accessibility of resources, from physical space to electronic access.

As mentioned previously, one of the purposes driving readers is the desire to identify with others who face similar situations in order to not feel alone and to make sense of their world. Patrons with disabilities are no exception to this desire. However, for patrons with disabilities the service is multifaceted. They and their families may be seeking information related to their specific disability; they may be seeking fiction and nonfiction about people with disabilities; or they may be seeking materials in formats that will enable them to engage with reading for pleasure.

Readers' advisors can begin by developing and maintaining fiction and nonfiction collections that offer materials in a variety of formats. The National Library Service for the Blind and Physically Handicapped (NLS) provides materials in braille and talking-book sound recordings to eligible patrons by mail free of charge. These materials can be obtained through the regional or subregional "talking book libraries." (The Talking Book Libraries go by many names. A state-by-state list of the agencies is available through a searchable database on the National Library Services Web site at www.loc.gov/nls/find.html.) NLS also has a searchable catalog on their Web site, which will help RA staff determine what books are available as either talking-book sound recordings or as braille translations. Braille and talking books feature the same range of genre fiction as the standard print fiction collection, with popular authors, bestsellers, and classics. Note, however, that talking books and the equipment required for playback are distributed only to eligible individuals.

Another option is to maintain a collection of large-print books for individuals with visual impairments or declining vision. Large-print books are typically slightly larger than trade-size publications and come in both hardcover and paperback. The font usually starts at 14 to 16 points, making it much larger than the standard 8- and 10-point font of the typical paperback (see Figure 13-1).

Figure 13-1: Font Size Comparisons	
8 point font	10 point font
14 point font	16 point font
20 point font	

More white space makes reading easier. According to reports in *Publishers Weekly* (Robbins, 2008), large-print books are rapidly gaining in popularity, with an increasing number of large-print titles being released simultaneously with the traditional trade editions. This is also a service much appreciated by the library's senior patrons.

Resources for Large-Print Books

Baker & Taylor: www.btol.com
Brodart Co.: www.brodart.com
Center Point Large Print: www.centerpointlargeprint.com
Follett Library Resources: www.titlewave.com
Gale, part of Cengage Learning: www.gale.com
HarperCollins Publishers: www.harpercollins.com
Ingram Library Services: www.ingramlibrary.com
Merriam-Webster, Inc.: www.Merriam-Webster.com
ReadHowYouWant: www.readhowyouwant.com
Ulverscroft Large Print USA: www.ulverscroft.com

Reading brings us into the lives of others who resemble ourselves. It introduces characters with similar thoughts and feelings, and ethnic and racial characteristics, who find themselves in situations the same as ours. This is no different for patrons with disabilities; they want to read stories that have characters resembling themselves, with disabilities, with triumphs, and with challenges. (See Table 13-2 for a sampling of titles that feature characters with disabilities.) The caveat, however, is to select books that are realistic in depicting individuals with disabilities and devoid of biases and prejudices. A number of readers' advisory staffs have prepared reading lists to meet these interests. Of note are the Seattle Public Library, Washington (www.spl.org/default.asp?pageID=audience_specialservices_booklist), the Johnson County Library, Kansas (www.jocolibrary.org/findagoodbook), and the Springfield City Library, Massachusetts (www.springfieldlibrary.org/reading/disabled.html). Each of these libraries provides

Table 13-2: A Sampling of Titles Featuring People with Disabilities in Fiction		
Author	Title	Alternate Formats
Karen Bender	*Like Normal People*	Large Print, Braille
Darryl Brock	*Havana Heat*	Audio Download, Audio CD, Audio Cassette
Carrie Brown	*Lamb in Love*	Large Print, Audio Cassette, Talking-Book Sound Recording
Rosellen Brown	*Tender Mercies*	Large Print, Talking-Book Sound Recording
Bebe Moore Campbell	*72 Hour Hold*	Audio Download, Talking-Book Sound Recording
Patricia Carlon	*The Whispering Wall*	Braille
David Cook	*Walter*	Braille
Rachel Cusk	*The Country Life*	Audio Download, Audio Cassette, Braille, Talking-Book Sound Recording
Iris Dart	*When I Fall in Love*	Large Print, Audio Cassette, Talking-Book Sound Recording
Debra Dean	*The Madonnas of Leningrad*	Audio CD, Braille, Talking-Book Sound Recording
Jeff Deaver	*A Maiden's Grave*	Audio Download, Talking-Book Sound Recording
Charles Dickinson	*The Widows' Adventures*	Talking-Book Sound Recording
Kim Edwards	*The Memory Keeper's Daughter*	Audio Download, Talking-Book Sound Recording
Dick Francis	*Whip Hand*	Audio Download, Braille, Talking-Book Sound Recording
Winston Graham	*The Walking Stick*	Audio Cassette, Braille
Joanne Greenberg	*Of Such Small Differences*	Large Print, Braille, Talking-Book Sound Recording
Winston Groom	*Forrest Gump: A Novel*	Large Print, Audio Download, Audio Cassette, Movie, Talking-Book Sound Recording
Mark Haddon	*The Curious Incident of the Dog in the Night-Time*	Audio Download, Audio CD, Braille, Talking-Book Sound Recording
Daniel Hecht	*Skull Session*	Large Print, Audio Download
Michael Ignatieff	*Scar Tissue*	Talking-Book Sound Recording
Frances Itani	*Deafening*	Audio Download, Braille
Molly Keane	*Time after Time*	Audio Cassette, Talking-Book Sound Recording
Margorie Kellogg	*Tell Me That You Love Me, Junie Moon*	Braille, Talking-Book Sound Recording
James Kelman	*How Late It Was, How Late*	Talking-Book Sound Recording
Daniel Keyes	*Flowers for Algernon*	Large Print, Audio Cassette, Braille, Talking-Book Sound Recording

Author	Title	Alternate Formats
Dave King	*The Ha-Ha*	Audio Download, Talking-Book Sound Recording
Joseph Klempner	*Flat Lake in Winter*	Large Print, Audio Cassette
Jonathan Lethem	*Motherless Brooklyn*	Large Print, Audio CD, Audio Cassette, Talking-Book Sound Recording
Bret Lott	*Jewel*	Audio CD, Audio Cassette, Large Print, Talking-Book Sound Recording
Ed McBain	*Hark! A Novel of the 87th Precinct*	Audio Download, Audio Cassette, Audio CD, Large Print, Braille, Talking-Book Sound Recording
Elizabeth McCracken	*The Giant's House: A Romance*	Large Print, Braille
Carson McCullers	*The Heart Is a Lonely Hunter*	Audio Cassette, Audio Download, Audio CD, Large Print, Braille, Talking-Book Sound Recording
Colleen McCullough	*Tim*	Audio CD, Large Print, Braille, Talking-Book Sound Recording
Elizabeth Moon	*The Speed of Dark*	Audio Download, Large Print, Talking-Book Sound Recording
Tawni O'Dell	*Coal Run*	Audio Download, Audio CD, Large Print, Braille
Belva Plain	*Daybreak*	Large Print, Audio Cassette, Talking-Book Sound Recording
Gwyn Rubio	*Icy Sparks*	Large Print, Audio CD, Audio Cassette, Talking-Book Sound Recording
William Safire	*Full Disclosure*	Braille, Talking-Book Sound Recording
Jose Saramago	*Blindness*	Audio Download, Audio CD, Large Print, Talking-Book Sound Recording
Vikram Seth	*An Equal Music*	Audio Download, Audio CD, Talking-Book Sound Recording
David Shields	*Dead Languages*	Talking-Book Sound Recording
Elizabeth Spencer	*The Light in the Piazza*	Audio Download, Braille, Talking-Book Sound Recording
Dalton Trumbo	*Johnny Got His Gun*	Audio Download, Audio CD, Braille, Talking-Book Sound Recording
Mary Webb	*Precious Bane*	Large Print, Audio Cassette, Braille, Talking-Book Sound Recording
Patricia Wood	*Lottery*	Audio Download, Audio CD, Large Print, Talking-Book Sound Recording
Stuart Woods	*Dead Eyes*	Audio Download, Large Print, Audio Cassette, Talking-Book Sound Recording

Note: Information for this table was gathered from the Johnson County Library, Seattle Public Library, Springfield City Library, and the National Library Services for the Blind and Physically Handicapped.

online access to lists of fiction about people with disabilities. The lists include mystery, romance, thrillers, literary fiction, and classics. Many of these titles also come in multiple formats, from movie tie-ins on audio-described DVD to braille and sound recording.

With imagination and willingness, readers' advisors can prepare readers' programs that are inclusive and take the interests and needs of patrons with disabilities into consideration. For example, book discussion groups can and should include patrons with disabilities. This may mean ensuring that the books selected by the reading groups are available in alternate formats, including audio, large print, braille, or film with closed captioning or audio descriptions. When planning "One Book, One Community" programs, a similar advanced preparation must take place to ensure the book selections are widely available through multiple copies and multiple formats. Complementary reading and study guides can be translated into Braille or created as large-print documents. Fostering a relationship with the talking-book library that serves the region or subregion will facilitate obtaining appropriate materials for programming as will relationships with local agencies serving the deaf and hearing impaired.

Reading lists and book annotations should be created as documents that can be easily scanned with screen magnifiers and screen readers. Plain black text on white backgrounds with minimal, simple graphics and large-font text are the most usable for individuals with low vision. Electronic versions of these documents can be disseminated to individuals who use specialized readers, making the information accessible. Many of these materials can be distributed to area agencies serving adults with disabilities as well as mailed to patrons identified as having disabilities.

Did You Know?

Georgia Tech provides an online series of tutorials for designing materials that are accessible to individuals with disabilities. The focus of the tutorials is distance learning; however, many of the modules provide practical information about creating Word and PDF documents, PowerPoint slides, video, and other resources that are accessible. Check out www.accesselearning.net/ for the ten free modules.

It is possible to serve patrons with disabilities in other ways as well. Many films are being released on audio-described DVD and video, including popular books with movie tie-ins. These specialized features provide narration of key visual elements (actions and gestures, costuming, facial expressions, scenery), which enables visually impaired and blind viewers to fully understand the film through sound. A wide selection of classic and popular film is available with audio descriptions, and resources are readily available through the talking-book libraries as well as a number of public libraries. Having direct access to or knowing who has these types of resources available can aid the readers' advisor in creating rich interactive engagement with the written word by reducing barriers to the reading experience. The Royal National Institute of Blind People (RNIB) provides an extensive list of recently released audio-described DVDs along with a fact sheet on choosing a DVD player on their Web site (www.rnib.org.uk/xpedio/ groups/public/documents/publicwebsite/public_videoandDVD.hcsp).

Communication with deaf or hearing-impaired patrons may be of greatest concern rather than their ability to access the collection or library catalog. A number of libraries now have access through community agencies to American Sign Language interpreters, who can then be engaged to assist with public programs and workshops. For deaf and hearing-impaired patrons, a wide selection of DVDs and video are available with closed captioning. Most movies and many television programs released during the past ten years are closed captioned, making a wide range of popular materials accessible to those with hearing impairments or who are deaf. As with audio-described films, the closed captioning allows the hearing-impaired patron to enjoy the full range of multimedia options by seeing the action and having text translation of the dialogue appear across the bottom of the screen. Many libraries are now providing telecommunications devices for the deaf (TDDs) to facilitate contacting the library without difficulty; much like text messaging with one's cell phone, the TDD allows users to send text messages back and forth via a keyboard (think IM reference and chat services).

American Sign Language

American Sign Language is a complete language that uses hands, movement, facial expressions, and body posture for communication. It is the first language of many deaf individuals in North America as opposed to spoken English. The following are some sources for information and education about American Sign Language.

The American Sign Language Phrase Book, 3rd edition, by Barbara Bernstein Fant, Lou Fant, and Betty Miller. McGraw-Hill Professional, 2008.
The American Sign Language Handshape Dictionary, by Richard A. Tennant, Marianne Gluszak Brown, and Valerie Nelson-Metlay. Gallaudet University Press, 1998.
ASL University: www.lifeprint.com
Handspeak: www.handspeak.com
National Institute on Deafness and Other Communication Disorders: www .nidcd.nih.gov/health/hearing/asl.asp

Assistive Technologies for Patrons with Disabilities

While not necessarily the purview of readers' advisory staff, they should be aware of a number of assistive technologies for patrons with disabilities. For many, the assistive technologies can open the world of reading and information access that may otherwise be limited to them. Assistive technology refers specifically to the special services and devices that make it possible for persons with visual, hearing, or speech impairments to access materials and services, including the library catalog. The devices can range from handheld magnifying glasses to highly complex computer systems that convert print into synthesized speech, large print, or braille. Assisted-listening devices (ALDs) are designed to amplify sound to make it easier for hearing-impaired patrons to enjoy and participate in library programs. Closed-circuit television (CCTV) uses a camera system integrated with a television to enlarge and magnify images. It also allows the user to alter contrast of the background (white text on black background, or black text on white background, for example). Job Access with Speech (JAWS) is another powerful software application designed to work with speech synthesizers to read documents aloud for the blind and visually impaired. Finally, Zoom Text is a magnification and reading software that enables computer users to enlarge the text they are viewing on the monitor.

A Few Sources for Assistive Technology

A number of companies provide assistive technology solutions for libraries. Over the past several years, the American Library Association has included an Assistive Technology Pavilion on the exhibits floor at both the Mid-winter and Annual Conferences. Some of the companies in attendance include:

EVAS: www.evas.com/cgi-bin/start.exe/Main.htm
HumanWare: www.humanware.com
ReadHowYouWant: www.readhowyouwant.com

In addition, *Library Journal* GoldBook (http://goldbook.libraryjournalcom) features a searchable directory of library vendors, including a list of companies providing assistive technology for libraries.

CONCLUSION

Serving patrons who might not be considered traditional library users provides satisfaction in meeting the needs of all members of the community. Individuals learning to read and acquiring language skills need the assistance of the readers' advisory staff to continue to make connections with reading for pleasure. The readers' advisor can encourage them to continue through their reading apprenticeship, transforming them into readers through "real" books. Patrons with disabilities need books and resources that match their interests in formats that enable them to engage with reading effectively and with pleasure. Meeting the needs of these specialized clients creates an inclusive and open community for everyone.

Many of the activities and services that readers' advisors create for their every-day patrons are easily adapted to extend the reach to other user groups. The key is to include the special populations in the conversation by asking them what they need and want. Providing services to adult learners and to patrons with disabilities is a winning situation for the entire community. Increased access to reading materials and information encourages lifelong learning, which ultimately improves the overall health of the community.

WORKS CONSULTED

American Library Association. 2006. "Federal Law—The Rehabilitation Act." Available: www.ala.org/ala/aboutala/offices/oitp/emailtutorials/accessibilitya/04.cfm (accessed September 10, 2009).

Bloem, Patricia L., and Nancy D. Padak. 1996. "Picture Books, Young Adult Books, and Adult Literacy Learners." *Journal of Adolescent & Adult Literacy* 40, no. 1 (September): 48–53.

Florez, MaryAnn Cunningham, and Lynda Terrill. 2003. "Working with Literacy-level Adult English Language Learners." Center for Adult English Language Acquisition. Available: http://www.cal.org/caela/esl_resources/digests/litQA.html (accessed September 10, 2009).

Hickok, John. 2005. "ESL (English as a Second Language) Web Sites: Resources for Library Administrators, Librarians, and ESL Library Users." *Journal of Library Administration* 43, no. 3/4: 247–262.

Mates, Barbara T. 2003. "AccessAbility @ Cleveland Public Library." *Public Libraries* 42, no. 1 (January/February): 28–31.

McCaffery, Laura Hibbets. 1998. *Building an ESL Collection for Young Adults: A Bibliography of Recommended Fiction and Nonfiction for Schools and Public Libraries*. Westport, CT: Greenwood Press.

Riechel, Rosemarie. 2009. *Easy Information Sources for ESL, Adult Learners and New Readers*. New York: Neal-Schuman.

Robbins, Sarah J. 2008. "Large Print Up Close." *Publishers Weekly* (May 19). Available: www.publishersweekly.com/article/CA6561932.html (accessed September 10, 2009).

Rosenthal, Nadine. 1995. *Speaking of Reading*. Portsmouth, NH: Heinemann.

Rosow, LaVergne. 1996. *Light 'n Lively Reads for ESL, Adult, and Teen Readers: A Thematic Bibliography*. Englewood, CO: Libraries Unlimited.

_____. 2006. *Accessing the Classics: Great Reads for Adults, Teens and English Language Learners*. Genreflecting Advisory Series. Westport, CT: Libraries Unlimited.

Ross, Catherine Sheldrick, Lynne E. F. McKechnie, and Paulette M. Rothbauer. 2006. *Reading Matters: What the Research Reveals about Reading, Libraries, and Community*. Westport, CT: Libraries Unlimited.

U.S. Department of Education, Institute of Education Sciences. 2003. *National Assessment of Adult Literacy*. Available: http://nces.ed.gov/naal/kf_demographics.asp (accessed September 10, 2009).

_____. 2006. *Digest of Education Statistics.* Available: http://nces.ed.gov/programs/digest/index.asp (accessed September 10, 2009).

U.S. Department of Justice. 2008. "Americans with Disabilities Act of 1990." Available: www.ada.gov/pubs/ada.htm (accessed September 10, 2009).

U.S. Rehabilitation Act of 1973. Public Law 93-112 93rd Congress, H. R. 8070, September 26, 1973.

Weibel, Marguerite Crowley. 1996. *Choosing and Using Books with Adult New Readers.* New York: Neal-Schuman.

_____. 2003. *Joining the Conversation: An Anthology for Developing Readers.* Upper Saddle River, NJ: Prentice Hall.

_____. 2007. *Adult Learners Welcome Here: A Handbook for Librarians and Literacy Teachers.* New York: Neal-Schuman.

FURTHER READING

Burt, Miriam, Joy Kreeft Peyton, and Rebecca Adams. 2003. *Reading and Adult English Language Learners: A Review of the Research.* Washington, DC: Center for Applied Linguistics.

Dawkins, Susan. 2008. "Tutors as Cultural Brokers: Some Thoughts on Library Literacy Councils and ESL Learners." *Bookmobile Outreach Services* 11, no. 2: 9–18.

Lewis, Laurie, and Bernard Greene. 2002. *Programs for Adults in Public Library Outlets.* Statistical Analysis Report NCES 2003-010 (November). Washington, DC: U.S. Department of Education, Office of Educational Research and Improvement.

Public Library Association. 1999. "1999 Top Titles for Adult New Readers." *Public Libraries* 38, no. 5 (September/October): 320–321.

Rubin, Rhea Joyce. 2002. "Serving People with Disabilities." OLOS Preconference Different Voices, Common Quest: Adult Literacy & Outreach in Libraries. American Library Association Conference, Atlanta, GA. Available: www.ala.org/ala/aboutala/offices/olos/outreachresource/docs/people_with_disabilities.pdf (accessed September 10, 2009).

Sibley, Carol H. 1999. "High Interest–Low Vocabulary Books Located at Livingston Lord Library, Minnesota State University Moorhead." Available: www.mnstate.edu/cmc/Bibliographies/HighLowBooks.htm (accessed September 10, 2009).

_____. 2002. "Bibliography." OLOS Preconference Different Voices, Common Quest: Adult Literacy & Outreach in Libraries. American Library Association Conference, Atlanta, GA. Available: www.ala.org/ala/aboutala/offices/olos/outreachresources/docs/disabilities_bibliog.pdf (accessed September 10, 2009).

U.S. Department of Justice. 1994. "ADA Standards for Accessible Design." *Code of Federal Regulations* (28 CFR Part 36). Available: www.ada.gov/adastd94.pdf (accessed September 10, 2009).

Venetis, Mary Jo. 2002. "Library Services for People with Disabilities." OLOS Preconference Different Voices, Common Quest: Adult Literacy & Outreach in Libraries. American Library Association Conference, Atlanta, GA. Available: www.ala.org/ala/aboutala/offices/olos/outreachresources/docs/services_disabilities.pdf (accessed September 10, 2009).

Part IV

Notate Bene

Chapter 14

List Culture

. . . the bestseller list from day one, has always represented a reliable mixture of the good and the bad, of quality and trash, of literature for the ages and self-improvement schemes that now seem merely weird . . .

—Michael Korda, *Making the List: A Cultural History of the American Bestseller 1900–1999* (2001)

OVERVIEW OF LIST CULTURE

We live in a list-based culture with lists for everything from the "Top 10 Beaches in Hawaii" on the Travel Channel to "1,000 Places to See before You Die" (television broadcast on Discovery Channel and book by Patricia Shultz). We rush to the newsstands to obtain the latest copies of *U.S. News & World Report*'s Rankings and *Fortune Magazine*'s "400 Richest Americans" and "Fortune 500 Companies." Lists provide the best and worst of contemporary culture, and they are a way of measuring value. From a sales and marketing perspective, lists offer extraordinary powers of influence and authority, showcasing what Edward Pooley of *Time*'s European edition calls the "top of the pops" along with the rising stars (quoted in Aitken, 2004: 39).

Books and reading are dominated by lists, ranging from the industry standards, such as *New York Times* Best Sellers, published weekly in the *New York Times* Review of Books to Amazon.com's "Listmania," which is a user-generated list of titles (books, music, and/or films). Book clubs, readers' advisory resources, publishers' Web sites, magazines, and a host of Internet resources publish and disseminate books lists on every conceivable subject. Lists serve an important function for the adult services librarian in identifying new and popular titles in specific genres, in creating "what to read next" recommendations, and in aiding readers to develop their literary tastes. These same lists are also used by the readers to learn about new titles and authors (Saricks, 1998: 15).

The lists can be divided into several distinct types, each with specific purposes (Wright, 2007: n.p.):

1. Bestsellers lists or popular literary tastes (*New York Times* Best Sellers, *Publishers Weekly* Bestsellers, *USA Today* Top 150 Best Sellers).
2. Publishers' lists on publishing house Web sites featuring their own titles and authors. For example, Random House and HarperCollins feature lists of their own bestselling titles garnered from the industry standards, such as *New York Times* Best Sellers.
3. Canonical or guide lists or lists of books with lasting literary merit; proscribed lists of books for self-enlightenment and intellectual growth (for example, Clifton Fadiman, *The New Lifetime Reading Plan*, 1997, or Martin Seymour-Smith, *The 100 Most Influential Books Ever Written: The History of Thought from Ancient Times to Today*, 1998).
4. "As Chosen by You" lists or reader participation lists that focus on readers' preferences rather than literary critics' recommendations (Listmania on Amazon.com, MySpace, and other social networking resource lists).
5. Fiction and nonfiction lists created by genre-specific organizations and associations (for example, "The 100 Favorite Mysteries of the 20th Century," as selected by members of the Independent Mystery Booksellers Association, or "RWA Honor Roll" from the Romance Writers of America).
6. Read-alike lists created by librarians (and avid readers) to help guide readers to other books they may enjoy; books with similar characteristics—protagonists, settings, pacing, time periods, etc. (What Do I Read Next? and other electronic databases, Fiction-L listserv and archives, BookSpot.com, and library Web sites, etc., are all sources for read-alikes.)

The difference in the first five types of lists and the librarian-generated read-alike lists is the purpose for which they are created. Bestsellers lists are promotional and marketing tools created by publishers for the purpose of selling books; canonical lists are created by scholars and literary critics for the education and enlightenment of the reader; "as chosen by you" lists are more democratic in nature and are created by the reader based on his or her own reading preferences. The genre fiction lists, especially those generated by associations, such as Independent Mystery Booksellers Association, seem to hover somewhere between canons (or at least guides) and read-alike lists.

The read-alike lists and the lists created by readers ("as chosen by you") have a superficial resemblance, especially those found through resources such as Amazon.com. However, the read-alikes are carefully selected to match specific criteria. They may focus on themes, places, characters, or plots (Library Booklists, 2007). The purpose of the read-alike lists is to answer one of the most popular requests made by public library users and bookstore frequenters: "Are there any other books/authors just like . . . ?" Listmania (Amazon.com) and other reader-generated lists are typically lists of books read or owned by the individual and grouped by author or theme (all the authors who have written books about cats that solve murders) without significant consideration of other elements that make books read alike.

INSIDE THE BESTSELLERS LISTS

The first American bestseller list was published in 1895 in a book industry publication titled *The Bookman: A Literary Journal.* Then-editor Harry Thurston Peck contacted individual booksellers around the country, asking them what new books had sold the best during the previous month. Thurston did not term his list a "bestsellers" list as we know it today. Rather, the list was ranked in "order of demand as sold between January 1 and February 1, 1895" (Peck, 1895: 64). It was not a singularly compiled and ranked list, but it did provide multiple rankings of titles for specific cities nationwide (e.g., New York, Uptown; New York, Downtown; Cincinnati, Ohio; and Portland, Oregon), and it did not distinguish between works of fiction and nonfiction. Many of the titles were common across the individual cities with *Trilby* by George Du Maurier appearing most frequently in the number one spot on this first bestsellers list.

A Selection of Titles from the First American Bestseller Lists

American Commonwealth, by James Bryce
Sherlock Holmes, by Arthur Conan Doyle
Trilby, by George DuMaurier
The Prisoner of Zenda, by Anthony Hope
The Jungle Book, by Rudyard Kipling
Bonnie Brier Bush, by Ian Maclaren
Golden House, by C. D. Warner

Source: Peck, 1895: 64–65.

What makes a bestseller is not a new discussion, and neither is the argument about the literary quality of bestsellers. In 1905 Henry Dwight Sedgwick called the bestsellers "mob novels" or popular novels of "lower bourgeois" literary tastes that are read with frantic enthusiasm by the general populace (Sedgwick, 1905: 9). He likened the phenomenon to the "spread of contagion." Sedgwick also suggested that "advertisements, publishers, wholesale booksellers, retail dealers, book agents, news-stands, parlor-car peddlers, and *circulating libraries*" (Sedgwick, 1905: 11—emphasis added) were factors in the perpetuation of "mob" novels and the eagerness with which readers devour them. This can be compared to the avid reading of *The Da Vinci Code* by Dan Brown (2003) and its impressive longevity on the contemporary bestsellers lists, remaining on the *New York Times* (*NYT*) bestsellers list for 166 weeks (more than three years) and at one point featuring two different versions (one traditional hardcover and the other an illustrated special edition hardcover) on the list. Interestingly, titles that might be described as Western canons have reappeared on contemporary bestsellers lists. For example, Tolstoy's *Anna Karenina*, published originally in 1887, appeared on the *NYT* Best Sellers List in 2007 (120 years after publication) after being recommended by Oprah Winfrey on her popular television book club.

Seen today as important measures of popularity of titles and authors, the regularly published bestsellers lists offer weekly and biweekly lists of titles, categorized by hardcover, paperback, children's, fiction, and nonfiction. These lists are based on the sales figures of titles as gathered from bookstores and wholesalers, and other retailers. According to Michael Korda, these lists "tell us what we're *actually* reading (or, at least, what we're actually *buying*) as opposed to what we think we *ought* to be reading, or would like other people to believe we're buying" (Korda, 2001: x). Titles and authors on these lists are the ones that garner the most attention by readers, critics, booksellers, and librarians. The goal for authors and publishing houses is to gain the #1 spot on the lists and to remain in that spot for more than a one-week run, thus generating revenue, fostering recognition, and creating a loyal reader base and, ultimately, more sales. Some of the major bestsellers lists include:

- *Library Journal* Bestsellers (the books most borrowed in U.S. libraries)
- *New York Times* Best Sellers
- *Publishers Weekly* Bestsellers
- *USA Today* Top 150 Best Sellers
- Amazon.com Bestsellers, Hot Releases, and Movers & Shakers
- Barnes & Noble Bestsellers

They can be accessed on the publishers' Web sites, through Amazon.com and BarnesandNoble.com, and through a variety of print publications. (See Appendix 2 for a more comprehensive list of bestsellers lists resources and Web addresses.)

Designation as a bestseller does not imply literary value today any more than it did in 1895; it is related only to commercial value and popular taste. This can best be evidenced by the appearance of John Steinbeck's *East of Eden* on the *NYT* bestsellers list on July 6, 2003, along with *The Beach House* (James Patterson and Peter de Jong) and *Hard Eight* (Janet Evanovich). *East of Eden* entered the *NYT* list ranked #1 and is classified in Bowker's Books in Print as literary fiction; *The Beach House* and *Hard Eight* are both popular mystery and suspense fiction with no pretensions of literary value (or of being highbrow). What the bestsellers lists do suggest are the current popular cultural climate, tastes, and values, and they are as changeable as the readers themselves.

GENRE LISTS AND PROFESSIONAL ASSOCIATIONS

The organizations and associations supporting the mainstream genres (e.g., Romance Writers of America or Mystery Readers International) are great generators of lists. While neither bestsellers lists nor canonical lists, the genre lists fulfill the role of recommending those titles thought to be the best or most representative of the genre. The titles on the genre lists are the benchmarks of the genre, or represent those titles and authors that are timeless. For readers' advisors, the books on these lists provide an excellent opportunity to become familiar with the range and depth of a genre. The RWA Honor Roll (www.rwanational .org/cs/authors_and_books/rwa_honor_roll), for example, features authors from all subgenres of romance fiction that have appeared on one or more of the bestsellers lists, including *New York Times* Top 20, *Publishers Weekly* Top 15, and *USA Today* Top 50.

The Collection Development and Evaluation Section (CODES) of the Reference and User Services Association (RUSA) established "The Reading List: Best Adult Genre Fiction" in 2007. This list intends to highlight outstanding genre fiction of all types. The titles are ones that The Reading List Council (a panel of librarians who are considered to be experts in readers' advisory and collection development) believes merit special attention by adult readers and the librarians who serve them. The list includes selections from eight categories, including science fiction, fantasy, historical fiction, women's fiction, and more. One book is selected for each of the eight categories and includes both debut novels and established authors. The published annual lists (www.ala.org/ala/mgrps/divs/ rusa/awards/readinglist/index.cfm) include the eight honored titles as well as the other titles nominated. To be included on "The Reading List," books must be pleasurable to read and strongly represent the elements that define the genre.

The Adult Reading Round Table (ARRT) of Illinois is another source for popular reading lists. The ARRT is an association of adult service and readers' advisory librarians who participate in genre studies in order to learn about each of the genres in depth. Every two years the association undertakes a new genre study, examining individual authors and titles along with the associated subgenres. The lists generated by ARRT (www.arrtreads.org/genrestudy.htm) are extremely useful in identifying the hallmarks of the genre and making connections between titles and even across genres. The genre studies frequently include read-alike and read-around lists that are useful for suggesting additional titles to individual readers.

Combined, these types of genre lists provide well-rounded examinations of the individual genres and their relationships to one another. The lists are extremely useful in guiding readers to the next good read. They also serve as informal professional development resources to become familiar with the range of genre reading. Many of the lists are prepared either by librarians or by genre experts, adding a level of selectivity to the lists, representing the standards of each genre. The lists tend toward highly readable books that best illustrate the features of each genre.

100 BOOKS TO READ BEFORE YOU DIE, OR CANONICAL LITERATURE

Unlike bestselling fiction and nonfiction, the canons are those works that scholars and literary critics tell us we *must* read in order to be fully educated. In the broadest terms the canons are those works that explore the history of thought and the human condition. They include religion and philosophy; science, technology, and medicine; arts, poetry, and literature; humanities and history; novels and nonfiction. The canons represent the work of the world's greatest philosophers and explorers, and others who have had the most influential impact on the greater world. Lists of "great books" abound in print and on the Web. They are created by individuals, boards and associations, and libraries. Titles vary, new ones are added, and old ones drop off with each new era. Books identified as great books at the start of the twentieth century might not be the same ones identified at the start of the twenty-first. Regardless of the list's creator or era, the canons, or "great books," are intended to "stretch your thinking, stir your soul, and maybe even offer some startling insights" ("The Loose Canon," Utne Reader).

Oxford English Dictionary Evolution of the Term "Canon"

c890: a rule, law, or decree of the Church; esp. a rule laid down by an ecclesiastical Council

1382: the collection or list of Books of the Bible accepted by the Christian Church as genuine and inspired; also any set of sacred books; or those writings of a secular author accepted as authentic

1601: a standard or judgement [sic] or authority; a test criterion, means of discrimination

1833: a chief epoch or era, serving to date from; a basis for chronology

1929: literary criticism: a body of literary works traditionally regarded as the most important, significant, and worthy of study; those works of esp. Western literature considered to be established as being of the highest quality and most enduring value; the classics. Also (usu. with qualifying word): such a body of literature in a particular language, or from a particular culture, period, genre, etc.

1977: literary criticism: in extended use (esp. with reference to art or music): a body of works, etc., considered to be established as the most important or significant in a particular field.

It should be noted that canons are not intentionally written. Fitzgerald and Hemingway did not awake one morning with the intent of becoming a part of twentieth century U.S. literary canon. Rather, canons are born through a process of critical evaluation and judgment. Many of the great works frequently started out as part of the national bestsellers of popular fiction. Hemingway and Steinbeck, for example, were both featured on the *New York Times* bestsellers fiction lists before being canonized by literary critics and academicians.

The canon lists serve an important function for the readers' advisor in identifying those works that are considered significant. Individuals who are intent on becoming serious readers and engaging in lifelong learning want recommendations for the great books that can help "stir their souls." (See Table 14-1 for sources of canonical lists.) For some book discussion groups, "Great American Literature" forms a basis for their discussions. The canons are the foundational materials of many college freshmen and high school summer reading lists.

Despite the criticism of popular fiction, a relationship exists between classic literature and popular novels. The argument is twofold: popular fiction does have its foundations in canonical and literary works, and, despite suggestions

Table 14-1: Sample Resources for Canons or "Great Books"
Library Lists
New York Public Library, Books of the Century: www.nypl.org/research/chss/events/booklist.html
Boston Public Library, 100 Most Influential Books of the Century: www.bpl.org/research/AdultBooklists/influential.htm
Books and Magazines
Clifton Fadiman and John S. Major, *The New Lifetime Reading Plan*, 4th edition, 1997.
LaVergne Rosow, *Accessing the Classics: Great Reads for Adults, Teens, and English Language Learners*, 2006
Martin Seymour-Smith, *The 100 Most Influential Books Ever Written: The History of Thought from Ancient Times to Today*, 1998
Sharon Steel, "Dead White Females: From Fall Out Boy to One Night in Paris, modern pop culture is what it is today thanks to 10 long-expired ladies." *The Phoenix* (August 8, 2007). http://thephoenix.com/article_ektid45248.aspx
Other Resources
The Great Books List: A Progressive Exploration of the Great Books: http://thegreatbookslist.com/index.html
Modern Library, 100 Best Novels, 100 Best Nonfiction, Radcliffe's Rival 100 Best Novels List: www.randomhouse.com/modernlibrary/100bestnovels.html
Robert Teeter, Great Books Lists: www.interleaves.org/~rteeter/greatbks.html
Utne Reader: "The Loose Canon: 150 Great Works to Set Your Imagination on Fire." Web Specials Archive. www.utne.com/web_special/web_specials_archives/articles/330-1.html

that people do not read literary classics, they are well exposed to the classics through reading popular fiction and encounters through mass media, film, and performing arts, preparing them to understand the allusions and references found in their everyday reading and communications. Herald, in the current edition of *Genreflecting: A Guide to Popular Reading Interests*, explains that "the roots of genre fiction are in the distant past, when storytellers and bards held audiences enraptured by their tales and ballads of wondrous adventure, larger-than-life heroes and heroines, and magical beasts" (Herald, 2006: 32). The argument can be traced as follows:

> Dante's *Inferno* is represented in the closing chapters of Mark Twain's *The Adventures of Huckleberry Finn*; and Mark Twain's *The Adventures of Huckleberry Finn* is the literary base for John Clinch's *Finn*; or, Edgar Allan Poe's character M. Auguste Dupin serves as the first model of a classic detective, followed by Sir Arthur Conan Doyle's Sherlock Holmes, whose stories are then represented in Michael Chabon's *The Final Solution* and Doyle himself appears as a protagonist in Julian Barnes' *Arthur and George*. (Maatta, 2008: n.p.)

In order for these leaps to be made by the reader, he or she must have some familiarity with the classic literature upon which the popular fiction is based. The reader will either have read the classic foundations or have been exposed to the literature in other ways (film, plays, and even popular Saturday morning cartoons).

AUTOMATION, ALGORITHMS, AND RECOMMENDATIONS

A contemporary phenomenon is the automated recommendations and list generation features offered by many of the online booksellers, especially the mega bookstores. Amazon.com, BarnesandNoble.com, and a host of other bookseller and book collector resources use proprietary automation and algorithms to generate book recommendations. In the case of the booksellers, the lists are generated from the matching of aggregated book sales and individual online browsing patterns to individual purchasing records. When a member signs into one of the bookseller Web sites (Amazon.com for example), the entry page is customized for the member. Lists of recommended books, movies, music, and other types of products are presented. Specific to Amazon.com (see Figure 14-1), the recommended titles are selected based on previous purchases. Interestingly, some of the suggestions do not appear to have a direct relationship to the recommended title (e.g., *Bones to Ashes: A Novel*—a forensics novel—compared to John Grisham's latest, *Playing for Pizza*—general adult fiction). The only common element appears to be that they are both newly released novels, and have common prior purchases where the individual had bought other books by Reichs and by Grisham even though the purpose of the purchases may have been quite different (gifts for others versus personal reading choices).

Figure 14-1: Sample Recommendations from Amazon.com
Recommended for You
Bones to Ashes: A Novel by Kathy Reichs (Author) **Our Price: $14.27** **Used & new** from **$8.50**
Because you purchased ...
The Xibalba Murders: An Archeological Mystery (Archaeological Mysteries) (Paperback) by Lyn Hamilton (author)
Cross Bones (Temperance Brennan Novels) (Hardcover) by Kathy Reichs (Author)
Maltese Goddess: An Archeological Mystery (Archaeological Mysteries) (Paperback) by Lyn Hamilton (author)
Lean Mean Thirteen: (Stephanie Plum Novels) (Hardcover) by Janet Evanovich
Deadline (Mass Market Paperback) by John Dunning (Author)
Playing for Pizza (Hardcover) by John Grisham (Author)
Note: The recommendations were generated based on this book author's own purchasing and reading patterns and are not necessarily typical of other readers.

Readers' advisors and other adult services librarians caution against using the automated lists to make patron recommendations. Cassell and Hiremath advise, "While these suggestions do pick up readalikes, they are generated through patterns of associative buying, not designed by a careful analysis of the appeal factors of particular books and, depending on the query, can be as misleading as helpful" (2006: 258). But for the readers themselves, the automated lists are a starting point, and they do make use of the recommendations. Because the individual reader is faced with an increasing number of books, authors, and genres, the automated lists are useful when attempting to make selections when a librarian is not available. Casual remarks from fellow readers indicate that they have found some limited success in finding other "good reads" based on the recommendations, but the lists are no substitute for the recommendations from someone who knows books and authors.

LibraryThing.com is a member-based Web resource for book collectors and readers, offering cataloging and tagging services (see Chapter 4 for detailed discussion). It also offers personalized book suggestions based on book ownership. LibraryThing searches for similar tags and topics across individual members' libraries and identifies the most significantly matching tags to make suggestions about other titles that might be of interest (see Figure 14-2). Similarly to the book recommendations generated by Amazon.com, the suggestions need to be used with some skepticism. Again, the site does not really analyze theme, content, pacing, or other appeal characteristics of the books; suggestions are based on personal ownership and tagging. But much like the Amazon.com lists, this resource is a starting point for finding other "good reads."

While discussed in more detail in other chapters of this book, "What Do I Read Next?" (product of Gale Cengage Learning), NoveList (product of Ebsco Industries, Inc.), and Fiction Connection (a Bowker product) also generate lists of titles and authors. These are meticulously built electronic databases that are designed specifically to match readers' interests with possible book and author

Figure 14-2: Sample Suggestions from LibraryThing.com

LibrarySuggester. Book recommendations for readerx

- People with your books also have: fiction / non-fiction books

People with your books also have: fiction

1.	The bookman's promise : a Cliff Janeway novel by John Dunning 356 copies. 11 reviews. Average rating 3.76. Why?
2.	The haunted bookshop; by Christopher Morely 305 copies. 6 reviews. Average rating 3.77. Why?
3.	Unprintable by Julie Kaewert 48 copies. 1 reviews. Average rating 2.67. Why?
4.	The browser's ecstasy : a meditation on reading by Geoffrey O'Brien 73 copies. Average rating 3.33. Why?
5.	Marginalia : readers writing in books by H. J. Jackson 80 copies. 2 reviews. Average rating 5. Why?

Note: The recommendations were generated based on this book author's own collection, tags, and reading patterns and are not necessarily typical of other readers.

selections. Each of the resources provides multiple methods and levels of searching and combining terms to create extensive reading lists. Several of the databases also provide options to generate lists of award winners, bestsellers, and other criteria-based lists. Unlike the more generic matches of Amazon.com and LibraryThing.com that identify associated purchasing and/or ownership patterns, the recognized readers' advisory tools use relational databases to cross-match qualitative criteria, such as genre, character, or setting.

BOOKLISTS AND SOCIAL NETWORKING UTILITIES

Social networking utilities have added a new dimension to finding booklists of all types and genres. MySpace, Facebook, Shelfari, LibraryThing, and many others have created broader access to what people are reading here and now. The value of the online sites lies not in the attention to the finer details of character, setting, or genre, but in real readers' responses to books. In addition to user-contributed suggestions, these resources frequently include tags of individual descriptions rather than "librarian-speak." The social networking resources have the added dimension of allowing members to discuss and communicate about books, reading, and authors through discussion boards and virtual chat and instant messaging.

The added value of the social networking utilities for libraries is the ability to market services to readers at no cost (or at least minimal cost). Numerous public libraries subscribe to MySpace and Facebook and provide links to readers' advisor services, such as lists for Teen Read Week or other special events and celebrations of reading (Banned Book Week, National Library Week, etc.). LibraryThing and Shelfari offer similar membership subscriptions that allow libraries to promote their services and allow their local users to contribute content to the library's online resources. For example, RavenousReaders (Pima County Public Library, AZ) offers book reviews, staff picks, and book club resources through their LibraryThing account, making book lists and reading choices more accessible.

Blogs and wikis (B&Ws) are two additional social networking utilities that have great popularity among readers. Much like the tagging and organizing utilities of LibraryThing and Shelfari, blogs and wikis are user-oriented and user-contributed tools. Overbooked, GoodReads, and BookLust are among the more popular and robust reading wikis on the Web, but they differ wildly in approach and creation:

- *Librarian created:* Typically these B&Ws, while appealing to the reading public, are crafted by professional librarians with an eye toward truly helpful reading guidance. Overbooked, for example, was created by a collection management librarian and offers authoritative lists and resources as well as encourages user participation. It must be noted that many of the librarian-created B&Ws are not necessarily official products of the associated library systems, but may be volunteer or independent projects designed to bring reading and books to a wide audience. BookLust is another similar wiki created by Nancy Pearl, complementing her successful series of publications by the same title. Overbooked and BookLust offer author interviews, links to reliable and authoritative book reviews, and access to other readers.

- *Reader created:* Typically these B&Ws mirror other social networking utilities such as MySpace and Facebook, offering accounts and creation of friend networks. Their strength lies in reader reactions to books and accessibility to other people with similar reading tastes and patterns. The reader-created resources rely heavily on personal tagging and classification rather than more formal schema, which allow for the creation of narrowed lists, such as "Food-Related Nonfiction about food, cooking and eating" or "Best Books to Become an Informed Voter."

Some of the features the B&Ws offer include author interviews, book reviews, and discussion forums. Members can join groups and book clubs of all types within individual B&Ws. In addition, the B&Ws offer links to off-site resources for a great reach and access to books and reading. The greatest challenge in using the blogs and wikis: getting lost in the richness of resources.

PUBLISHING HOUSE RESOURCES

A final consideration for booklists is the publishing houses. The Web sites and their myriad features are commercial in nature and the purpose and function is to highlight and sell books from their own slate of authors. Publishers provide information not only for acquisition and collection librarians and booksellers, but to the reading public as well. The advantage for libraries is in the unique and subject specific lists that can be located on the publishers' sites. For example, Random House includes sections for "Libros en Español," exclusive signed first editions, and reading group guides, as well as lists of their bestselling titles appearing on *NYT* bestsellers and in other national, regional, and local newspapers as well as by sales figures based on various booksellers. Random House also offers booklists by category, such as African-American Interests, Books to Film, or E-books. The limitation, of course, is that only publications of the individual publishing houses and their affiliates are included on the Web sites.

Another strong feature of the publishers' Web sites is the access to authors. Some sites offer podcasts and streaming audio components that include live author interviews. Most will provide information about when and where authors will be signing books and alerts about upcoming new titles by favorite authors. And for fans, publishers' Web sites typically include links to the authors' official Web sites, which abound with biographical information, FAQs, tour schedules, photographs, and television and audio clips.

CONCLUSION

Booklists of all types offer a variety of ways to access good reads. More importantly, they suggest something for every taste and every reader. For the reader, lists provide a "do it yourself" approach to answering the "what do I read next" question. For the readers' advisor, lists suggest ways to make connections between titles across genres and to understand what contemporary readers are selecting from the library and purchasing from their favorite booksellers. The array of reading lists can become an informal professional development tool to learn about the genres for readers' advisors and other adult services librarians, especially in the genres not normally read.

Library 2.0 innovations have expanded the access to reading lists and resources that make reading a more holistic activity. Genre standards and niche reading lists are readily located through Web searches and on social networking sites as well as the more traditional RA databases and tools. All of these resources are another way to keep up with the book buzz and stay informed about authors and titles.

WORKS CONSULTED

Aitken, Lucy. 2004. "For the Love of Lists." *Campaign* (October 15): 39.

"Blog: Worth Reading." Library Booklists and Bibliographies. Available: www .librarybooklists.org (accessed September 10, 2009).

Cassell, Kay Ann, and Uma Hiremath. 2006. *Reference and Information Services in the 21st Century: An Introduction.* New York: Neal-Schuman Publishers.

Herald, Diana Trixler. 2006. *Genreflecting: A Guide to Popular Reading Interests,* edited by Wayne A. Wiegand. Westport, CT: Libraries Unlimited.

Korda, Michael. 2001. *Making the List: A Cultural History of the American Bestseller 1900–1999 as Seen through the Annual Bestseller Lists of Publishers Weekly.* New York: Barnes & Noble Books.

"The Loose Canon: 150 Great Works to Set Your Imagination on Fire." Utne Reader, Web Specials Archive. Available: www.utne.com/web_special/web_specials_archives/ articles/330-1.html (accessed September 10, 2009).

Maatta, Stephanie. 2008. "Loose Canons & Contemporary Canon Fodder: Exploring the Relationship between Great Literature and Popular Novels through the Eyes of Librarians." Paper presented at Popular Culture/American Culture Joint Annual Conference, San Francisco, CA, April 8, 2008.

Oxford English Dictionary. 2007. "Canon." Oxford University Press. Available University of South Florida Libraries. Available: http://dictionary.oed.com.ezproxy.lib.usf.edu/cgi/ enry/50032546?query_type=word&queryword=canon (accessed September 10, 2009).

Peck, Harry Thurston. 1895. "Sales of Books during the Month." *The Bookman: A Literary Journal* 1 (February 1): 64–65.

Saricks, Joyce G. 1998. "Providing the Fiction Your Patrons Want: Managing Fiction in a Medium-Sized Public Library." In *Fiction Acquisition/Fiction Management: Education and Training* (pp. 11–28), edited by G. N. Olson. Binghamton, NY: The Haworth Press.

Sedgwick, Henry Dwight. 1905. "The Mob Spirit in Literature." *Atlantic Monthly* 96 (July): 9–15.
Wright, David. 2007. "Big Read, Long Tail: Literary Taste and List-Culture in a Time of 'Endless Choice.'" Paper presented at Beyond the Book: Contemporary Culture of Reading, Birmingham, UK, September 2007.

FURTHER READING

Diamond, Edward. 1994. *Behind the* Times*: Inside the New York Times.* New York: Villard Books.
Hackett, Alice Payne, and James Henry Burke. 1977. *80 Years of Best Sellers: 1895–1975.* New York & London: R. R. Bowker Company.
Inge, M. Thomas, ed. 1988. *Handbook of American Popular Literature.* New York, Westport & London: Greenwood Press.

Chapter 15

Book Awards
and Award-Winning Books

Everybody has won and all must have prizes.

—from *Alice's Adventures in Wonderland* by Lewis Carroll (1865)

If the bestsellers lists denote popular taste, then book awards and literary prizes must certainly represent literary taste. Awards are pervasive throughout reading culture; *The Bowker Annual Library and Book Trade Almanac* (Bogard, 2007) details approximately 140 unique literary prizes, and *2009 Writer's Market* (Brewer, 2008) lists another 230 awards for fiction and nonfiction. Myriad awards for poetry, screenplays, children's and young adult materials, and journalism abound online and in writer's guides and directories. However, much like the array of booklists, awards range from the literary to pop fiction and genre-specific to readers' choice awards. The awards encompass international, national (i.e., United States, Canada, and the United Kingdom), state, and industry-related achievement. They include books for all ages and reading interests.

For the authors, book awards and literary prizes bring recognition (both fame and infamy) for the quality of their writing along with financial gain. James English, throughout his book *The Economy of Prestige* (2005), suggests that the major cultural awards legitimize an author's work and contribute to the establishment of literary canon along with being a commercial tool for marketing. Frequently a flurry of increased book sales occur simultaneously with the announcements of nominations and award winners, bringing additional commercial and critical attention to the authors. Tom Holman, of *The Bookseller,* explains, "the award has been the main catalyst for success, bringing the books to wider attention by generating masses of valuable media interest. The value of the awards in terms of free advertising are immeasurable [*sic*]" (Holman, 2003: 11).

In an unusual phenomenon, books not nominated or awarded literary prizes, but that have received high critical and/or popular acclaim, also benefit from the book award announcements through the ensuing scandal of being ignored by the judges. These titles reap publicity for the accolades they *did not* receive,

spurring readers to check out the titles at the library or purchase them from local bookstores to determine if the books meet or exceed the readers' standards
of literary quality compared to professional juries. When the Nobel Prize for Literature, for example, was first awarded in 1901, Tolstoy, who was considered to
be one of the greatest authors of the time, was bypassed for a lesser-known poet,
Sully Prudhomme, who has since slipped into anonymity. Interestingly, *Anna
Karenina* resurfaced on the U.S. bestsellers lists in 2007 with Oprah's "rediscov-
ery" of Tolstoy, while nothing has been published by or about Prudhomme since
1925. In another instance jurors of the National Book Award in 1986 passed over
Toni Morrison's *Beloved*—a solid, critically acclaimed bestseller—for Robert
Heinemann's *Paco's Story*, which is now out of print. Morrison went on to receive
several of the highly visible, prestigious literary awards, including a Pulitzer Prize
for Fiction (1988) and the Nobel Prize for Literature (1993). Both of these instances of passing over the author drew outcry from literary critics and the reading public alike.

The general reader consults the book awards announcements for a variety of
purposes. By far the most popular use is to identify new authors, genres, and titles. With the array of books being published annually (Bowker reported a U.S.
book output of 411,422 books, of which 50,071 were new fiction titles, in 2007),
the task of wading through the bookshelves searching for something new to read
can be daunting. Janelle Zauha of the Pacific Northwest Library Association
states, "Awards serve as guideposts for readers stunned by the magnitude of published materials in any given year" (Zauha, 2006: 5). The award nominee lists
and finalists, in this aspect, serve a similar function to the bestsellers lists.

In an informal discussion fellow readers agreed that the various awards, especially the international awards, introduce them to new authors of note and
sometimes new and experimental forms of writing that they might not otherwise
read. Joyce Saricks suggests that readers, especially literary fiction readers, "like
to evaluate the books that have won awards for themselves. Is it really good
enough by their standards?" (Saricks, 2001: 134). The reader allows himself or
herself to be a critic.

As a librarian, it is all but impossible to read every book that comes into the library (even if we really want to). Along with bestsellers lists, the book awards provide a source of information about current titles that have achieved critical
notice. The award lists also identify the titles that readers hear about on the
news, online, and in bookstores. The readers will ask for the award winners when
they visit the library, and they look to their favorite librarian as a source of information about what constitutes a good read. Of particular note to librarians serving adult readers are the genre-specific awards, such as the Edgars (mystery) and
RITAs (romance). Awarded annually, these prizes recognize the best of the
genre while also introducing new authors and first novels to the reading public.
Combined, the literary awards and the genre awards provide a well-rounded
view of contemporary publishing and readers' interests.

Beyond current awareness, the literary awards provide a range of resources for readers' advisors. Several of the book award Web sites, such as the Man Booker Prize, offer reading guides and materials for book discussion groups. The international, non-English awards present opportunities to serve foreign-language speakers by identifying books in their native tongue that have both literary excellence and popular appeal.

THE MAJOR LITERARY AWARDS

Without a doubt, several awards for literature are immediately recognizable by anyone who has an acquaintance with books and reading: The Nobel Prize for Literature, the Pulitzer Prize for Fiction, the National Book Award for Fiction, and the Man Booker Prize (see Table 15-1 for a sampling of major international and national literary prizes). While it is impossible to detail all of the major cultural awards of the twentieth and twenty-first centuries, a few of the most recognizable ones are considered in this chapter. All of the international and national book awards intend to honor the "best of," "the ideal," or "excellence in writing." They also honor experimental writing, excellence in representation of a time, place, or person, social consciousness, and even old-fashioned readability.

Historically, these awards represent the best of the world's literature. According to Louis Menand, "The Nobel Prize in Literature was the first of the major modern cultural prizes. It was soon followed by the Prix Goncourt (first awarded in 1903) and the Pulitzer Prizes (conceived in 1904, first awarded in 1917)" (Menand, 2005: 136). The James Tait Black Memorial Prize, the United Kingdom's oldest literary award, was established in 1919. The period between the 1970s and mid-1990s saw another flurry of new awards arise, with substantial prize money, especially among publishers and literary foundations in the United States. Australia, Canada, and the United Kingdom also experienced an increasing number of literary prizes replete with substantial monetary awards. In an unusual turnabout, both the Hemingway Foundation/PEN Award and the PEN/Faulkner Award for Fiction were established by the authors' estates with the proceeds from each having won the Nobel Prize for Literature. Additional awards and recognitions emerged again in 2000 and 2005 with the establishment of the independent booksellers awards (Book Sense Book of the Year) and the Quill Award, a readers' choice award, and the Man Booker International Prize. (The Quill Award was discontinued in 2008.) All of these awards are intended to celebrate the best of the year's literature and encourage opportunities to read and explore life through literature.

The literary awards on the whole have a lengthy and intricate decision-making process that involves many people. The process is governed by rules and by-laws unique to each awarding entity. The Nobel Prizes are perhaps the most stringently regulated of awards, with carefully selected nominators and deliberation about merit. (Nominators must be invited to participate in order to nomi-

Table 15-1: Major Literary Awards		
Name of Prize/Award	Date Established	Country of Origin
The Nobel Prize for Literature	1901	Sweden
Prix Goncourt	1903	France
Pulitzer Prize for Fiction	1917	United States
The James Tait Black Memorial Prizes	1919	Scotland
Premio Nacional de Ciencias y Artes	1935	Mexico
Governor General's Literary Awards	1937	Canada
The National Book Awards for Fiction	1950	United States
Xavier Villaurrutia Award	1955	Mexico
Miles Franklin Literary Award	1957	Australia
The Man Booker Prize	1968	Ireland
National Book Critics Circle Award	1974	United States
Hemingway Foundation/PEN Award	1976	United States
American Book Awards	1978	United States
Premio Miguel de Cervantes	1978	Spain
PEN/Faulkner Award for Fiction	1980	United States
Commonwealth Writer's Prize	1987	British Commonwealth
PEN/Malamud Award and Memorial Reading	1988	United States
American Booksellers Book of the Year	1991	United States
The Scotiabank Giller Prize for Fiction	1994	Canada
Orange Prize for Fiction	1996	United Kingdom
Book Sense Book of the Year	2000	United States
Man Booker International Prize	2005	Ireland
Orange Prize for New Writers	2005	United Kingdom

Note: This table represents some of the most recognized and prestigious of the literary awards. There are many others awarded by the publishing industry and other book-related associations.

nate potential laureates.) The Nobel is international in scope, assessing literary works for all nations and in all languages. The Pulitzer Prizes accept nominations from anyone, including the authors themselves, but small juries of three to five individuals review and make recommendations to the larger Pulitzer Prize board. The Pulitzer Prize for Fiction is awarded only to American authors. The James Tait Black Memorial Award and the Commonwealth Writer's Award consider only authors who published or co-published their work in the United Kingdom, while the Man Booker Prizes have an award for an author who is a citizen of the British Commonwealth or Republic of Ireland and an international award for fiction published in the English language. In almost all instances the awards are given to singular works of fiction published in the preceding or current year, rather than being awarded as lifetime achievements.

The Nobel Prize for Literature

Along with prizes for physics, chemistry, medicine, economics, and the Nobel Peace Prize, Alfred Nobel's will (upon his death in 1895) established the Nobel Prize for Literature. Nobel specified that the award "was intended for the person who, in the literary field, had produced the most outstanding work in an ideal direction" (Espmark, 1999: n.p.). At the heart of the prize is the "challenge that very few minds in history have been able to solve, and then only erratically: to know which literary works truly surpass others now, and will continue to stay alive for generations to come" (Feldman, 2000: 66). These sentiments have created the drama and suspense that are inherent in the awarding of the Nobel Prize.

The Nobel Prize is frequently criticized as elitist, Eurocentric, and snobbish; critics contend that the judges are politically and morally biased and motivated. Nobel intended that the award be international and that the nationality of the nominees not be considered in the deliberations; however, it was 1968 before a work from an Asian author was selected. And, since its inception, the laurel has been awarded to only nine authors from the United States. Despite the criticisms the Nobel continues to be one of the significant cultural prizes for literature. While the early prizes celebrated idealism, it also celebrates unknown masters, experimentalists, and "literature of the whole world" (Espmark, 1999: n.p.). Recipients of the prize receive an inscribed gold medal, a monetary award (approximately $1.3 million in U.S. dollars in 2008), and a place in literary history.

In 1901 approximately 25 names were nominated for consideration; in 2008 estimates suggest that well over 200 authors were nominated. The judging and final decisions are shrouded in secrecy and politics. Authors nominated for the award and the ensuing deliberations are tightly guarded; names of nominees and short-listed authors are not released to the public until 50 years after the current year's award is given. Rumor and speculation about nominees and winners abound and motivate the odds-makers and bookies. (J. M. G. Le Clézio, the 2008 Nobel Laureate for Literature, was the odds-on favorite at 1:2 odds, according to *The Guardian*, when the announcement was finally made in early October; Flood, 2008.)

The Nobel Prize Web site (www.nobelprize.org) is the most comprehensive resource for information about the prizes and awarding process. Extensive historical information and lists of all prize winners in all categories including biographies, bibliographies, and resource lists are located on the site. Nominations and reports authored by various members of the Swedish Academy provide a detailed record of the evolution of the prizes from 1901 through the early twenty-first century. Links to contemporary Nobel Lectures delivered by the recipient are available as well as citations for the compiled volumes of the lectures.

The Man Booker Prizes for Fiction

In the long litany of literary prizes, the Man Booker Prizes for Fiction rise to the top among awards coveted by authors. The Man Booker Prize for Fiction was established in 1968 to recognize and reward the best novel of the year written by a citizen of the British Commonwealth or the Republic of Ireland. In 2005 the Man Booker Prize for International Fiction was created to celebrate literary excellence internationally among authors who publish their work in the English language. The international prize is awarded every two years, allowing the judges sufficient time to review works by foreign authors. The Man Booker Prize for Fiction carries an award worth £50,000, or approximately $80,000 U.S. dollars; the international award is worth £60,000 (approximately $95,000 U.S. dollars, depending upon current foreign exchange rates). In celebration of the fortieth anniversary of the Man Booker Prize, a "Best of the Booker" novel was selected from each of the 41 winning entries (one for each year of the Man Booker). A panel of judges selected a short list of six titles for the "Best of the Booker," and then the final award was chosen by popular vote.

Unlike the Nobel Prize for Literature, the Man Booker Prize process is much more transparent and open to the public. The five judges change each year and are selected for balance among the individuals—age, interests, background, views. All judges review each entry and do not use a preselection process by outsiders, or previewers, to eliminate unlikely candidates. Publicizing both the long list, which began in 2001, and the short list of candidate novels assists not only in maintaining the integrity of the award but also fosters huge commercial value through increased book sales and worldwide recognition and the occasional purchase of film and television rights. Candidates enjoy the limelight and become fodder for discussion, heated debate, and odds-making (a seemingly common occurrence among British bookies surrounding literary events). Jonathan Ruppin states, "The Man Booker Prize is like some sort of global book group, a tasting menu for some of the best fiction around, always full of classics and unexpected pleasures" (Ruppin, 2007: n.p.). The features that distinguish the Man Booker Prize novels from other literary awards, as described by Michael Portillo (Chairman of the Man Booker judges), are that "These novels are intensely readable, each of them extraordinary examples of imagination and narrative. These fine page-turning stories nonetheless raise highly thought-provoking ideas and issues" (Portillo, 2008: n.p.).

The Man Booker Prize Web site (http://themanbookerprize.com) is the most comprehensive resource for information about the Man Booker Prize for Fiction and the Man Booker Prize for International Fiction. One of the most useful features is the Library Resources. This includes downloadable toolkits and reading group guides for the current Man Booker Prize for Fiction (2008) short-list novels and a downloadable reading guide that covers the six novels selected for the "Best of Booker" fortieth anniversary. A complete list of all Man Booker Prize for Fiction short-listed novels, winners, and judges from 1969 through 2008 is also available. A unique feature of the Man Booker Prizes Web site is the inclusion of public blogs in which general readers can post their opinions, recommendations, and predictions about the awards, especially when the long and short lists are made public.

Orange Prize for Fiction

Established in 1992 and first awarded in 1996, the Orange Prize for Fiction recognizes literary excellence in fiction written by women. The prize is open to any full-length novel; short stories and novellas are not eligible. Entries must be written in English and published in the United Kingdom during the year prior to the awarding of the prize (between April 1 and March 31). Women of any nationality are eligible as long as the book is written in English. Books may also be published in other countries as long as the U.K. publication falls within the specified dates between April and the following March.

The Orange Prize jury consists of only women drawn from a variety of backgrounds, including writers, critics, broadcasters, and librarians. Books are judged on their "accessibility, originality, and excellence in writing by women" (Orange Prize for Fiction, 2009: n.p.). During the review process judges create a long list and a short list and ultimately select a winner. (The long lists and short lists are readily available on the Orange Prize Web site at www.orangeprize.co.uk/ along with the winner announcements.) As judging begins, jurists are advised to forget about book reviews, author reputations, and publicity, but to read for pleasure and to select books that move them and that they truly enjoy.

In 2005 the Orange Prize for Fiction was expanded to include the Orange Award for New Writers. Entries are open to all first works of fiction, including novels, short story collections, and novellas. The books must be published in the United Kingdom; however, women of any nationality are eligible to enter. The prize emphasizes emerging talent and evidence of future potential. Like the Orange Prize for Fiction, the Award for New Writers represents writings by women that exhibit excellence, originality, and accessibility.

Both the Orange Prize for Fiction and Orange Award for New Writers carry monetary awards of £30,000 and £10,000, respectively (approximately $49,350 and $16,450 USD). Winners of the Orange Prize for Fiction also receive a limited edition bronze figurine called the "Bessie," which was created by Grizel Niven. Like many of the other British-based literary awards, the Orange Prize is closely followed by the reading public and bookmakers alike, with odds published and updated regularly as the lists are announced.

The Orange Prize Web site (www.orangeprize.co.uk) includes comprehensive information about the prizes and the processes. Particularly useful features of the Web site include the lists of winners and short lists along with news articles and events surrounding the Orange Prize for Fiction and Orange Award for New Writers. One of the most unique features of the Orange Prize is a newly created youth panel who will shadow the Orange Prize judges throughout the process, reading and discussing the 20 books selected for the long list with the judges. (The panel's responses are posted in an online book community called Spinebreakers; see www.Spinebreakers.co.uk.) The Orange Prize also offers a small award and tickets to the awards ceremony to the book group who best promotes and supports the social nature of reading.

Pulitzer Prizes in Letters

The Pulitzer Prizes are among the truly American awards granted to American authors and poets writing on topics of American life and history. Conceived by American journalist Joseph Pulitzer, the Pulitzer Prizes were to be "an incentive to excellence . . . in journalism, letters and drama, and education" (Topping, 1999: vii). Awards for journalism, letters and drama, education, and scholarships were the first of the prizes, and more recently additional ones were added for poetry, music, and photography, along with online journalism and public service in journalism. The first of the Pulitzer Prizes was awarded in 1917, with the first Pulitzer for Novels (renamed Fiction in 1947) awarded to Ernest Poole in 1918 (*His Family*, 1917, Macmillan).

Unlike other awards, such as the Nobel Prize for Literature, authors may receive more than one Pulitzer Prize for Fiction since the prize is awarded to individual works. Booth Tarkington, William Faulkner, and John Updike each received two Pulitzer Prizes for Fiction, and numerous other authors have appeared on the finalist lists with great frequency. The Pulitzer Prizes provide a modest monetary award, with winners receiving $10,000 in cash and a certificate, but without a doubt the prizes focus attention on the award winners, propelling books up the bestsellers lists and bringing them into the public eye. (Estimates by the *New Yorker* and *Los Angeles Times* suggest book sales can double and triple once the Pulitzers are announced—see Surowiecki, 2001, and Rutten, 2002.)

Approximately 2,400 entries are received for the 21 awards given, and of these entries more than 1,000 are books vying for the awards in Letters. Much like the other international and national literary awards, the Pulitzer Prizes are administered by a board of experts, and selections are determined by the deliberation of a jury. Similar to the Man Booker Prizes, the Pulitzer jury members are selected with professional excellence and diversity in mind and are drawn from publishers, journalists, and scholars of distinction. Each individual jury deliberates on their specific category and makes recommendations to the Pulitzer Prize Board, with the board taking the final vote and selection. As with the other prizes, the Pulitzers are held in strict confidence, but unlike the Nobel Prize nominations, which are not released for 50 years, the jury nominations (finalists), board members, and jurors' names are released at the time of the prize announcements.

The Pulitzer Prizes (www.pulitzer.org) winners, administration, and history are located on the Pulitzer Web site. Like the other literary award Web sites, it is a comprehensive resource that includes information about all of the Pulitzer Prizes, including entry criteria and entry forms. The links to press releases and "In the News" provide additional access to news articles, interviews, and commentary on the prizes, authors, and jurors.

Other National Awards of Note across the United States and Canada

The National Book Award (NBA) and the National Book Circle Critics Award (NBCCA) are two additional literary awards that generate discussion and recognition among readers and writers alike. According to the Web site, the mission of the National Book Awards "is to celebrate the best of American literature, to expand its audience, and to enhance the cultural value of good writing in America" (National Book Foundation, 2008). The National Book Awards were established in 1950 and have undergone several transformations, with many publisher-sponsored awards being added, and ultimately reduced to six significant awards: Fiction, Nonfiction, Poetry, Young People's Literature, Distinguished Contribution to American Letters, and the Literarian Award. The NBA is essentially a jury of one's peers, with authors and writers judging the entries that have been submitted by publishers. The five judges on each panel must be published authors in their category, and they must have been nominated for this honor by past award winners, finalists, and judges. NBA entries consist only of books written by American citizens and published in the United States during the current year (December 1 through November 30). The NBA finalists are announced in October and culminate with the winner announcement, awards dinner, and ceremony in mid-November. Like the Pulitzer Prizes, the NBA is worth $10,000 in cash and significantly increases book sales.

The National Book Critics Circle Award (NBCCA), by comparison, is judged and awarded by book critics. It has been awarded annually since 1975 for five different categories: fiction, general nonfiction, biography/autobiography, poetry, and criticism. Entries may be submitted by publishers or placed into nomination by the NBCCA board of directors. Like the other literary awards, it is a lengthy and time-consuming process involving long discussions, many differences of opinion, and creation of long lists and short lists. Criteria are limited to those books which have been published in the United States; citizenship of the author is not a consideration. The short list of five fiction titles, along with the other award finalists, typically becomes public in January, and the award winner is announced in March.

Combined, the Pulitzer Prize for Fiction, the National Book Award for Fiction, and the National Book Critics Circle Award for Fiction celebrate the best of American fiction or works published in the United States. They range from cultural inclusion to postapocalyptic America. These awards honor first novels as well as renowned authors. In addition, they represent some of the finest literary reads available.

Canada celebrates literary excellence through two highly recognized awards: Governor General's Literary Awards (the GGs) and the Scotiabank Giller Prize. The GGs were established in 1937 by then-Governor General Lord Tweedsmuir (more commonly known as John Buchan, author of *The Thirty-Nine Steps*) and the Canadian Authors Association. Tweedsmuir's intent was to honor the best books published in the previous year. The award originally included only works of fiction, nonfiction, poetry, and drama written in English or translated from French into English. Additional prizes were added for works written in French (beginning in 1959) and children's literature (text and illustration, beginning in 1987). The GGs are open only to authors who are Canadian citizens or permanent residents, and books must be first published in Canada. Similarly to the U.S. Pulitzer Prize, the Governor General's Literary Award is granted to individual works, and authors may receive multiple awards across their publishing lifetime. Margaret Atwood, Alice Munro, and Michael Ondaatje are among a lengthy list of literary luminaries receiving multiple honors. Entries for the Governor General's Award are judged by a "committee of peers" (Governor General's Literary Awards, 2009: n.p.) that includes writers, critics, and independent book professionals. Winners of the GGs receive approximately $25,000 CAD and a handcrafted leather-bound copy of the winning book, while finalists are recognized with $1,000 (CAD); publishers of the winning books also receive a small award ($3,000 CAD).

Canada's other renowned national literary award, the Scotiabank Giller Prize, was established in 1994 in honor of Doris Giller, a literary journalist. The prize recognizes excellence in Canadian fictional novels and short stories. In 2005 the Giller Prize partnered with the Scotiabank to promote literature and literary excellence throughout Canada. The partnership resulted in what is now the richest of the Canadian literary awards, granting the winner $50,000 CAD and $5,000 CAD to each of the four finalists. Each year a distinguished panel of judges is selected to adjudicate the entries. Interestingly, the judges are chosen from an international slate of authors, journalists, and scholars, including individuals from the United States and United Kingdom as well as Canadians. Much like the Governor General's Literary Award, the Giller Prize is awarded to a singular title; thus authors may receive the award more than once. Not only has the Scotiabank Giller Prize celebrated literary achievement, it has also generated significant book sales as a result of the prize, increasing awareness and exposure of Canadian literary talent.

Many other nations support and recognize the literary achievements of their citizens. Globally the awards hold many commonalities, including works written in the native language of the country; written by citizens or permanent residents of the nation; and celebrating the history, literature, and poetry of the nation. The Government of Mexico, for example, awards the *Premio Nacional de Ciencias y*

Artes (PNCA; The National Prize of Arts and Sciences) annually, including the prize for language and literature. The PNCA winners receive a gold medal and 520,000 pesos (approximately $39,000 USD). Another prestigious Mexican award is the Xavier Villaurrutia Award, granted to a Latin-American writer published in Mexico.

The Language Academies of the Spanish-speaking countries established and annually award the *Premio Miguel de Cervantes* (Miguel de Cervantes Prize) to honor lifetime achievements of writers in the Spanish language (specifically Castilian). Nominations for the award are made by the Spanish Royal Academy, the Language Academies, and former prize winners. Recipients come from Spain, Cuba, Argentina, Uruguay, Mexico, and Paraguay. The prize recognizes the recipient's overall body of work and is awarded to a writer only once, similarly to the Nobel Prize in Literature. It was first awarded in 1976, and today carries a prize of 90,000 euros (approximately $127,000 USD).

Australia also has a strong literary tradition, recognizing excellence in children's literature, fiction, nonfiction, and poetry. Awards range from genre awards, such as the Aurealis Awards for science fiction, fantasy, and horror to the Australian Prime Minister's Literary Awards recognizing the importance of literature to national identity and cultural and intellectual life. The most prestigious of the Australian awards, the Miles Franklin Literary Award, recognizes a novel of the "highest literary merit" and its "contributions to the richness of Australian cultural life" (Trust Foundation, 2009: n.p.). The Miles Franklin Literary Award was established in 1957 with a bequest from the author Miles Franklin (*My Brilliant Career*, 1901, William Blackwood and Sons). Today the award is valued at $42,000 AUD and guarantees increased book sales.

Quick Search Tip

A quick search on your favorite Web search engine for "literary awards" AND the name of the country you're interested in (for example, Australia AND "literary awards") yields a number of great links to international book awards. An added benefit is access to information about the many reading associations and book events held globally to support reading and literacy.

INDUSTRY AND LIBRARY ASSOCIATION AWARDS

Industry and association awards make up a second category of book awards that are watched by librarians and readers alike. Many of these awards are less literary in nature and more in tune with reader preferences. Like the literary awards, enumerating all of them defies possibilities, but several bear in-depth discussion. (See Table 15-1 for a comprehensive list of major literary awards.) These awards carry a little less drama and controversy, but like the more renowned awards they also represent the best of the book trade and publishing industry. Judging of the nominees is accomplished by active members of the book trade, publishing industry, and librarians, many of whom focus on readability and excellence in writing.

Independent Booksellers and Publishers

The American Booksellers Association (http://bookweb.org/index.html) is the not-for-profit organization that represents independent booksellers nationwide. It was established in 1900 and offers "education, services and products, advocacy, and relevant business information" for members. The Web site is designed with two audiences in mind: the ABA members, with members-only resources, and readers and librarians who want to select materials from a broader range of authors and publishers, especially the small publishers and presses. Of particular interest are the links to IndieBound, which "is a community-oriented movement that brings together booksellers, readers, indie retailers, local business alliances— anyone with a passionate belief that healthy local economies help communities thrive." IndieBound features a range of recommendations and bestsellers lists.

Numerous awards are given to authors whose works celebrate the diversity of American literary culture without limitations or restrictions and that are recommended by independent booksellers and publishers. Award recipients include recognized authors, though few of the popular blockbuster authors appear (John Grisham, Dan Brown, James Patterson, etc.), "under-recognized" authors, and first novels. These awards include American Book Awards, American Booksellers Book of the Year (ABBY), which evolved into Booksellers Book of the Year Awards (BSBY), and Book Sense Book of the Year Awards. This array of literary awards was established by the American Booksellers Association, who represents and supports the independently owned bookstores with real storefronts (not virtual bookstores) nationwide. Combined, the awards granted by the independents recognize outstanding literary achievement and the "hidden treasures" (American Booksellers Book of the Year Award, 2008: n.p.) among American literature. The ABBY/BSBY Awards are selected by independent booksellers and represent the books that the ABA members "most enjoyed recommending to their customers during the previous years" (ABA Booksellers Association, 2008: n.p.).

The United States is not the only nation to offer awards from independent booksellers associations. In 2008 Australia independent booksellers established the "Best Australian Book" Indie Award to honor the best of Australian authors. The Canadian Booksellers Association (similar to the ABA) sponsors the CBA Libris Awards to honor outstanding achievements by authors, editors, booksellers, and other book professionals. The CBA Libris Awards are nominated and selected by CBA members. Great Britain also offers similar awards through the Booksellers Association, an association of independent booksellers, to recognize the best in fiction and nonfiction books and authors.

Library Association Awards

The American Library Association (ALA) and librarians nationwide dedicate themselves to promoting reading and literacy. One of the most recognizable of the ALA awards is Reference and User Services Association (RUSA) Notable Books for America's Readers. The Notable Books Council was established in 1944 with the charge to "make available to the nation's readers a list of 25 very good, very readable, and at times very important fiction, nonfiction, and poetry books for the adult reader" (Reference and Users Services Association, 2008: n.p.). Any book submitted for consideration must be published in the United States, though translations and editions previously published in foreign countries are eligible. In order to be considered "notable," books must "possess exceptional literary merit; expand the horizons of human knowledge; make a specialized body of knowledge accessible to the non-specialist; promise to contribute significantly to the solution of a contemporary problem" (Reference and User Services Association, 2008). Books represented on the Notables list include well-known and emerging authors and titles from independent and small presses side by side with the major publishing houses.

The Notable Books Web site is the best and most current source for information about the notable books from 1998 to the present (www.ala.org/ala/mgrps/divs/rusa/resources/notablebooks/index.cfm). A brief history of the award along with individual lists of titles by year may be accessed. For a comprehensive listing of titles from 1944 to 1996, read the ALA's *50 Years of Notable Books*, listed in the section on Further Reading. Each summer at the ALA Annual Conference, Notable Book recipients are honored at the "Literary Tastes" breakfast, reading from their works and signing books.

Other divisions and affiliates of the American Library Association feature their own book awards and reading lists. For example, The Black Caucus of the American Library Association (BCALA) Literary Awards recognizes outstanding fiction and nonfiction for adult readers by African-American authors. BCALA designates awards for authors for fiction, nonfiction, first novelist, and outstanding contributions to publishing along with recognition of honor awards (www.bcala.org/awards/literary.htm). The Asian Pacific American Librarians Association offers a similar award for literature, titled Asian Pacific American Award for Literature (www.apalaweb.org/awards/awards.htm).

Many of the regional library associations, such as the Southeastern Library Association (SELA) or Border Regional Library Association (BRLA), offer regional awards for works of literary merit. Typically the authors must be official residents of one of the states encompassed by the regional association, and many regional awards consider only books written about the specific region. These are joined by the regional independent booksellers associations (similar to ABA with a regional focus), such as the Mountain and Plains Independent Booksellers Association or the Great Lakes Booksellers Association, who also offer similar categories of awards for regional authors.

Quick Search Tip

A quick search on your favorite Web search engine for "independent booksellers association" AND "book awards" yields a number of great links to regional book awards around the country. An added benefit is access to information about the many book events held in local communities to support reading and literacy.

Fifty States, Fifty Books

Across the nation, state literary and humanities councils and state library associations recognize excellence in fiction, nonfiction, and poetry by authors who were born in the state, who are permanent residents of the state, or have some significant tie to the state. Without a doubt these are some of the hidden gems in publishing; hidden not only in awareness of the awards' existence but in locating the awards and their yearly list of winners. The Alabama Library Association Author Awards sums up the intent of the state awards, saying they "seek to encourage and recognize [local] authors and promote interest in local authors' books, whether the books are about [the state] or another subject" (Alabama Library Association, 2008: n.p.). The state book awards play a crucial role in promoting community and supporting local authors, reading, and literacy.

Each state takes its own approach to the type of awards to be given and the process for selecting and disseminating the award winners' names. In general the types of awards include general and popular or genre fiction, nonfiction about the state, juvenile and young adult fiction, biography/autobiography and memoir, translations and/or foreign language books (e.g., Florida Book Awards includes a category for Spanish-language books), and book design. Some states, such as Idaho, award only one book annually with the honor of being the best of the best in the state; others make awards in multiple categories. Still others, such as Kansas, follow a similar style of "Notable Books" as the American Library Association Notable Books for Adults, which encompasses both fiction and nonfiction selections.

The real challenge is in locating information about the locally presented awards. According to Janelle Zauha of the Pacific Northwest Library Association, the statewide awards "are generally absent" from the available print and electronic resources for finding literary awards (Zauha, 2006: 5). Essential starting points include the state and regional library associations, the state's Center for the Book, the state's humanities council, the state historical society, and the state library. (See Appendix 3 for a compilation of statewide adult book awards with Web addresses.) Local independent booksellers and bookseller associations will include links to the award winners on their Web sites, and in some cases the local independent bookstores offer the most comprehensive collections of statewide and local book award winners. (A wonderful indie bookstore in southwest

Florida has one of the most extensive collections of books about Florida—fiction, nonfiction, cookbooks, photographic journals, etc.—that I have had the pleasure of browsing.)

THE GENRE AWARDS

By far the largest category of awards for fiction is the genre classification (see Table 15-2). Almost every conceivable genre has awards for excellence, lifetime achievement, and recognition of contributions to and support of the genre. Similarly to the other categories of awards, the genre awards recognize both established authors and first-time novelists. What differentiates the genre awards from others is, first, they are honorary recognition without large cash awards, and second, they carry far less public controversy than the Nobels, Bookers, and Pulitzers. The primary genres that honor authors include mystery, science fiction, crime, horror, Westerns, and romance, though many others exist, including those for poetry (Walt Whitman Award), humor (Thurber Prize), gay/lesbian/bisexual/transgender literature (Lambda Literary Awards), and cooking (James Beard/KitchenAid Award).

Mystery, Crime, and Horror Awards

Four primary awards presented annually recognize mystery writing: Agatha Award, Edgar Award, Macavity Award, and Shamus Award. While each is devoted to mystery writing, the lines become blurred between mystery and horror and mystery and crime fiction. Each of the major awards feature numerous subcategories and specialty awards that highlight mysteries written in particular styles, agencies and institutions that support mystery writing and authors, and memorial awards.

The Agatha Awards are presented at the annual fan convention Malice Domestic, which celebrates traditional mystery writing, best characterized by Agatha Christie's body of work. Malice Domestic "loosely defines [traditional mysteries] as mysteries which contain no explicit sex or excessive gore or violence; and usually (*but are not limited to*) featuring an amateur detective, a confined setting, and characters who know one another" (Malice Domestic, 2008). Awards are given for Best Novel, Best First Novel, Best Nonfiction, Best Short Story, and Best Children's/Young Adult Mystery.

The Web site is not searchable, but in the Awards section, the complete list of Agatha Award winners is available from 1988 to the present (www.malicedomestic.org/aboutmalice.html). One additional feature that is worth a look is Malice Domestic's newsletter, *The Usual Suspects*, which contains information about upcoming conventions, authors, awards, and grant programs.

The Edgars are sponsored by Mystery Writers of America (MWA), an association for mystery and crime-fiction writers. It is among the oldest and most presti-

Table 15-2: Genre Awards

Name of Award	Genre	Sponsoring Association	Year Established	Web Site
Agatha Awards	Mystery Writing	Malice Domestic	1988	www.malicedomestic.org/aboutmalice.html
Arthur C. Clarke Award	Science Fiction	Arthur C. Clarke	1987	www.clarkeaward.com
Bram Stoker Awards	Horror	Horror Writers Association	1987	www.horror.org/aboutus.htm
Edgar Awards	Mystery and Crime Fiction	Mystery Writers of America	1946	www.mysterywriters.org/
Hammett Awards	Crime Writing	International Association of Crime Writers	1991	www.crimewritersna.org/hammett/index.htm
Hugo Awards	Science Fiction	World Science Fiction Society	1953	www.thehugoawards.org/
Macavity Awards	Mystery Writing	Mystery Readers International	1987	www.mysteryreaders.org/index.html
Mythopoeic Awards	Fantasy and Mythic Literature	Mythopoeic Society	1971	www.mythsoc.org/
Nebula Award	Science Fiction	Science Fiction and Fantasy Writers of America	1965	www.sfwa.org/awards/
Philip K. Dick Award	Science Fiction and Fantasy		1982	www.philipkdickaward.org/
RITA Awards	Romance	Romance Writers of America	1982	www.rwanational.org/cs/home
Romantic Novel of the Year (UK)	Romance	Romance Novelists' Association	1960	www.rna-uk.org/
Shamus Awards	Private Eye Writing	Private Eye Writers of America	1982	www.thrillingdetective.com/trivia/triv72.html#2000
Spur Awards	American West	Western Writers of America	1953	www.westernwriters.org/awards.htm
Western Heritage Awards	American West	National Cowboy & Western Heritage Museum	1961	www.nationalcowboymuseum.org/events/wha/Default.aspx
WILLA Awards	American West	Women Writing the West	1999	www.womenwritingthewest.org/willaaward.html

Note: This table represents the most recognized and prestigious of the genre awards. There are many others awarded by the publishing industry and other book-related associations.

gious of the genre-specific awards, established in 1946 to recognize mystery and crime writing. The Edgars limit themselves to works published in the United States; the Best First Novel is limited to a U.S.-born novelist. Along with the more commonplace Best Novel and Best First Novel categories, MWA also recognizes short stories, plays and screenplays, movies, and television episodes. An additional award is presented for novels written in the Mary Higgins Clark tradition.

Mystery Writers of America (www.mysterywriters.org/) is the home of the Edgar Awards. A comprehensive Web site, it has something for everybody, from readers to authors to librarians. New and forthcoming mystery and crime titles are prominently featured. A good section for book clubs discusses the establishing of book clubs and a page of general discussion questions that can be used to guide a book discussion. The strongest feature of the Web site is its link to a searchable database (www.theedgars.com) that provides searches of winners and nominees from 1946 to the present.

The Macavity Awards, named for T. S. Eliot's mystery cat in *Old Possum's Book of Practical Cats*, are awarded annually by Mystery Readers International (MRI). They were established in 1987 and are awarded for Best Mystery Novel, Best First Mystery, Best Mystery Short Story, Best Mystery Nonfiction, and Best Historical Mystery (Sue Feder Memorial). Members of MRI nominate and vote on their favorite mysteries. The Web site (www.mysteryreaders.org/index.html) provides extensive information about the organization itself as well as its awards. This is a useful tool for collection development and mystery acquisition since it includes information about mystery periodicals, author interviews (an extensive list of well-known mystery writers being interviewed by their equally well-known peers), and the complete list of award winners from 1987 to the present. An additional feature is a state-by-state listing of mystery reader book clubs along with a few international inclusions (Canada, England, and Spain) and a link to information about starting mystery book clubs.

The Shamus Awards were established in 1982 by the Private Eye Writers of America (PWA). They recognize excellent writing of novels, first novels, original paperbacks, and short stories in the private eye genre. PWA "defines a 'private eye' as any mystery protagonist who is a professional investigator, but not a police officer or government agent" (PWA, 2007). In 1986 PWA partnered with St. Martin's Press, a prominent publisher for this genre, to present the St. Martin's Press/Private Eye Writers of America Best First Private Eye Novel. Private Eye Writers of America's Web site (www.thrillingdetective.com/trivia/triv72.html #2000) provides a list of the Shamus Awards presented annually from 1982 to 2007 for excellence in private eye writing. Links are also provided to the list of St. Martin's Press/Private Eye Writers of America Best First Private Eye Novel contest. The most useful part of the Web site is the link to "Murder in the Library: Bibliography," which features a comprehensive resource of periodicals, books, anthologies, as well as reference materials (www.thrillingdetective.com/trivia/biblio.html).

The crime genre is closely related to mystery. Distinct crossover occurs among some of the awards, especially the Hammett Prize, the Edgars, and the Shamus Award. The International Association of Crime Writers, North American Branch, defines crime writing as "any published work of adult fiction or narrative nonfiction that encompasses such areas as 'crime,' 'suspense,' 'thriller,' 'mystery,' or 'espionage' as those terms are normally understood in the writing and publishing fields" (International Association of Crime Writers, North American Branch, 2008). The Hammett Prize, named in honor of Dashiel Hammett, was established in 1991 to honor literary excellence in crime writing. The award is specific to books, although collections of short stories by a single author may be considered. Criteria for consideration include books published in the English language in the United States and Canada. Unlike the other mystery-crime awards, The Hammett Prize nominees are solicited from association members and distinguished crime specialist booksellers and critics. A particularly useful feature of the Web site is a link to a bibliography of crime fiction in translation from other languages (www.crimewritersna.org/hammett/index.htm).

Hovering by the side of mystery and crime, but a well-developed genre of its own, is horror writing. At its finest horror fiction "elicits an emotional reaction that includes some aspect of fear or dread" (Horror Writers Association, 2007: n.p.). The Bram Stoker Awards are presented annually by the Horror Writers Association, an international association devoted to the genre of fear and terror (www.horror.org/index.htm). The awards were established in 1987 to recognize "superior achievement in horror writing" (Horror Writers Association, 2007: n.p.). Bram Stoker Awards are given in approximately eight literary categories and for lifetime achievement, specialty press, librarian of the year, and volunteer service (all in support of bringing the horror genre to the eye of the reading public).

Science Fiction Awards

Science fiction devotees will note the range of awards for this genre, at least six major awards and many subcategories and related awards. Combined, they encompass science fiction, fantasy, and mythic literature for adults and children. Several of the awards are among the oldest of the established genre awards. Like the others, the science fiction genre awards recognize excellence in science fiction and fantasy writing. Nominations and voting are typically a function of association membership along with the occasional genre specialist and critic.

The Hugo Award is the oldest of the science fiction awards. Established in 1953, the Hugos are sponsored and presented by the World Science Fiction Society at the annual Worldcon convention. The award was named in honor of Hugo Gernsback, the founder of *Amazing Stories*, the first magazine devoted to science fiction. Awards are presented in at least a dozen categories, ranging from Best Novel to Best Fan Artist. They are international in nature, without limitation of place of publication or nationality of writer. The Hugos are not limited to science fiction, but also include fantasy and horror. Again, like crime, mystery, and horror, a level of flexibility exists in defining the category with crossing between science fiction, fantasy, horror, and mystery.

The Hugo Awards Web site (www.thehugoawards.org/) is a blog site devoted to information about the awards. Hugo Award Categories and Hugo Award History are the two most useful sections of the resource. The history section provides lists of Hugo Award Winners and Nominees from 1953 to the present, and it includes an award titled Retro Hugo that recognizes excellence in science fiction written 50 to 100 years prior to the establishment of the Hugo.

Another major science fiction and fantasy award is the Nebula Award. This award is presented annually and sponsored by Science Fiction and Fantasy Writers of America (SFWA). Like the Hugo Awards, the Nebula Award recognizes the best novels, novellas, novelettes, and short stories along with the best movie script. Along with the Nebula Awards, SWFA also sponsors awards for lifetime achievement, young adult science fiction and fantasy, and author emeritus. In order to be eligible for consideration, submitted works must be published, released, or aired in the United States. The Web site provides links to the lists of nominees and winners from 1965 to the present (www.nebulaawards.com/index.php/awards/nebulas/). It also provides links to resources covering the craft and business of writing and recommended reading.

The premier prize for science fiction literature in the United Kingdom is the Arthur C. Clarke Award. The award is presented annually for the best science fiction novel of the year. It was established with a grant from Sir Arthur C. Clarke with the intent to promote science fiction in Britain. The winning author receives a small monetary award and engraved bookends. The competition is open to any full-length novel written in English by an author of any nationality. The novel must be published for the first time in the United Kingdom between January 1 and December 31 of the year prior to the awarding of the prize. Margaret Atwood was the first winner in 1987, for *The Handmaid's Tale*. Judges for the award are selected from the British Science Fiction Association, the Science Fiction Foundation, and SF Crowsnest. The complete list of winners from 1987 through 2009 along with the short list and judges is available on the award Web site (www.clarkeaward.com/).

Other longstanding science fiction awards include the Mythopoeic Awards for fantasy and mythic literature (www.mythsoc.org/), Philip K. Dick Award (www.philipkdickaward.org/) for original science fiction paperback, and the Skylark Award, recognizing individual contributions to science fiction. While the focus of each is adult literature, the Mythopoeic Awards include children's literature. Nominations and selection range from fan-based suggestions to nomination and selection by writers and academics.

Ah, Romance

Romance is another of the genres that experiences blurred lines and intergenre relationships. It covers historical, paranormal, inspirational, and traditional romances, romantic comedy, and romantic mysteries, suspense, and adventure, along with many other descriptions and subgenres. Romances come in series and single titles. At the center of romance writing is the human relationship, or central love story, and in the end all romances by definition must be emotionally satisfying and optimistic.

The most recognizable and prestigious genre award for romance writing is the RITA, established in 1982. This award, sponsored by Romance Writers of America (RWA), celebrates the best of romance writing along with numerous other awards for lifetime achievement, bookselling, publishing, industry, and service. The RWA also recognizes a librarian of the year for support in promoting the reading of romance. Two categories of romance awards are presented each year: RITA Awards for published romance novels and the Golden Heart for unpublished romance novel manuscripts. Nominations for the awards are judged by other published romance authors, and up to 1,200 entries in 12 categories are judged each year.

Romance Writers of America (www.rwanational.org/cs/home) offers a robust Web site that covers all aspects of writing romance fiction. It serves as an advocate and network for romance writers at all levels of their writing career. A portion of the Web site is directed at librarians to support romance fiction promotion and acquisition. Lists of books and authors and links to bestsellers lists are readily available. One of the more interesting components details romance literature statistics for sales, readership, and market share based on book sales.

The Romance Novelists' Association (RNA) is the United Kingdom's answer to RWA. Much like the RITAs, RNA sponsors several awards to honor romance writing, including Romantic Novel of the Year, RNA Love Story of the Year, New Writers Award, and the Elizabeth Goudge Trophy. The Romantic Novel of the Year was established in 1960. Awards encompass full-length novels, short stories, and thematic competitions for first chapters. The panel of judges is comprised of ordinary members of the reading public, and each book is read and scored by three readers. Only those books receiving the highest scores for romantic content, readability, dialogue, characters, plot, style, and setting move to the long list, which is then narrowed to a short list and final vote for the winning entry.

The RNA Web site (www.rna-uk.org/) features lists of winners from 1960 through 2009, resources for new writers, and author biographies. Much like the RWA Web site, RNA offers statistics and information about the romance genre in the United Kingdom and the relationship between the U.K. and U.S. readership. The site offers a range of useful links for writers to find publishers and agents as well as writing groups and workshops.

Westerns or American West Literature

The final genre awards to be considered in this chapter are for Westerns, or novels about the American West. Along with the Hugo Awards for science fiction, the Spur Awards are among the oldest of the genre awards. The Spur Award has been presented annually since 1953 by Western Writers of America (WWA), recognizing the best in writing about the American West. The Web site (www .westernwriters.org/index.html) features links to award winners from 1953 to the present, current lists of judges, and access to the association's online journal. In addition to the Spur Awards, WWA gives awards for lifelong contributions in support of the literature of the American West and includes luminaries such as John Jakes, John Wayne, Louis L'Amour, and Clint Eastwood. While offering the more traditional range of "best of" awards, Spur Awards are also presented for juvenile literature, history, TV or motion-picture drama, and TV or motion-picture documentaries. Entries for the Spur Awards are not limited to historical representations of the American West; they may be contemporary (considering the years 1900 to the present) or historical (up to 1900). All entries must be set in the American West, the early frontier, or be related to one or the other.

In celebration of women authors writing about the West, the Women Writing the West association (www.womenwritingthewest.org) was established in the early 1990s. WWW is a nonprofit organization comprised of authors and other professionals who write about and promote Western literature. Their specific purpose is to support and recognize authors who write stories featuring women and/or girls set in the American West. In that vein the WWW established the WILLA Literary Awards to honor fiction, historical fiction, nonfiction, poetry, and children's/YA books. The panel of judges for the WILLA Literary Awards is composed of librarians who deliberate about the qualities of submissions that best represent the role of women in the American West.

A final award for the representation of the American West in literature is presented by the National Cowboy and Western Heritage Museum (www .nationalcowboymuseum.org/events/wha/Default.aspx). The award was established in 1961 to honor significant stories of the American West. The fiction entries are evaluated on originality and creativity, as are many other genre awards; the evaluation, more importantly, considers the story's faithfulness to the facts, legends, and myths of the West. The Western Novel category considers all genres inclusively, and they may be historical or contemporary in nature.

While discussed previously in this chapter, several of the regional independent bookseller awards and library association awards support and recognize fiction and nonfiction works in the Western genre. These awards celebrate not only authors who are bona fide residents of the American West, but many also follow similar criteria to the Spur Awards and others in selecting books that are representative of either the American West or the early frontier.

CONCLUSION

Book awards provide another way to celebrate the interest and popularity of reading. They range from the recognition of a lifetime of achievement, especially the Nobel Prize for Literature, to the next best thing in popular fiction. While the major literary awards bring recognition to the authors, the smaller genre awards place the books and authors squarely in the sight of the everyday reader. For readers and librarians alike, the awards are one more way to find new reads that might not be considered on first glance in the book shelves. More important than the annual awards themselves are the Web sites that provide incredible depth of information about authors, reading lists, and resources. These are ready-made reading lists, especially for the genre fiction, to help guide readers to books that might match their mood.

WORKS CONSULTED

Alabama Library Association. 2008. "Author Awards." Available: http://allanet.org/about_author_awards.cfm (accessed September 10, 2009).

Bogard, Dave, ed. 2007. *The Bowker Annual Library and Book Trade Almanac 2007*. Medford, NJ: Information Today.

"Bowker Reports U.S. Book Production Flat in 2007." 2008. Available: www.bowker.com/index.php/press-releases/66-corporate2008/526-bowker-reports-us-book-production-flat-in-2007 (accessed September 10, 2009).

Brewer, Robert Lee, ed. 2008. *2009 Writer's Market*. Cincinnati, OH: Writer's Digest Books.

"Canadian Literary Awards." 2008. Canadian Authors Association. Available: www.canlitawards.com/caa.html (accessed September 10, 2009).

English, James F. 2005. *The Economy of Prestige: Prizes, Awards, and the Circulation of Cultural Value*. Cambridge, MA: Harvard University Press.

Espmark, Kjell. 1999. "The Nobel Prize in Literature." (December 3). Available: http://nobelprize.org/nobel_prizes/literature/articles/espmark/index.html   (accessed September 10, 2009).

Fein, Esther B. 1992. "Even in Book Awards, to Victors Go the Spoils." *The New York Times*, Late Edition East Coast (March 16): D8.

Feldman, Burton. 2000. *The Nobel Prize: A History of Genius, Controversy, and Prestige*. New York: Arcade Publishing.

Flood, Alison. 2008. "Nobel Prize for Literature Goes to Author of Poetic Adventure." *The Guardian* (October 9). Available: http://www.guardian.co.uk/books/2008/oct/09/nobelprize.awardsandprizes (accessed September 10, 2009).

Governor General's Literary Awards. 2009. "About the GGs." Available: www.canadacouncil.ca/prizes/ggla (accessed September 10, 2009).

Holman, Tom. 2003. "The Race for the Prize." *The Bookseller*, no. 5106 (December 5): 10–11.

Horror Writers Association. 2007. "The Bram Stoker Awards." Available: www.horror.org/hwaawards.htm (accessed September 10, 2009).

International Association of Crime Writers, North American Branch. 2008. "The Hammett Prize." Available: www.crimewritersna.org/hammett/index.htm (accessed September 10, 2009).

Johns, Derek. n.d. "Ensuring a World-Wide Audience for Fiction." Available: www
.themanbookerprize.com/perspective/articles/1139 (accessed September 10, 2009).

Malice Domestic. 2008. Available: www.malicedomestic.org/aboutmalice.html (accessed
September 10, 2009).

Menand, Louis. 2005. "All That Glitters: Literature's Global Economy." *The New Yorker* 81,
no. 42 (December 26): 136.

National Book Foundation. 2008. "About Us—History of the National Book Foundation." Available: www.nationalbook.org/aboutus_history.html (accessed September
10, 2009).

Orange Prize for Fiction. 2009. Available: www.orangeprize.co.uk/ (accessed September
10, 2009).

Portillo, Michael. 2008. "Man Booker Prize Announces 2008 Shortlist." Available: www
.themanbookerprize.com/news/stories/1134 (accessed September 10, 2009).

Private Eye Writers of America. 2007. Available: www.thrillingdetective.com/trivia/triv72
.html#2000 (accessed September 10, 2009).

Reference and User Services Association. 2008. "Notable Books for Adults." American
Library   Association.   Available: www.ala.org/ala/mgrps/divs/rusa/awards/
notablebooks/index.cfm (accessed September 10, 2009).

Ruppin, Jonathan. 2007. "What Good Booksellers Do Best: A Bookseller's View of the
Man Booker Prize." Available: www.themanbookerprize.com/perspective/articles/
1133 (accessed September 10, 2009).

Rutten, Tim. 2002. "Big Book Prizes—The Velvet Salesmen." *Los Angeles Times* (October
19): E1.

Saricks, Joyce G. 2001. *The Readers' Advisory Guide to Genre Fiction.* Chicago: American Library Association.

The Scotiabank Giller Prize. 2009. Available: www.scotiabankgillerprize.ca/about.htm
(accessed September 10, 2009).

Surowiecki, James. 2001. "The Power of the Prize." *The New Yorker* 77, no. 15 (June 18): 67.

Topping, Seymour. 1999. "Foreword: Joseph Pulitzer and the Pulitzer Prizes." In *Who's
Who of Pulitzer Prize Winners* (pp. vii–xiv), by Elizabeth. A. Brennan and Elizabeth C.
Clarage. Phoenix, AZ: The Oryx Press.

Trust Foundation. 2009. "Miles Franklin Literary Award." Available: www.trust.com.au/
awards/miles_franklin (accessed September 10, 2009).

Zauha, Janelle M. 2006. "Reading the Region: Award Books from the Pacific Northwest."
PNLA Quarterly 71, no. 1 (Fall): 5–7.

FURTHER READING

American Library Association. 1996. *50 Years of Notable Books.* Chicago: American Library
Association. Also see the American Library Association Web site (www.ala.org/ala/
mgrps/divs/rusa/resources/notablebooks/index.cfm) for a "Brief History" and links
to "The Current List," covering winners from 1998 through the current year.

Herald, Diana Trixler. 2006. *Genreflecting: A Guide to Popular Reading Interests,* edited by
Wayne A. Wiegand. Westport, CT: Libraries Unlimited.

National Book Foundation. 2002. *The National Book Awards: Winners and Finalists 1950–
2001.* New York: National Book Foundation.

"The Year in Awards." 2007. *Publishers Weekly* 254, no. 52 (December 31): 17–20.

Chapter 16

Reading Groups Old and New

I suppose you could say that the real, hidden subject of a book group discussion is the book group members themselves. I think they are quite brave. They are ready to reveal, in semi-public, their own reactions, their own biases and doubts and convictions, and above all their own tastes; not everyone dares.

—from *The Book Group Book*, foreword by Margaret Atwood (1995)

Shared reading through book discussions carries a long tradition and history. Early readers shared the written word through oral traditions. The written word was intended to be heard. In the tenth century AD, the oral tradition shifted and silent reading and solitary reading became accepted practices, but reading continued to be shared through the process of intensive reading and debate about ideas and through the sharing of the books themselves among groups. (Books were held dear and few could afford to purchase their own personal copies; thus books were passed among friends and colleagues.)

As early as the mid-sixteenth century, but firmly in the seventeenth and eighteenth centuries, salons emerged as fashionable social gatherings, and more importantly as forums for scientific, political, and literary discussion and intellectual education, especially for women. The salons were attended by writers and poets, philosophers and scientists, where their work was read and discussed both furtively and openly, depending upon who was in political power. The salons provided a haven for ideas not accepted or held by the nobility. In France, the salons were the cradle of the French Revolution and the birth of a democratic society. In England, the salons encouraged women to become intellectuals, or "Bluestockings." In the fledgling nation of America, in salons and literary circles the notions of freedom and democracy were explored and tested. The salons provide the first inkling of what was to come with book discussion groups and social activism. (See Murray, 2002, in the Further Reading list and Long, 2003, for detailed discussions of the history of book discussion groups.)

With the rise of the popular novel in the nineteenth century along with increased leisure time for the working class came the burgeoning of book discussion groups in a form that contemporary readers will recognize. Groups, especially women, gathered together to discuss books for both the pleasure de-rived from a social gathering and for intellectual pursuit and improvement. These book discussion groups held the same elements of empowerment, educa-tion, and political activism as the early salons of France and England. This gath-ering of likeminded individuals to discuss books and ideas continues today with the contemporary reading group.

The difference, however, between book clubs or literary societies and salons falls in the purpose of the gathering. Members of the salons, while discussing lit-erature (books, sermons, scientific treatises), did not intentionally read the same works prior to a salon gathering with the purpose of fostering discussion. Rather, the discussion was free-form and free-flowing. The hallmark of the book discussion group, on the other hand, is the common reading with the purpose of shared dialogue.

However, with the evolution of mass media and the Internet, the traditional book discussion group has grown and split into other iterations of shared read-ing. Starting with the early television talk shows featuring author interviews and remodeling their forms into Oprah's Book Club, *Good Morning America*'s Read This!, and the *Today* Show Books, among others, broadcast media book clubs have come alive and firmly captured the attention of readers. The Internet also offers opportunities for readers and other book lovers to connect and communi-cate worldwide with one another and within the culture of books and reading.

TRADITIONAL BOOK DISCUSSION GROUPS

Can we really call a book discussion group traditional? For purposes of this dis-cussion, traditional book discussion groups meet face-to-face as a social gather-ing with the intent to discuss books, for a variety of purposes. The groups meet not only in libraries but in members' homes, bookstores, places of worship, cafés or pubs, on college campuses, and anywhere a group can gather comfortably. Rough estimates suggest more than 500,000 book groups exist in the United States, and many report significant longevity, having been in existence for 30 or more years (Hartley, 2002; Sandra and Spayde, 2001; Moore and Stevens, 2004). The overwhelming response to questions about why people participate in book clubs (discussion groups, literary circles, or literary societies) is to satisfy a need for community and to share experiences and ideas found in reading.

The traditional book clubs, as we know them today, emerged in the late-nine-teenth and early twentieth centuries. Membership was, and still is, predomi-nantly women, though men also formed their own discussion groups and often joined the women's groups. But what was the purpose of these grassroots organi-zations? Suffrage, community-building, intellectual growth, or all of the above? For many women, for whom a university education was denied, the reading groups provided opportunities to read and discuss the important ideas of the day and to indulge in self-education. Long suggests that these women "were aflame with the then revolutionary desire for education and self-development" (2003: 38), and reading groups offered these women the opportunity to engage in intellectual growth. The reading groups also allowed women to share their experiences and find a sense of communal support for their needs and interests.

A Few Novels Featuring Book Clubs

The Book Class, by Louis Auchincloss
The Used Women's Book Club, by Paul Bryers
The Jane Austen Book Club, by Karen Joy Fowler
Pure Fiction, by Julie Highmore
The Reading Group, by Elizabeth Noble
And Ladies of the Club, by Helen Hooven Santmyer
The Guernsey Literary and Potato Peel Pie Society, by Mary Ann Shaffer
   and Annie Barrows

The earliest known women's reading group in the United States occurred in approximately 1634. Anne Hutchinson gathered together a group of women for regular "sermon discussions" in her home in the Massachusetts Bay Colony. She encouraged her group to discuss theology and literature and steep themselves in self-education. Moving against the Puritanical belief by suggesting that faith alone, and not hard work, was necessary to attain salvation and enter heaven, Hutchinson was tried in a court of law and charged as a heretic, and her reading group was determined to be subversive and participating in "seditious crimes" (Hartley, 2002; Moore and Stevens, 2004). While Hutchinson's all-female gathering was not a book discussion group as they are known today, "it inaugurated a tradition of serious discussion of serious texts by women" (Sandra and Spayde, 2001: 149).

These same groups played a critical role in the development of the public library as a civic organization, raising funds to build libraries and purchase materials for collections, and promoting education and literacy for all. They were frequently considered dangerous, encouraging members to question societal norms and to take political action, or in the case of Hutchinson religious action. Yet they also served as conduits to improve society through fund-raising, education, and communal support of those needing assistance (physical, financial, and spiritual).

In a smaller, less visible movement, African Americans formed their own literary societies in the nineteenth century for many of the same purposes that women's literary societies were formed. Particularly in the urban Northern cities, the African-American societies became a place to read and explore communal and personal identities. In her book *Forgotten Readers*, Elizabeth McHenry presents African-American literary societies as a way for free blacks and former slaves to find a "voice for their demands for full citizenship and equal participation in the life of the republic" (2002: 23). Evolving from these early literary societies, contemporary black women's reading groups are strong communities that come together for social and intellectual discussions. They continue to carry the tradition of activism and self-education, but the reading groups also provide opportunities to explore relationships and to discover writers of African descent who can speak to the members' own experiences.

In her groundbreaking work, Elizabeth Long explores the purposes of the contemporary women's reading groups. She suggests that today's groups come together more for the "companionable discussion of books, ideas, and experiences" (2003: 69) since most members are already well-educated and have less need for the self-education and development that the early women's groups offered. She also suggests that the need for social reform and consciousness-raising has been relegated to other organizations, and contemporary reading groups devote themselves to books and ideas. The notion of self-improvement still exists, but it is intertwined with the "exploration of personal identity . . . and dedicated to the discussion of ideas, meaning, and values in the company of equally dedicated companions" (Long, 2003: 73). Throughout, the emphasis is on companionship and personal support as well as intellectual discussion.

Every book group has its own flavor, dependent upon the personalities that make up the membership. Book groups run the gamut from children and teen reading groups to groups for seniors; they divide by gender and ethnicity as well as bring together wildly diverse groups of individuals. Some combine the social gathering with food and drink (tea to wine) in a relaxed and informal atmosphere, while others are highly formal with recognized etiquette and procedure. The range of reading choices approaches the same level of diversity as the groups themselves: fiction, nonfiction, literary classics, everyone reading the same book (also known as single-title groups), or everyone reading different books (also referred to as multi-title clubs) but with the same theme or topic.

Planning for Successful Book Discussion Groups

There is no real wrong way to conduct a book discussion group, though some discussion groups are more successful and fruitful than others. Thoughtful planning provides the key to a stimulating and enjoyable discussion. Numerous resources provide guidance on how to start and maintain book groups (see Appendix 4 for a list of resources in print and online formats). Common parameters include developing an identity for the group: what kind of discussion group on a continuum of highly social to seriously intellectual, size of the group, and the type of books to read that fit the social or intellectual intent. Common wisdom suggests "to be clear about your goals for the group: Are you a serious book-study circle, or are the books intended as a jumping-off place for sociability? Are you going to read mainly fiction, nonfiction, poetry, plays—or a bit of everything?" (Sandra and Spayde, 2001: 154). Organizational structure also has a role in a productive discussion group. Some issues to consider include the format and length of the group meetings, how to conduct the discussions, and basic ground rules.

By far the most crucial element of the discussion group focuses on the selection of the titles. The choice of what to read must first reflect the goals of the book club. Any of the book discussion how-to guides offer methods for selecting titles. Some of the common suggestions include exploring themes (specific authors, travel, etc.), mixing genres, selecting related books you can read together (The Seattle Public Library suggests the examples of *Reading Lolita in Tehran* by Azar Nafisi and *Lolita* by Vladimir Nabokov) or books that raise social issues. The most consistent recommendation advises that book discussion groups avoid popular genre fiction (romance, mystery, science fiction) and focus on books with complex characters and issues that readers can explore deeply. Remain flexible in book selections, choosing only two or three months of reading in advance, to accommodate new discoveries. Consensus, majority vote, and rotating selections all encompass effective methods of choosing titles by group members. Other recommendations include choosing books available in multiple formats (audio, downloadable, large print) to meet the varying preferences of group members.

Many of the resources for starting book groups also include lists of possible titles appropriate for all types of groups. Book club resources abound on the Web and provide extensive lists of titles for all types of reading preferences (see Appendix 4 for a small selection of resources). Chapter 14, "List Culture," presents a number of resources for booklists, as does Chapter 15, "Book Awards and Award-Winning Books." Consulting other librarians, booksellers, and book discussion groups may yield surprising recommendations and new approaches.

Go On Girl! Book Club

An extraordinary book discussion group was founded in 1991 to support the needs and interests of African-American women. Go On Girl! Book Club is the largest African-American women's book club in the United States with more than 30 chapters across 12 states. The intent of the book club, while providing an intellectual and social outlet for women, is to celebrate the legacy of black literature. Among other events, Go On Girl! chapters gather to honor authors of black literature, including Gloria Naylor, Bebe Moore Campbell, and Pearl Cleage, with an Author of the Year and New Author of the Year award.

The Go On Girl! Web site (www.goongirl.org/) features annual reading lists and suggested readings. The site also features a selection of resources for magazines, book reviews, and literary club resources. Along with the annual author awards, the club sponsors writing awards for unpublished authors and educational scholarships for aspiring young authors.

Tools for Enhancing the Book Discussion

Book discussions present numerous opportunities to learn about authors and the social issues explored in the selected books. This can be accomplished by developing or obtaining reading guides and discussion questions to support and guide the discussion group. Many of the publishing houses create support materials for book discussion groups and make them freely available to book groups (frequently downloadable from the Web site and in a PDF format). Many of the popular reading group title selections include discussion guides as part of the book when they are published. (Check out the reading guides included in *The Secret Life of Bees* by Sue Monk Kidd, Penguin Books, 2002, and *Reading Lolita in Tehran* by Azar Nafisi, Random House, 2004, for example. Both include conversations or interviews with the author, brief background materials, and discussion group questions.) Numerous public libraries include reading guides on their Web sites, or at least access to Web resources for obtaining reading guides. Web sites devoted to books, readers, and reading groups offer comprehensive resources, including book reviews, reading guides, author notes, and other materials to enhance the reading experience. (See Appendix 4 for a list of reading guide resources along with resources for titles.)

Some public libraries that sponsor or support reading guides prepare "book club kits" that patrons can check out. These kits include several copies of a book, sometimes in multiple formats, reading guides, book reviews, and other materials that might enhance the reader's understanding of issues, time, and place. The kits have extended circulation periods to accommodate reading and discussion schedules, generally six to eight weeks. Book discussion kits (also called book club to go, book discussion sets, and book club sets) offer many advantages for libraries and book clubs by facilitating access to resources and ensuring availability of titles for readers. They make it easy for discussion groups to enjoy the experience of reading without the challenges of finding resources. Kits also lend themselves to meeting the interests and needs of a variety of reading groups, from children and teens to seniors to business and professional groups. Initially creating the kits comes with some cost (money, time, and staff), but the libraries justify the expense by providing "a popular, cost-effective use of library tax support for a broad cultural benefit" (Hermes, Hile, and Frisbie, 2008: 33).

Promoting and marketing book discussion groups are essential to the group's success. Besides the standard public service announcements in local newspapers and on the library Web site, libraries of all sizes are actively creating wikis, blogs, and social networking pages to promote their book discussion groups and the resources available for supporting book discussion groups. Not only do these online resources provide general information about group meetings (often in the form of a calendar of events) and selected titles, but they also provide a forum to reach readers who might not come into the library. More common use of the online resources includes links to author Web sites and book reviews and reading guides.

BROADCAST MEDIA AND TALK SHOW BOOK CLUBS

Television has been a boon to authors and publishers, promoting books and reading. It has been a longstanding tradition for talk show hosts to invite authors to discuss their books in front of a studio audience and in live broadcast. Historically, these were not billed as book clubs and occurred irregularly throughout the broadcast season. Beginning in the early 1960s, *The Mike Douglas Show* and *The Merv Griffin Show*, popular afternoon talk shows, featured numerous authors, including Dr. Joyce Brothers, Robert Frost, Charles Schulz, and Sidney Sheldon. The show's host chatted informally with the author, but the audience did not have occasion to interact or respond to the guest. This format continues today with many of the talk shows following a similar style.

Enter Oprah Winfrey and Oprah's Book Club, *Good Morning America*'s Read This!, *Today* Show Books, and *Live with Regis and Kelly*'s Reading with Ripa. In September 1996, Winfrey began a reading segment on her wildly popular talk show with the intent of getting the nation reading—and not reading just anything, but good books with a message. The format of Oprah's Book Club consisted of an announcement of the selected title at the beginning of the month and taped segment at the end of the month of a dinner party including Winfrey with the author and four invited guests from the studio audience.

After a little more than five years of an almost monthly selection, Winfrey discontinued the book club in 2002, indicating that she wanted to be able to read without the pressure of having to pick a selection each month and wanted to choose only books that truly moved her. In summer 2003 the book club resumed with classics as its focus, starting with John Steinbeck's *East of Eden* and an enhanced book club Web site. The model changed in autumn 2005 when she once again began inviting authors to join her on the live broadcast to discuss their books. The remodeled book club now includes in-depth interviews with the authors following a two-week advanced announcement of the selected title to ensure availability of the book through bookstores, libraries, and other retail outlets. Winfrey invites the studio audience to participate through question-and-answer sessions, and the at-home viewers are encouraged to join in the conversation through a robust Web-based book club resource.

Through the book selections and the companion Web site, reading becomes a holistic experience that allows Winfrey's viewers to explore books and share their experiences and reactions. After members register as Oprah Web site users, they may log in and explore the archived titles of recommendations from past years. Members have access to information about face-to-face book clubs in their area. As part of the reading experience, they can view one of many lecture videos relating to the book, participate in online reading groups, or contribute to message board discussions. Oprah's Book Club Web site even allows members to complete mini-learning modules and to take a quiz on what they have read and learned.

Finally, Oprah's Book Club book selections have not been "dumbed down" (consider, for example, *Anna Karenina* by Tolstoy). Winfrey does not select summer beach reading (unlike Reading with Ripa). She assumes that her audience is capable of reading literature and learning something from it. The books may be hard to read or understand, but they are intellectually reachable for Winfrey's audience, especially if they make use of the myriad Oprah Web resources, including the learning modules. Winfrey's book selections highlight her belief in the power of books to change lives.

When Winfrey decided to discontinue her book club in 2002, other talk shows raced to fill the niche. Among these were the clubs on *Good Morning America* (GMA) and the *Today* show, each with a unique format and distinct appeal. GMA's reading program consisted of inviting one regional book club to recommend a book to another, following a round-robin format. The *Today* Show Book Club also began its broadcast in 2002 after Oprah's Book Club ceased. The *Today* format allowed a well-known author to select books of relatively unknown authors each month. For example, John Grisham selected Stephen L. Carter's debut novel *The Emperor of Ocean Park* as the first *Today* Show Book Club selection. The second club selection was *You Are Not a Stranger Here* by Adam Haslett, selected by Jonathan Franzen. At the end of each month, members of book groups nationwide were invited to go on the show and talk with the author. Neither of these television book clubs, however, achieved the same status in their viewers' lives as Winfrey's has, and the respective book clubs did not have the same luster or sales impact as Oprah's Book Club.

GMA and *Today* more closely resemble the early talk shows, such as *The Mike Douglas Show* or *The Merv Griffin Show*, offering less personal interaction with authors and more in the way of journalistic interviews. *GMA* and *Today* select books that have already been highlighted by the media critics in some way. The books are readily known in the marketplace, and the recommendations are additional promotion for the titles and authors. Many critics predicted that none of these clubs would reach the "monolithic success garnered by Winfrey's original" book club (Rooney, 2005: 182); in fact, *GMA* and *Today* no longer feature their television book clubs, but do continue to feature authors as guests.

In a sense, Oprah's Book Club, *GMA*'s Read This!, and the *Today* Show Books are not traditional book clubs, though Oprah's contains many of the more formal elements of a book discussion group. Readers do not gather together and discuss books guided by discussion questions. Rather, the television book clubs more closely resemble book recommendations or, in library terms, readers' advisory activities. Oprah's Book Club and the others fulfill a need for people who have difficulty in finding new books to read when faced with the profusion of books available through online booksellers and the mega-bookstores. Regardless of the delivery format, however, media book clubs, especially Oprah's Book Club, fulfill a need for shared community, or at least acknowledge that others are reading the same books and sharing similar thoughts and reactions.

For librarians serving adult readers, the television book clubs provide opportunities to connect readers with books they may not have considered in the past. The demand for Oprah selections in particular continues to be high, but mentions of books and authors on other talk shows also promote reading. By linking the library users to the reading lists and supplemental resources, the reading experience has been extended into the local community (supporters of the local library). Connecting to the book club Web sites through links on the library's pages also connects the reader to the authors and fellow readers through learning modules, interviews, and discussion boards, further supporting the shared nature of the reading experience. The lists of talk show selections also points to the books that people are reading, which is a core piece of knowledge for readers' advisors to have on hand.

Richard and Judy's Book Club

What Oprah did for American publishing, Great Britain's "The Richard and Judy Book Club" did for the U.K. publishing industry. Richard Madeley and Judy Finnigan began their on-air book club in 2004 under the direction of Amanda Ross of Cactus TV. From the start it was wildly popular and exceedingly successful in promoting book sales. The intent of the television book club was to turn the Brits into a nation of readers, foregoing the "telly" for a good read. Ross never dreamed that Richard and Judy's Book Club would have a similar effect on book sales to the "Oprah effect." Initially the program would have a ten-week run and culminate in the Richard and Judy's Best Read award, which would be presented at the British Book Awards. The Richard and Judy Book Club was discontinued on Cactus TV in late 2008 when Madeley and Finnigan moved to another television station.

Unlike Oprah, who personally selects the featured titles, Richard and Judy did not choose the books. Amanda Ross, the show's producer, and her production team selected the books for the club from titles submitted by publishers. The first season a total of 269 titles were submitted, with the final short list narrowed to 20 titles. Madeley and Finnigan had little to do with the initial selection; however, they were provided with synopses of the short list, which they read. The selected titles ranged from popular fiction to literary fiction, with no distinction being made about improving or enlightening readers beyond introducing them to a broad range of books. Many of the titles are also ones that appeared on U.S. bestseller lists.

Each broadcast began with a brief film clip of the author discussing the selected book, but the author was not invited to attend the on-air book discussion. Rather, other well-known celebrities and political figures joined Madeley and

Finnigan on the set to share their opinions and reactions to the selected titles. Guests were given freedom to offer both positive and negative opinions of the book, and Madeley and Finnigan often disagreed about the selected books, adding a little excitement to the book discussions. By not inviting the author, Ross believed that guests and the hosts would offer honest critiques of the books.

The first book to be featured on the show was *Toast* by Nigel Slater. Sales of the book more than doubled the week after being discussed on the broadcast. Much like Oprah's impact, as soon as titles were announced, book sales for titles soared. If the on-air guests and Richard and Judy endorsed the book, sales continued to soar; if they panned the book, sales dropped. Estimates suggested that *The Star of the Sea* by Joseph O'Connor gained 350 percent in sales and bestseller status for a book that would have otherwise gone unnoticed by the general reading public (Feay, 2005: n.p.).

Selections from The Richard and Judy Book Club

Half of a Yellow Sun, by Chimamanda Ngozi Adichie
Brick Lane, by Monica Ali
Perdita: The Life of Mary Robinson, by Paula Byrne
The Promise of Happiness, by Justin Cartwright
The Jane Austen Book Club, by Karen Joy Fowler
Love in the Present Tense, by Catherine Ryan Hyde
The Time Traveler's Wife, by Audrey Niffeneger
The Star of the Sea, by Joseph O'Connor
My Sister's Keeper, by Jodi Picoult
The Interpretation of Murder, by Jeb Rubenfeld
The Lovely Bones, by Alice Sebold
The American Boy, by Andrew Taylor
Lucia, Lucia, by Adriana Trigiani
The Shadow of the Wind, by Carlos Ruis Zafon

Amazon.co.uk (the U.K. affiliate of Amazon.com) began featuring a "Richard and Judy's Book Club" list, much as appears on Amazon.com and other U.S. resources for Oprah's Book Club Selections. Publishers rushed to add "Richard and Judy's Book Club" labels to their titles as soon as the selections were announced. Many of the titles went into second and third print runs to meet the demand by the reading public. An active "Richard and Judy's Book Club" Web site was developed to enhance the reading experience through interactive discussion groups, reading lists, and multimedia components.

The role of these types of broadcast media book clubs has added a new layer to the reading research, especially considering how people select the books they want to read. Many of the television clubs cannot maintain the same level of intensity and longevity that Winfrey has accomplished. But without a doubt these broadcasts do influence readers' selections, both at the bookstore and at the library.

ONLINE BOOK DISCUSSION GROUPS

With the development of the Internet and social networking sites, the nature of book clubs and book discussion groups has changed to some extent. In recent years online book clubs have turned to discussion boards and blogs for communication and discussion. A prime example of the changed nature of book clubs is Book-Clubs-Resource.com, which hosts as well as links to numerous book discussion groups of all types and genres. It also covers tips for creating and maintaining online book discussion groups. Another example, LibraryThing.com, allows members to catalog their personal libraries and join a variety of discussion groups, and it serves as a hosting site for book discussion groups. These electronic sources allow individuals to participate in book discussions at their convenience and without the limitations of time and geographic boundaries. Online book clubs have capitalized on the broad reach of the Internet to encompass greater engagement with reading by linking readers to events and festivals and access to other resources to enhance the reading experience as well as connecting fellow readers.

Library online book discussions take a variety of forms. The most common and familiar are Web pages with hot link navigation to other resources either on the library Web site or to external sites. Many now incorporate blogs and wikis residing on external hosting sites (see, for example, Brooklyn Public Library's Brooklyn Book Talk at http://brooklynbooktalk.blogspot.com/) that allow and encourage readers to participate in discussions. Libraries have embraced online discussion groups and forums as a method to connect with local readers. Online book discussions promote the library and its resources as well as make it easy for library users (and even nonusers) to share their thoughts about books. With the availability of both commercial and grassroots discussion tools, libraries that have small staffs and limited experience in Web design and implementation can enjoy the promise of expanded access as their larger counterparts do.

One of the most popular online book clubs available through a variety of library Web sites is DearReader.com. DearReader offers two options for participation: e-mail subscription to the book club or the book forum. Adult readers can register for an online e-mail subscription. By agreement with a variety of publishers, DearReader provides portions of chapters of popular books to readers through e-mail each weekday. Dear-Reader offers a range of book club types, including mystery, fiction, romance, nonfiction, etc. The other option is to participate in a book forum through DearReader.com, which features online discussions about selected titles. One of the features of the Online Book Clubs section is a link to nearby public libraries that offer online book clubs. (For example, I plugged in my zip code and it located my closest public library branch should I want to check out the book I received the excerpts for; and it works, too, as I quickly placed a hold on the excerpted title.)

Quick Search Tip

A quick way to find examples of public libraries' book discussion groups and resources is to use your favorite search engine. Using the phrase "online book discussion" and "public library" yielded approximately 1,500 links (far more than I really needed, but great examples nonetheless). The following are a few commercial resources that provide information and access to online book discussion groups of various types. Most of them do require registration in order to access the resources.

Book-Clubs-Resource.com: www.book-clubs-resource.com
DearReader.com: www.dearreader.com/index.html
GoodReads: www.goodreads.com/
LibraryThing: www.librarything.com
Reading Groups Online: www.readinggroupsonline.com/
Shelfari: www.shelfari.com

Several of the online resources offer suggestions on creating and maintaining successful online book discussion groups. The first step requires planning and preparation. Like traditional book discussion groups, the online version needs to have an identity and a purpose. Define a theme or the types of books to be discussed; identify appropriate books and authors. Finding and using reading guides to prompt discussion is a familiar strategy, echoing traditional book discussion group activities. Several resources suggest that the most challenging component of the online book discussions is to keep the conversation moving. Discussions quickly lag and stagnate if the forum falls behind in currency and interesting commentary. This requires both new materials added regularly and a high degree of responsiveness to participants. Unlike traditional book club members who have committed themselves to a meeting, online users enter and leave sites quickly. The Web interface needs to grab the user's attention quickly with visual appeal and high-quality content to keep them there and to encourage them to return.

Social networking resources, such as Facebook and MySpace, offer another option for promoting and participating in online book discussion groups. In a recent personal exploration, more than 20,000 groups identifying themselves as reading groups or book groups had pages on MySpace. They covered every conceivable topic, genre, and author. The groups included ones that disliked a particular author or book as well as fan sites that celebrated these same aspects. Many were promotional in nature, touting print-on-demand and self-published works in order to find an audience. Size of membership ranged from extremely small (six to eight members) to very large (numbering in the thousands). The level of activity swings from the rare posting to members who interact regularly and frequently.

Searching for book and reading groups on MySpace and Facebook offers an interesting sociological study of readers. Groups vary widely in terms of depth and quality of member interaction; some are very superficial, responding to questions like, "What are you reading now? or "Did you like *Wicked*?" without any comprehensive discussion of content or issues. Other online book groups, however, engage in highly sophisticated dialogue, not only about individual books or authors, but about publishing and bookselling in general. Given the somewhat anonymous nature of the social networking spaces, it appears impossible to determine demographic characteristics of the online reading membership, but the common denominator seems to be that each has a personal relationship with books and reading.

Even virtual worlds, such as Second Life, are attempting to implement book discussion groups. For example, The Gazebo at Mystery Manor, an RA site for the mystery genre in Second Life, features a monthly book discussion. In April 2009 the discussion focused on international crime fiction set in Cuba and the book *Havana Black* by Leonardo Padura Fuentes. Along with a book description and review excerpts, the virtual library includes links to book reviews and articles about the author.

While distinctly different in purpose and intent, online discussion groups through the library Web site and through personal social networking sites offer library users and other members of the community broad access. Connecting readers to books in ways that are convenient for the end user is the real key for the online resources. More importantly, the online discussion groups and the traditional book discussion groups bring readers together to share their experiences and promote the library as the best resource for all things related to books and the pleasures of reading.

CONCLUSION

Reading continues to be celebrated as a shared activity. More importantly, it now encompasses more than just the book itself. Readers look to others to support and debate their personal responses to individual authors and titles (Fish's [2002] and Iser's [2002] interpretive communities, discussed in Chapter 3). They also look to many other resources not only to learn about books, but to explore ideas and to engage with other readers. While traditional book discussion groups encourage local participation in the local community, social networking sites and the Internet in general have created a global reading community. Broadcast media (television and radio) have enhanced the opportunities to learn about books, especially the programming that exploits the Internet along with the airwaves, such as Oprah's Book Club, and that has developed a strong presence on the Web, through print publication, and on television.

WORKS CONSULTED

Feay, Suzi. 2005. "So What's the Best Read? The Answer's in Grotty South London." *The Independent* (January 16). Available: http://license.icopyright.net/user/viewFreeUse .act?fuid=MjUzMDk3OQ%3D%3D (accessed September 10, 2009).

Fish, Stanley. 2002. "Interpreting the Variorum." In *The Book History Reader*, 2nd edition (pp. 450-458), edited by David Finkelstein and Alistair McCleery. London: Routledge.

Hartley, Jenny. 2002. *The Reading Groups Book 2002–2003 Edition*. Oxford, UK: Oxford University Press.

Hermes, Virginia, Mary Anne Hile, and Johnetta L. Frisbie. 2008. "Reviving Literary Discussion: Book Club to Go Kits." *Reference & User Services Quarterly* 48, no. 1 (Fall): 30–34.

Iser, Wolfgang. 2002. "Interaction between Text and Reader." In *The Book History Reader*, 2nd edition (pp. 391–396), edited by David Finkelstein and Alistair McCleery. London: Routledge.

Long, Elizabeth. 2003. *Book Clubs: Women and the Uses of Reading in Everyday Life*. Chicago: The University of Chicago Press.

McHenry, Elizabeth. 2002. *Forgotten Readers: Recovering the Lost History of African American Literary Societies*. Durham, NC: Duke University Press.

Moore, Ellen, and Kira Stevens. 2004. *Good Books Lately: The One-Stop Resource for Book Groups and Other Greedy Readers*. New York: St. Martin's Griffin.

Rooney, Kathleen. 2005. *Reading with Oprah: The Book Club That Changed America*. Fayetteville, AR: The University of Arkansas Press.

Sandra, Jaida N'Ha, and Jon Spayde. 2001. *Salons: The Joy of Conversation*. Gabriola Island, BC: New Society Publishers.

Slezak, Ellen, ed. 1995. *The Book Group Book: A Thoughtful Guide to Forming and Enjoying a Stimulating Book Discussion Group*. Chicago: Chicago Review Press.

FURTHER READING

American Library Association. 2009. "Professional Tips: Book Discussion Groups." Available: http://wikis.ala.org/professionaltips/ index.php/Book_Discussion_Groups (accessed September 10, 2009).

Green, Hardy. 2005. "Why Oprah Opens Readers' Wallets." *Business Week* (October 10): 46.

Laskin, David, and Holly Hughes. 1995. *The Reading Group Book: The Complete Guide to Starting and Sustaining a Reading Group, with Annotated Lists of 250 Titles for Provocative Discussion*. New York: Plume. (Chapter 1, "A Brief History of the Reading Group in America," offers an engaging discussion about the history of reading groups, especially women's groups.)

Murray, Heather. 2002. *Come, Bright Improvement! The Literary Societies of Nineteenth-Century Ontario*. Toronto: University of Toronto Press.

Saal, Rollene. 1995. *The New York Public Library Guide to Reading Groups*. New York: Crown Publishers.

Chapter 17

Reading Events—A Celebration of Reading, Books, and Authors

A great book combines enlightenment with enchantment. Literature awakens our imagination and enlarges our humanity. It can even offer harrowing insights that somehow console and comfort us.

—Dana Gioia, Chairman, National Endowment for the Arts, on "The Big Read"
(November 2008)

What better way to celebrate reading than by throwing a party—a large, full-out, A-list (with A standing for All) gala? Nationwide, communities and organizations along with bookstores and libraries sponsor reading events intended to celebrate the joy of reading, books, and lifelong learning. The events take the form of street fairs and festivals, community "one book" reading programs, author signings, and a host of other fêtes and celebrations complete with the glitter and literati and the everyday reader. Not only do the festivals take place on the city streets and in the local parks, but they take place online in electronic forums. Above all, these activities bring individuals together to find common ground and explore diversity while sharing an appreciation for the written word.

CENTER FOR THE BOOK

A wide range of agencies and organizations sponsor book festivals and reading events. Most notably, the National Center for the Book and its state affiliate centers organize and implement or support many of these types of programs. The Center for the Book at the Library of Congress was established by President Jimmy Carter on October 13, 1977, when he signed Senate Bill 95 S. 1331 into law (P.L. 95–129). The purpose of the Center was to use the cachet and resources of the Library of Congress to stimulate public interest in books and reading. The mission of the Center has since expanded to promote literacy and

291

P.L. 95–129

Signed into law on October 13, 1977
S. 1331, from which the public law was enacted, was sponsored by Senator Howard W. Cannon of Nevada
An Act to provide for the establishment of a Center for the Book in the Library of Congress, and for other purposes

Section 1. The Congress hereby finds and declares—,

(1) that the Congress of the United States on April 24, 1800, established for itself a library of the Congress;
(2) that in 1815, the Congress purchased the personal library of the third President of the United States which contained materials on every science known to man and described such a collection as a "substratum of a great national library";
(3) that the Congress of the United States in recognition of the importance of printing and its impact on America purchased the Gutenberg Bible in 1930 for the Nation for placement in the Library of Congress;
(4) that the Congress of the United States has through statute and appropriations made this library accessible to any member of the public;
(5) that this collection of books and other library materials has now become one of the greatest libraries in civilization;
(6) that the book and the printed word have had the most profound influence on American civilization and learning and have been the very foundation on which our democratic principles have survived through our two hundred-year history;
(7) that in the year 1977, the Congress of the United States assembled hereby declares its reaffirmation of the importance of the printed word and the book and recognizes the importance of a Center for the Book to the continued study and development of written record as central to our understanding of ourselves and our world.

It is therefore the purpose of this Act to establish a Center for the Book in the Library of Congress to provide a program for the investigation of the transmission of human knowledge and to heighten public interest in the role of books and printing in the diffusion of this knowledge.

Note: Full text of the enactment is available through Thomas Legislative Bills & Resolutions.

libraries for all ages, and the historical study of the book and the printed word through a variety of academic and research agencies.

Beginning in 1984 state affiliate centers were established in each of the 50 states and the District of Columbia to promote books and reading on a local basis. In addition, the Center and its state affiliates created reading promotion partnerships with civic and educational organizations across the United States and through other federal agencies, currently numbering close to 100 different associations. The Center also has an international reach, inspiring and influencing the creation of reading promotion centers globally, most recently in South Africa and Russia. The National Book Festival and "One Book" community reading projects, which encompass both public library and academic institution programs, are among the Center's most recognizable events. Other hallmarks include "Letters about Literature," "River of Words," and the "National Ambassadors for Young People's Literature." Along with the reading promotion projects, the Center has sponsored or cosponsored the publishing of numerous books and pamphlets about reading, literacy, and book history.

Major Center for the Book Projects

- *Books & Beyond:* An author series of public talks presenting authors whose works are related to the Library of Congress's holdings. Held at the Library of Congress. Many of the book-sponsored events are Webcast and may be accessed through The Center for the Book Web site (www.loc.gov/loc/cfbook/cyber-cf.html).
- *Letters about Literature:* National reading and writing promotion program for children and young adults, grades 4 through 12. Presented in partnership with Target stores and in cooperation with the state affiliate centers (www.loc.gov/loc/cfbook/letters/).
- *Read More About It!:* Reading list companion for adults, children, and young adults from the Library of Congress's American Memory Project (http://learning.loc.gov/learn/collections/book/cntrbook.html).
- *River of Words:* An international environmental poetry and art contest for young people designed to increase awareness and understanding of the natural world (www.riverofwords.org/).

The Center for the Book through the Library of Congress features an extensive Web site (http://www.loc.gov/loc/cfbook/) offering access and links to affiliates and partner programs. In recent years many of the events held at the Center for the Book in the Library of Congress have been created as Webcasts and made available on the Center's Web site. The Webcasts feature interviews with authors, readings, and a variety of discussions about books, libraries, and reading. In addition, links to an exhaustive list of literary events sponsored by state affiliate centers along with "One Book" projects are available.

State Affiliates Program

State affiliate centers are established in the 50 states and the District of Columbia (use www.loc.gov/loc/cfbook/statecen to link to each of the state centers' Web site and contact information). Their purpose is to develop activities that promote each state's own literary heritage. This includes hosting and cosponsoring a variety of events and programs that call attention to the importance of literacy, reading, and libraries. The state centers are granted affiliate status with the Center for the Book in the Library of Congress for three years with the option for three-year renewal periods. Along with the Library of Congress, the state libraries form the major partner for each state affiliate center, guiding, sponsoring, and promoting statewide reading events and activities.

Among other activities, the state affiliate centers participate in communitywide reading events, book festivals, and state book award projects. The state affiliate centers prepare and distribute reading lists that celebrate the literary heritage of the state, focusing on local authors and poets and books about the state. Discussed in a previous chapter, one of the most popular state center projects includes state book awards that are frequently cosponsored with other state humanities and arts councils, reading councils, and state library associations. The primary directive of the state affiliate centers requires each state center to develop and carry out reading and literacy programming appropriate to the individual state's needs.

The United Kingdom's Booktrust

Booktrust is an agency similar to the Library of Congress's Center for the Book. However, it is an independent charity rather than a governmental agency. The purpose of Booktrust is to encourage reading among all ages and all cultures in Great Britain. It promotes literature, reading, and writing in the United Kingdom. Among other programs, Booktrust provides recommendations for adult readers, including books, short stories, special reading events such as Get London Reading, and translated fiction that is published in the United Kingdom. Their Web site (www.booktrust.org.uk/) features numerous reading lists, ranging from recommendations by Booktrust staff to newspaper round-ups (much like the *New York Times* bestsellers lists or *USA Today* bestsellers).

Booktrust's sister agency, Scottish Book Trust (www.scottishbooktrust.com) provides similar lists and resources. The Scottish Book Trust features a "Book of the Month," "Favourite International Books," and "Quick Reads." Along with reading lists and searchable databases, Scottish Book Trust offers audio and video podcasts of interviews with authors and illustrators, including many familiar to U.S. readers, such as Neil Gaiman.

BOOK FESTIVALS AND FAIRS

Book festivals and fairs are popular forums to link readers to authors and books through communitywide events. They typically feature author readings and signings for all ages and genres, fiction and nonfiction. Event planners also attempt to offer a variety of venues to appeal to a broad range of participants. For example, the St. Petersburg Reading Festival, held each October, sponsors a ticketed gala event as a festival fund-raiser the evening before the festival for adults and free storytelling events for the families throughout the festival day. Along with opportunities to purchase new and used books, festival-goers with a creative bent can consult with writer's guilds and writer's association representatives, as well as identify possible writing contests and writing education programs to further creative efforts.

Quick Search Tip

The Center for the Book Web site has an extensive list of book fairs and other literary events held nationally and around the world. For additional links use "book fair," "book festival," or "literary event" along with the location name (city, state, or region) in your favorite search engine. This will retrieve local book events along with some international ones, including ones with specific themes, such as the Green Book Festival for books on environmental issues. You can also use the American Booksellers Association and their regional association Web sites to find links to trade shows for the independent booksellers and publishers.

Festivals vary in size and length. The Miami Book Fair International, for example, is a ten-day-long celebration, while the National Book Festival is a one-day event. Some festivals draw thousands of attendees. They also range in theme or focus, from storytelling to antiquarian book fairs to children's festivals. Frequently libraries of all types, especially public and academic libraries and their Friends of the Library groups, will co-sponsor or at least be represented with an exhibit, promoting library services to the community. Regardless of length or size, the book festivals offer opportunities to buy, sell, hear, see, and learn about books and authors.

National Book Festival

The Center for the Book sponsors the National Book Festival (NBF), a one-day street fair on the National Mall in the District of Columbia. Established in 2001, former First Lady Laura Bush hosts the event, featuring author signings, the Pavilion of the States, and entertainment for the entire family. The event occurs in late September and draws more than 100,000 participants from around the United States. What makes this festival unique is that it features pavilions for each of the 50 states, District of Columbia, and U.S. territories, with each pavilion hosting authors, books, and other products representing the literary heritage of each state. Along with the day-long street fair, the NBF includes a gala event and a White House breakfast.

The National Book Festival Web site (www.loc.gov/bookfest/index.html) provides access to an exhaustive array of resources for information about the festival. Webcasts and podcasts are readily available from many of the event activities. Web users can listen to interviews with some of the authors, read biographies and excerpts, and view video and audio. (For those able to attend the American Library Association conferences, the annual National Book Festival poster and information are readily available at the Library of Congress exhibit booth.)

COMMUNITY-WIDE READING PROGRAMS

Increasingly popular, communitywide reading programs promote widespread reading and literacy across communities throughout the United States and its territories. The programs promote dialogue and explore diversity among community members. Two programs—"One Book," supported and cosponsored by the State Affiliate Centers for the Book, and "The Big Read," an initiative of the National Endowment for the Arts (NEA), Institute for Museum and Library Services (IMLS), and Arts Midwest—enjoy high visibility and participation in communities large and small. Among the goals of these programs are the following:

- Promotion of widespread literacy
- Shared love of reading
- Shared ideas through reading and discussion
- Creation of forums to promote tolerance and acceptance
- Fostering intergenerational dialogue and multicultural dialogue

Public and academic libraries along with other local organizations collaborate to sponsor the community reading events. Most events last four to six weeks and include numerous events and activities centered upon the chosen book. During the planned communitywide reading events, sponsors and supporters attempt to include movie screenings for novels with movie tie-ins, author visits complete with readings and signings, essay- and poetry-writing contests, and ongoing discussion groups. Book discussion groups are encouraged to select the community's chosen title for members. Librarians, scholars, and others prepare and produce reading and discussion guides and brochures to help explore the topics and themes of the chosen title. Frequently the communitywide reading event will be enhanced by comprehensive, rich Web resources, including Web sites, Webcasts and podcasts, blogs, and online discussion boards.

"One Book, One Community" Reading Events

The first "One Book, One Community" (OBOC) event was conceived and implemented by the Washington Center for the Book at The Seattle Public Library in 1998. Titled "If All Seattle Read the Same Book," which quickly evolved into "Seattle Reads," the program is "designed to foster reading and discussion of works by authors of diverse cultures and ethnicities" (Seattle Reads, 2009). The first book chosen for "Seattle Reads" was *The Sweet Hereafter* (HarperCollins, 1991) by Russell Banks, and the popularity of the event continues with the selection of *My Jim* (Three Rivers Press, 2005), by Nancy Rawles for the 2009 community event.

With the success of "Seattle Reads," library systems across the nation followed suit, with events being sponsored in each of the 50 states and featuring a wide range of authors and themes. Librarians, educators, booksellers, and local community members come together to select books of both popular interest and literary excellence for the reading event that also have cultural and social significance for the community. Reviewing the Author/Title list for the "One Book" Reading Promotion Projects at the Center for the Book shows that *To Kill a Mockingbird* by Harper Lee ranks as the most popular selection for the communitywide reading events, encompassing both the OBOC programs and The Big Read program. Other top choices have included Mitch Albom's *Tuesdays with Morrie*, Ray Bradbury's *Fahrenheit 451*, and Ernest J. Gaines' *A Lesson before Dying*.

Library systems each have their own criteria for selecting titles to feature in the OBOC events. Common recommendations include choosing a major author with a body of work and who would be willing to engage in discussion with readers. Books should also offer potential for discussion relevant to social issues within the local community. Select titles that have film and theater adaptations and that are available in multiple formats (print, audio, large print, etc.). If the community is multilingual, choose titles that might have readily available translations. The multidimensional nature of the selected books contributes to the success of the OBOC events, encouraging intergenerational and multicultural discussions.

One Book, One College Common Reading Programs

With a purpose similar to that of the "One Book, One Community" communitywide reading programs, colleges and universities nationwide have begun instituting common reading programs for incoming freshmen. These programs go by many names, including "One Book, One Campus," "Common Reading," or "Common Read." Most frequently the common reading programs form a component within the new student orientation or first-year experience course. These programs are intended to help ease the student's transition from high

Quick Tips for Successful "One Book" Programs

1. Create or obtain reading group materials that include author biographies, sample questions, annotated bibliographies, tips for book discussions, and a calendar of events. Make the materials freely available through a range of sources, including the public or academic library, local bookstores, and on the library's Web site.
2. Organize multidimensional programs and activities, such as screenings of film or theater adaptations and radio readings. Allow the readers to experience the book in many ways and through multiple vehicles.
3. Develop promotional materials, including bookmarks, postcards, buttons, brochures, and posters. Many of these items related to the book can be obtained from the publisher. Don't forget to obtain the publisher's permission for use of book jacket art in promotional materials.
4. Find partners and sponsors, including local media and bookstores. Funding, space, and volunteers will be necessary for the successful implementation of the event.
5. Plan social events where readers meet the author and enjoy interviews and readings. These might include luncheons or evening receptions with the author.
6. Prepare suggestion/evaluation sheets for participants to complete. This will help plan for future events. Include questions about what worked, what didn't and why, and what books/authors participants would like to include in the future.

Consult the following sources for planning and implementing a successful "One Book" program: "Community-wide Reading Event Planner" from HarperCollins, "Following Seattle's Read: Citywide Book Clubs Sprout up Throughout the U.S." from Bookselling This Week, and One Book, One Community Resource Disc from the American Library Association.

school to college by opening dialogue on a new intellectual level through provocative reading. Representatives from Eastern Michigan University's Fusion: New Student Orientation program state that "a common reading experience is designed to contribute to the retention of new students by building a sense of community among students, faculty, and staff through common experience, to encourage participation in the intellectual life of campus in a stimulating and interactive way, and to increase the development of necessary college skills in critical reading and reflection" (Eastern Michigan University, 2007: n.p.). This sentiment echoes across college campuses nationwide and from major public institutions to small private colleges.

Unlike the "One Book, One Community" programs, the "one college" book choices tend toward popular culture and contemporary issues students are likely to encounter, such as the environment, social justice, diversity, and multiculturalism. Some of the popular titles from academic year 2008 include *Three Cups of Tea* by Greg Mortenson and David Oliver Relin, *A Long Way Gone: Memoirs of a Boy Soldier* by Ismael Beah, and *The Kite Runner* by Khaled Hosseini. (Note, however, that Mortenson and Hosseini do appear on the "One Book, One Community" reading lists.) Much like the multidimensional experience of the OBOC programs, the "one college" programs tie the reading to other experiences in the first-year experience, including the relationship to library research, essay-writing contests, films and performances, and exhibits across campus. The college programs also call upon the chosen author to provide a culminating event for students through on-campus visits and lecture series.

Numerous resources abound on the Web for the "One Book, One College" programs. Gustavus Adolphus College in Minnesota provides access to an extensive list of programs on the college Web site (http://homepages.gac.edu/~fister/onebook.html), including the titles chosen by each institution. The National Resource Center for the First Year Experience and Students in Transition maintains a range of resources and reading lists through the University of South Carolina (www.sc.edu/fye/resources/fyr/index.html). One of the particularly useful features is the link to Publisher Resources Web sites that support college-wide and first-year-experience reading programs. Currently eight major publishing houses, including HarperCollins, Houghton Mifflin, Random House, and Simon & Schuster Academic publish books and curriculum guides to support the college programs. (Many of these publishing houses also offer similar resources for the nonacademic communitywide reading events.) Curriculum and teaching guides may be downloaded and printed from their Web sites.

"One Festival, One Book"

The Magna cum Murder Conference, a crime-writing festival at Ball State University, includes a "One Festival, One Book" event as part of the conference festivities. Each year conference planners select a mystery title to serve as a touchstone for events. Magna cum Murder 2008 selected Josephine Tey's *Brat Farrar* as the "One Festival, One Book" title.

The Big Read

With the release of the 2004 National Endowment for the Arts (NEA) report *Reading at Risk* came a huge outcry and rush to encourage literary reading among the adult population of the United States. The NEA report indicated that literary reading for pleasure among adults had dropped from previous levels reported in 1982 and 1997. "The Big Read" (TBR), sponsored by the National Endowment for the Arts along with the Institute for Museum and Library Services and Arts Midwest, was a response to *Reading at Risk*, intending to revitalize a love of literature and reading among adults. While similar in purpose to the OBOC programs, "The Big Read" focuses its attention on literature and literary excellence as opposed to popular culture and literature. (See Table 17-1 for a brief comparison of the two programs.)

TBR is a federally funded grant program. As such, the grant application process is open only to 501(c)3 nonprofit agencies or divisions of state, local, or tribal government. However, the applicant organizations must partner with a library if they are not libraries themselves. Selected applicants receive a number of resources and services with their grant: financial support to attend a national orientation meeting; reader's, teacher's, and audio guides for the selected title; promotional materials; online organizer's guide for developing and managing the program; and inclusion of the organization and its events on the Big Read Web site (NEA, 2007: 25).

Unlike the OBOC programs, a panel—the Readers Circle—recommends the titles for "The Big Read," from which participants choose for their program. The panel is comprised of librarians, professors, journalists, authors, and poets. Readers Circle panelists include James Lee Burke (author), Michael Dirda (book critic), Anne Fadiman (author/essayist), Ted Kooser (U.S. Poet Laureate, 2004–2006), Azar Nafisi (author and professor), and Nancy Pearl (author and librarian), among many others (NEA, 2007: 4). The Readers Circle recommendations are reviewed by the National Endowment for the Arts literature staff for final selection.

In 2007, TBR initiated international partnerships to "deepen dialogue and cultural understanding with other countries through the reading of great literature" (NEA, 2008: vii). The international partnership began with Russia in coor-

Table 17-1: Comparing "One Book, One Community" and "The Big Read"		
	One Book, One Community	The Big Read
Year Started	1998	2004
Types of Books Selected	Popular culture and literature	Literature from predetermined list
Book Selectors	Local librarians, educators, booksellers, and members of the community	Readers Circle—panel of 22 literary experts and laypeople with a passion for literature
Funding	Obtained locally and through various charitable foundations	Federally funded grant program
Duration	Four to six weeks	Four to six weeks
Eligible Organizations	Public and academic libraries, booksellers, arts/humanities councils, reading councils, schools, colleges and universities	Literary centers, libraries, museums, colleges and universities, art centers, historical societies, arts/humanities councils, tribal governments, literary festivals. MUST partner with library if organization is not one itself

dination with the Open World Leadership Center and the Library for Foreign Literature in Moscow. In 2008 and 2009 the partnership expanded to Egypt and a pilot program with Mexico. This is a cross-cultural exchange of literary excellence with the U.S. selections of *To Kill a Mockingbird* (Harper Lee), *Fahrenheit 451* (Ray Bradbury), and *The Grapes of Wrath* (John Steinbeck). The international selections include *The Death of Ivan Ilyich* (Leo Tolstoy, Russia), *The Thief and the Dogs* (Naguid Mahfouz, Nobel Laureate, Egypt), and *Sun, Stone, and Shadows: 20 Great Mexican Short Stories* (Fondo de Cultura Económica, Mexico).

Since the program's inception the National Endowment for the Arts reports more than 500 TBR grants have been awarded to more than 360 cities across the United States, District of Columbia, and the U.S. territories, with eight statewide Big Reads. NEA estimates that more than 2 million people have participated in Big Read events. Currently 26 authors are represented in the featured books, with additional titles added yearly as the program continues to expand.

Information and applications for "The Big Read" are available on the NEA's Big Read Web site (www.neabigread.org). Lists of titles and program descriptions and lists of cities and states hosting TBR events are readily available on the Web sites and in their print catalogs and brochures. Title descriptions include a synopsis of the book, its common themes, brief author biographical notes, film adaptations, documentaries, and performance venues, and availability of accessible materials (audio, large print, Braille).

"The Big Read" in Great Britain

In 2003 the British Broadcast Corporation (BBC) began its own "Big Read" activity. Unlike the community reading events in the United States, the BBC's "Big Read" was a nationwide search to identify the nation's best-loved novels. In an open invitation readers were asked to nominate and vote on their favorite novels of all time in order to generate a list of Great Britain's Top 100 Novels. From the resulting nominations the top 21 novels were selected as the focus of reading events and reading groups nationwide. More importantly, BBC's "Big Read" intended to encourage and highlight literacy for all by engaging the nation in the event.

Much like "The Big Read" and "One Book, One Community" events in the United States, the BBC's Big Read culminated in a variety of local events. Reading groups were established to discuss the top 21 novels. The Booktrust, a national charity, sponsored activities throughout the nation to explore the selected titles through poetry writing, food, and performance. A similar agency, The National Literacy Trust, focused on encouraging reading and literacy among reluctant readers, especially men and boys. The National Library for the Blind made all 21 of the top novels available in braille to include blind and visually impaired persons in the nationwide event, while other related agencies produced the titles as talking books.

Not surprisingly, J. R. R. Tolkien's *The Lord of the Rings* is officially the United Kingdom's best-loved book, followed by *Pride and Prejudice* by Jane Austen. While the list is dominated by British authors, many books with U.S. authors appear as well, including Harper Lee's *To Kill a Mockingbird*, J. D. Salinger's *The Catcher in the Rye*, and Margaret Mitchell's *Gone with the Wind*. Titles range from literary fiction to popular fiction. Rather than representing the tastes of literary critics, the BBC's Top 100 represents the taste of the British people.

The BBC's "Big Read" Web site includes an extensive set of resources (www .bbc.co.uk/arts/bigread/index.shtml). Along with the lists of the top novels, multimedia trailers from the BBC broadcasts of the "Book Champions" are available. The Web site also features a downloadable booklet titled "The Little Guide to Big Reading," which provides information about establishing Big Read book groups. The booklet is not unlike the materials provided for the U.S. "The Big Read" and "One Book, One Community" events, with reading guides to the books, thematic arrangements of titles, and suggestions for establishing the conversations.

Canada Reads

"Canada Reads" is another in a long line of literary events designed to celebrate reading. The program began in 2002 with the winning title *In the Skin of a Lion* by Michael Ondaatje. Unlike the U.S. and U.K. "Big Read" programs, "Canada Reads" is a weeklong radio series hosted by Canadian Broadcasting Centre (CBC) of Canada. A celebrity panel debates various books and their merits throughout the week, eliminating titles each day to find the one book that "All Canada Should Read." CBC's "Canada Reads" focuses on literary fiction rather than popular fiction. The CBC has a robust Web site (www.cbc.ca/canadareads/ index. html), with links to podcasts of the debates and discussions, moderated blogs, and discussion forums. Following the final selection, the Web site features live chats, interviews, videos, and forums devoted to the winning title. An extensive archive is available, featuring the selected titles from 2002 through the present.

OTHER RESOURCES AND VENUES FOR READING EVENTS

Many other reading events can be quickly located through local bookstores and online. The publishing houses also sponsor and promote author events around the country. Author and library Web sites as well as social networking resources provide easy access to book-signing dates and author discussions (online and at a location). Media resources, such as NPR, YouTube, and iTunes, offer downloadable podcasts and video of author interviews and book discussions.

Besides libraries, who better than a bookstore to connect readers with books and authors? Independent booksellers (indies) along with the bookstore chains frequently schedule book discussions and book-signing events with local and nationally recognized authors. Beyond a general Web search, LibraryThing.com and other social networking resources for books and readers offer lists of area events for members. LibraryThing.com combines indies with the chains to provide comprehensive listings of events along with maps displaying the approximate locations of the bookstores. Using the bookseller's Web site is another excellent method of finding local events. Powell's Bookstore, Barnes & Noble, Borders, and many others provide searchable event locators for their own store locations. Along with author readings and signings, many of the booksellers sponsor book groups and writing groups, musical performances, and poetry jams.

Publisher Web sites make excellent resources for finding when author events will occur in the area and when authors will appear at conferences. At the very least, the publisher's Web site provides brief biographical information about their authors, links to the authors' Web sites, and bibliographies of their work, including upcoming new releases. Frequently publishers will make podcasts of author events accessible through their Web sites or provide external links to social networking tools where additional author information resides. An important feature of the publishers' Web sites is the "Speakers Bureau" whereby libraries, local community organizations, universities, etc., can identify and schedule author visits. While the author typically receives an honorarium for speaking, the promotional materials are provided by the publisher at no cost. However, each publisher handles this individually, and it is best to contact the publisher directly for more information.

Similar to publishers' Web sites, television networks and broadcast media offer a range of resources to support the interests of readers and help connect readers to authors. The news media resources are particularly useful for linking readers to nonfiction materials covering business and finance, memoirs and biographies, travel, and a wide range of other interests. NPR (www.npr.org), for example, provides access to interviews with authors as well as book discussions from their various radio broadcasts. C-SPAN's Book TV (www.booktv.org) links viewers to broadcast episodes online along with interviews, Webcasts from book fairs and festivals, and in-depth materials on the authors and books featured on Book TV.

ONLINE RESOURCES FOR CONNECTING READERS, BOOKS, AND AUTHORS

It is impossible to list every resource available for reading events online. Given the dynamic nature of Web resources, new ones are posted daily and old ones fall into disuse. However, the following resources are currently available and active and provide a flavor of ways to enhance the reading experience.

Authors on Air, "Where Readers and Writers Listen and Connect" (www
.blogtalkradio.com/stations/AuthorsOnAir/splash.aspx), is an online audio resource that features a variety of authors and poets discussing their work and participating in on-air interviews. Authors on Air can be posted on the library's Web
site, on Facebook and MySpace accounts, and on other social networking resources that allow html embedding.

iTunes and iTunes University (www.apple.com/itunes) offer access to both
audio and video podcasts. Like many of the other resources that offer downloadable audio and video, the iTunes podcasts are freely available, though the user
must have a compatible playback component and set up an account with iTunes.
The ability to create and organize podcast "libraries" makes iTunes a unique resource. It also offers automatic downloads of current episodes to the user's library once he or she has subscribed to a particular series.

LibraryThing (www.librarything.com), a social networking resource for readers, librarians, and book lovers, features online chats with authors. The chats
take place across a week to ten days and are nominally interactive. In order to
participate, members post their questions and comments in a threaded discussion forum; the author and moderator check the discussion board throughout
the scheduled week and respond to the participant's postings. While the discussions may lack depth at times, the forum does offer opportunities for readers to
connect with authors.

Online Programming for All Libraries (OPAL) (www.opal-online.org) is an
international collaborative effort by all types of libraries. It provides online public access for programming and training for library users and library personnel.
OPAL sponsors live book discussions and literary events. These programs are
freely available, requiring no registration or fees, and they are open to library users worldwide. The searchable archive provides access to downloadable recordings and documents from previous programs.

YouTube (www.youtube.com) is a social networking tool that provides space
for members to upload and download video. While much of the content is user
created (and not always high quality), many television networks and news media
resources link official content to accommodate wide-range access. For example,
C-SPAN's Book TV (nonfiction author readings and discussions) has space on
YouTube where members are able to view and download episodes from the television broadcast. The American Library Association and other library organizations post materials, including episodes from the Auditorium Speakers forums,
which are freely accessible.

CONCLUSION

Reading can be celebrated in many ways, from book festivals to community-wide
reading events. Not unlike state fairs and church festivals, the reading events
have become ingrained in the fabric of the local community as a way to bring

writers, readers, and fellow book enthusiasts together. At a macro level, these types of events encourage social dialogue among community members and offer opportunities for shared understanding. More importantly, reading events are ways to discover new authors and titles through formats that best fit the reader's preferences (in person versus online). The key to discovering reading events is to look beyond the physical library building to the array of resources available online and in multimedia formats.

WORKS CONSULTED

"An Act to Provide for the Establishment of a Center for the Book in the Library of Congress, and for Other Purposes," P.L. 95-129 (1977). Available at Thomas Legislative Bills & Resolutions: http://thomas.loc.gov/cgi-bin/bdquery/z?d095:HR06214:| TOM:/bss/d095query.html (accessed September 10, 2009).

"The Center for the Book." Library of Congress. (2008). Available: www.loc.gov/loc/ cfbook (accessed September 10, 2009).

Eastern Michigan University. 2007. "Campus Life: Common Reading Experience at Eastern Michigan University." Available: www.emich.edu/campuslife/?p=orientation-reading (accessed September 10, 2009).

Ferguson, Michael. 2006. "Creating Common Ground: Common Reading and the First Year Experience." *Peer Review* 8, no. 3 (Summer). Available: www.aacu.org/ peerreview/pr-su06/pr-su06_analysis2.cfm (accessed September 10, 2009).

Fister, Barbara. 2008. "One Book, One College: Common Reading Programs." Gustavus Adolphus College. Available: http://homepages.gac.edu/~fister/onebook.html (accessed September 10, 2009).

"National Book Festival." Library of Congress. (2008). Available: www.loc.gov/bookfest/ index.html (accessed September 10, 2009).

National Endowment for the Arts. 2004. *Reading at Risk: A Survey of Literary Reading in America*. Research Division Report #46. Washington, DC: National Endowment for the Arts.

_____. 2007. *The Big Read*. Washington, DC: National Endowment for the Arts, Institute of Museum and Library Services.

_____. 2008. *The Big Read Catalog*. Washington, DC: National Endowment for the Arts, Institute of Museum and Library Services.

National Resource Center for the First Year Experience and Students in Transition. 2008. "First-Year Resources." University of South Carolina. Available: www.sc.edu/fye/resources/fyr/index.html (accessed September 10, 2009).

"News from the Center for the Book: 30th Anniversary Brings Fresh Look at Future." *Library of Congress Information Bulletin* 66, no. 10 (October): 215.

"Seattle Reads." 2009. The Seattle Public Library. Available: www.spl.org/default.asp? pageID+about_leaders_washingtoncenter_seattlereads (accessed September 10, 2009).

FURTHER READING

American Library Association. 2003. *One Book, One Community Resource Disc* (S.I.). Chicago: American Library Association.

Cole, John Y. 2002. "Communities Reading Together: State Centers for the Book Idea Exchange." *Library of Congress Information Bulletin* 61, no. 6 (June). Available: www.loc
.gov/loc/lcib/0206/stateideas.html (accessed September 10, 2009).

"Community-wide Reading Event Planner." 2009. HarperCollins. Available: www
.harpercollins.com/community/index.aspx (accessed September 10, 2009).

"Following Seattle's Read: Citywide Book Clubs Sprout Up Throughout the U.S." 2002.
Bookselling This Week (March 13). Available: http://news.bookweb.org/m-bin/printer
_friendly?article_id=306 (accessed September 10, 2009).

Halpern, Leslie. 2007. "Book Fairs and Reading Festivals: Six Reasons Why You Should Attend These Literary Events." Resources for Writers (April 29). Available: http://
resourcesforwriters.suite101.com/article.cfm/book_fairs_and_festivals   (accessed
September 10, 2009).

Laufgraben, Jodi Levine. 2006. *Common Reading Programs: Going Beyond the Book.* Colom-
bia, SC: National Resource Center for the First-Year Experience & Students in Transition, University of South Carolina.

"MBA Show: A Great Mix of Education, Authors & Events." 2008. *Bookselling This Week*
(September 30). Available: http://news.bookweb.org/news/ 6318.html (accessed
September 10, 2009).

"One Book, One Community: Duluth's Area-wide Reading Projects." Duluth Public Library. (2009). Available: www.duluth.lib.mn.us/Programs/OneBook.html (accessed
September 10, 2009).

Twiton, Andy. 2007. "Common Reading Programs in Higher Education: A Patricia
Lindell Scholarship Research Project." Gustavus Adolphus College (April). Available:
http://gustavus.edu/academics/library/Pubs/Lindell2007.html (accessed September 10, 2009).

Chapter 18

Reflections on the Future of Reading and Readers' Advisory

One faces the future with one's past.

—Pearl S. Buck (Nobel Prize in Literature, 1938)

We have come full circle in examining reading and services to readers. We looked at the history of reading and of readers' advisory services. We listened to readers tell us about their interests and needs and considered how best to serve them in the library. The current state of the art of reading and technological innovations was explored. The dynamic nature of genres was detailed. We looked to the tools and resources available in multiple formats to enhance the experience of reading. In the final chapter, we are left to explore the challenges ahead and how best to meet those challenges.

At the heart of this book is the fact that reading has fundamentally changed in the past several years, and that readers have greater expectations of the reading experience than they may have had in the past. It is no longer about picking up a print book and passively reading through page by page (maybe making notations in the margins), only to do it all over again when the next book is read. Reading is participatory; it is about engaging with the text in multiple ways and at multiple levels. Reading is about the meaning that it has in the life of the reader, and why he or she reads. Reading is about the reader, and not about the book as an object. It is through this lens that we consider the challenges ahead for readers' advisors.

CHALLENGE 1: BOOK AS FORM OR BOOK AS CONTENT?

It is both an exciting and a daunting time to be involved with books. The scope of authors and titles to meet the needs and interests of everyone stretches out before us. The choice of materials in print, audio, downloadable formats, and film is mind-boggling. For example, John Grisham's newest legal thriller, *The Associate*, released in January 2009, is available as a hardcover book, audio downloadable, audio CD, and large-print paperback. Then add access to Grisham's MySpace and Facebook fan pages, the official John Grisham community on Ning, and his official publisher's Web site. View online video interviews and reviews on Amazon.com, Borders' Web site, and YouTube. You probably know more about John Grisham and his writing than you ever thought possible, or wanted to know. If you follow Clive Cussler's newest novel, *Corsair*, you can add both an Amazon Kindle version and a Sony e-Reader version to the other format options along with public accessibility to Cussler's biographical information.

The question is not about whether the book is obsolete as many pundits have declared, but rather it is about how the reader engages with the written word. The physical book gives many hours of pleasure, and the structure and feel of it is comforting and familiar. The hand-operated codex has existed for centuries and has been an effective tool in carrying the ideas of the author to the minds of the reader. Old-fashioned book lovers own books for both the ideas they contain and for the pleasure of touching and handling beloved volumes. And people visit bookstores and libraries as much for the social contact with likeminded individuals as for the acquiring of reading material.

Can Kindle or the Sony e-Reader compete with that? For our technically savvy younger generations, reading electronically is attractive and easy. E-books are portable and environmentally friendly. Multiple books can be carried in one lightweight product. On the downside, the e-Readers are expensive and not transferable across delivery platforms (Amazon's Kindle titles are not compatible with Sony's e-Reader). Despite the downsides, however, e-books are increasingly popular, especially with the support of American icons such as Oprah Winfrey, who is also a great supporter of reading and literacy.

Reading is not about the medium—book or digital, print or audio. The consideration becomes one of content rather than container. Regardless of the distribution format, writers will continue to write and publishers will continue to produce their works. The form may change but the intent to convey ideas will not. Reports from publishers' associations (print and audio) indicate that people who use audiobooks are likely to read print books as well; they are as likely to visit the library as they are to visit a bookstore. This offers opportunities for outreach and interesting programming options that will appeal to a greater segment of the library user community.

The array of titles and formats requires the readers' advisory staff to refocus on whole library collections rather than a single component of it, from print to multimedia. They also need to be aware of how best to meet the needs of the individual reader. While once considered a dying art, readers' advisory services has resurged with the complexity of reading and the overwhelming number of resources to provide the best reading experience possible.

CHALLENGE 2: GENRE BLENDING, BENDING, AND SLIDING

At one time it was easy to fit authors and titles into a simple description—a romance, a Western, a mystery. Today genre blending has become the norm with an increasing number of authors using conventions from several genres in one book. The use of multiple characteristics makes for richer reading experiences, but it becomes challenging to suggest titles within a genre and to organize fiction collections around arbitrary classifications.

Genres are dynamic, not static. Today's genres reflect the cultural tastes and interests of readers. The fact is that traditional genres do not always meet the needs of contemporary society, and they must evolve in order to explore new issues and new situations. Elements of the genres have disappeared to meet the mercurial demands of contemporary readers, while new elements have been added for the same purpose. Westerns, for example, have undergone significant evolution from the cowboys and range wars of the early twentieth century to stories set in the West that explore social and cultural issues, including environmentalism and the role of women and of Native Americans. Chick lit arose out of women's fiction and the romance genre to provide stories that play out against the lives of contemporary, young career women, juggling love and job to make it on their own merits.

The lines between genres are blurred. With the commercial and literary success of novels such as Diana Gabaldon's Outlander series or Audrey Niffenegger's *The Time Traveler's Wife*, and even Cormac McCarthy's *The Road*, which combine and twist multiple genres, comes the challenge of describing the story in meaningful ways. Genre studies have been a mainstay of developing an understanding about the genres. While still relevant, it becomes much more critical to look across genres to find similarities, thus allowing readers' advisors to make more meaningful suggestions of books that will appeal to the reader's mood and interests.

The readers' advisor must rely upon other factors to match readers with a few good books. It is increasingly important to pay attention to the more subtle elements that create appeal. This also means that the readers' advisor must be willing to move outside of the comfortable range of genres to explore other connections. Being well-read in a genre simply is not sufficient anymore. Readers' advisors need to look to professional reviews, readers' reviews, and even nontraditional resources, such as blogs and discussion boards, to learn about the ways in which readers respond to titles. They also need to stay one step ahead in knowing what will be the newest, hottest trend in reading interest by paying attention to the publishing industry as a whole.

CHALLENGE 3: READING IN A DIVERSE COMMUNITY

Local communities increasingly expect that the public library will meet the reading, viewing, and listening demands of all community members. This means providing materials for adult new readers and for patrons who do not speak or read English as their first language and providing materials for a multicultural and ethnic community. Libraries must also be prepared to accommodate the interests of their patrons with disabilities through materials and programs that are accessible. All of this places greater pressure on shrinking budgets and over-extended staffing.

Popular fiction and literature alike celebrate the differences in our culture and remind us that we are not alone. According to Steven Fischer in his historical study of books, the "modern marginalized readers can now freely read what mirrors their unique place, experience, vulnerability" (2003: 315). This sentiment echoes the work done by Catherine Sheldrick Ross and colleagues (2006) and Nadine Rosenthal (1995) in their studies of readers, and Cynthia Lee Katona (2005) points out that reading allows us to know ourselves and to learn about others. The very diversity of the community provides opportunities to engage in cross-cultural dialogue within the library environment and to explore our differences and our similarities.

Yet this means that the readers' advisor must look beyond the standard tools to find resources that will match the reader's interests to good reads (or audio or film). Unlike the traditional genres, reading guides are not readily available that focus on issues of multiculturalism or that relate to the needs of disabled patrons. It takes creativity and an eye for subtlety to find just the right reading. The Internet becomes one of the best resources for locating titles of a nontraditional nature (e.g., protagonists with disabilities, private investigators who are people of color, or romances featuring gay couples). Above all, the readers' advisor must talk with library users to determine what interests them and what works or does not work when it comes to books.

CHALLENGE 4: READERS' ADVISORY SERVICES IN A 2.0 WORLD

Technological innovation has been both compelling and frustrating in the library environments. Library 2.0 innovations have presented more opportunities then ever before to reach library users and to invite them to participate in the reading experience. User participation places the reader at the heart of the service rather than the library. Incorporating Library 2.0 technologies into services allows readers to take advantage of all of the library's resources and to create content that is meaningful to the user. One of the functions of readers' advisory has been to listen to the reader and then to respond; Library 2.0 has facilitated this to even greater levels.

Blogs and wikis, along with social networking sites, provide excellent ways to communicate with readers and to build communities. These tools present options for developing reading groups who are independent of the bricks-and-mortar library. Information about events, new resources, and reading lists can be quickly pushed to the reading community through social networks and Web resources. Library users can access materials remotely, and they can connect with others with similar interests. They can also contribute their own reactions to books through readers' reviews and user-defined tagging, which then provides information to the readers' advisor about connections between books. Blogs and wikis can be used to provide other materials to enhance the reading experience, including podcasts, photographs, and video.

However, Web 2.0 innovations also provide challenges to the RA services. In many ways the social cataloging sites, such as LibraryThing and GoodReads, compete with the traditional RA services. They offer readers a "do it yourself" voyage for discovering similar read-alike titles. Through a variety of algorithms and pattern matching, these systems are set up to make reading recommendations based on personal catalogs. Amazon.com certainly uses this technique based on previous purchases. This effectively removes the human element from the suggestion process, which is ultimately the focus of readers' advisory in the library. What these sites cannot do is get at the emotional elements of books that create appeal for the reader.

Another issue considers user-defined tagging. While tagging provides opportunities to learn more about how readers define their interests, it is also imprecise. Language can be very subjective, with words having multiple and differing meanings to individuals. Readers' advisors do well to tap into the user-defined folksonomies and blend the tags with other pieces of knowledge that librarians have about books and authors. This will create an environment of suggesting books that is thoughtful, appropriate, and based on the individual reader rather than generalizations.

As with all other technology, Library 2.0 innovations are dynamic. Today's hot applications change tomorrow. By far the greatest challenge will be keeping up with the next best thing. Incorporating technological innovation into accessible resources requires a commitment of time and effort and requires the readers' advisory staff to maintain technical knowledge currency. It also requires ongoing environmental scanning to know where changes need to be made and to do it quickly.

CHALLENGE 5: REACHING THE READER

The greatest challenge lies not in providing readers' advisory services, but in reaching readers and thereby encouraging them to use the services. For any number of reasons, the library's community of readers can be reluctant to ask questions about leisure reading. These may range from the thought that reading fiction is frivolous and therefore one should not bother the librarian with questions to the fact that patrons simply may not know that they can avail themselves of readers' advisory services. It behooves the RA staff to ensure that the service is visible and viable.

Readers' advisors need to take the service to the reader. That means being visible in the library and ensuring that readers know who to ask about books. Well-planned and attractive book displays, reading lists, and bookmarks all promote the library services. Exciting and engaging programs, such as community-wide reading events or book festivals, keep the library in the eye of the reader. The purpose is to find ways to talk with readers about their reading interests and offer them opportunities to find other similar or satisfying books and resources and to encourage them to make use of all the library has to offer.

As the time of readers is stretched thin with obligation, it becomes increasingly difficult to come to the library for lengthy consultations. This means that Library 2.0 innovations can serve the library well by enhancing the services available in the library. Readers' advisory services can expand beyond the physical limitations of the library. Newsletters, e-mail services, and online discussion groups, for example, present opportunities for the reader to remain engaged with the library and to find resources for reading without making a trip to the public library.

Marketing and promotion should not be seen as business prototypes but as opportunities to meet the readers on the middle ground. RA services have value, and marketing is one way to ensure that they are seen as valuable to the community. The focus becomes one of meeting the needs of the community and showing the community of readers that materials and resources to meet their reading interests do indeed exist. In an era of tight budgets, staff reductions, and reduced services, low-cost marketing efforts may pay off in increased library usage and quantifiable outcomes.

CONCLUSION

The heart and soul of readers' advisory services is the reader. Regardless of whether he or she comes into the library or finds resources online, the intent of RA is to satisfy the needs of the reader by suggesting books based on his or her preferences and mood. Unlike early RA attempts, elevating the taste of the reader has little place in today's complex reading environment. The readers' advisor has become a guide through the complex maze of authors, titles, genres, and resources to find books that are satisfying and that meet the reader's criteria of mood and appeal. The skills and qualifications of today's RA librarian do not fit Samuel Swett Green's library clerk who "heartily enjoys works of the imagination, but whose taste is educated" (Green, repr. 1993: S5). Today it requires a readers' advisor who knows books and is well read, knows the resources to consult, and above all is interested in the reader.

Variety and complexity makes readers' advisory services exciting. It is now possible to help readers explore books in multiple ways through word, sound, and sight. It becomes possible to link readers with similar tastes to the authors who produce the stories that engage the readers' thoughts and imaginations. Reading has become a holistic, active, and global process. In the end, Ranganathan's "Five Laws of Library Science" (1931) still ring true with "Every reader his book; Every book its reader."

WORKS CONSULTED

Fischer, Steven Roger. 2003. *A History of Reading.* London: Reaktion Books.

Green, Samuel Swett. 1876. "Personal Relations between Librarians and Readers." *Library Journal* 1, no. 1 (October 1); reprinted in 118, no. 11 (June 15, 1993): S4–S5.

Katona, Cynthia Lee. 2005. *Book Savvy.* Lanham, MD: The Scarecrow Press.

Ranganathan, Shiyali Ramamrita. 1931. "The Five Laws of Library Science." Available: www.mcallen.lib.tx.us/library/ranganat.htm (accessed September 10, 2009).

Rosenthal, Nadine. 1995. *Speaking of Reading.* Portsmouth, NH: Heinemann.

Ross, Catherine Sheldrick, Lynne (E. F.) McKechnie, and Paulette M. Rothbauer. 2006. *Reading Matters: What the Research Reveals about Reading, Libraries and Communities.* Westport, CT: Libraries Unlimited.

Trott, Barry. 2008. "Building on Firm Foundation: Readers' Advisory over the Next Twenty-Five Years." *Reference and User Services Quarterly* 48, no. 2 (Winter): 132–135.

Appendix 1

Reference Resources for the Genres

Many reference resources exist to aid in discovering authors, titles, and series in each of the genres. The following is a selective bibliography of resources divided by genre and featuring materials that have been published since 1998. Numerous bibliographies and criticisms of individual authors and their bodies of work are available; they are not included here but may be located in several of the general guides. Many of the readers' advisory general guides and online resources include retrospective and historical resources that will supplement and extend this list. Readers' advisory guides for young adults may also produce titles of interest to adult readers, especially for adult new readers and adult ESL students.

GENERAL GUIDES AND OTHER RESOURCES TO THE GENRES

Herald, Diana Trixler. 2006. *Genreflecting: A Guide to Popular Reading Interests,* edited by Wayne A. Wiegand. Westport, CT: Libraries Unlimited. (For reviews and more see "Genrefluent," available at www.genrefluent.com.)

Husband, Janet, and Jonathan F. Husband. 2009. *Sequels: An Annotated Guide to Novels in Series,* 4th edition. Chicago: American Library Association.

Jacob, Merle L., and Hope Apple. 2000. *To Be Continued: An Annotated Guide to Sequels,* 2nd edition. Phoenix, AZ: Oryx Press.

Pearl, Nancy. 2003. *Book Lust: Recommended Reading for Every Mood, Moment, and Reason.* Seattle, WA: Sasquatch Books.

_____. 2005. *More Book Lust: 1,000 New Reading Recommendations for Every Mood, Moment, and Reason.* Seattle, WA: Sasquatch Books.

Pop Goes Fiction. Available: http://popgoesfiction.blogspot.com.

Saricks, Joyce G. 2001. *The Readers' Advisory Guide to Genre Fiction.* Chicago: American Library Association.

PROFESSIONAL JOURNALS FOR INDUSTRY ARTICLES AND REVIEWS

Booklist and *Booklist Online.* American Library Association. Available: www.booklistonline.com.

Bookmarks Magazine. Bookmarks Publishing. Available: www.bookmarksmagazine.com.

Kirkus Reviews. Available: www.kirkusreviews.com.

Library Journal. Reed Business. Available: www.libraryjournal.com.
Publishers Weekly. Reed Business. Available: www.publishersweekly.com.

ADVENTURE, SUSPENSE, AND THRILLERS

Conventions and Conferences

ThrillFest, sponsored by International Thriller Writers. Available: www.thrillwriters.org.

Guides and Manuals

Anderson, Patrick. 2007. *The Triumph of the Thriller: How Cops, Crooks, and Cannibals Captured Popular Fiction*. New York: Random House.
CheckerBee Publishing. 1999. *Legal Thrillers: A Reader's Checklist and Reference Guide*. Middletown, CT: CheckerBee.
Gannon, Michael B. 2004. *Blood, Bedlam, Bullets, and Bad Guys: A Reader's Guide to Adventure/Suspense Fiction*. Westport, CT: Libraries Unlimited.
Melton, H. Keith. 2002. *Ultimate Spy*. New York: DK.
Owen, David. 2002. *Hidden Secrets: A Complete History of Espionage and the Technology Used to Support It*. Buffalo, NY: Firefly Books.
Swanson, Jean, and James Dean. 1998. *Killer Books: A Reader's Guide to Exploring the Popular World of Mystery and Suspense*. New York: Reed.
Wheat, Carolyn. 2003. *How to Write Killer Fiction: The Funhouse of Mystery and the Roller Coaster of Suspense*. Santa Barbara, CA: John Daniel/Perserverance.

Magazines, Fanzines, Webzines

"The Big Thrill." A Webzine published online by International Thriller Writers, Inc.

Organizations

International Thriller Writers. 2009. Available: www.thrillerwriters.org.

Reviewing Resources

Reviewing the Evidence. Available: www.reviewingtheevidence.com.

HISTORICAL FICTION

Resources for and about subgenres of historical fiction will be found among the other genres listed here, particularly in mysteries and romance. A number of the organizations and associations will include sections and special-interest groups related to historical writing within the genre.

Bibliographies and Biographies

Mediavilla, Cindy. 1999. *Arthurian Fiction: An Annotated Bibliography*. Lanham, MD: Scarecrow Press.
Murphy, Roxanne C. 2000. *The English Civil War through the Restoration in Fiction: An Annotated Bibliography, 1625–1999*. Westport, CT: Greenwood Press.

Conventions and Conferences

Historical Novel Society. Available: www.historicalnovelsociety.org.

Guides and Manuals

Adamson, Lynda G., and A. T. Dickinson. 1999. *American Historical Fiction: An Annotated Guide to Novels for Adults and Young Adults*. Phoenix, AZ: Oryx Press.
_____. 1999. *World Historical Fiction: An Annotated Guide to Novels for Adults and Young Adults*. Phoenix, AZ: Oryx Press.
Burgess, Michael, and Jill H. Vassilakos. 2005. *Murder in Retrospect: A Selective Guide to Historical Mystery Fiction*. Westport, CT: Libraries Unlimited.
Burt, Daniel S. 2003. *What Historical Novel Do I Read Next?* Three volumes. Detroit: Gale Research.
Johnson, Sarah L. 2005. *Historical Fiction: A Guide to the Genre*. Genreflecting Advisory Series, edited by Diana T. Herald. Westport, CT: Libraries Unlimited.
Oliver, Marina. 2003. *Writing Historical Fiction*. Munslow: Tudor House.
_____. 2005. *Writing Historical Fiction: Creating the Historical Blockbuster*. Abergele: Studymates.

History and Criticism

Carnes, Mark C. 2001. *Novel History: Historians and Novelists Confront America's Past (and Each Other)*. New York: Simon and Schuster.
Rozett, Martha Tuck. 2003. *Constructing a World: Shakespeare's England and the New Historical Fiction*. Albany: SUNY Press.

Listservs and Other Electronic Resources

Astrodene's Historic Naval Fiction. Available: www.historicnavalfiction.com.
Histfict. Available: http://groups.yahoo.com/group/Histfict.
Historical Fiction Network. Available: www.histfiction.net.
Historical Fiction Online. Available: www.historicalfictiononline.com.
Historical Fiction Writers. Available:
    http://groups.yahoo.com/group/historical-fiction-writers/.
Historical Mystery Fiction Writers. Available:
    http://groups.yahoo.com/group/Historical-Mysterywriters/.
Historical Novel Society listserv. Available:
    http://groups.yahoo.com/group/HistoricalNovelSociety/.
Historical Novelist Center. Available: http://groups.yahoo.com/group/HistNov/.
Writing Historical Fiction. Available:
    http://groups.yahoo.com/group/writinghistoricalfiction/.
Yesterday Revisited. Available: http://yesterdayrevisitedhere.blogspot.com.

Magazines, Fanzines, Webzines

Historical Novels Review. Historical Novel Society. Available:
    www.historicalnovelsociety.org/the-review.htm.
Solander: The Magazine of the Historical Novel Society. Available:
    www.historicalnovelsociety.org.

Organizations

Historical Novel Society. Available: www.historicalnovelsociety.org.

HORROR

Collections and Anthologies

Baldick, Chris. 2001. *The Oxford Book of Gothic Tales.* Oxford: Oxford University Press.

Berry, Mary, and Alex Madina. 1998. *Tales from Times Past: Sinister Stories of the 19th Century.* New York: Cambridge University Press.

Chizmar, Richard T., and Robert Morrish. 2000. *October Dreams.* Baltimore, MD: Cemetery Dance Publications.

Crow, Charles L. 1999. *American Gothic: An Anthology, 1787–1916.* Malden, MA: Blackwell.

Henderson, Eric, and Madeline Sonik. 1998. *Fresh Blood: New Canadian Gothic Fiction.* Winnipeg: Ravenstone.

Jones, Stephen. 2008. *The Mammoth Book of Best New Horror: No. 19.* London: Robinson Publishing.

Link, Kelly, Gavin Grant, and Ellen Datlow. 2008. *The Year's Best Fantasy and Horror 2008: 21st Annual Collection.* New York: St. Martin's Griffin.

Massey, Brandon. 2004. *Dark Dreams: A Collection of Horror and Suspense by Black Writers.* New York: Kensington.

Monteleone, Elizabeth E., and Thomas F. Monteleone. 2003. *Borderlands 5: An Anthology of Imaginative Fiction.* Grantham, NH: Borderlands Press.

_____. 2004. *From the Borderlands: Stories of Terror and Madness.* New York: Warner Books.

_____. 2005. *The Best of Borderlands, Vols 1–5: An Anthology of Imaginative Fiction.* Baltimore, MD: Borderlands Press.

Pelan, John, ed. 2002. *The Darker Side: Generations of Horror.* New York: Roc.

Silva, David B., and Richard T. Chizmar. 2001. *Night Visions 10.* Burton, MI: Subterranean Press.

Conventions and Conferences

World Horror Convention. Available: www.worldhorrorconention.com.

Guides and Manuals

Burgess, Michael, and Lisa. R. Bartle. 2002. *Reference Guide to Science Fiction, Fantasy and Horror,* 2nd edition. Westport, CT: Libraries Unlimited.

Fonesca, Anthony J., and June Michele Pulliam. 2009. *Hooked on Horror III: A Guide to Reading Interests.* Westport, CT: Libraries Unlimited.

Hawk, Pat. 2001. *Hawk's Science Fiction, Fantasy and Horror Series and Sequels.* Greenville, TX: Hawk's Enterprises.

Spratford, Becky Siegel, and Tammy Hennigh Clausen. 2004. *Horror Readers' Advisory: The Librarian's Guide to Vampires, Killer Tomatoes and Haunted Houses.* Chicago: ALA Editions.

Wiater, Stanley. 1998. *Dark Thoughts: On Writing, Advice and Commentary from Fifty Masters of Fear and Suspense.* Nevada City, CA: Underwood Books.

History and Criticism

Bleiler, Richard. 2003. *Supernatural Fiction Writers: Contemporary Fantasy and Horror,* 2nd edition. New York: Charles Scribner's Sons.

Bloom, Clive. 1998. *Gothic Horror: A Reader's Guide from Poe to King and Beyond.* New York: St. Martin's Press.

_____. 2007. *Gothic Horror: A Guide for Students and Readers,* 2nd edition. New York: Palgrave Macmillan.

Jones, Stephen, and Kim Newman. 1998. *Horror: The 100 Best Books.* New York: Carroll and Graf.

_____. 2005. *Horror: Another 100 Best Books.* New York: Carroll and Graf.

Listservs and Other Electronic Resources

Dark Echo. Available: www.darkecho.com.

Horror World. Available: www.horrorworld.org.

Magazines, Fanzines, Webzines

Locus Magazine. Available: www.locusmag.com.

Organizations

Horror Writers Association. Available: www.horror.org.

International Horror Guild. Available: www.horroraward.org. (*Note:* The International Horror Guild Awards ceased in 2007. A list of recipients from 1994 through 2007 continues to be available on the Web site.)

World Horror Society. Available: www.worldhorrorsociety.org.

Reviewing Resources

Necropsy: The Review of Horror Fiction. Available: www.lsu.edu/necrofile/.
Horror is also included in reviews of science fiction and fantasy.

MYSTERIES AND CRIME FICTION

Bibliographies and Biographies

Sobin, Roger M. 2007. *The Essential Mystery List: For Readers, Collectors and Librarians.* Scottsdale, AZ: Poisoned Pen Press.

Collections and Anthologies

Gorman, Edward, and Martin H. Greenberg. 2005. *The Adventure of the Missing Detective: And 19 of the Year's Finest Crime and Mystery Stories.* New York: Carroll and Graf Publishers.

Conventions and Conferences

Bouchercon, the World Mystery Convention. Available: www.bcon2010.com. (*Note:* Each convention maintains its own annual Web site.)

Left Coast Crime Convention. Available: www.leftcoastcrime.org/2009/index.html. (*Note:* Each convention maintains its own annual Web site.)

Magna cum Murder. Available: www.magnacummurder.com.

Malice Domestic. Available: www.malicedomestic.org/aboutmalice.html.

Encyclopedias and Dictionaries

Herbert, Rosemary, ed. 1999. *The Oxford Companion to Crime and Mystery Writing.* Oxford: Oxford University Press.

Murphy, Bruce F. 1999. *The Encyclopedia of Murder and Mystery.* New York: St. Martin's Minotaur.

Guides and Manuals

Anderson, Patrick. 2007. *The Triumph of the Thriller: How Cops, Crooks, and Cannibals Captured Popular Fiction.* New York: Random House.

Bleiler, Richard. 1999. *Reference Guide to Mystery and Detective Fiction.* Englewood, CO: Libraries Unlimited.

Breen, Jon L. *Novel Verdicts: A Guide to Courtroom Fiction,* 2nd edition. Lanham, MD: Scarecrow Press.

Burgess, Michael, and Jill H. Vassilakos. 2005. *Murder in Retrospect: A Selective Guide to Historical Mystery Fiction.* Westport, CT: Libraries Unlimited.

Charles, John, Joanna Morrison, and Candace Clark. 2002. *The Mystery Reader's Advisory: The Librarian's Clues to Murder and Mayhem.* ALA Reader's Advisory Series. Chicago: American Library Association.

Emerson, Kathy Lynn. 2008. *How to Write Killer Historical Mysteries: The Art and Adventure of Sleuthing through the Past.* McKinleyville, CA: Perseverance Press.

Grape, Jan, with Dean James and Ellen Nehr. 1998. *Deadly Women: The Woman Mystery Reader's Indispensable Companion.* New York: Carroll and Graf Publishers.

Heising, Willetta L. 1998. *Detecting Men.* Dearborn, MI: Purple Moon Press.

_____. 1999. *Detecting Women 3.* Dearborn, MI: Purple Moon Press.

Nichols, Victoria, and Susan Thompson. 1998. *Silk Stalkings: More Women Write of Murder.* Lanham, MD: Scarecrow Press.

Niebuhr, Gary Warren. 2003. *Make Mine a Mystery: A Reader's Guide to Mystery and Detective Fiction.* Westport, CT: Libraries Unlimited.

Swanson, Jean, with Dean James and Anne Perry. 1998. *Killer Books: A Reader's Guide to Exploring the Popular World of Mystery and Suspense.* New York: Berkley Books.

Histories and Criticism

Collins, Max Allan. 2001. *The History of Mystery.* Tigard, OR: Collectors Press.

Kawana, Sari. 2008. *Murder Most Modern: Detective Fiction and Japanese Culture.* Minneapolis: University of Minneapolis Press.

Klein, Kathleen Gregory. 1999. *Diversity and Detective Fiction.* Bowling Green, OH: Bowling Green State University Press.

Knight, Stephen Thomas. 2004. *Crime Fiction, 1800–2000: Detection, Death, Diversity.* New York: Palgrave Macmillan.

Lachman, Marvin. 2000. *The American Regional Mystery.* Minneapolis, MN: Crossover Press.

Landrum, Larry N. 1999. *American Mystery and Detective Novels: A Reference Guide.* Westport, CT: Greenwood Publishing.

Lehman, David. 1999. *The Perfect Murder: A Study in Detection.* Expanded edition. Ann Arbor: University of Michigan.
Rzepka, Charles J. 2005. *Detective Fiction.* Cambridge: Polity.
Walton, Priscilla L., and Manina Jones. 1999. *Detective Agency: Women Rewriting the Hard-Boiled Tradition.* Berkeley, CA: University of California Press.
Winks, Robin W., and Maureen Corrigan. 1998. *Mystery and Suspense Writers: The Literature of Crime Detection and Espionage.* New York: Charles Scribner's Sons.

Listservs and Other Electronic Resources

Dorothy-L. Available: www.dorothyl.com/index.html.
In Reference to Murder. Available: www.inreferencetomurder.com/index.html.
Reviewing the Evidence. Available: www.reviewingtheevidence.com.
Sisters in Crime. Available: www.sistersincrime.org. Members-only discussion list; paid membership required.
Stop! You're Killing Me. Available: www.stopyourekillingme.com.

Magazines, Fanzines, Webzines

Crime Time Magazine. Available: www.crimetime.co.uk/mag/index.php.
Deadly Pleasures Mystery Magazine. Available: www.deadlypleasures.com.
Mystery Readers Journal: The Journal of Mystery Readers International. Available: www.mysteryreaders.org/journal.html. (*Note:* The journal is not available in full text without a subscription; however, tables of contents and sample articles are on the Web site.)
Mystery Scene. Available: www.mysteryscenemag.com.
The Strand. Available: www.strandmag.com.

Organizations

International Association of Crime Writers. Available: www.crimewritersna.org.
Murder Readers International. Available: www.mysteryreaders.org/index.html.
Private Eye Writers. Available: www.thrillingdetective.com.
Sisters in Crime. Available: www.sistersincrime.org/index.html.

MULTICULTURAL FICTION

Encyclopedias and Dictionaries

Malinowski, Sharon. 1998. *The Gale Encyclopedia of Native American Tribes.* Four vols. Detroit: Gale.
Waldman, Carl. 2006. *Encyclopedia of Native American Tribes,* 3rd edition. New York: Facts on File.

Guides and Manuals

Bosman, Ellen, John P. Bradford, and Robert B. Ridinger. 2008. *Gay, Lesbian, Bisexual, and Transgendered Literature: A Genre Guide.* Westport, CT: Libraries Unlimited.
Dawson, Alma, and Connie Van Fleet. 2004. *African American Literature: A Guide to Reading Interests.* Englewood, CO: Libraries Unlimited.

Fleming, Robert. 2000. *The African American Writers Handbook: How to Get in Print and Stay in Print*. New York: One World.
Reisner, Rosalind. 2004. *Jewish American Literature: A Guide to Reading Interests*. Englewood, CO: Libraries Unlimited.
"Urban Fiction/Street Lit/Hip Hop Fictions Resources for Librarians." 2009. Library Success: A Best Practices Wiki. Available: www.libsuccess.org/index.php?title=Urban_Fiction/Street_Lit/Hip_Hop_Fiction_Resources_for_Libraians.

Listservs and Other Online Resources

Rawsistaz. Available: www.rawsistaz.com/index.html.
Street Fiction. Available: www.streetfiction.org.
The Urban Book Source. Available: www.theurbanbooksource.com/main.html.
Urban Reviews. Available: www.urban-reviews.com.

Magazines, Fanzines, Webzines

Black Issues Book Review. Available: www.bibookreview.com.
Essence. Available: www.essence.com/news_entertainment/.
QBR: The Black Book Review. Available: www.qbr.com.

ROMANCE FICTION

Conventions and Conferences

Romance Novelists' Association Annual Awards Luncheon, United Kingdom.
Romance Writers of America Annual National Conference. Several of the RWA chapters sponsor state and regional events, including workshops, conferences, and contests.

Guides and Manuals

Bouricius, Ann. 2000. *The Romance Reader's Advisory: The Librarian's Guide to Love in the Stacks*. Chicago: American Library Association.
Charles, John, and Shelley Mosley, eds. 2006. *Romance Today: An A-to-Z Guide to Contemporary American Romance Writers*. Westport, CT: Greenwood.
Grant, Vanessa. 2007. *Writing Romance*, 3rd edition. North Vancouver, BC: Self-Counsel Press.
Knight, Angela. 2007. *Passionate Ink: A Guide to Writing Erotic Romance*. La Vergne, TN: Lightning Source.
Lanigan, Catherine. 2006. *Writing the Great American Romance Novel*. New York: Allworth Press.
Michaels, Leigh. 2007. *On Writing Romance: How to Craft a Novel That Sells*. Cincinnati, OH: Writer's Digest Books.
Mussell, Kay, and Johanna Tunon, eds. 1999. *North American Romance Writers*. Lanham, MD: Scarecrow Press.
Ramsdell, Kristin. 1999. *Romance Fiction: A Guide to the Genre*. Englewood, CO: Libraries Unlimited.
_____. 1999. *What Romance Do I Read Next? A Reader's Guide to Recent Romance Fiction*. Detroit: Gale Group.

Vinyard, Rebecca. 2004. *The Romance Writer's Handbook*. Waukesha, WI: Writer Books.

History and Criticism

Hardin, Richard F. 2000. *Love in a Green Shade: Idyllic Romances Ancient to Modern*. Lincoln, NE: University of Nebraska Press.
Kaler, Anne K., and Rosemary E. Johnson-Kurek. 1999. *Romantic Conventions*. Bowling Green, OH: Bowling Green State University Popular Press.
Pearce, Lynne. 2007. *Romance Writing*. Cambridge, MA: Polity.
Ramsdell, Kristin. 1998. *Romance Fiction: A Handbook for Readers, Writers and Librarians*. Englewood, CO: Libraries Unlimited.

Listservs and Other Electronic Resources

All about Romance. Available: www.likesbooks.com.
Good Ton: A Resource for Readers of Regency Romance Novels. Available: www.thenonesuch.com.
Historical Romance Writers. Available: http://historicalromancewriters.com/index.cfm.
Paranormal Romance. Available: www.paranormalromance.org.
Paranormal Romance Writers. Available: www.paranormalromancewriters.com.
The Romance Reader. Available: www.theromancereader.com.
Romance Reader at Heart. Available: http://romancereaderatheart.com.
Romance Reviews Today. Available: www.romrevtoday.com.
Romancing the Blog. Available: www.romancingtheblog.com/blog/.
Romantic Times Book Reviews. Available: www.romantictimes.com.
Yahoo! Groups RRA-L. Available: http://groups.yahoo.com/group/rra-l/.

Magazines, Fanzines, Webzines, and Reviewing Resources

Affaire de Couer. Available: www.affairedecoeur.com.
Romance Matters. Romance Novelists' Association. Available: www.rna-uk.org.
Romance Writers Report. Romance Writers of America. Available: www.rwanational.org.
Romantic Times. Available: www.romantictimes.com.

Organizations

Romance Novelists Association. Available: www.rna-uk.org.
Romance Writers of America. Available: www.rwanational.org.

SCIENCE FICTION AND FANTASY

Bibliographies and Biographies

Harris-Fain, Darren. 2002. *British Fantasy and Science-Fiction Writers, 1918–1960*. Detroit: Gale Group.
_____. 2002. *British Fantasy and Science-Fiction Writers Since 1960*. Detroit: Gale Group.
Ivison, Douglas. 2002. *Canadian Fantasy and Science-Fiction Writers*. Detroit: Gale Group.
Lockhart, Darrell B. 2004. *Latin American Science Fiction Writers: An A-to-Z Guide*. Westport, CT: Greenwood Press.

324 A Few Good Books

Marcus, Leonard S., ed. 2006. *The Wand in the Word: Conversations with Writers of Fantasy.* Cambridge, MA: Candlewick Press.

Stevens, Jen, and Dorothea Sala. 2008. *Fantasy Authors: A Research Guide.* Author Research Series. Westport, CT: Libraries Unlimited.

Collections and Anthologies

Arment, Chad, ed. 2008. *Flora Curiosa: Cryptobotany, Mysterious Fungi, Sentient Trees, and Deadly Plants in Classic Science Fiction and Fantasy.* Landisville, PA: Coachwhip Publications.

Bova, Ben. 2004. *The Science Fiction Hall of Fame, Volume Two A.* New York: Tor Books.

_____. 2008. *The Science Fiction Hall of Fame, Volume Two B: The Greatest Science Fiction Novellas of All Time.* New York: Tor Books.

Datlow, Ellen. 2008. *The Del Rey Book of Science Fiction and Fantasy: Sixteen Original Works by Speculative Fiction's Finest Voices.* New York: Del Rey/Ballantine Books.

Link, Kelly, Gavin Grant, and Ellen Datlow. 2008. *The Year's Best Fantasy and Horror 2008: 21st Annual Collection.* New York: St. Martin's Griffin.

Morrow, James, and Kathryn Morrow. 2007. *The SFWA European Hall of Fame: Sixteen Contemporary Masterpieces of Science Fiction from the Continent.* New York: Tor Books.

Silverberg, Robert. 2003. *The Science Fiction Hall of Fame: Volume One, 1929–1964.* New York: Tor Books.

Conventions and Conferences

FantasyCon, British Fantasy Society. Available: www.britishfantasysociety.org.uk.

MythCon. Available: www.mythsoc.org.

World Fantasy Convention. Available: www.worldfantasy.org.

Worldcon. Available: www.anticipationsf.ca/English/Home/. (*Note:* Worldcon is a traveling convention and changes location annually. Each Worldcon will have its own Web site.)

Encyclopedias and Dictionaries

D'Ammassa, Don. 2005. *Encyclopedia of Science Fiction.* New York: Facts on File.

_____. 2006. *Encyclopedia of Fantasy and Horror Fiction.* New York: Facts on File.

Joshi, S. T., and Dziemianowicz, Stefan R. 2005. *Supernatural Literature of the World: An Encyclopedia.* Westport, CT: Greenwood Press.

Mann, George, ed. 2001. *The Mammoth Encyclopedia of Science Fiction.* New York: Carroll and Graf.

Prucher, Jeff. 2007. *Brave New Worlds: The Oxford Dictionary of Science Fiction.* Oxford and New York: Oxford University Press.

Stableford, Brian M. 2005. *Historical Dictionary of Fantasy Literature.* Lanham, MD: Scarecrow Press.

_____. 2006. *Science Fact and Science Fiction: An Encyclopedia.* New York: Routledge.

Westfahl, Gary. 2005. *The Greenwood Encyclopedia of Science Fiction and Fantasy: Themes, Works and Wonders.* Westport, CT: Greenwood Press.

Guides and Manuals

Barron, Neil. 1998. *What Fantastic Fiction Do I Read Next? A Reader's Guide to Recent Fantasy, Horror and Science Fiction.* Detroit, MI: Gale Group.

Buker, Derek M. 2002. *Science Fiction and Fantasy Readers' Advisory: The Librarians Guide to Cyborgs, Aliens and Sorcerers.* Chicago: ALA Editions.
Burgess, Michael, and Lisa R. Bartle. 2002. *Reference Guide to Science Fiction, Fantasy and Horror,* 2nd edition. Westport, CT: Libraries Unlimited.
Card, Orson Scott. 2001. *How to Write Science Fiction and Fantasy.* Cincinnati, OH: Writer's Digest Books.
Fichtelberg, Susan. 2006. *Encountering Enchantment: A Guide to Speculative Fiction for Teens.* Westport, CT: Libraries Unlimited.
Gerrold, David. 2001. *Worlds of Wonder: How to Write Science Fiction and Fantasy.* Cincinnati, OH: Writer's Digest Books.
Gunn, James E. 2000. *The Science of Science-Fiction Writing.* Lanham, MD: Scarecrow Press.
Hawk, Pat. 2001. *Hawk's Science Fiction, Fantasy and Horror Series and Sequels.* Greenville, TX: Hawk's Enterprises.
Herald, Diana Trixler, and Bonnie Kunzel. 2002. *Strictly Science Fiction: A Guide to Reading Interests.* Greenwood Village, CO: Libraries Unlimited.
_____. 2008. *Fluent in Fantasy: The Next Generation.* Westport, CT: Libraries Unlimited.
Hollands, Neil. 2007. *Read On . . . Fantasy Fiction: Reading Lists for Every Taste,* Read On Series. Westport, CT: Libraries Unlimited.
Kunzel, Bonnie, and Suzanne Manzuk. 2001. *First Contact: A Reader's Selection of Science Fiction and Fantasy.* Lanham, MD: Scarecrow Press.
Longyear, Barry B. 2002. *Science Fiction Writer's Workshop-I: An Introduction to Fiction Mechanics.* Lincoln, NE: iUniverse.
Sheffield, Charles. 2000. *Borderlands of Science: How to Think Like a Scientist and Write Science Fiction.* Riverdale, NY: Baen.

History and Criticism

Barron, Neil, ed. 1999. *Fantasy and Horror: A Critical and Historical Guide to Literature, Illustration, Film, TV, Radio and the Internet.* Lanham, MD: Scarecrow Press.
_____. 2004. *Anatomy of Wonder: A Critical Guide to Science Fiction.* Westport, CT: Libraries Unlimited.
Bleiler, Richard. 2003. *Supernatural Fiction Writers: Contemporary Fantasy and Horror,* 2nd edition. New York: Charles Scribner's Sons.
Broecker, Randy. 2001. *Fantasy of the 20th Century: An Illustrated History.* Portland, OR: Collectors Press.
Disch, Thomas M. 1998. *The Dreams Our Stuff Is Made Of: How Science Fiction Conquered the World.* New York: Free Press.
O'Keefe, Deborah. 2003. *Readers in Wonderland: The Liberating Worlds of Fantasy Fiction: From Dorothy to Harry Potter.* New York: Continuum.
Westfahl, Gary, George Slusser, and Dvaid Leiby, eds. 2002. *Worlds Enough and Time: Explorations of Time in Science Fiction and Fantasy.* Westport, CT: Greenwood Press.

Listservs and Other Electronic Resources

The Dark Network, SciFi Section. Available: www.scifisection.com. (*Note:* Focus of this social network is on cataloging science fiction movies and television shows.)
Encyclopedia Mythica. Available: www.pantheon.org.
Fantasy 100. Available:
http://home.austarnet.com.au/petersykes/fantasy100/lists_books.html.

Fantasy Book Critic. Available: www.fantasybookcritic.blogspot.com.
Feminist Science Fiction, Fantasy and Utopia. Available: www.feministsf.org/femsf/.
Green Man Review. Available: www.greenmanreview.com.
Internet Speculative Fiction Database. Available: www.isfdb.org/cgi-bin/index.cgi.
Pat's Fantasy Hotlist. Available: http://fantasyhotlist.blogspot.com.
Reader's Robot Fantasy Page. Available: www.tnrdlib.bc.ca/rr/fa-menu.html.
Recommended Fantasy Author List. Available:
    www.sff.net/people/Amy.Sheldon/listcont.htm.
Sci Fi Wire. Available: scifiwire.com/index.php.
SciFan. Available: www.scifan.com.
SF Crowsnest Hivemind, the social network for science fiction and fantasy fans. Available:
    www.sfcrowsnest.com/hivemind/home.php.
SF Site: The Home Page for Science Fiction and Fantasy. Available: www.sfsite.com.
SFFWorld. Available: www.sffworld.com.
Urban Fantasy Land. 2009. Available: http://urbanfantasyland.wordpress.com.

Magazines, Fanzines, Webzines

Analog Science Fiction and Fact. Available www.analogsf.com.
Asimov's Science Fiction. Available: www.asimovs.com.
Fantasy and Science Fiction. Available: www.sfsite.com/fsf/.
Locus Magazine. Available: www.locusmag.com.
New York Review of Science Fiction. Available:
    http://ebbs.english.vt.edu/olp/nyrsf/nyrsf.html.
Weird Tales. Available: www.weirdtales.net.

Organizations

British Fantasy Society. Available: www.britishfantasysociety.org.uk.
British Science Fiction Association. Available: www.bsfa.co.uk.
European Science Fiction Society. Available: www.esfs.info/index.html.
Mythopoeic Society. Available: www.mythsoc.org.
Science Fiction and Fantasy Writers of America. Available: www.swfa.org.
SF Canada. Available: www.sfcanada.ca.

WESTERN FICTION

Resources for historical fiction and romance frequently include sections devoted to stories about the American West or set in the American West. In addition to the resources listed below, be sure to consult the general genre guides as well as those for history and romance.

Collections and Anthologies

Barnes, Kim, and Mary Clearman Blew, eds. 2004. *Circle of Women: An Anthology of Contemporary Western Women Writers.* Norman, OK: University of Oklahoma Press.
Estleman, Loren, ed. 2001. *American West.* New York: St. Martin's.
Gorman, Ed, and Martin H. Greenberg, eds. 2002. *Stagecoach.* New York: Berkley Books.
Jakes, John, ed. 2001. *A Century of Great Western Stories.* New York: Forge Books.

Lyon, Thomas J. 1999. *The Literary West: An Anthology of Western American Literature*. New York: Oxford University Press.

McMurtry, Larry, ed. 2000. *Still Wild: Short Fiction of the American West*. New York: Simon and Schuster.

Piekarski, Vicki, ed. 2001. *No Place for a Lady*. Waterville, ME: Five Star.

Randisi, Robert J., ed. 2002. *Boot Hill: An Anthology of the West*. New York: Forge Books.

Walker, Dale, ed. 2002. *The Western Hall of Fame Anthology*. Thorndike, ME: Center Point Publications.

_____. 2004. *Westward: A Fictional History of the American West*. New York: Forge Books.

Guides and Manuals

Barton, Wayne. 1999. *What Western Do I Read Next? A Reader's Guide to Recent Western Fiction*. Detroit: Gale Group.

Hawk, Pat. 1999. *Western Series and Sequels: With Pseudonyms and Author Attribution*. Greenville, TX: Hawk's Enterprises.

Mort, John. 2006. *Reading the High Country: Guide to Western Books and Films*. Genreflecting Advisory Series, edited by Diana Trixler Hearld. Westport, CT: Libraries Unlimited.

History and Criticism

Allmendinger, Blake. 1998. *Ten Most Wanted: The New Western Literature*. New York: Routledge.

Lackmann, Ronald W. 2006. *Women of the Western Frontier in Fact, Fiction and Film*. Jefferson, NC: McFarland.

Rogers, Kenny. 2007. *The Real West: The Cowboys and Outlaws*. DVD. A and E Home Entertainment.

Magazines, Fanzines, Webzines

Roundup. Available: www.westernwriters.org.

Organizations

National Cowboy Hall of Fame and Western Heritage Center. Available: www.cowboyhalloffame.org.

Western Writers of America. Available: www.westernwriters.org.

Women Writing the West. Available: www.womenwritingthewest.org.

Reviewing Resources

Western Fiction Review. Available: http://westernfictionreview.blogspot.com.

WOMEN'S FICTION AND CHICK LIT

Very few guides and resources specific to women's fiction and chick lit exist. In addition to the resources listed here, consult the general guides for genre fiction along with resources for romance and historical fiction. A number of studies and books have been written about women writing mysteries and detective fiction; be sure to consult the section on Mysteries and Crime Fiction for resources. The Western fiction genre includes a large portion of women writing about the American West and fiction focused on the female protagonist in the West.

Collections and Anthologies

Baratz-Logsted, Lauren. 2005. *This Is Chick Lit.* Dallas, TX: BenBella Books.
Merrick, Elizabeth. 2006. *This Is Not Chick Lit: Original Stories by America's Best Women Writers.* New York: Random House.

Guides and Manuals

Ferriss, Suzanne, and Mallory Young. 2005. *Chick Lit: The New Woman's Fiction.* New York: Routledge.
Mylnowski, Sarah, and Farrin Jacobs. 2006. *See Jane Write: A Girl's Guide to Writing Chick Lit.* Philadelphia, PA: Quirk Books.
Reynolds, Guy. 1999. *Twentieth-Century American Women's Fiction: A Critical Introduction.* Revised edition. New York: Palgrave Macmillan.
Smith, Caroline J. 2008. *Cosmopolitan Culture and Consumerism in Chick Lit.* New York: Routledge.
Yardley, Cathy. 2006. *Will Write for Shoes: How to Write a Chick Lit Novel.* New York: Thomas Dunne Books.

Listservs and Other Online Resources

BookReporter. Available: www.bookreporter.com/womens_fiction/index.asp.
Candy Covered Books. Available: www.candycoveredbooks.com.
ChickLitClub. Available: www.chicklitclub.com.
ChickLitWriters. Available: www.chicklitwriters.com.
Sisters in Crime. Available: www.sistersincrime.org.
Women Writing the West. Available: www.womenwritingthewest.com.

Appendix 2

Bestsellers Books and Reading Lists

Online book/reading lists are too numerous to mention all of them. The following are representative of the resources that are available in print and online. A generic search on a favorite search engine using "bestsellers lists" yields hundreds of possible options for all tastes and interests. This can be limited by adding terms for regional lists and genres or topics.

INDIEBOUND BESTSELLERS

- An online product of the American Booksellers Association
- According to the Web site: The Indie Bestsellers List puts the diversity of America's independent bookstores on display. It's produced just two days after the end of the sales week and is the most current snapshot of what's selling in indie bookstores nationwide. Prior to June 2008 the list was part of Book Sense with the 2007 and 2008 lists still available online.
- Available: www.bookweb.org/indiebound/bestsellers/archives
- Published weekly, featuring:
  Hardcover fiction
  Hardcover nonfiction
  Trade paperback fiction
  Trade paperback nonfiction
  Mass market
  Children's illustrated
  Children's interest

LIBRARY JOURNAL BESTSELLERS (the books most borrowed in U.S. libraries)

- Published biweekly, featuring fiction and nonfiction
- Compiled from data on books borrowed and requested at public libraries throughout the United States
- Available online through www.libraryjournal.com/. Scroll down to the link for bestsellers.

NEW YORK TIMES BESTSELLERS

- Published weekly, featuring:
    Hardcover fiction
    Hardcover nonfiction
    Hardcover advice
    Children's books
    Paperback fiction
    Paperback nonfiction
    Paperback advice
    Inside the list
- "Rankings reflect sales, for the week ended [two weeks prior], at many thousands of venues where a wide range of general interest books are sold nationwide. These include hundreds of independent book retailers (statistically weighted to represent all such outlets); national, regional and local chains; online and multimedia entertainment retailers; university, gift, supermarket, discount, department stores and newsstands." (*NYT*, 2008)
- Available online at www.nytimes.com/pages/books/index.html

PUBLISHERS WEEKLY LATEST BESTSELLERS

- Published weekly, featuring:
    Hardcover fiction
    Hardcover nonfiction
    Mass-market paperback
    Trade paperback
    Audio fiction
    Audio nonfiction
    Children's picture books
    Children's fiction books
    Children's series and tie-ins
    Religious hardcover
    Religious paperback
- Rankings are based on previous week's sales from a variety of chain and independent booksellers and other retail outlets.
- Available at www.publishersweekly.com/. Use the link at top for bestsellers lists.

USA TODAY TOP 150 BESTSELLERS

- Published weekly, featuring:
    Fiction
    Nonfiction
    Paperback
    Hardcover
- Rankings are based on sales through the previous week.
- Available in an online searchable database at http://asp.usatoday.com/life/books/booksdatabase/default.aspx; can sort list by Rank, Title, or Author.

AMAZON.COM BESTSELLERS

- Features the most popular items in a category, updated hourly.

- Does not categorize books by age, reading level, or format like publishers' lists (*A Thousand Splendid Suns* by Khaled Hosseini appears on the same list as *Harry Potter and the Deathly Hallows* by J. K. Rowling).

- Added features include editorial reviews (*Library Journal* or *Booklist*, etc.) as well as reader reviews, podcasts, links to author's Web site, exclusive online excerpts, and downloads.

- Other Amazon bestsellers lists include Movers & Shakers (books that have gained the most in sales on Amazon.com) and Hot New Releases (newly released books and preorders with the highest sales on Amazon.com).

- Available at www.amazon.com. Bestsellers link at top of home page.

BARNES & NOBLE.COM TOP 100 IN BOOKS

- Features the books with highest sales or preorders on Barnes & Noble.com.

- Does not categorize books like publishers' lists.

- Added features include editorial reviews, reader reviews, book synopses from the publisher, and biographical information about the author.

- Other B&N bestsellers lists include Barnes & Noble Recommends, Daily Top 10 Books by Subject, and Best Sellers of 2007.

- Available: www.barnesandnoble.com/index.asp?z=y. Bestsellers link at top of home page.

OTHER POSSIBILITIES

- BookSpot.com, which, according to their Web site, is a "free resource center that simplifies the search for the best book-related content on the Web. Featured sites are hand selected by BookSpot.com editors and organized into intuitive categories, such as bestseller lists, genres, book reviews, electronic texts, book news and more." Available at www.bookspot.com/about.htm.

- Your local and regional newspapers: Perfect for finding local favorites as well as national and international bestsellers lists. See, for example, *The Boston Globe, San Francisco Chronicle, Creative Loafing,* or *Chicago Tribune.*

- Wikis and blogs: Perfect for finding reviews, broad range of lists, and discussion groups. For example, check out Overbooked at www.overbooked.com/index .html, GoodReads at www.goodreads.com/, or BookLust at http://booklust .wetpaint.com/.

Appendix 3

Statewide Adult Book Awards

*These awards are not available in all states. Only those with awards for adult fiction and nonfiction are represented.

Alabama
Alabama Library Association Author Awards
http://allanet.org/about_author_awards.cfm

Arizona
Arizona Book Awards
http://azbookpub.com/onews/glyph-awards/

California
The California Book Awards
www.commonwealthclub.org/features/caBookAwards/about.php

Colorado
Colorado Book Awards
www.coloradohumanities.org/ccftb/Colorado_Book_Awards.htm

Connecticut
Conneticut Book Awards
www.hplct.org/cfb/cba.htm

Florida
The Florida Book Awards
http://floridabookawards.lib.fsu.edu/index.php

Georgia
Georgia Author of the Year Award
www.georgiawriters.org/

Georgia Center for the Books Award
www.georgiacenterforthebook.org/Awards/index.php

Idaho
Idaho Book Award
www.idaholibraries.org/bookaward

Illinois
Illinois Art Council Literary Awards Program
www.state.il.us/agency/iac/guidelines/guidelines.htm#lia

Indiana
Best Books of Indiana
www.in.gov/library/icb.htm

Kansas
Kansas Notable Books
http://skyways.lib.ks.us/orgs/kcfb/

Kentucky
Kentucky Literary Awards
www.sokybookfest.org/BookFest07/kylitawardgeneralinfo.htm

Louisiana
Louisiana Writer Award
www.state.lib.la.us/la_dyn_templ.cfm?doc_id=18

Louisiana Literary Award
www.llaonline.org/as/

Maine
The Lupine Award
http://mainelibraries.org/aw_lupine.php?mi=7&page_mi=4

Massachusetts
Massachusetts Book Awards
www.massbook.org/bookawards.html

Michigan
Michigan Notable Books
www.michigan.gov/notablebooks

Minnesota
Minnesota Book Awards
www.thefriends.org/mnbookawards_index
.html

Mississippi
Mississippi Author Awards
www.misslib.org/index.php/awards-
scholarships/mla-awards-scholarships/
mississippi-authors-awards/

Missouri
MLA Literary Award
http://molib.org/Awards.html#literary

Montana
Montana Book Award
www.montanabookaward.org/index.html

Nebraska
Nebraska Book Awards
www.nlc.state.ne.us/publications/
ncbawards.html

Mari Sandoz Award
www.nebraskalibraries.org/awards.html

New Hampshire
New Hampshire Literary Award
www.nhwritersproject.org/newfiles/
SpecialEvents.html

New Jersey
NJCH Book Award
www.njch.org/awards_bookaward.html

New Mexico
New Mexico Book Awards
www.nmbookcoop.com/page5/page5.html

New York
New York State Author & Poet Awards
www.albany.edu/writers-inst/webpages4/
programpages/awardees.html

North Carolina
North Carolina Book Awards
www.history.ncdcr.gov/affiliates/lit-hist/
awards/awards.htm

Linda Flowers Literary Award
www.nchumanities.org/flowers.html

Roberts Award for Literary Inspiration
www.ecu.edu/cs-lib/lithomecoming/
authorinfo.cfm

Ohio
Ohioana Book Award
www.ohioana.org/awards/book.asp

Ohio Arts Council Individual Excellence
Awards
www.oac.state.oh.us/grantsprogs/
guidelines/individualcreativity.asp

Oklahoma
Oklahoma Book Awards
www.odl.state.ok.us/ocb/obaward.htm

Oregon
Oregon Book Awards
www.literary-arts.org/awards/

South Carolina
The SC Center for the Book Awards
www.sccenterforthebook.org/books/
awards/the-sc-center-for-the-book
-awards.html

Tennessee
Tennessee History Book Award
www.tnla.org/displaycommon.cfm?an=1&
subarticlenbr=86

Texas
Texas Institute of Letters Literary Awards
www.texasinstituteofletters.org/awards/

Utah
Utah Book Award
www.slcpl.lib.ut.us/details.jsp?parent_
id=15&page_id=137

Utah Original Writing Contest
www.utahhumanities.org/BookFestival/
UtahLiteraryAwards.htm

Virginia
Library of Virginia Literary Awards
www.lva.lib.va.us/whatwedo/awards/index
.htm

Jefferson Cup Award
www.vla.org/demo/Youth-Serv/cyart/
    jefferson_cup/Jeffersoncup_index
    .html

Washington
Washington State Book Awards
www.spl.org/default.asp?pageID=about_
    leaders_washingtoncenter_
    awardwinners

West Virginia
West Virginia Library Association Book
    Award
www.wvla.org/awards/index.html

Wisconsin
RR Donnelley Award
www.wla.lib.wi.us/readers/WLAC/
    RRDonelley_Award_Index_CRriteria
    .html

Wyoming
Neltje Blanchan and Frank Nelson
    Doubleday Memorial Awards
http://wyoarts.state.wy.us./IndArtist/
    Literature.asp

Appendix 4

Resources for Book Discussion Groups

This appendix provides a list of the books, articles, and Web resources available to assist with the forming and maintaining of lively, successful reading groups. Most of them are readily available through libraries in your local communities. Searching through Amazon.com and other online booksellers, publishers, library catalogs, and general Web sites yields many additional titles, far too many to enumerate here.

PRINT RESOURCES

Burns, Martha, and Alice Dillon. 1999. *Reading Group Journal: Notes in the Margin*. New York: Abbeville Press.

Contarino, Ann-Marie. 2008. "Establishing a Parish Book Discussion Group." *Catholic Library World* (March): 203–206.

Dodson, Shireen. 1997. *The Mother-Daughter Book Club*. New York: HarperCollins.

Ellington, H. Elisabeth, and Jane Freimiller. 2002. *A Year of Reading: A Month-by-Month Guide to Classics and Crowd-Pleasers for You and Your Book Group*. Naperville, IL: Sourcebooks.

Fineman, Marcia. 1997. *Talking about Books: A Step-by-Step Guide for Participating in a Book Discussion Group*. Rockville, MD: Talking about Books.

Gardner, Sarah. 2005. *Read it and Eat*. New York: Hudson Street Press.

Greenwood, Monique. 1999. *The Go on Girl! Book Club Guide for Reading Groups: Works Worth Reading, Chats with Our Favorite Authors, Tips for Starting and Sustaining a Literary Circle, Questions and Topics to Get You Talking—and More*. New York: Hyperion.

Healy, Anna. 2002. "Giving Readers a Voice: Book Discussion Groups." *Book Links* 11, no. 4 (February/March).

Jacobsohn, Rachel W. 1998. *The Reading Group Handbook: Everything You Need to Know to Start Your Own Book Club*, Revised edition. New York: Hyperion.

John, Lauren Zina. 2006. *Running Book Discussion Groups: A How-To-Do-It Manual*. New York: Neal-Schuman.

Laskin, David, and Holly Hughes. 1995. *The Reading Group Book: The Complete Guide to Starting and Sustaining a Reading Group, with Annotated Lists of 250 Titles for Provocative Discussion*. New York: Plume.

Loevy, Diana. 2006. *The Book Club Companion: A Comprehensive Guide to the Reading Group Experience*. New York: Berkley Books.

McMahon, Susan I., and Taffy Raphael. 1997. *The Book Club Connection: Literacy, Learning and Classroom Talk.* New York: Teachers College Press.

McMains, Victoria Golden. 2000. *The Reader's Choice: 200 Book Club Favorites.* New York: Quill.

Moore, Ellen, and Kira Stevens. 2004. *Good Books Lately: The One-Stop Resource for Book Groups and Other Greedy Readers.* New York: St. Martin's Griffin.

Nelson, Sara. 2003. *So Many Books, So Little Time: A Year of Passionate Reading.* New York: G. P. Putnam's Sons.

Saal, Rollene. 1995. *The New York Public Library Guide to Reading Groups.* New York: Crown Publishers.

Sauer, Patrick. 2000. *The Complete Idiot's Guide to Starting a Reading Group.* Indianapolis, IN: Alpha Book. (Also available as an e-book.)

Slezak, Ellen, ed. 1995. *The Book Group Book: A Thoughtful Guide to Forming and Enjoying a Stimulating Book Discussion Group,* 2nd edition. Chicago: Chicago Review Press.

Soltan, Rita. 2006. *Reading Raps: A Book Club Guide for Librarians, Kids, and Families.* Westport, CT: Libraries Unlimited.

ONLINE RESOURCES

American Library Association. 2009. "Book Discussion Groups." Available: http://wikis.ala.org/professionaltips/index.php/Book_Discussion_Groups.

"Book Club Tips for Author Chats." 2009. Blogpost. Available: http://lisamm.wordpress.com/2008/01/17/book-club-tips-for-author-chats.

"Book Discussion Club." 2009. Wikipedia. Available: http://en.wikipedia.org/wiki/Book_discussion_club. (If nothing else, the Wikipedia article includes a list of external links to reading and book discussion group resources, which is highly useful.)

"Book Group How-Tos." 2009. The Seattle Public Library. Available: www.spl.org/default.asp?pageID=collection_readinglists_bookclub_howtos.

"Books about Reading Groups." 2009. Reading Group Guides. Available: www.readinggroupguides.com/roundtable/aboutrgg.asp.

Go On Girl! Book Club. 2009. Available: www.goongirl.org.

Jacobsohn, Rachel. "Ten Tips for Starting and Running a Successful Book Club." Available: www.readinggroupchoices.com/readinggroups/leaders.cfm.

"Love to Read: Finding Books & Book Clubs." 2009. Internet Public Library. Available: www.ipl.org/div/pf/entry/48523.

RESOURCES FOR TITLE LISTS AND READING GUIDES

Amazon.com Book Clubs. Available: www.amazon.com/Book-Clubs-Books/b?ie=UTF8&node=292203.

Book Browse. Available: www.bookbrowse.com/reading_guides/.

Book Lust: A Community for People Who Love Books. Available: http://booklust.wetpaint.com.

Book Movement. Available: www.bookmovement.com/info/about.php (requires a subscription; free).

Book Muse. Available: www.bookmuse.com/index.asp (requires a subscription; free).

Book Spot. Available: www.bookspot.com/readingguides.htm.

Book-Clubs-Resource.com. Available: www.book-clubs-resource.com.

Booklist Online Book Group Buzz. Available:
bookgroupbuzz.booklistonline.com/book-club-resources.

The Bookreporter. Available: www.bookreporter.com.

Harcourt Trade Publishers. Available:
www.harcourtbooks.com/booksearch/readingguides.asp?source=topnav.

HarperCollins Reading Groups. Available:
www.harpercollins.com/readers/readingGroups.aspx.

Hatchette Book Group Book Club Reading Guides. Available:
www.hachettebookgroup.com/books_reading-group-guides.aspx.

Houghton Mifflin Reader's Guides. Available:
www.houghtonmifflinbooks.com/readers_guides/.

LitLovers. Available: www.litlovers.com.

Morton Grove Public Library. Available: http://webrary.org.

National Endowment for the Arts Big Read. Available: www.neabigread.org.

National Resource Center for the First Year Experience and Students in Transition. Available: www.sc.edu/fye/resources/fyr/index.html.

Penguin Reading Guides. Available:
http://us.penguingroup.com/static/pages/bookclubs/index.html.

Random House Reading Guides. Available: www.randomhouse.com/rgg/.

Reader's Circle. Available: www.readerscircle.org.

The Reading Club (a British site). Available: www.thereadingclub.co.uk.

Reading Group Choices. Available: www.readinggroupchoices.com.

Reading Group Guides. Available: www.readinggroupguides.com.

Simon & Schuster. Available: www.simonsays.com/content/index.cfm?sid=519.

W. W. Norton & Company. Available:
http://books.wwnorton.com/books/reading-guide-list.aspx?tid=3288.

Author, Series, and Title Index

Page numbers followed by "f" indicate figures; those followed by "t" indicate tables.

Danticat, Edwidge, 201
Dark series, 176t
Dark Thicket, 192t
Darker, 167t
Darkest Part of the Woods, The, 167t
Darkest Powers, 167t
Dark-Hunter series, 176t
Darkness Demands, 167t
Darkness series, 150t
Darkover series, 157
Dart, Iris, 230t
Darwin series, 150t
Daughter of Time, The, 181
Dave Brandstetter series, 140
Dave Robicheaux series, 139, 141t
Davidson, Andrew, 89f
Davidson, Diane Mott, 140, 141t
DaVinci Code, The, 131, 241
Day of the Jackal, 132t
Daybreak, 231t
Daybreak 2250 AD, 151
Daybreakers, 191
de Jong, Peter, 242
de Lint, Charles, 158, 160t
de Scudéry, Madelein, 9
Dead Cert, 142t
Dead Eyes, 231t
Dead Languages, 231t
Deadline, 247f
Deafening, 230t
Dean, Debra, 230t
Dearly Departed, The, 202t
Death Angel, 176t
Death Gate, 161t
Death Gate Cycle, The, 157
Death of Ivan Ilyich, The, 301
Death on Demand series, 124, 141t
Death on the Nile, 138
Deaver, Jeffery, 132t, 230t
DeBerry, Virginia, 208t. *See also* Grant, Donna
Debt to Delia, A, 176t
Deed of Paksenarrion, 150t
Deep Blue Sea for Beginners, The, 202t
Deep Dish, 202t
Defoe, Daniel, 9
Delinksy, Barbara, 202t
Deliverance Valley, 188
DeMille, Nelson, 132t, 134

Demon Seed, 167t
Denslow, W.W. *See* Baum, L. Frank
Dereske, Jo, 140
Destry Rides Again, 191
Devil Wears Prada, The, 204t
Diamond, De'neshan, 208t. *See also* Mink, Meesha
Diary of a Mad Mom to Be, 204t
Diaz, Junot, 214
Dicey's Song, 224t
Dick, Philip K., 150, 152
Dickens, Charles, 121, 183, 209
Dickey, Eric Jerome, 208t
Dickinson, Charles, 230t
Dietz, William C., 150t, 152, 153
Digital Fortress, 136
Dillard, Annie, 192t
Dim Sum of All Things, The, 204t
Dirda, Michael, 300
Dirk Pitt series, 131, 132t
Dirty Girls Social Club, The, 204t
Discworld series, 122, 158, 160t
Dispatch, 167t
Do Androids Dream of Electric Sheep?, 151
Do Right Man, A, 208t
Doc Ford series, 111, 133t
Doig, Ivan, 192t
Don Quixote, 9
Donai, Sara, 183t
Donald Duk, 212t
Donaldson, Stephen, 157
Donovans series, 130
Doona, 150t
Dopefiend, 310
Dorsey,Tim, 141t
Doss, James D., 195, 290
Double Bind, The, 202t
Dow, Candice, and Daaimah S. Poole, 208t
Doyle, Arthur Conan, 21, 101, 129, 138, 139, 140, 149, 241, 246
Draco Tavern, 152
Dracula, 89f, 164
Dragon King, 160t
Dragonfly in Amber, 178. *See also* Outlander series
Dragonlance Chronicle, 157
Dragonlance Legends Trilogy, The, 157
Dragonriders of Pern, 160t
Dragon's Tears, 167t

Subject Index

Page numbers followed by "f" indicate figures; those followed by "t" indicate tables.

About the Author
and Contributors

Stephanie L. Maatta earned her bachelor's degree in English and American Literature from Michigan State University and her master's and doctorate in Library and Information Studies from Florida State University. She is a faculty member at the School of Library and Information Science at the University of South Florida. She is active in ALA and RUSA, serving on various committees. She is also an active member in the Popular Culture Association. Her current research interests focus on books and reading as social and cultural phenomenon and services to students with disabilities. When Dr. Maatta is not teaching or reading, she enjoys exploring social networks and making connections with fellow readers.

* * *

Leila Martini holds a Master of Public Health and a Master of Arts in Library and Information Science from the University of South Florida. She co-authored a paper for the Beyond the Book Conference held at the University of Birmingham, Birmingham, UK, titled "Something about Oprah: Television Book Clubs & Intimate Connections," which will be published in *Journal of Popular Culture*. She prefers literary fiction to genre fiction, and she recently finished reading *Agent Zigzag* by Ben Macintyre.

Bruce G. Smith holds a Bachelor of Science degree in Horticulture from Penn State University, a Bachelor of Science degree in Biological Sciences from Florida State University, and a Master of Science in Library and Information Science from Florida State University. He maintains Carpe Biblio, an online source for book reviews and more, and he is an avid reader and researcher of science fiction, fantasy, and horror.